Enslavement

For Anita, cherished companion, lifesaver, with all my love and gratitude

"Whoever saves a life saves an entire world,"
Tractate Sanhedrin 4.5; Quran 5:32

Enslavement
Past and Present

Orlando Patterson

polity

Copyright © Orlando Patterson 2025

The right of Orlando Patterson to be identified as Author of this Work has been asserted in accordance with the UK Copyright, Designs and Patents Act 1988.

First published in 2025 by Polity Press

Polity Press
65 Bridge Street
Cambridge CB2 1UR, UK

Polity Press
111 River Street
Hoboken, NJ 07030, USA

All rights reserved. Except for the quotation of short passages for the purpose of criticism and review, no part of this publication may be reproduced, stored in a retrieval system or transmitted, in any form or by any means, electronic, mechanical, photocopying, recording or otherwise, without the prior permission of the publisher.

ISBN-13: 978-1-5095-6175-9
ISBN-13: 978-1-5095-6176-6(pb)

A catalogue record for this book is available from the British Library.

Library of Congress Control Number: 2024934471

Typeset in 10.5 on 12 pt Sabon LT Pro by
Cheshire Typesetting Ltd, Cuddington, Cheshire
Printed and bound in Great Britain by CPI Group (UK) Ltd, Croydon

The publisher has used its best endeavours to ensure that the URLs for external websites referred to in this book are correct and active at the time of going to press. However, the publisher has no responsibility for the websites and can make no guarantee that a site will remain live or that the content is or will remain appropriate.

Every effort has been made to trace all copyright holders, but if any have been overlooked the publisher will be pleased to include any necessary credits in any subsequent reprint or edition.

For further information on Polity, visit our website:
politybooks.com

CONTENTS

Acknowledgments	viii
Introduction	1

Part I: The Nature and Study of Slavery

1. On the Institution of Slavery and Its Consequences	15
The distinctive features of slavery	15
The modes of enslavement	20
The acquisition of slaves	24
Treatment of the enslaved	25
Manumission as an integral element of slavery	28
Agency and resistance	31
The enduring consequences of slavery	36
2. Revisiting Slavery and Property as a "Bundle of Rights"	41
Property as a bundle of rights (or sticks)	42
Property and slavery across time and societies	51
3. Beyond "Slave Society": The Structural Articulations	
of Slavery in Pre-Capitalist and Capitalist Social Formations	65
Approaches to the study of slave societies	65
An alternative framework for the study of slave societies	69
Large-scale passive articulation: The case of Korea	78
Conclusion	81
4. The Denial of Slavery in Contemporary American Sociology	83
Introduction	83
The historical significance of slavery	85
The silence of the sociological clan	87

CONTENTS

Part II: Slavery in the Premodern and Early Christian Worlds

5. The Origins of Slavery and Slave Society: A Critique of
   the Nieboer-Domar Hypothesis and Case Study of Ancient
   Athens 95
      The origins of slavery as institution 95
      The origin of slave society: Athens 800–300 BCE 126
      Appendix 140

6. The Social and Symbolic Uses of Slavery in Ancient Rome
   and Early Christianity 145
      Coda 153

Part III: Slavery in the Modern World

7. Slavery and Slave Revolts: The Maroon Slave Wars of
   Jamaica, 1655–1739 157
      Introduction 157
      The British conquest and the failure of White settlement,
      1655–1700 159
      Early Black marronage and slave revolts, 1655–1700 163
      Black solidarity between enslaved rebels and maroons,
      1700–1720 169
      Toward victory: The defeat of the British slaveholder
      class, 1720–1739 173
      Snatching betrayal from the jaws of victory: Cudjoe and
      the Treaty of 1739 182
      Explaining slave revolts 185
      Conclusion 195
      Appendix A 196
      Appendix B 198

8. Slavery and Genocide: The US South, Jamaica, and the
   Historical Sociology of Evil 201
      The nature of genocide and ethnocide 201
      Slavery and genocide in history 212
      Slavery and protracted genocide in Jamaica, 1655–1838:
      A counterfactual comparison with US slavery 215
      Coda 226

vi

CONTENTS

Part IV: Slavery Today

9. Human Trafficking, Modern-Day Slavery, and Other Forms
   of Servitude   231
        Servitude, slavery, trafficking, and smuggling   233
        Forms of servitude   242
        Measuring servitude   261
        Explaining the rise of modern servitude   269
        Conclusion   273

Credits   278
References   280
Index   318

ACKNOWLEDGMENTS

I am deeply grateful to Professor Loïc Wacquant, distinguished Professor of Sociology at Berkeley, whose encouragement and insightful guidance were instrumental in bringing this collection to fruition. His unwavering support and generosity exemplify a rare camaraderie among scholars, an act I hold in high regard and will always cherish. I further extend my heartfelt appreciation to Professor Chris Muller, who also urged me to publish these essays and whose valuable feedback on the introduction contributed significantly to its refinement.

Earlier renditions of Chapters 2 and 6 found their roots in discussions sparked by contributions to a collection of papers on my book *Slavery and Social Death* (2018 [1982]), edited by the classical scholars John Bodel, Professor of Classics and History at Brown University, and Walter Scheidel, Professor of History and Classics at Stanford. The scholarly discourse surrounding this work, notably during the Brown University conference in 2012 and the subsequent publication *On Human Bondage: After Slavery and Social Death* (2017), greatly enriched my understanding of comparative slavery and enhanced my interpretations of the symbolic role of slavery in Christian doctrine.

Chapter 2's evolution was further shaped by insights gleaned from responses to my keynote lecture at the University of Dayton School of Law's conference on "Property and Subordination" in 2017, efficiently organized by Professor Eleanor Brown, now of Fordham Law School. I am indebted to Professor Brown and the distinguished legal scholars in attendance for their invaluable perspectives.

Chapter 4 was written for a special issue of *Theory and Society*, edited by Professors Fiona Greenland of the University of Virginia

ACKNOWLEDGMENTS

and George Steinmetz of the University of Michigan. Their astute observations greatly contributed to honing the final draft.

I am grateful for the intellectual stimulation provided by conversations over three days on my work with members of Berkeley's Matrix Institute for Cross-disciplinary Social Science, brilliantly led by Professor Marion Fourcade. Special thanks to Professor Scott Strauss for his extensive and invaluable feedback on an early version of Chapter 8 delivered at the conference.

The revision of several chapters benefited significantly from discussions at the conference on my work organized by Professors Bruce Kapferer and Michael Rowlands of University College London. Their meticulous planning and insightful observations were invaluable, making this conference one of the highlights of my career. The 2023 Daryll Forde memorial lecture at UCL, delivered as part of the conference proceedings, provided valuable feedback on Chapter 5, thanks to Professor Martin Holbraad's chairmanship and learned interventions as well as the engaged audience's probing questions.

Professor David Wengrow's perceptive questions and observations during our meeting at the Royal Anthropological Institute, which he chaired, prompted new insights that influenced the revisions of several chapters, as did the penetrating comments and novel perspectives brought to the meeting by the anthropologists from the University of Bergen, Professors Knut Rio, Bjørn Bertelsen, and Rolf Scott, whose university generously co-sponsored the conference.

The Harvard Sociology workshop in History, Culture, and Society, which I co-chair with Professors Ya-Wen Lei and Chris Muller, has been a constant source of inspiration and intellectual exchange, shaping many ideas reflected in these chapters.

I remain grateful to the late Professor Sidney Mintz of Johns Hopkins University and the late Professor Arnie Sio of Colgate University for their invaluable feedback on the manuscript of Chapter 7, offered some fifty years ago, but still remembered.

Any errors or shortcomings of style or substance in these chapters are solely my responsibility and should not be attributed to the scholars mentioned above.

Lastly, I thank my wife Anita Patterson, for her patience and support, both emotional and intellectual, during the long nights and months spent on the revision of these chapters.

Initially the enslaver is perceived as the essential truth, an independent self-consciousness existing for itself, though not quite as its [the enslaved's] own. However, enslavement does eventually entail the enslaved accepting this purely negating truth of the enslaver's existence for itself; and making it an essential component of itself. This [other-directed] consciousness is not so much a fear for the particular or momentary, but for its utmost being; for it has experienced the fear of death, of absolute subjection. It has been internally dissolved in this, has trembled through and through in itself, and everything fixed has been shaken within it. This pure universalizing movement, the absolute dissolution of all [previous] existence, now simply becomes the essence of self-consciousness, an absolute negativity. (¶42) ... This negative medium or formative activity is simultaneously the particularity of pure [sublated] consciousness existing for itself, which now through [enslaved] labor steps outside itself into something permanent; and through this laboring consciousness, the contemplation of independent being [freedom] as its own is attained. (¶43)

G. W. F. Hegel, (1807). *Phenomenology of Spirit*, selected from Chapter IV, ¶¶42, 43

He can only understand the effect of this combat on my spirit, who has himself incurred something, hazarded something, in repelling the unjust and cruel aggressions of a tyrant. Covey was a tyrant, and a cowardly one withal. After resisting him, I felt as I had never felt before. It was a resurrection from the dark and pestiferous tomb of slavery, to the heaven of comparative freedom. I was no longer a servile coward, trembling under the frown of a brother worm in the dust, but my long-cowed spirit was roused to an attitude of manly independence. I had reached the point at which I was not afraid to die. This spirit made me a freeman in fact, while I remained a slave in form.

Frederick Douglass, (1855). *My Bondage and My Freedom*, selected from Chapter 17

[Western] Mankind has liberated itself not so much *from* enslavement as *through* enslavement.

G. W. F. Hegel (1917–20 [1840]). *Lectures on the Philosophy of World History*, p. 875

INTRODUCTION

Along with man's inhumanity to woman, slavery is one of humanity's most ancient and persistent inequities. It predates the rise of civilization, and its traces can be seen in archaeological findings, pre-literate legends and myths, and observations of surviving hunter-gatherer societies (Biermann and Jankowiak, 2021; Lane and MacDonald, 2011). Slavery played a foundational role in the ancient rise and growth of Western and Islamic civilizations and was significant in other cultures such as those of Africa, pre-Columbian America, Korea, and Southeast Asia. It also had a critical role in the emergence and global spread of capitalism. Given its historical significance, it is not surprising that the problem of Atlantic slavery is still passionately debated in the Anglo-American world today, more than a century and a half after its abolition in America, with modern-day trafficking and servitude being major concerns worldwide.

The ongoing debate surrounding the implications of Atlantic slavery reflects its deep-rooted social, economic, and political consequences. Echoes of the slave trade and plantation slavery continue to resonate in contentious discussions about racial inequality, systemic racism, and reparations. *The 1619 Project* (Hannah-Jones, 2019) an initiative by the *New York Times*, has brought attention to this legacy by reframing American history, highlighting the consequences of slavery and the contributions of Black Americans. Several major American universities, such as Harvard, Brown, and Georgetown, have recognized the role of slavery in their founding and development, taking steps such as removing statues, names, and objects associated with slavery, as well as providing funds for reparations and commemorations. However, these efforts have ignited controversy, with conservative critics arguing that they present a revisionist view of

INTRODUCTION

history, while supporters maintain that they shed light on previously neglected aspects of the American narrative. The debate has even entered mainstream American politics, leading to the censorship of many books on race and slavery in schools and libraries, as well as high school exams on Black history.

In Britain, the debate has been equally intense and increasingly acrimonious. Attempts to reassess the role of the Atlantic slave trade in British imperial and domestic economic history, including its contribution to the rise of prominent elite families such as that of former British Prime Minister David Cameron, have been condemned as attempts to belittle and tarnish British history. Several British universities, notably Glasgow, Bristol, and Oxford, have acknowledged the importance of slavery in their past and have taken steps to make amends, with Glasgow agreeing to pay £20 million as reparations for benefiting from the Atlantic slave trade. However, academic backlash has emerged, particularly at the University of Cambridge, where a researcher studying Cambridge's connection to Atlantic slavery faced criticism in the national press from anonymous academics who labeled them a "woke activist" with an agenda (according to the *Guardian* newspaper).

The claim by some scholars and politicians that modern scholarship on slavery, which acknowledges its evils and enduring impact, amounts to the imposition of value judgments on historical events is epistemologically disingenuous and historiographically inaccurate. Some subjects are inherently normative, and slavery is undoubtedly one of them. The historiography of slavery indicates that the study of the subject has always been influenced by values and ideologies. A brief look at the historiographies of ancient and Atlantic slavery makes this abundantly clear.

The study of slavery in Europe is as old as post-classical Western history itself. Discussions on "the moral problem of slavery continued incessantly during the Middle Ages," according to Malowist (1968: 161). From the sixteenth to the eighteenth century, numerous major works focused on the moral aspects of ancient slavery, mainly in the form of Latin dissertations (Vogt, 1973: 1–7).

Starting in the late eighteenth century, there was a surge of studies on slavery that resulted from the abolitionist movement and the interest of Marxian and non-Marxian scholars in both ancient slavery and the iniquities of the contemporary institution. Studies on ancient slavery were related to the abolitionist controversy in two ways: the role of slavery in biblical and early Christian times and its role in ancient Greece and Rome. The first aspect, highly polemical

2

INTRODUCTION

in nature, sought to justify or condemn slavery based on scriptural grounds. Proponents of slavery argued that it was morally acceptable since it was sanctioned by the Old Testament, Pauline theology, and the patristic thinkers of the early Church. Antislavery writers, however, attempted to show that early Christianity, while not ideologically critical of slavery, was historically and structurally opposed to it, and there was a correlation between the institutionalization of Christianity and the decline of slavery. The antislavery thesis led to the development of a more sophisticated historiography on this aspect of ancient slavery (Davis, 1966: Chs. 10–12; Davis, 1975: Ch. 11; Patterson, 1977: 408).

Regarding ancient Greece and Rome, the early nineteenth century saw debates over the then accepted fact that classical European antiquity was based on slavery. Enlightenment scholars condemned the ancients for their reliance on slavery, while others argued that the great civilizational breakthroughs of the Greeks were made possible only by slavery. These debates continued throughout the nineteenth century, with scholars questioning the foundations of ancient Greek civilization and arguing for or against its dependence on slavery (Vogt, 1965). Over time, scholarly opinion shifted, and it is now widely accepted that ancient Greek civilization was indeed based on slavery (Finley, 1960: 53–72).

Parallel to these debates, Marxian scholars, evolutionary historians, and anthropologists also explored the role of slavery in human development. Slavery was seen as a major stage in the emergence of socialism within the cruder materialistic conception of history. Marx himself recognized the limitations of this view and developed the concept of the Asiatic mode of production specifically to address the problem of slave society. Engels, influenced by Morgan, later abandoned this qualification and developed the untenable periodization theory that all societies went through five stages, including slavery. This theory had a detrimental impact on historical scholarship in the Soviet Union and China (Patterson, 1977: 410–13).

In the United States, the study of slavery has always been a morally, ideologically, and emotionally charged subject (Elkins, 1975). From the early twentieth century, US slave studies revolved around two main themes: the economic structure, efficiency, and profitability of slavery, and the socioeconomic stability and cultural integrity of the slaveholding world and its consequences for the enslaved. The dominant school for the first half of the twentieth century, led by Ulrich Phillips (1918), argued that slavery was pre-capitalist, socially stable, morally benign, and culturally progressive for the enslaved.

3

INTRODUCTION

Black American historians, led by W. E. B. DuBois (1935: Chs. 1–4), strongly resisted this racist interpretation but faced institutional marginalization within the segregated historically Black university system (see Smith, 1980). Kenneth Stampp (1989 [1956]), influenced by the civil rights movement, challenged the dominant school, emphasizing the capitalistic and profitable nature of slavery, its social instability, and its moral perversity. Robert Fogel and Stanley Engerman's cliometric school, drawing on earlier work by economic historians, argued that slavery was capitalist, profitable, socially stable, and culturally progressive for both enslaver and enslaved, generating further debate (Walton, 1975; Haskell, 1975; David and Temin, 1974). Eugene Genovese (1965) partly returned to the Phillips thesis, highlighting the pre-capitalist nature of the system while emphasizing its social stability and cultural integration (see also Genovese, 1976). Herbert Gutman (1976) and John Blassingame (1972) likewise argued for the social stability and moral integrity of the Black segment of the enslaved community, but expressed less enthusiasm for the system as a whole; indeed, they strongly suggested that it was brutal, although the two theses rest uneasily alongside each other.

This positive emphasis on Black culture, community, and agency, as well as the stability of the Black family under slavery, was in part a response to the work of the earlier tradition of liberal scholarship that emphasized the injuries of slavery and Jim Crow for Blacks (see, for example, Frazier, 1951 [1939]; Myrdal, 1944; and Kardiner and Ovesey, 1951). Stanley Elkins's (1959) controversial study of the psychological response of American slaves was written in that tradition. The infantilized Sambo image of Southern lore, Elkins claimed, was the tragic result of the totally oppressive institution of slavery, similar to the response of many Jewish inmates of the Nazi concentration camps. In the mid-1960s, a policy brief written by a non-historian, Patrick Moynihan (Rainwater and Yancey, 1967), argued that slavery had been destructive of Black institutions, especially their marital and familial relations, which persisted in contemporary economic and social problems of the inner cities. Although this argument was largely a revision of positions held by earlier liberal scholars, noted above, including contemporary Black scholars such as Kenneth Clark (1965), Moynihan was condemned as a racist who was blaming the victim, in complete disregard of the fact that the report was written as a rationale for quite radical intervention by the Johnson Administration on behalf of the Black poor. In a balanced evaluation of this period of historical writing on slavery and its legacies, Peter Kolchin (1983) has noted that, "in destroying the myth that slaves were depersonalized Sambos

INTRODUCTION

and in focusing on the enslaved as actors who helped shape their own world," historians have "tended increasingly toward celebration and even mystification of slave life." This danger has persisted, one Black American historian claiming that slavery was a mere "predicament" for Black slaves, over which they triumphed (Brown, 2009).

The latest controversy surrounding slavery arises from the New History of Capitalism (NHC) school of thought, which claims that slavery was not only closely related to, but also generative of, modern capitalism, particularly nineteenth-century American industrial capitalism (among its leading proponents: Beckert, 2014; Beckert and Rockman, 2016; Schermerhorn, 2015; Baptist, 2014; Rockman, 2014). This viewpoint has sparked disagreement from conservatives and nearly all economic historians, and also from liberal and even some left-leaning historians, and feminists. Critics argue that the NHC, in addition to repeating as new discoveries long-established findings by economic historians on the capitalistic nature of US slavery (Conrad and Meyer, 1958; Fogel and Engerman, 1974), has tended to "mishandle historical evidence and mis-characterize important events in ways that affect their major interpretations on the nature of slavery, the workings of plantations, the importance of cotton and slavery in the broader economy, and the sources of the Industrial Revolution and world development" (Wright, 2016). The polemical assertion of several of NHC's least defensible claims in one of the most widely cited articles of *The 1619 Project*, authored by Matt Desmond, a qualitative sociologist with no formal historical training, has been fodder for critics of both *The 1619 Project* and, somewhat unfairly, the entire NHC school. No one now doubts that Southern slavery was highly profitable and enriched the slaveholder class, and that its social, cultural, political, and racial consequences for America were transformative and, for many, catastrophic. Whether it contributed significantly to US economic development during the nineteenth century or actually retarded the South as a region are still open questions, with nearly all economic historians critical of the NHC (on which, see Wright, 2022). Some left-leaning scholars, particularly those focusing on the West Indies, have also criticized the NHC for its America-centric approach and its neglect of the Caribbean and sugar in favor of North America and cotton. The NHC's treatment of the region and its history, especially the fact that the entire debate on slavery and capitalism was initiated some eighty years ago by Eric Williams (2021 [1944]) and C. L. R. James (1963 [1938]; see also Beckles, 1997), the two great heroes of West Indian scholarship, has been viewed as "neglectful and erasing, marginalizing intellectual

5

communities that have long nurtured Caribbean studies" (Hudson, 2018; see also Burnard and Riello, 2020). It is extraordinary that Seth Rockman, a leading member of the NHC, in a long review of earlier explorations of the history of capitalism with "competing accounts of the field's genealogy" (2014: 442) almost completely neglects the large Caribbean historiography on the subject, with one miserly, almost slighting, reference to Eric Williams and the vast transatlantic literature this work generated. One conservative commentator has gleefully accused the NHC of having a "Whiteness problem," declaring that the "Caribbean-centric black radical school of historical thought ... is now in direct tension with the predominantly White and Ivy League-centric NHC school" (Magness, 2019). Feminists have also criticized the NHC for neglecting the role of gender in the rise of capitalism and nonrecognition of female historians of the subject (O'Sullivan, 2018).

The study of slavery today also encompasses contemporary trafficking and modern forms of servitude. While slavery is now illegal everywhere and is universally condemned, there is debate about its definition, and about the extent and political commitment to its abolition (Patterson and Zhuo, 2018; Allain, 2012). Additionally, debates arise concerning what forms of exploitative relationships should be considered slavery or "slave-like" labor. Feminists have engaged in intense arguments regarding the morality of sex work, with different perspectives on whether it is akin to slavery or a woman's right to choose (MacKinnon, 2011). The distinction between emotionally abusive relationships and outright marital slavery also remains blurry (Patterson and Zhuo, 2018).

In summary, the study of slavery encompasses a wide range of debates and perspectives. It involves examining economic, social, cultural, and moral aspects of the subject, in both its historical forms and its enduring presence in contemporary societies. The subject has always been morally and intellectually contentious and this continues to shape academic scholarship and public discourse. Understanding the history of slavery is crucial for acknowledging the profound injustices endured by millions of enslaved individuals and the need to take seriously the demand for a consideration of the nature and extent of moral, political, and other forms of reparation. It is a reminder of humanity's capacity for both cruelty and resilience and serves as a catalyst for ongoing efforts to combat inequality and build a more inclusive society for all.

*   *   *

INTRODUCTION

The nine chapters in this book traverse the author's lifelong study of the subject. All but one of them (Chapter 4) have been revised to bring them up to date, or have been completely rewritten. They all reflect the distinctive viewpoint of a comparative and historical sociologist which, at the very least, means a sensitivity to theoretical issues and the importance of defining terms carefully. This is one of the main shortcomings of too much traditional historical scholarship on slavery.

What is slavery? Why slavery? How did slavery originate? What were its different levels of development in society? What was slave society? What were the institutional and cultural mechanisms by which it was maintained? How did it come to an end? What was the role of gender in the rise and maintenance of slavery? What did it mean to be enslaved? Why, how, and when did the enslaved resist? Why did some slave societies experience relatively few large-scale revolts, while others experienced many, forcing slaveholders to yield, or the system to collapse? Why was slavery so closely linked to some religions? Why is slavery and redemption from slavery the central metaphor of Christian doctrine? What was the relation between slavery and freedom? Is slavery to be defined in terms of the absence of freedom, as is traditionally done, or is it more historically accurate, and philosophically less essentialist, to understand freedom as the absence of slavery? Why was slavery the critical institution at all the great turning points of Western civilization, from the rise of ancient Greece and Rome to the rise of capitalism in the Atlantic system and the emergence of America? What were the consequences of slavery for our present times, for the descendants of the enslaved, their enslavers, and the societies in which they continue to coexist?

These are some of the deeper theoretical and substantive issues that any serious engagement with the subject should raise. While several historians have made notable contributions to these theoretical issues, it is striking how they are avoided in typical works on the subject. Indeed, a disdain for theory and definition is even hailed as a hallmark of the new history of slavery and capitalism, one of its leading advocates declaring that it "has opened new vistas on the past by pursuing its questions differently from earlier scholarship," the first of these being that "the current scholarship has minimal investment in a fixed or theoretical definition of capitalism"(Rockman, 2014: 442).

Part I, "The Nature and Study of Slavery," explores theoretical, definitional, and disciplinary issues in slave studies. Like all enduring social structures, slavery exists on different levels of abstraction: the micro level of relationships, the meso level of groups and institutions,

INTRODUCTION

and the macro level of entire societies, states, and civilizations. Chapter 1 summarizes major findings on slavery as a relation of domination amounting to a state of social death. A significant point of contention addressed here is the prevailing definition of the enslaved as human property, and slavery as ownership of one person by another. I challenged this approach in *Slavery and Social Death* (Patterson, 2018 [1982]), not for being wrong, but for being limited in its application only to Western and capitalistic systems. A better conception of property that embraces all forms of slavery, I argued, is the relativistic one that views property as a bundle of rights (or "sticks," as some legal theorists prefer). Chapter 2 develops this approach, drawing on recent legal theory. I show that the bundle-of-rights approach is consistent with the views and practices of slavery in all premodern and modern slave systems and is increasingly adopted by economists and legal theorists in the study of the changing nature of property, especially in our postindustrial digital age.

Chapter 3 examines the problem of slavery at the macro-structural level, often referred to as the problem of slave society, or what Finley (1968) called "genuine slave societies." I begin with a review of past and present approaches to the problem, including a critique of the Marxian concept of the slave mode of production, the first important attempt to examine what constitutes slave society. I then propose that a better way of understanding this set of societies is to consider what I call "patterns of articulation," or ways in which societies become dependent on the institution. This approach seeks to answer three basic questions. First, what was the nature of the dependence on slavery? Was it economic, military, administrative, lineage-based, status enhancement, or ritualistic? Second, what was the degree of dependence? This refers to the number and proportion of the enslaved in the population. And third, what was the direction of dependence? Was slavery an active and transformative force, influencing most other institutions, or was it passive and noninvasive? The answers to these three questions together determine the various patterns of articulation of slavery. These patterns are briefly discussed with examples.

The problem of inequality is central to sociology, particularly American sociology, which focuses largely on class, race, and inequality. However, it is puzzling that American sociology has shown the least interest in the problem of slavery, both domestically and internationally, compared to other social and historical disciplines. Economics, for instance, has shown great interest in slavery, with one of its members winning a Nobel Prize partly for work on the subject. Chapter 4 attempts to explain this puzzle, suggesting that it is due

8

INTRODUCTION

in part to a pervasive presentist and parochial bias in the American practice of the discipline and a special reluctance to provide historical explanations for contemporary racial problems, due to the fear of being maligned with the charge of blaming the victim.

Part II, "Slavery in the Premodern and Early Christian Worlds," presents two studies on slavery in the premodern world. Chapter 5 critiques the theory – independently developed by the Dutch historical anthropologist Herman Nieboer and the MIT economist Evsey Domar – that slavery arises as a result of a high ratio of land to people. The first part of the chapter retests this theory with data from George Murdock's sample of world societies, using statistical methods that were not available when the paper was first published in 1977. I propose an alternate model that takes into account social, economic, and resource factors, paying special attention to the role of women as wives, reproducers, and producers, and of warfare and male violence in competing for status and power. I suggest that slavery emerges for quite different reasons in different sociohistorical contexts. The second part of Chapter 5 not only offers a historical case study that confirms my critique, but also presents a brief historical sociology of the first-known large-scale slave society in human history: that of ancient Greece, especially Athens between 800 and 300 BCE.

In an important comment on the concept of slavery as a state of social death, the distinguished classicist John Bodel (2017) argued that death, being the ultimate final state, is too static a metaphor to account for the fact that slavery was demographically a temporary status in ancient Rome, given its high rate of manumission and the anticipation of it by most of the enslaved. As a metaphor, he argues, the idea of social death does not comport well with the celebratory triumph over slavery reflected in the monumental inscriptions of freedmen. In Chapter 6, I show that social death, far from being conceived metaphorically as a static condition, was understood dynamically as a prelude to liberation by those who did achieve their freedom. We find the association of manumission with death and rebirth in many cultures, including Han China. However, it was most powerfully expressed in the central metaphor of the religion that was refashioned in the midst of Roman slave society: Christianity. The urban poor, including the enslaved, were significant segments of the early Christian congregations. Freedmen and freedwomen occupied important leadership roles in its organization and the development of its creed. The most important social and emotional experience of these freedmen was their redemption (Latin *redemptionem*, "a buying back, redemption, releasing, ransoming") from the social and spiritual

INTRODUCTION

death of slavery. Christianity introjected this powerful secular metaphor of redemption, making it the center of its creed. The writings of St. Paul, the religion's "second founder," fully expressed the centrality of spiritual death, not simply as a prelude, but as a condition to be transcended by the life-giving, redemptive death of Christ. There could be no clearer demonstration of death as a dynamic symbolic state than the belief that salvation came to the Christian by dying in Christ and living his death. I draw on the symbolic theory of Charles Peirce in interpreting Paul's complex, dynamic vision of death, and argue that Christianity's power as a creed inheres in the fact that its central metaphor has equal appeal to both conservative elites and the dispossessed throughout the ages of Western history, depending on how it is interpreted.

Part III, "Slavery in the Modern World," focuses on Jamaica and the US South, the paradigmatic large-scale plantation systems of the Americas, the problem of slave revolts, and the surprisingly unexplored question of the relation of genocide to slavery.

The question of slave revolts has long concerned historians of slavery in the Americas and antiquity. Was it the case that there were relatively few slave revolts in Graeco-Roman antiquity? If so, why? What were the causes of slave revolts? Why did some parts of the Americas, such as Jamaica, the Dominican Republic, Haiti, Cuba, and Brazil, have high rates of rebellion, while other areas, such as Barbados and the US South, have relatively low rates? Emphasizing the attitudes of the enslaved is inadequate, as the enslaved everywhere resented their condition and resisted in various ways, with outright collective slave wars being the most extreme form. Chapter 7 focuses on Jamaica and argues that demographic, ethnic, and geographic factors, in addition to the genocidal brutality of the system and absenteeism of the slaveholder class, were key variables in accounting for slave revolts. These were genuine slave wars and should not be confused with maroon communities established by runaways in other parts of the Americas.

Chapter 8 reviews the field of genocide studies and distinguishes between ethnocide, the destruction of a people's culture, and genocide, the physical elimination of all or part of a people. Slavery in the US South exemplified the historic crime against humanity of ethnocide without physical decline due to the unique pattern of demographic reproduction and growth of its enslaved population. From 1655, when the British captured the island, to 1838, when slavery was abolished, Jamaica experienced one of the highest mortality rates of any slave society in the modern world. The chapter argues that

INTRODUCTION

the destruction of the enslaved African population amounted to a form of protracted genocide. Using the demographic history of the United States as a counterfactual case, the genocidal death toll over the course of 133 years of slavery was estimated at nearly 6 million, including those who died prematurely from overwork, and miscarriages due to harsh conditions or the premature death of the mother, and the anti-natal policies of the planters.

Part IV, "Slavery Today," is a single long chapter examining slavery in our times. The revival of slavery, other forms of forced servitude, and human trafficking in recent times have engendered widespread activism and a substantial body of literature. While there are valid concerns about the conflation of terms, exaggerated empirical claims, and a shortage of evidence-based work, modern-day slavery and other forms of servitude are undeniably real and shockingly widespread, the UN's International Labour Office estimating some "50 million people in situations of modern slavery on any given day" (ILO et al., 2022). Although contemporary slavery is universally considered illegal and evil, its actual practice, and genuine political commitment to its abolition, vary across different countries. Forms of servitude such as debt bondage, extreme child labor, domestic servitude of immigrant labor, as well as marital slavery, are widespread in countries like Pakistan, India, Thailand, and the Gulf States, despite formally advocating human rights and having laws against slavery (Patterson and Zhuo, 2018; Allain, 2012). Among the world's advanced nations, the United States is unique in being both a major destination for, and the source of, thousands of modern slaves, in its brothels, restaurants, construction sites, homes, and farms. This chapter clarifies the basic terms in the field of contemporary studies of the subject – servitude, forced labor, modern-day slavery, trafficking, and smuggling – and examines all forms of servitude to evaluate the extent to which they can be classified as slavery proper or other forms of exploitation. It also addresses methodological problems in measuring servitude and provides a brief analysis of the factors contributing to its contemporary revival.

I

The Nature and Study of Slavery

— 1 —

ON THE INSTITUTION OF SLAVERY AND ITS CONSEQUENCES

Slavery is the most extreme form of the relations of domination. In the totality of the enslaver's power, their exclusion from the rights, privileges, and duties of the society of the free, and the denial of any recognition of their human worth and dignity, the enslaved and their descendants suffered the condition of social death.

Slavery has existed, at some time, in most parts of the world and at all levels of social development. This chapter examines seven aspects of the institution: its distinguishing features; the means by which persons were enslaved; the means by which owners acquired them; the treatment and condition of the enslaved; manumission; slave resistance; and the enduring consequences of slavery.

1.1: The distinctive features of slavery

The traditional, and still conventional, approach is to define slavery in legal-economic terms, typically as "the status or condition of a person over whom any or all the powers attaching to the right of owner-ship are exercised" (UN OHCHR, 1926). In this view, the enslaved is, quintessentially, a human chattel. This definition is problematic because it adequately describes mainly Western and modern, capi-talistic systems of slavery. The conception of the enslaved as chattel originated in the practices and legal thought of ancient Rome, where it was quite appropriate. However, in many non-Western parts of the world, several categories of persons who were clearly not enslaved, such as unmarried women, concubines, debt bondsmen, indentured servants, sometimes serfs, and occasionally children, were bought and sold. Conversely, in many slaveholding societies certain categories of

THE NATURE AND STUDY OF SLAVERY

the enslaved, such as those born in the household, or women who had given birth to sons by their enslavers, were not treated as chattels to be bought and sold. Other societies not directly influenced by Roman legal thought also developed an alternate conception of property that more appropriately described the condition of slavery and other forms of possession. Sir Moses Finley (1964) has shown that, even in Athens of the classical era, a relativistic, bundle-of-rights approach was more appropriate for an understanding of the relation of slavery. This alternate approach to property will be considered in the next chapter.

Slavery is a relation of domination that is distinctive in three respects. First, the power of the enslaver was usually total, if not in law, almost always in practice. Violence was the basis of this power. Even where laws forbade the gratuitous killing of the enslaved, it was rare for enslavers to be prosecuted for murdering them, due to their universally recognized right to punish their slaves, and to severe constraints placed on the enslaved in giving evidence in courts of law against their enslavers, or free persons generally (Fede, 2017; Jacobs, 2024 [1855]: 23–7).

The totality of the enslaver's claims and powers in them meant that the enslaved could have no claims or powers in other persons or things, except with the enslaver's permission. A major consequence of this was that the enslaved had no custodial claims on their children; they were genealogical isolates, lacking all recognized rights of ancestry and descent. As the self-liberated formerly enslaved John Swanson Jacobs noted: "He owns nothing – he can claim nothing. His wife is not his – his children are not his" (2024 [1855]: 6). From this flowed the hereditary nature of their condition. They had no more legal rights to or claims on their children and parents than to other persons or things. Another distinctive consequence of the slaveholder's total power was the fact that they often treated the enslaved as their surrogates, and hence could perform functions for them as if they were legally present, a valuable trait in premodern societies with advanced commodity production and long-distance trading, such as ancient Rome, where laws of agency, though badly needed, were nonexistent or poorly developed. However, even in slave societies where the law of agency was well developed, slaveholders sometimes used the enslaved as their agents in commercial transactions, as not infrequently happened in the antebellum South. The practice contradicted the custom of White supremacy and was sometimes challenged, although the views of the slaveholder usually prevailed on the grounds that the enslaved, having no formal existence outside of the slaveholder, could act on his behalf with his permission (Tippett, 2021).

THE INSTITUTION OF SLAVERY AND ITS CONSEQUENCES

Slaveholders' power over their slaves had a distinctly carnal aspect. The enslaver possessed the body of the enslaved. Among cannibal peoples, this entitled them to literally consume the enslaved's body. In early Christian texts, the enslaved were often referred to as "the bodies" (Glancy, 2006). While the ancient Romans did not eat their slaves, their possession of them was so extreme that they used the term *abusus* to describe their ownership, meaning that the enslaved's body was not just used, but *used up*. This was similar to how patriarchal men felt about women, and it is not accidental that in many societies slavery was closely associated with marriage and sexuality, the rituals of marriage and divorce often being similar to those of enslavement and manumission.

Second, the enslaved were universally considered as outsiders, this being the major difference between them and serfs, servants, and other exploited people. They were natally alienated people, deracinated in the act of their, or their ancestors', enslavement, who were held not to belong to the societies in which they lived, even if they were born there. They lacked all legal or recognized status as independent members of a community. In kin-based societies, this was expressed in their definition as kinless persons; in more advanced, state-based societies, they lacked all claims to and rights of citizenship. Because they belonged only to their enslaver, they could not belong to the community; because they were bonded only to their enslaver's household, they could share no *recognized* bond of loyalty and love with the community at large. To be sure, this does not mean that they had no informal personal and communal relations among themselves. They most certainly did, but all human beings need formal recognition of their deeply held relations, especially with kin, and assurances that they could not be arbitrarily terminated by others, because they belonged to, and were included in, relations beyond their superiors, and this the enslaved did not have. The most ancient words for the enslaved in the Indo-European and several other families of languages translate to mean, "those who do not belong," or "not among the beloved," in contrast to non-enslaved members of the community (OED): a "stranger by necessity, the slave is designated in the Indo-European languages, even modern ones, either by a foreign word (Gr. *doulos*, Lat. *servus*) or by the name of a foreign people (slave<Slav) . . . In the ancient civilizations, the status of a slave puts him outside the community . . . There are no slaves who are citizens" (Benveniste, 1973, Ch. 5). For all their communal interactions among themselves, like the enslaved everywhere, American slaves felt this denial of social recognition acutely. Jacobs recalled that his "mental

suffering had become such that it made life a burden to me" and that, upon snatching his freedom, "the first thing I strove to do was to raise myself up above the level of the beast, where slavery had left me, and fit myself for the society of man" (2024 [1855]: 50–1).

Third, the enslaved were everywhere considered to be dishonored persons. They had no honor that a non-slave person need respect. What DuBois wrote of the Black slave was true of the experience of all enslaved persons: "They represented in a very real sense the ultimate degradation of man . . . the tragedy of the black slave's position was precisely this; his absolute subjection to the individual will of another" (1935: 9–10). Slaveholders could violate all aspects of their slaves' lives with impunity, including by raping them. "A slave's wife or daughter," wrote the ex-enslaved Jacobs, "may be insulted before his eyes with impunity; he himself may be called on to torture them, and dare not refuse" (2024 [1855]: 6). In most slaveholding societies, injuries against the enslaved by third parties were prosecuted, if at all, as injuries against the person and honor of the enslaver. Where an honor-price, or *wergild*, existed, as in Anglo-Saxon Britain and other Germanic lands, its payment usually went to the slaveholder rather than to the injured slave. Universally, slavery was considered the most extreme form of degradation, so much so that the enslaved's very humanity was often in question. In ancient Greece they were called human-footed animals (i.e. animals who walked on two feet), in Rome "vocal instruments"; if they were Greek slaves, they were contemptuously called "Graeculus," meaning "little Greek," the ancient version of the American term "boy," "bound to some one," no matter their age, or infantilized "Sambos" (Cartledge, 1985). Among the Tuareg, the generic term for a man, *ahalis*, was never applied to a male slave, who was usually called *akli*, or boy (Winter, 1984: 12).

The honorlessness of the enslaved served other ends than their debasement. It was a form of human parasitism in that it enhanced the ego and honor of the enslaver (Patterson, 2018 [1982]: Ch. 12). In many tribal and hunter-gathering societies, such as the Tupinamba of Brazil, the glorification of the slaveholder and his kin was often its sole function, since the enslaved were of little economic value and may even have been an economic burden. However, in many advanced societies, the honorlessness of the enslaved, the fact that they were mere surrogates of their enslavers, served both honorific as well as useful economic and political functions. In ancient Rome, the enslaved parasitically projected the honor and *dignitas* of their enslavers, "a precious marker of respectability" (Harper, 2011). In the American South, male enslavers were obsessed with honor, which

THE INSTITUTION OF SLAVERY AND ITS CONSEQUENCES

defined their identity as men, and, because the enslaved was quintessentially defined as a person without honor, "all issues of honor relate to slavery" (Greenberg, 1997: xiii). This parasitism was extended to the meanest of non-enslaved persons, who reveled in the fact of not being a slave, to the benefit and security of the slaveholder. As DuBois noted of the poor White both during and after slavery, their non-slave status and Whiteness "fed his vanity because it associated him with the masters," and "while they received a low wage, were compensated in part by a sort of public and psychological wage" (DuBois, 1935: 700).

For all these reasons, there was a general tendency for enslavers and the non-enslaved to conceive of and treat the enslaved as socially dead persons. The enslaved themselves were acutely conscious of this conception and the socio-legal definition of their condition by the free. And, while in their own eyes, and in relations with fellow slaves, they did not consider themselves socially dead, it was a permanent, dehumanizing affliction imposed on them that they often referred to when describing their degradation and relating why real death was preferable to the unfreedom and degradation of social death. Harriet Jacobs wrote that "I had rather live and die in jail, than drag on, from day to day, through such a living death" (Jacobs, 1861: 63). Her contemporary, Frederick Douglass, repeatedly returned to the description of his enslavement as a kind of death, describing his sense of freedom as "glorious resurrection from the tomb of slavery" (Douglass, 1855: 73). Throughout the Americas, the enslaved celebrated rather than mourned the death of kinsmen and friends, since physical death brought a merciful end to the living, social death of slavery and the hope of return to Africa (Roediger 1991; Patterson 2022 [1967]: 195–202). Among slaveholders and the free, in societies at all levels of development, the social death of the enslaved was often represented symbolically in ritual signs and acts of debasement, death, and mourning: in clothing, hairstyles, naming practices, and other rituals of obeisance and nonbeing (Patterson, 2018 [1982]: 51–62; Thompson, 2003: 241–4; Santos-Granero, 2017).

Although, as we will discuss below, the enslaved everywhere sought ways of relieving, escaping, and even violently resisting this imposed condition, and of exercising agency, the consequences of social death could be devastating, given the power of enslavers and their support from the free as well as those controlling the levers of communal and state power. It threatened the core social motives that psychologists have identified as essential for effective social functioning and well-being: *belonging* – the need to freely affiliate and bond with others in

19

strong, stable relationships and groups with shared common goals and interests that are not arbitrarily severed or disrupted; *understanding* – the need to make sense of one's social environment and "predict what is going to happen in case of uncertainties"; *control* – the feeling of being effective in dealing with one's environment and in setting and realizing normal, everyday goals; *self-enhancement* – maintaining self-esteem; and *trust* – "seeing the world as a benevolent place," with confidence in the reliability of others (Fiske, 2010). In the absence or persistent disruption of these basic human motives, the most fundamental of which is belonging, the psychological wellbeing and survival of individuals through belonging in groups is threatened. What DuBois wrote of the American slave held true for the enslaved of all times and places: "The hurt . . . was not only his treatment in slavery; it was the wound dealt to his reputation as human being. Nothing was left; nothing was sacred" (1935: 39).

Few formerly enslaved wrote more searingly than John Jacobs, the brother of Harriet Jacobs, of the tragic struggle they experienced each day reconciling their inherent humanity with the endless onslaught on it by the slaveholder and his society's socially erasing definition of them as socially dead or, more acutely, "murdered." "Human nature will be human nature," he wrote; "crush it as you may, it changes not." But "slavery is unnatural, and it requires unnatural means to support it. Everything droops that feels its sting. Hope grows dimmer and dimmer until life becomes bitter and burthensome. At last death frees the slave from his chains, but his wrongs are forgotten. He was oppressed, robbed, and murdered" (2024 [1855]: 73).

1.2: The modes of enslavement

Free persons became enslaved in one of eight ways: capture in warfare, kidnapping, through tribute and taxation, indebtedness, punishment for crimes, abandonment and sale of children, self-enslavement, and birth (for detailed discussion of these methods see Patterson, 2018 [1982]: 105–31). Capture in warfare is generally considered to have been the most important means of acquiring slaves, but this was true mainly of simpler, small-scale societies, and of certain volatile periods among politically centralized groups. Among even moderately advanced premodern societies, the logistics of warfare often made captivity a cumbersome and costly means of enslaving free persons.

Kidnapping differed from captivity in warfare mainly in the fact that enslavement was its main or sole objective, and that it was

THE INSTITUTION OF SLAVERY AND ITS CONSEQUENCES

usually a private act rather than the by-product of communal conflict. Other than birth, kidnapping in the forms of piracy and abduction was perhaps the main form of enslavement in the ancient Near East and the Mediterranean during Greek and Roman times; and this was true also of free persons who were enslaved in the trans-Saharan and transatlantic slave trades.

Debt bondage, which was common in ancient Greece up to the end of the seventh century BCE, the ancient Near East, and in Southeast Asia and Latin America down to the twenty-first century (see Chapter 9), could sometimes descend into real slavery, although nearly all societies in which it was practiced distinguished between the two institutions in at least three respects: debt bondage was nonhereditary; bondsmen remained members of their community, however diminished; and they maintained certain basic rights, in relation both to the bondholder and to their spouses and children.

The paying of tribute or taxes by means of slaves from vassal states was not uncommon although it was a major source mainly in the Islamic world and among several of the more advanced states of precolonial Africa. Often persons sent as tribute were already enslaved, although vassal states sometimes had to send free persons as Korea was required to do when it was a client of the Mongols during the thirteenth century. The most famous case of vassal states paying tribute with free persons involved the Christian peoples of the Ottoman empire, mainly in the Balkans, whose children were periodically recruited by means of the *devshirme* to reproduce the elite slave corps of Janissaries (Agoston, 2017)

Punishment for crimes was a major means of enslavement in small, kin-based societies; China and, to a lesser extent, Korea were the only advanced societies in which it remained the primary way of becoming enslaved. Nonetheless, it persisted as a minor means of enslavement in all slaveholding societies and became important historically in Europe as the antecedent of imprisonment for the punishment of crimes.

The enslavement of foundlings was common in all politically centralized premodern societies, though rarely found in small-scale slaveholding communities. It was the humane alternative to infanticide and was especially important in China, India, European antiquity, and medieval Europe. It has been argued that it ranked second to birth as a source of slaves in ancient Rome from as early as the first century CE until the end of the Western empire.

Self-enslavement, or autodedition as it was known in medieval Europe, was often the consequence of extreme penury or catastrophic loss. It occurred on a significant scale in East Asia. In premodern

Korea the extreme burdens of taxes, *corvée* labor, and military service on the rural poor resulted in a substantial number of people taking the extreme step of commending themselves to slavery, to which we return in Chapter 3. One of the most extreme cases of this in the history of the institution was the rapid growth in China of the *nubi* or slave population during the late Ming period (1368–1644) by commendation or "voluntary" enslavement as a means of survival or paying off debts. While contemporaries often attempted to write off this development as a kind of contractually based welfare for the impoverished, Claude Chevaleyre (2023: 297–317) has shown definitively that this was a classic case of "extrusive" slavery in which locally born free persons were expelled from the world of normal, "good" people to the category of the debased and socially dead. Like the enslaved of the ancient world and modern Americas, what "distinguished *nubi* . . . was that enslavement produced a total and unique form of excommunication from the standards of belonging to society and of membership in the household, which reduced people permanently to the sole function of 'serving' others and to one single direct social relationship [with their master]" (Chevaleyre, 2023: 314). The myth of this development being a special kind of Chinese welfarism was exploded by the extraordinary succession of *nubi* revolts in China between the 1630s and 1660s associated with the collapse of Ming, the Manchu conquest, widespread peasant revolts, and the rise of Qing rule (1644–1911).

The common modern Western view that self-enslavement is contrary to nature has, in Alice Rio's view, distorted historical views on the extent of its occurrence in medieval Europe (Rio, 2012). It was, in fact, not uncommon. Free people bargained away their status for economic improvement throughout medieval Europe and it was a major source of slaves for the church up to the twelfth century (Sommar, 2020). In early and central medieval Bavaria, its frequency was increasingly due to the practice of local slave raiding and the threat of what was termed "unjust servitude" by unscrupulous lords, in which single and widowed women were usually targeted, accounting for the disproportionate number of them in autodeditions. By donating themselves to powerful monasteries, they gained the protection of the church against the far worse fate of unjust servitude to rapacious lords who would exploit them economically and not hesitate to rape them (Sutherland, 2017).

In nearly all slaveholding societies where the institution was of any significance, birth rapidly became the most important means by which persons became enslaved, and by which the enslaved were

THE INSTITUTION OF SLAVERY AND ITS CONSEQUENCES

acquired. Contrary to a common misconception, this was true even of slave societies in which the enslaved population did not reproduce itself naturally. The fact that births failed to compensate for deaths, or to meet the increased demand for the enslaved – which was true of most of the slave societies of the New World up to the last decades of the eighteenth century – does not mean that birth did not remain the main source of slaves (see Chapter 8 on slavery and genocide in Jamaica).

However, the role of birth as a source of slaves was strongly mediated by the rules of status inheritance, which took account of the complications caused by mixed unions between the enslaved and free persons. There were four main rules:

1   The child's status was determined by the mother's status only, regardless of the father's status. This was true of most modern and premodern Western slave societies, and of nearly all premodern non-Western groups with matrilineal rules of descent.
2   Status was determined by the father only, regardless of the mother's status. This unusual pattern was found mainly among certain rigidly patrilineal groups, especially in Africa, where it was the practice among groups such as the Migiurtini Somali, the Margi of northern Nigeria, and among certain Ibo tribes. The practice, however, was not unknown in the West. It was the custom in Homeric Greece and was the norm during the seventeenth century in a few of the North American colonies, such as Maryland and Virginia, and in South Africa and the French Antilles up to the 1680s.
3   Status was determined by the principle of *deterior condicio*, that is, by the mother or father, whoever had the lower status. This was the harshest inheritance rule and was the practice in China from the period of the Han dynasties up to the reforms of the thirteenth and fourteenth centuries. It found its most extreme application in Korea, where it was the dominant mode down to 1731. The rule also applied in Visigothic Spain and medieval and early modern Tuscany. The only known case in the New World was that of South Carolina in the early eighteenth century.
4   The fourth principle of slave inheritance, that of *melior condicio*, is in direct contrast to the last mentioned, in that the child inherited the status of the free parent, whatever the gender of the parent, as long as the father acknowledged his paternity. This is the earliest known rule of slave inheritance and may have been the most widely distributed. It was the norm in the ancient Near

23

East and, with the exception of the Tuareg, it became the practice among nearly all Islamic societies. The rule was supported among Muslims by another Quranic prescription and practice: the injunction that a slave woman was to be freed, along with her children, as soon as she bore a son for her enslaver.

The only known cases in Europe of the *melior condicio* rule both emerged during the thirteenth century. In Sweden, it was codified in the laws of Ostergotland and Svealand as part of a general pattern of reforms. In Spain, religion was the decisive factor in the appearance of a modified version of the rule. Baptized children of a Saracen or Jewish-owned slave and a Christian were immediately freed. Throughout Latin America, although the legal rule was of the first type – the children of enslaved women were to become slaves – the widespread custom of concubinage with enslaved women, coupled with the tendency to recognize and manumit the offspring of such unions, meant that, in practice, a modified version of the *melior condicio* rule prevailed where the free person was the father, which was usually the case with mixed unions.

1.3: The acquisition of slaves

Slaves not born to, or inherited by, an owner were acquired mainly through external and internal trading systems, as part of bride and dowry payments, as money, or as gifts. There were five major slave-trading systems in world history. The Indian Ocean trade was the oldest, with records dating back to 1580 BCE, and it persisted down to the twentieth century CE. Slaves from sub-Saharan Africa were transported to the Middle and Near East as well as to Southern Europe. It has been estimated that between the years 800 and 1800 CE approximately 3 million slaves were traded on this route, and more than 2 million were traded during the nineteenth century.

The Black Sea and Mediterranean slave trade supplied slaves to the ancient European empires and flourished from the seventh century BCE through to the end of the Middle Ages. More than a quarter of a million slaves may have been traded in this system during the first century of our era. The European slave trade flourished from the early ninth century CE to the middle of the twelfth century, and was dominated by the Vikings. One of the two main trading routes ran westward across the North Sea; the other ran eastward. Celtic peoples, especially the Irish, were raided and sold in Scandinavia. Most

THE INSTITUTION OF SLAVERY AND ITS CONSEQUENCES

of the enslaved traded on the eastern routes were of Slavic ancestry. It was the Viking raiding, and wide distribution, of Slavic slaves throughout Europe that accounts for the common linguistic root of the term "slave" in all major European languages.

The trans-Saharan trade has persisted from the mid-seventh century CE down to the twenty-first and involved the trading of sub-Saharan Africans throughout North Africa and parts of Europe. It has been estimated that some 6.85 million persons were traded in this system up to the end of the nineteenth century. Although it declined substantially during the twentieth century, largely under European pressure, significant numbers of Africans were, until recently, still being traded in Sudan and Mauritania.

The transatlantic slave trade was the largest in size and certainly the most extensive of all these systems. The most recent evidence suggests that between the years 1500 and 1870, some 11.5 million Africans were taken to the Americas. Of the 10.5 million who were forced from Africa between 1650 and 1870, 8.9 million survived the crossing. Although all the maritime West European nations engaged in this trade, the main traders were the British, the Portuguese, and the French. Four regions account for 80 percent of all slaves going to the New World: the Gold Coast (Ghana), the Bights of Benin and Biafra, and West-Central Africa. Overall, 40 percent of all slaves landed in Brazil and 47 percent in the Caribbean. Although only 7 percent of all slaves who left Africa landed in North America, by 1810 the United States had, nonetheless, one of the largest slave populations due to its unusual success in the reproduction of its slave populations. For the entire three and a half centuries of the Atlantic slave trade, approximately 15 percent of those forced from Africa died on the Atlantic crossing (some 1.5 million), with losses averaging between six and eight thousand per year during the peak period between the years 1760 and 1810.

1.4: Treatment of the enslaved

It is difficult to generalize about the treatment of the enslaved, since this varied considerably not only between societies but also within them. There was no simple correlation of favorable factors. Furthermore, the same factor may operate in favor of the enslaved in one situation, but against them in the next. Thus, in many small kin-based societies, the enslaved were relatively well treated and regarded as junior members of the enslaver's family, but could nonetheless be sacrificed brutally on special occasions, such as potlatches or the death of the slaveholder, as was true of Indigenous peoples of the northwest coast of North America such as the Haida and Tlingit. In advanced premodern societies such as Greece and Rome, as well as modern slave societies such as Brazil, the enslaved in the mines or latifundia suffered horribly short lives, while skilled urban slaves were often virtually free and sometimes even pampered. In the Caribbean, the provision ground system, by which the enslaved supported themselves, led to high levels of malnutrition compared to the US South, where slaveholders provided nearly all the enslaveds' provision. Nonetheless, Caribbean slaves cherished the provision ground system for the periods of self-determination and escape from the slaveholder's direct control that it offered.

In general, the most important factors influencing the condition of the enslaved were the uses to which they were put, their mode of acquisition, their location – whether urban or rural – absenteeism of owners, proximity to the slaveholder, and the personal characteristics of the the enslaved. Slaves were acquired for purely economic, prestige, political, administrative, sexual, and ritual purposes. The enslaved who worked in mines or in gangs on highly organized farming systems were often far worse off than those who were employed in some skilled craft in urban regions, especially where the latter were allowed to hire themselves out independently. Slaves acquired for military or administrative purposes, as was often the case in the Islamic world – the Janissaries and Mamelukes being the classic examples – were clearly at an advantage when compared with lowly field hands or aging concubines. Newly bought slaves, especially those who grew up as free persons and were new to their enslaver's society, usually led more wretched lives than those born to their owners. High levels of absenteeism among owners – which was true of the owners of slave latifundia in ancient Rome as well as the Caribbean slave societies and some parts of Latin America – often meant ill-usage by managers and overseers who were paid on a commission basis.

Proximity to the slaveholder cut both ways with respect to the treatment of the enslaved. Household slaves were usually materially better off, and in some cases close ties developed between them and their enslavers – for example, between owners and their former nannies, or with a favored concubine. However, proximity meant more sustained and direct supervision, which might easily become brutal.

Ethnic and somatic or perceived ethnoracial differences between enslavers and enslaved operated in complex ways. Intra-ethnic slavery was uncommon in world history, although by no means nonexistent,

THE INSTITUTION OF SLAVERY AND ITS CONSEQUENCES

while it was frequent between peoples of different perceived "racial" groups. The common view that New World slavery was distinctive in that enslavers and the enslaved belonged to different perceived races is incorrect. Where there were somatic differences, the treatment of the enslaved depended on how these differences were perceived and, independently of this, how attractive the enslaved was in the eyes of the enslavers. Scandinavian women were prized in the slave harems of many Islamic Sultans, but so were attractive Ethiopian and sub-Saharan women. Furthermore, in Muslim India and eighteenth-century England and France, dark-skinned slaves were the most favored, especially as young pages. In the New World, on the other hand, mulatto and other light-skinned female slaves were often better treated than their more African-looking counterparts.

Two other factors should be mentioned in considering the treatment of the enslaved: laws and religion. Slightly more than a half of all slave societies on which data exist had some kind of slave laws, in some cases elaborate servile codes, the oldest known being those of ancient Mesopotamia. Slightly less than a half had none. Laws did make a difference; a much higher proportion of societies without any slave codes tended to treat the enslaved harshly. Nonetheless, the effectiveness of laws was mediated by other factors such as the relative size of the enslaved population, and religion.

The degree to which religion, especially Islam and Christianity, influenced the treatment of the enslaved is a controversial subject. Islam had explicit injunctions for the treatment of the enslaved, and these were sometimes influential, especially those relating to manumission. Although racism and strong preference for light complexion were found throughout the Islamic lands, it is nonetheless the case that Islam as a creed has been more assimilative and universalist than any other of the world religions, and has rarely been implicated in egregiously racist movements similar to those that have tarnished the history of Christianity such as Nazism, apartheid, the Ku Klux Klan, Southern Christianity during the era of segregation, and the ethnic cleansing of Eastern Europe. However, Islam never developed any movement for abolition, and, in general, strongly supported the institution of slavery, especially as a means of winning converts.

For most of its history up to the end of the eighteenth century, Christianity simply took slavery for granted, had little to say about the treatment of the enslaved, and generally urged the enslaved to obey their enslavers. This changed radically with the rise of evangelical Christianity in the late eighteenth and early nineteenth centuries,

THE NATURE AND STUDY OF SLAVERY

during which it played a critical role in the abolition of both the slave trade and slavery in Europe and the Americas. Throughout the world, Christianity appealed strongly to the enslaved and to ex-slave populations, and in the Americas their descendants are among the most devout Christians. While Christianity may have had conservative influences on converted slaves, it is also the case that nearly all the major slave revolts from the late eighteenth century were influenced strongly by rebel leaders, such as Daddy Sharp in Jamaica and Nat Turner in America, who interpreted the faith in radical terms, or by leaders of syncretic Afro-Christian religions.

1.5: Manumission as an integral element of slavery

With a few notable exceptions, manumission, the release from slavery, was an integral and necessary element of the institution wherever it became important (Patterson, 2018 [1982]: Ch. 8). The reason for this is that it solved the incentive problem implicit in slavery. The promise of redemption proved to be the most important way of motivating the enslaved to work assiduously on their enslaver's behalf. In many parts of the world, the act of manumission was culturally interpreted as a gift-exchange in which the enslaver bestowed the treasured gift of freedom on the enslaved in exchange for eternal gratitude, respect, and often services to the former enslaver (Patterson 2018 [1982]: 214–19).

The enslaved were manumitted in a wide variety of ways, the most important being: self-purchase or purchase by others, usually free relatives; through the postmortem or testamentary mode; through cohabitation or sexual relations; through adoption; through political means or by the state; and by various ritual or sacral means. Self-purchase or purchase by relatives or friends of the enslaved into freedom was by far the most important means in the advanced slave economies of Greece and Rome, as well as in the modern capitalistic slave regimes. However, it was not the most widespread in other kinds of slave systems, and in parts of the world such as Africa it was uncommon. Postmortem manumission by wills and other means was common in Islamic lands and in many parts of Africa. This form of manumission was usually intimately linked to religious practices and with expectations of religious returns for what was often defined as an act of piety.

As indicated earlier, in many slave societies concubines sometimes gained freedom for themselves and their children. Manumission by

28

the state for acts of heroism or for military action was an important, though episodic, form of manumission not only in the ancient world, but also in many New World slave societies. Thousands of slaves gained their freedom in this way, not only in Latin America, but also in North America during the American war of independence and in wars against Spain in the Southern United States. In 1807, in what was possibly the largest mass manumission in the history of slavery, some ten thousand slave soldiers of the West India Regiment, located in various slave colonies of the region although purchased in Africa, were manumitted by the British army, thirty-one years before the final abolition of slavery in the British empire.

Manumission by adoption was unusual, but in certain societies, such as ancient Rome, it constituted the most complete form of release from slavery. The enslaved were sometimes manumitted for ritual or religious reasons, or on special celebratory occasions. Although thousands of slaves were manumitted at Delphi, ostensibly by being sold to Apollo, such manumissions had become merely legal formalism by the second century BCE, although the practice may have harked back to an earlier era when they were genuinely religious in character. In other societies, religious or ritual manumissions were often substitutes for earlier practices in which the enslaved were sacrificed. Since manumission meant the negation of slavery, freeing the enslaved was, for many peoples, symbolically identical to killing them; the sacrifice of their social death made them socially alive, a gift of freedom analogous to the sacrificial gift of the slave's physical life to the gods. Such practices were common in some parts of Africa and the Pacific islands, and among some Indigenous tribes of the northwest coast of America slaves were either killed or given away in potlatch ceremonies. There is an extension of this primitive symbolic logic in Christianity, where Christ's sacrificial death is interpreted as a substitute for the redemption of mankind from enslavement to sin and eternal death, "redemption" (from Latin *redemptionem*; nominative *redemptio*) literally meaning "purchasing," or "buying back" someone out of slavery.

In all slave societies, certain categories of slave were more likely to be manumitted than others. The most important factors explaining the incidence of manumission were gender, the status of parents, age, skill, residence and location, the means of acquisition, and, where relevant, skin color. These factors are similar to those influencing the treatment of the enslaved and will not be discussed further. They were also important in explaining varying rates between societies. Thus, societies with relatively higher proportions of skilled slaves, a greater

THE NATURE AND STUDY OF SLAVERY

location of the enslaved in urban areas, higher ratios of female to male slaves, and higher rates of concubinage between enslavers and the enslaved were more likely to have higher rates of manumission than those with lower levels of these attributes. Added to this is another critical variable: the availability of slaves, either internally or externally, to replace manumitted slaves. As long as such sources existed and the replacement value of the manumitted slave was less than the price of manumission, it suited slaveowners to manumit the enslaved, especially when the slaves in question were nearing, or had already reached, the end of their useful life.

However, on rare occasions, the supply of slaves was cut off when demand remained high or was on the increase. This always resulted in very low rates of manumission. The most striking such case in the history of slavery was the US South, where the rise of cotton-based, capitalistic slavery in the early nineteenth century came within a few years of the termination of the Atlantic slave trade to America. Planters responded by reducing the manumission rate to near zero. A similar situation, though not as extreme, developed in the Spanish islands of the Caribbean during the nineteenth century, when the plantation system developed in the context of British enforcement of the abolition of the slave trade in the region. The result was that previously high rates of manumission plunged to very low rates.

A final point concerns the status of freed persons. This varied considerably across slave societies and bore little relation to the rate of manumission. Thus manumission rates were high in the Dutch colonies of Curaçao and in nineteenth-century Louisiana, but the condition of freedmen was wretched. Conversely, in the British Caribbean, where manumission rates were relatively low, the condition of freedmen was relatively good, some groups achieving full civil liberties before the end of slavery. The main factor explaining the difference in treatment was the availability of economic opportunities for freedmen, and the extent to which the dominant planter class needed them as allies against the enslaved. In the Caribbean, the small proportion of slaveholders and Europeans and the existence of a vast and rebellious slave population gave much political leverage to the small but important freed population. No such conditions existed in the United States, where the free and White population greatly outnumbered the enslaved, and conditions for rebellion were severely restricted. In the ancient world, ethnic barriers meant generally low status and few opportunities for the manumitted in the Greek states, in contrast with Rome, where cultural and economic factors favored the growth and prosperity of a large freedmen class, a group that

THE INSTITUTION OF SLAVERY AND ITS CONSEQUENCES

eventually came to dominate Rome demographically and culturally, with major implications for Western civilization.

1.6: Agency and resistance

Non-resistive agency

The social death of the enslaved did not mean that they considered themselves to be in that condition, or that they did not exercise agency. Their agency was made possible and exercised in three basic ways. First, it was often in the interest of the enslaver to permit their slaves some exercise of agency. In fact, an agentless slave was likely a useless one. In all but the simplest of tasks, it suited the slaveholder that the enslaved exercised some agency in doing what the enslaver wanted. Adam Smith was famously of the view that the enslaved were inherently inefficient because they were unmotivated workers, and that, as a result, the complex slave systems, such as the capitalistic structures of the Americas, would collapse of their own accord. He was wrong. Economic historians such as Fogel and Engerman (1974) may have gone too far in claiming that US slaves were more efficient than free Northern US workers, but there is now little doubt that the plantations of the antebellum South and the Caribbean were highly profitable, as were the wine-producing latifundia and commercial enterprises of ancient Rome and the craft shops of classical Athens, which were all dependent on slave labor. Indeed, in ancient Athens, most of the civil servants – policemen, court clerks, archivists, and accountants – were *dēmosioi* or publicly owned slaves (Ismard, 2017). This worked because slaveholders permitted their slaves to make decisions on their own and to exercise some control over the immediate outcomes of their actions. To be sure, if these outcomes were unsuccessful, the enslaved, unlike other agents, could be corporally punished, unlike free agents who would be punished in other ways, such as being fired. But this reflects the dishonorable condition of the enslaved rather than their lack of agency. The fact that the whip was used in the cane and cotton fields of the Americas reinforces the point. This was laborious drudge work, offering the enslaved little or no incentive to exercise their sense of control over the outcome. However, in the many skilled occupations on the sugar and cotton plantations, drivers with whips were conspicuously absent.

It is precisely because the enslaved yearned for activities that enabled them to exercise their agency that they performed these tasks without immediate compulsion. Nothing better illustrates the point than the fact that they sometimes did so even when it was not in their immediate material interest. The best illustration of this was the provision ground system of the larger islands of the Caribbean. In Jamaica, planters, in their greed to make more profit, allowed their slaves one day off every two weeks, plus Sundays (out of the crop season, when they were allowed only one day), to grow their own food on the marginal lands of the plantation. The enslaved eagerly accepted the offer to do so, entirely because it provided them with unsupervised time on their own in which they exercised their own agency in the provision of their basic necessities. It was, in fact, a cruel bargain. There was not enough time to farm the land, which was located in the infertile, mountainous backlands of the plantation. The result was that most slaves, especially children, were malnourished and, in the event of hurricanes, hundreds, sometimes thousands, died of starvation. And yet, the enslaved greatly valued these provision grounds and even managed to establish Sunday markets where they exchanged some of the foods they had grown in what were more social than profitable economic practices. They did so because for one, and sometimes two, days they exercised agency and had some control over the outcomes of their actions (Patterson, 2022 [1967]: 83–4, 103–4).

The second area in which the enslaved exercised agency was in those situations or periods of time that were of no interest to their enslavers. Most slaves had to be given time off to rest and it was then that they extended and enjoyed relations with each other beyond the eye and supervision of drivers and other controllers. Between sundown and sunup, and on the few holidays as well as less intensive periods of work, the enslaved established familial bonds and friendships, played, prayed, and fashioned songs, stories, dance, religious rituals, and other cultural creations. Nothing better expresses human resilience and adaptability of humanity than the survival of slave populations under all but the most brutally oppressive systems. At the same time, it is important that we do not exaggerate the costs of survival and the sometimes explicit, more often covert, experience of trauma that always accompanies the social death of slavery. As I noted in the introduction, too many historians, especially in the United States, desperate for a usable past, impose on the iniquitous moral, mental, and physical exploitation of slavery an interpretation of social harmony and normalcy that amounts to an idealization of their experience. In applauding the resiliency of the enslaved, we should never neglect the trauma of their social death.

THE INSTITUTION OF SLAVERY AND ITS CONSEQUENCES

Resistance

There were many occasions, however, when the enslaved exercised violent agency against the interests of the slaveholder. Here we enter the realm of resistance, which were of two broad kinds: passive or covert, and violent or overt. Covert resistance existed in four sub-types: go-slow or work stoppage, deliberate inefficiency, sabotage, and evasion; satire; running away; and suicide. These were the slaves' equivalent of the peasants' "weapons of the weak," studied by James Scott (1985). Overt resistance was usually violent and of two sub-types: individual and collective.

Throughout the Americas, the enslaved, especially those doing the most arduous work in the fields, practiced a form of slowdown by deliberately cutting back on the amount of effort they put into their tasks, or "malingering," as the enslavers preferred to call it. They had ways of doing so even while appearing to be working hard. Enslavers were sometimes aware of this and responded by whipping, but this often had the opposite effect. The universal complaints of enslavers was that the enslaved were inherently lazy and could only be made to work efficiently under the threat of being beaten. The enslaved everywhere, and in all times, engaged in various strategies such as tool-breaking, mistreatment of draft animals, and theft. Observers of eighteenth-century Jamaica claimed that as much as a sixth of the entire sugar crop was taken by the enslaved and sold on the local market. When caught, a standard response was that it was not possible for the enslaved to steal from their enslavers, since everything they owned belonged to the slaveholder (Patterson, 2022 [1967]), or, as Frederick Douglass famously put it, the enslaved was merely "taking meat out of one tub [of the enslaver] and putting it in another" (Douglass, 1855).

The use of satire and trickery consisted of cultural forms of resistance found in all slave societies, from ancient times to the modern plantation. Satirical songs and mimicry were used all over the Americas to lampoon enslavers and other free persons (Pierson, 1976). The Sambo stereotype controversially studied by Elkins (1959) did indeed exist, and can be found in other slave societies of the Americas and the ancient world. Elkins's error was to believe that the infantilized playing the fool behavior reported by slaveholders reflected the real personality of the enslaved when, in fact, it was a form of lampooning of the enslavers and other free people, of subversively flattering them into believing that their stereotype was real, as a way of getting what the enslaved wanted. As Bertram Wyatt-Brown (1988: 1242))

33

remarked: "The survivor was the conscienceless 'chameleon' who adopted the coloration that the totalitarian slave regime – or the master's whim – imposed." Sambo could be found in the Quashee stereotype of the Jamaican slaves, in the "Graeculus" stereotype of Greek slaves in ancient Rome, and in the enslaved characters of the ancient Greek and Roman comic writers (Patterson 2022: 174–81; Harsh, 1955; McCarthy, 2004). The enslaved of Jamaica spoke for all the enslaved of all times when they summed up the real meaning of their buffoonery in one of their pithiest proverbs: "play fool to catch wise."

Running away was another prime weapon universally used by the enslaved. It was pervasive in Greece and Rome, in spite of harsh laws to prevent it. Some twenty thousand slaves are said to have fled Attica near the end of the Peloponnesian War (Cartledge, 1985: 9); and a hundred thousand are estimated to have fled the antebellum South, many to Canada and Mexico (Blackett, 2018). In Jamaica and Latin America, thousands not only fled, but formed maroon settlements, some of which persisted for decades, such as the famous Palmares quilombo in Brazil (Patterson 2022: 262–4; Reis and dos Santos, 2010).

Suicide was the most extreme form of passive resistance. Southern slaveholders propagated the belief that the enslaved rarely took their own lives, partly to blunt abolitionist arguments that Blacks suffered psychologically under slavery. Terry Snyder's (2015) study has undermined this claim. Suicide was ubiquitous during the middle passage (Mustakeem, 2016); it was also frequent among Africans who were newly arrived, during their period of seasoning. It was therefore more common during the earlier periods of North American slavery, when there was a higher proportion of newly arrived African-born slaves, though it continued until late in the history of Caribbean and Latin American slavery, where Africans constituted a significant proportion of the slave populations until the very end. There were several dramatic cases of mass suicide among slave rebels who chose death over being defeated and recaptured in Jamaica (Patterson 2022: 264–5). Although suicide was not uncommon among the free people of ancient Greece and Rome, where it was considered an honorable way to end one's life in the face of humiliation, cases of slave suicide are not reported in the sources, which does not mean that it did not occur.

The enslaved everywhere also resisted violently. We do not know how many slaveholders were murdered by the enslaved in the antebellum South, since this was usually done furtively, but it did occur,

34

THE INSTITUTION OF SLAVERY AND ITS CONSEQUENCES

especially in cases where the enslaved were pushed beyond their limits of physical or emotional endurance. Celia, a slave in Missouri, was typical of cases that came to light. Repeatedly raped from the age of fourteen by her much older enslaver, as a result of which she had a child, Celia demanded that the assaults end when she fell in love with another slave. When the slaveholder persisted, she clubbed him to death and burned his body, for which she was hanged in 1855 (Linder, 1995). The murder of enslavers was more frequent in the Caribbean and Latin America, especially Brazil, where the last person to be executed was a slave, in 1876. Poisoning was the preferred means of surreptitiously killing enslavers and other Whites, the techniques brought from Africa and kept alive by the relatively higher proportion of Africans in these slave populations, compared with the United States. The skill of poisoning, strongly associated with female slaves, was integral to African-derived medicine, as well as to the practice of witchcraft or Obeah. As Karol Weaver (2006: 75) has pointed out, "the practice of herbalism by slaves was a powerful tool and a symbol of political resistance" in Haitian slave society, which was equally true of Jamaica (Patterson 2022 [1967]: 186–90). Fear of being poisoned sometimes generated mass panic among Whites, as happened in the Sarah Bassett conspiracy of Bermuda in the late 1720s, the Mackandal terror of St. Domingue during the 1750s, and in Martinique in 1826 (Maxwell, 2000; Paton, 2012; Savage, 2007). There are few reported cases of enslavers being killed by their slaves in Graeco-Roman antiquity, which does not mean that it did not happen. The Romans, however, had a brutal and apparently effective means of preventing it: should a slave kill their enslaver, the entire household of slaves would be executed, as happened during the reign of Claudius when some four hundred slaves of a wealthy murdered enslaver were crucified (Hopkins, 1993).

The threat or actual occurrence of slave revolts was a common feature of most advanced slave societies. There is little evidence of it in small-scale kin-based societies, and ancient Greece was unusual in the relative absence of data on the subject, except for the problematic case of Spartan helotage (Cartledge, 1985). The view of Moses Finley that, other than the three great servile wars of the second and first centuries BCE, slave revolts were rare in all Western antiquity, has been challenged by more recent scholars, especially Theresa Urbainczyk (2008), who persuasively shows that, in addition to these three great revolts, significant slave uprisings occurred in other regions and periods of the Roman Empire. While not a major feature of the Islamic world, the fourteen-year revolt of mainly

African slaves in ninth-century Iraq, known as the Zanj, ranks as one of the great slave revolts in world history.

Slave revolts against European slave traders and colonists were widespread in the Atlantic and the Americas, beginning on the slave ships, in which some 485 rebellions occurred (Richardson, 2001). Starting in 1521 in what became the Dominican Republic, major revolts occurred throughout the hemisphere, though far more frequently in the Caribbean, Central America and Brazil. Long before the celebrated Haitian revolt, there were several successful revolts in Jamaica and Haiti, if by success is meant the defeat of the slaveholder class in battle leading them to recognize the freedom of the rebels and their right to live independently on their own maroon communities (Rodriguez, 1997; Price, 1996).

The causes of slave revolts will be discussed in Chapter 7 – which examines one of the most successful series of slave uprisings in history, that of the First Maroon slave wars in Jamaica during the late seventeenth and early eighteenth centuries. For now, we should note that the occurrence of slave revolts was due less to the propensity of the enslaved of a given region to rebel, and more to the existence of demographic, economic, and geographical factors. Thus, one should not assess the willingness of a slave population to rebel against the system of their oppression in terms of the occurrences of revolts, since conditions may simply have been unfavorable to successful outcomes. The US South well illustrates this. Conditions there strongly disfavored armed uprisings. At the same time, the impressively large number of plots and conspiracies, in addition to revolts, numbering over 260, as well as their activities during the American revolutionary war and in the Union Army during the American Civil War, clearly indicate that their propensity to overturn the slave system was as great as that of the enslaved elsewhere; they were correctly viewed by antebellum Whites as the "domestic enemy" (Taylor, 2014; Genovese, 1980) a description true of the enslaved everywhere and in all times. An ancient Roman proverb, told by Seneca, expressed it best: "*totidem hostes esse quot servos*: there are as many enemies as there are slaves" (Seneca, Letter 47: 5–11).

1.7: The enduring consequences of slavery

The exercise of agency and resistance by the enslaved against their oppression and social death are remarkable testaments to the resilience and strength of the human spirit and the unquenchable need not simply to survive but to preserve some modicum of humanity and dignity.

However, slavery and its aftermath had enduring consequences which must be recognized and understood. As Bloome and Pace (2024: 1126) demonstrated in an innovative recent study: "Even when circumstances change across historical time, the past shapes the present through intergenerational legacies." We already noted that slavery was an assault on every one of the basic needs of human beings. The endless physical, social, economic, and psychic abuse amounted to a deep unfathomable individual and collective trauma, a constant sense of loss and grief even among the few who, through sheer superhuman will and luck, succeeded in breaking away from the "tomb of slavery," as Douglass did. But, as Douglass himself confessed, reflecting on his "first glimmering conception of the dehumanizing character of slavery," long after he had gained his freedom: "I can never get rid of that conception." Just hearing a few notes from a slave song reduced him to tears (1855: 14).

We know that sustained, unremitting trauma has layered and complex intergenerational consequences for descendants (see Danieli, 1998: Introduction, Chs. 1–2; Graff, 2014). It is reasonable to assume that slavery is somehow related to both the external inequalities and persisting personal and structural racism that descendants of slaves experience throughout the world, as well as the internalized oppression of problematic social and psychological coping mechanisms and distrust that hampers their self-advancement (Fanon, 2008; Smith, 2010; Nunn, 2011). Among a growing number of scholarly descendants of the enslaved in the Americas, especially the United States, there has emerged a vision of the persistence of social death into the living present, called "Afropessimism" by Frank Wilderson (2021), its main theoretician, that finds no solace in the advancement of the few or the achievements of the civil rights movements and postcolonial Black majority states. "Slavery persists as an issue in the political life of black America," Saidiya Hartman (2007) writes, "because black lives are still imperiled and devalued by a racial calculus and political arithmetic that were entrenched centuries ago. This is the afterlife of slavery."

It is important, however, to distinguish origin from consequences. Assuming an afterlife of slavery is one thing; demonstrating the direct and indirect causal pathways by which slavery persisted, where it persisted, among which group of descendants, and for how long, are related but separate matters that raise difficult issues concerning the nature of causality and continuity (on which, see Patterson,

2004; Ermakoff, 2019). As Frans van Lunteren (2019: 324) aptly stated: "We do not just want to know where we came from; we also want to know how we got here." Fortunately, in recent years some scholars have begun to address the issue of "the legacy of slavery" and its immediate consequences in a rigorous manner, instead of simply assuming continuity, relying mainly on statistical and archival analyses of place-based (Acharya et al., 2018; Baker, 2022) and inter-generational approaches (Bloome, 2014) as well as a combination of both approaches (Bloome and Pace, 2024) to probe the imputed effects of slavery on several contemporary outcomes.

Thus, Martin Ruef and Ben Fletcher (2003) found a clear pattern of institutional reproduction of inequality in the translation of the inequalities of slavery into the inequalities of the crop lien and share-cropping system. To be sure, mediating factors such as migration and education ruptured institutional reproduction and, increasingly, Black mobility was determined by structural features of the postbel-lum capitalist system, but Ruef and Fletcher found that substantial barriers to Black mobility can be attributed to the direct legacies of slavery.

In the United States, the sharecropping and broader Jim Crow system was a powerful mediating institution in the transmission of the effects of slavery, but it did so in complex and often indirect ways and its role is sometimes the opposite of what is often assumed. Thus, Michelle Alexander's (2010) popular attribution of present-day mass incarceration of Black Americans to the persistence of the Jim Crow era is problematic. As Christopher Muller (2018, 2021) has shown, there was a relatively low rate of incarceration of Blacks during the Jim Crow era of the South, much lower than in the Northern states. Because Southern planters needed Black labor, they rigged the system to prevent Blacks from being incarcerated so as to make them more readily available for labor exploitation on the sharecropping farms. This racist exploitation of Black labor was, to be sure, a direct legacy of slavery, but it explains the low Southern rate of incarceration, which illustrates the point that slavery's legacy works through com-plex, not readily obvious, mediating causal pathways.

The sharecropping system also mediated the legacy of slavery on Black gender relations and familial fragility. As those who argue against any connection between slavery and present gender relations and familial disruption like to point out, there was a relatively high, seemingly stable, rate of early marriage among Blacks on the share-cropping farms, suggesting a modern origin of present problems. But, as Deirdre Bloome and Christopher Muller (2015) have demonstrated,

THE INSTITUTION OF SLAVERY AND ITS CONSEQUENCES

the pattern of early marriage resulted from the desperate economic plight of Black women who were patriarchally denied access to land and the crop lien arrangement – a denial rooted in the misogyny of slavery – and thus were forced to marry, work on the farm, and produce laboring children as the only means of survival. Far from being an indication of familial stability, early marriage and gender exploitation resulted in deep resentment, reflected in high rates of marital disruption. As soon as other economic opportunities opened in the post-sharecropping era, Black women chose being single over patriarchal domination.

Other works have shown a clear legacy of slavery in the persisting political disenfranchisement of Black Americans in the South (Acharya et al., 2018); in the much higher rates of economic disparities and poverty among Southern Blacks (O'Connell, 2012; Bertocchi and Dimico, 2014); in the racial education gap (Bertocchi and Dimico, 2012); in racial disparities in education enrollment rates (Reece and O'Connell, 2016); in anti-Black hate crimes, amplified by residential segregation (Gunadi, 2019; Bailey and O'Neill, 2023); in the pattern of violent crime among both Blacks and Southern Whites (Gouda and Rigterink, 2017); in racial disparities in arrest rates (Ward, 2022) and executions (Vandiver et al., 2007); in the exclusion of Blacks from labor markets and reduction in the returns to investment in education (Jung, 2019); and in explaining much higher rates of heart disease mortality in the US South (Kramer et al., 2017). Other work has shown a more direct influence of the extent of slavery in a region on the likelihood of pretrial detention, and the chance and length of incarceration (Gottlief and Flynn, 2021). Apart from its effects on crime, these works have largely avoided the legacy of slavery for present problems of internal oppression. A notable exception concerns the effects of slavery on colorism and skin-tone stratification among Black and White Americans (Reece, 2018), which an increasing number of studies have shown to be far more severe in their economic and health consequences than previously acknowledged (Monk, 2021).

The deleterious effects of slavery have also been documented for other areas of the world, especially the Americas and Africa (for an overview, see Bertocchi, 2016). In general, the greater the presence of slavery in Africa and the societies of the Americas, the lower the long-term level of economic and social development. While initially generating enormous riches for the slave-traders and slave-holding minorities during the seventeenth and eighteenth centuries, slavery led to defective institutional outcomes that retarded modern economic development (Acemoglu et al., 2001; on Africa, see Nunn, 2008, 2011; on the Americas see Engerman et al., 2002; on Jamaica, see Patterson, 2019). Similar to the United States, the countries and other sub-regions that had greater levels of slavery are those that today show the worst social and economic outcomes for Blacks. In Colombia, for example, the former presence of slavery is associated with higher levels of poverty, greater land inequality, lower school enrollment and vaccination coverage, and far less provision of public goods among the Black population. These effects have been present for more than a hundred years and, sadly, seem to have gotten worse more recently (Acemoglu et al., 2012).

While providing welcome scientific evidence for the afterlife of slavery, these works have a major limitation. The statistical strategy they use confines their results to a comparison of those areas where slavery existed with others where it was absent in 1865. This precludes an understanding of the diffusion of slavery's legacy to non-slave areas of the societies studied (for a major exception that addresses this problem, see Bloome and Pace, 2024). But we know that such diffusion was rampant. Whites in the north and the west of the United States, especially post-abolition immigrants, were quick to embrace the racist advantages of Whiteness, of being non-Black; the descendants of slaveholders and their allies transmitted the evils of slavery and social death in policies that institutionalized racist disparities everywhere. Ohio had no slavery; it is today among the most racist states of America. Most Blacks today would rather live in Richmond and Atlanta than in Levittown, New York, built after World War II, where the language of its racist home covenants is still engraved in many of its deeds.

For those descendants of slavery who have made it in America's distinctive, top-down mode of racial integration, Afropessimism may seem outmoded. After all, did not a president of America, the most powerful man on earth, rise from their midst? And also governors and senators and entertainers of vast wealth? But to the mass of the descendants of the enslaved in the favelas and shanty-towns of the Black Atlantic, the rural Black belts, and the hyper-segregated ghettoes behind the hidden walls of glittering liberal American cities, the afterlife of slavery is all too real. In and out of these vast ghettoes, the lingering shadows of social death – the social impotence, disparities, and daily harassment by agents of the state; the exclusions, slights, micro aggressions, and injustices; the degradation of impoverishment in the richest of all lands; the self-destructive violence – loom large on every corner, in every patch of cluttered space that passes for a home.

— 2 —

REVISITING SLAVERY AND PROPERTY AS A "BUNDLE OF RIGHTS"

The traditional Western conception of slavery has always made the treatment of persons as the exclusive and absolute property of the slaveholder the defining feature of the institution. In *Slavery and Social Death* (1982), I challenged this view, arguing that the most common Western conception of property, while certainly important for advanced Western systems of slavery, is insufficient for the comparative study of slavery, on two grounds.

First, it does not adequately designate a distinct category of persons, since there are numerous societies in which persons clearly considered and treated as slaves were nonetheless not bought and sold. Thus, in many Islamic societies, several categories of the enslaved were not treated as chattels; among the Tuareg of Mali, for example, only captives were bought and sold, never the locally born Eklan (Winter, 1984), and the same was the case with slave concubines in the Ottoman empire who had borne the slaveholder a son who automatically transitioned to the status of *ümm-i veled* (Aykan, 2017: 15). In the Indigenous societies of the Americas and New Zealand, where slaveholding was not uncommon, the enslaved were usually not bought and sold, although there was no question that they were socially dead; indeed, they were not infrequently sacrificed and, in some cases, even eaten (Cameron, 2018; Santos-Granero, 2017). Second, the conception of property as absolute ownership is itself inadequate even for Western societies, since it refers to the Roman derived civil law conception of property, which is problematic in the common law tradition, does not apply to non-Western notions of possession, and is increasingly of limited relevance in the modern digital age.

David Lewis (2017), an historian of slavery in the ancient Mediterranean, has stoutly defended the traditional approach in his critique of my position. Lewis relies entirely on Tony Honore's (1961) widely cited concept of property, which he assumes, wrongly, is now the accepted view among legal theorists, and he asserts that it is universally applicable. As will become clear shortly, he seems unaware of the complexities of the property concept in the West, especially the Anglo-American world, and the fact that it has been a bone of considerable contestation among legal theorists for more than a century, a contestation that has heated up in recent decades as a result of the digital and internet revolutions.

The remainder of this chapter is in two sections. In the first section I take a closer look at the property concept in Western legal and philosophical thought, especially the idea of property as a bundle of rights. The second section examines a continuum of cases in light of what we have concluded from the first section. I conclude with a brief examination of the problem that advanced industrial slavery, especially in the antebellum South, posed for the property concept.

2.1: Property as a bundle of rights (or sticks)

Property, broadly defined, refers to a relationship involving three elements: (a) a proprietor (which may be a person or collective entity), (b) a set of rights or, to use Hohfeldian realist language (Hohfeld, 1913), a set of claims, powers and/or privileges with respect to other persons, in relation to (c) an object, which may be tangible or intangible. Beyond this point, major contestations emerge: questions of who or what can be an owner and the nature of ownership; the extent, nature, and limits on these rights; the persons against whom these rights or claims are made; and, especially in recent years, the nature of the objects regarding which rights can be made.

In global, comparative terms, we may distinguish two basic approaches to property. One, the more widespread and, indeed, the default position found in all non- and pre-Western societies, and increasingly in the Anglo-American world, is the relational, in which property is viewed as a set of relations among persons with regard to an object, and "possession and ownership may more or less explicitly include notions of usufruct, shared access and many other legitimate forms of use of goods and resources that do not imply exclusive, private ownership" (Turner, 2017: 26). The other is the absolute approach in which property is viewed as the possession of the proprietor, to the exclusion of all others, with the emphasis placed on the relation between an owner and an object. This approach was first socially and legally constructed by the ancient Romans and was inherited via the Middle Ages by continental Europeans who adhere to the statute-based civil law tradition. However, as Bertram Turner (2017: 26) has emphasized, anthropologists "from a comparative point of view, often argued that the prominence – some might call it an obsession – with the exclusivity of (individual) private property is not a central aspect of the understanding of property in most societies or cultures." This has long been evident from the data of the Murdock World Sample (Murdock and White, 1969; Divale, 2004) although surprisingly few anthropologists working on this problem have used it. Of the seventy-six societies on which data permitted coding on the property variable, 78 percent had no private property. While I found no relationship between the presence/absence of private property and slavery, it is nonetheless noteworthy that 84 percent of societies with non-hereditary slavery and 78 percent with hereditary slavery existed in societies with no notion of private property. If we focus on access to land, we find that rights to its use are fully communal in the major-ity (53 percent) of premodern societies and are partly communal in a quarter of cases. In only 22 percent of all premodern human societies in history was access to land predominantly private. The presence or absence of slavery bears no significant relation to the existence of private property rights.

The Anglo-American legal tradition differs from the absolute tradi-tion of continental civil law in its embrace of both the relative and absolute approaches to property. The dominant tradition in British law is the common law, which vigorously maintained the pre-Roman relative approach to property. However, civil law absolutism did penetrate the British legal system through several conduits. The work of the glossators, the early commentators and teachers of Roman law following the discovery of the Digest in the late eleventh century, inevitably made its way to England; more important was Canon law, itself strongly influenced by Roman law, the influence of which went beyond religion to issues such as marriage and the family, wills, and even some kinds of contracts. These infusions were strongly resisted by common law practitioners, centered on the Inns of Court, especially after the Tudor reformation, but the civil law influence lin-gered in areas such as maritime and ecclesiastical law and also came through academic dialog with continental philosophers and legal theorists such as Hugo Grotius (1583–1645), Samuel von Pufendorf (1632–94), and Jean-Jacques Burlamaqui (1694–1748), especially their reflections on natural rights and law.

There are at least four ways in which the property concept has been used in Anglo-American legal thought and common parlance. The first is the colloquial layman reference to that which is owned, usually tangibles, as property, such as when a person points to his house and says, "That's my property." In many ways, it is closest to the continental civil law view. Few Anglo-American legal analysts regard this usage as anything but colloquial, an exception being the British legal theorist J. E. Penner (2011), who asserted that "the layman is essentially right" (in a deliberately contentious, but "essentially" qualified argument). It also finds expression in the strand of legal theory that emphasizes the right to exclude as the most critical and necessary element in defining property, theorists varying in what ancillary factors are deemed to be also important (Thomas and Smith, 2007).

There is, secondly, a broad property concept that Donald Kochan (2013) has called the "Lockean-Madisonian definition of property." It may be traced back to Locke (or one interpretation of Locke), but its most forceful expression comes from James Madison, who opens his essay on property by contrasting his own "larger and juster meaning" with the more technical Blackstonian view as follows:

> This term in its application means "that dominion which one man claims and exercises over the external things of the world, in exclusion of every other individual." In its larger and juster meaning, it embraces every thing to which a man may attach a value and have a right; and which leaves to every one else the like advantage. In the former sense, a man's land, or merchandize, or money is called his property. In the latter sense, a man has a property in his opinions and the free communication of them. He has a property of peculiar value in his religious opinions, and in the profession and practice dictated by them. He has a property very dear to him in the safety and liberty of his person. He has an equal property in the free use of his faculties and free choice of the objects on which to employ them. In a word, as a man is said to have a right to his property, he may be equally said to have a property in his rights. (1962 [1792]: 266–8)[1]

This is a quite radical view of the subject, derived intellectually from Locke. The argument that people had a property in their rights

---

[1] Cf. Locke: "Man, by being master of himself, and proprietor of his own person, and the actions or labour of it, had still in himself the great foundation of property; and that, which made up the great part of what he applied to the support or comfort of his being, when invention and arts had improved the conveniencies of life, was perfectly his own, and did not belong in common to others" (*Second Treatise*, Sec. 44). Note, however, that Thomas Jefferson did not share Madison's expansive view of intellectual property. See his letter to Isaac McPherson, August 13, 1813, at: http://press-pubs.uchicago.edu/founders/documents/a1_8_8s12.html.

REVISITING SLAVERY AND PROPERTY AS A "BUNDLE OF RIGHTS"

attached the traditional reverence for property and its force in law to the protection of rights. The essay has had a profound effect on American political life in its influence on the Constitution, and subsequently on Americans' reverence for the Bill of Rights, especially the right of free expression. His view that majorities could threaten the property rights of minorities also influenced the institution of constitutional safeguards for minorities and minority views, although it also limited democratic governance in significant ways. The fact that this influential interpretation of property came from a slaveholder who would later own more than one hundred slaves, none of whom he manumitted in his will, may seem breathtaking in its irony, and downright paradoxical. However, once the origin of freedom in the first large-scale slaveholding society of ancient Athens and subsequent historical construction in the West is understood, the paradox dissolves (on which, see Patterson, 1991; see also Scott and Patterson, 2023). The enslaved came closest to an existential grasp of freedom in the face of their social death. The slaveholder similarly discovered the power and meaning of freedom in imposing its loss and in experiencing, as Hegel was the first to intimate, the perverse, dialectical pleasure of the absence of its absence in his being-as-master:

> The master relates himself to the bondsman mediately through independent existence, for that is precisely what keeps the bondsman in thrall; it is his chain, from which he could not in the struggle get away, and for that reason he proved himself to be dependent, to have his independence in the shape of thinghood [social death?]. The master, however, is the power controlling this state of existence, for he has shown in the struggle that he holds it to be merely something negative. (Hegel, 2016 [1807]: 182)

Madison, especially in his very close relationship with one of his household slaves, his valet Paul Jennings, who shaved him every day and catered to his most private needs for sixteen years and later wrote the first biography of the fourth president, would have come to discover existentially, even without the intellectual provocation of Locke or the tradition of thought forged by Athens, the feeling and sense of having a property in his being and rights as a person. He saw and felt it every day in Jennings's yearning. He enjoyed it every day in deliberately denying it to him, and could write with a straight face of that sweet property that "Heaven, in decreeing man to earn his bread by the sweat of his brow [is he thinking of Jennings?], kindly reserved to him [Madison]." Herein lies the grim origin of America's passion for the property in their rights. It is, however, an origin too dark and confounding for most American legal theorists to contemplate, not to mention ordinary Americans. As the eminent British legal anthropologist, Dame Marilyn Strathern (2005: 136), has tersely observed, Western property law "is surrounded by assumptions that act out the idea that one can have property in persons, or aspects of persons, even though the law is built on its denial." Madison's view, as Kochan correctly notes, also erodes the traditional textbook distinction between property and contract. Viewing rights as property complicates notions of agency and bodily integrity: if one's person is a property, it means that every contract to provide a service entails renting or leasing out one's property. Further, since a contract is a legally binding promise and a promise is an expressed idea to do something, the distinction between contracts and the exercise of one's property rights in one's opinions is eroded. Violating a person's rights and failure to fulfil the terms of a contract end up being similar violations of property law. I could continue, but let's move on.

The third major property concept – the "more particular" one to which Madison referred – is the traditional common law view, originating in the late Middle Ages, that found its classic exposition in Blackstone's *Commentaries on the Laws of England*, especially Book 2. Blackstone opens his discussion of property with a definition completely at odds with the common law tradition, writing that it is "that sole and despotic dominion which one man claims and exercises over the external things of the world, in total exclusion of the right of any other individual in the universe," which, he wryly comments, "so generally strikes the imagination and engages the affections of mankind" (Blackstone, 1979 [1766]: 2). However, there can be few introductory definitions that are more misleading than this, in light of what follows. It clearly aligns with the continental, civil law view of exclusive, absolute ownership derived from the Roman notion of dominium, which Blackstone promptly abandons after the generalities of the second book's first chapter. Beginning with Chapter 2, he offers the classic analysis and systemization of the common law's contrasting, more complex, and relational approach to property, one that allows for various persons having different kinds of claims and powers in the same piece of property. Regarding the same parcel of land, for example, one person may have a leasehold interest, another person a life estate, another an easement, and another a reversionary interest. His distinctions between, and detailed expositions of, real and personal property, of the means by which persons gained title to property, of wrongs and remedies, and of rights and limitations, all thoroughly based on the English common law relational tradition, strongly influenced how property was understood in all common law jurisdictions thereafter.

Blackstone's stated view that the common law embodied the "perfection of reason" is rhetorical flattery of English legal custom, inconsistent with the contradictions and changes in opinions that inevitably appeared over the centuries. The title of the book notwithstanding, Blackstone's work went well beyond mere commentary on common law since much of what he wrote were inferences from custom and court decisions as well as his interpretations of statutory law enacted by Parliament. Frederick Whelan observes that Blackstone's work was innovative not simply in his interpretations but in his theory of the social origin of laws and the ways they are created. Although he cites Locke's social contract theory favorably, his own considered view was that, "from an analytic point of view, property institutions are the creatures of civil societies, and they in fact vary, reflecting in their rules and the rights they confer the character of different sorts of society. Public recognition and (in principle) enforcement of rights is regarded as essential to the concept of property" (1980: 126). This perspective was more influenced by his contemporary, Hume, than by Locke, and was, for its time, an original and quite radical approach, anticipating the modern social constructionist view "that is both collective and political: property rights and institutions are to be evaluated by reference to social ends, and they may properly be modified, as they were at first invented, by public authority for such purposes" (1980: 126). Blackstone's influence was less pronounced during the eighteenth century, especially in the American colonies where Locke's natural rights theory prevailed, particularly among the revolutionary generation. His influence grew in the nineteenth century and in many respects his strong advocacy of the relational foundation of common law anticipated the realist and progressive theorists of the late nineteenth and twentieth centuries who developed or, more properly, explicated the bundle-of-rights view of property, sometimes called the "bundle-of-sticks" view, as part of a broader intellectual assault on the rampant laissez-faire ideology of their day (on which, see Fried, 1998).

The fourth approach to property we consider – the bundle of rights or sticks – is presently the dominant theory of property among American legal theorists, academics, and jurists (Johnson, 2007: 247). Jane Baron has summed it up as follows:

> The bundle-of-rights metaphor emphasizes that property is not "sole dominion," but involves, in many cases, only relatively better rights.

THE NATURE AND STUDY OF SLAVERY

The bundle metaphor also highlights that property involves not just "one man" and his "external things," but multiple parties tied together in relationships that are social as well as legal. Seen as a bundle of rights, property is not monolithic but is composed of pieces (sometimes called "sticks") that are combined together but can be disentangled. Property is not about the connection between people and things, but about the connections between and among people. (2014: 58–9, see also 62–70; for a symposium of criticisms and counterarguments, see Klein and Robinson, 2011)

Bundle theorists are a varied bunch. Several have argued that there is a basic distinction among them between "essentialists," who claim that their bundle of attributes constitutes one unified, correct, and universally applicable meaning of property, and nominalists, who hold that there is no defining element or universally applicable meaning of the term "property," its identification being entirely a function of context and social convention, often involving the use of different words (Merrill, 2011). The difference is so great between the two, however, that it makes little sense including them under the same rubric; the only thing they have in common is their emphasis on a bundle of attributes, or sticks, instead of a single factor, such as exclusion, in talking of property. All genuine bundle theorists are relationists, nominalists, or contextualists, and many of the criticisms aimed at bundle theory are more properly confined to the essentialists. Be that as it may, Honore is squarely located in the essentialist category of theorists, his bundle of eleven sticks or rights being: the right to *possess*, which is having exclusive control or occupancy of the property; the right to *use* the property as one sees fit; the right to *manage*, defined as the authority to decide how the property will be used; the right to *income*, being the ability to derive income from the property, such as renting it out; the right to the *capital*, being the ability to consume, waste, modify, or even destroy the essential resources of the property; the right to *security*, being assurance that ownership will endure and will not be subject to challenge or confiscation; the right to *transmissibility of ownership* which is the power to transfer ownership to others, either during one's lifetime or upon death; the *absence of term*, meaning that ownership is not constrained by a predetermined period; the *duty to prevent harm*, being the obligation to ensure the property doesn't harm others; the *liability to execution*, which is the fact that the property can be taken if the owner owes a debt and fails to pay it; and the *residuary character of property*, meaning that if certain rights are not exercised, they revert to the owner by default (1961: 16–59).

48

Honore's taxonomy has been criticized by both so-called nominalist bundle theorists and critics of bundle theory. Thus Eric Claeys, a critic of bundle theorists, finds that his "taxonomy simply begs the question why rights to possess, use, or transfer a thing are property rights. Honore's taxonomy assumes an integrated conception of property without supplying one" (2011: 206). Another criticism comes from the exclusionist theorist Thomas Merrill, coauthor of one of the most respected textbooks in the law of property (Merrill and Smith, 2007), who is concerned "whether we attach the label 'property' to the whole bundle or to each of the sticks," and, of even greater concern to exclusionists, whether "at least one stick is essential or all sticks are optional." A taxonomy such as Honore's, he writes, "does not answer this question and provides no assistance about how to answer it." (Merrill, 2011: 248). Another criticism, while aimed at all bundlers, is especially damaging to essentialists such as Honore – that his bundle of attributes is too atomistic and neglects the critical factor of relations between elements: it "treats property in atom-counting fashion. It sees property as a bundle of sticks but misses the trees, not to mention the forest" (Smith, 2011: 279). The most serious criticism, however, is the fact that Honore's bundle of rights, to the degree that it is useful, is of relevance only to one kind of economic system and, more particularly, one period of capitalist development. It fails as a taxonomy in all but a few pre-capitalist systems and is of little use in understanding the new forms of wealth generated by postindustrial economies. Tom Grey (1980), the distinguished Stanford legal theorist, has pointed out that thing-focused views of property and ownership worked well in economies where the predominant forms of wealth were land and tangible objects. This was true of the agrarian phase of capitalism as well as early industrialism up to about the third quarter of the nineteenth century. To this, I would add pre-capitalist economic systems with highly developed commodity production, most notably ancient Rome and possibly the urban and mining sectors of classical Greece, as well as the more advanced economies of the Near East and Eastern societies (see Scheidel, 2012; Finley, 1981). With the rise of mature industrialism in the late nineteenth century, more and more wealth was created in exchange rather than tangible commodities, and by new forms of enterprises involving radically new forms of entitlement. It was to meet the challenge of this later phase of mature capitalism, Grey argued, as well as the severe moral and distributional problems it created, that the realists and progressive legal thinkers turned to non-essentialist bundle theories of property.

> The theory of property rights held by the modern specialist tends both to dissolve the notion of ownership and to eliminate any necessary connection between property rights and things. Consider ownership first. The specialist fragments the robust unitary conception of ownership into a more shadowy "bundle of rights." Thus, a thing can be owned by more than one person, in which case it becomes necessary to focus on the particular limited rights each of the co-owners has with respect to the thing. Further, the notion that full ownership includes rights to do as you wish with what you own suggests that you might sell off *particular aspects* of your control – rights to certain uses, to profits from the thing, and so on. Finally, rights of use, profit, and the like can be parceled out along a temporal dimension as well – you might sell your control over your property for tomorrow to one person, for the next day to another, and so on. (1980: 69)

By the 1980s, when Grey wrote his seminal paper, a new era of capitalism – postindustrial society (Bell, 1976) – was already in progress, leading to even greater fragmentation and dissolution of the traditional forms, and related conceptions, of property. But the personal computer, the internet, and bio-technology revolutions were yet to come. These were to change even more traditional notions of property. As the Berkeley legal theorist Peter Menell (2011) argues, what "characterizes the intellectual property landscape" in the digital age with rapid changes in technological innovation, expressive creativity, and the means for the dissemination of creative work is "disintegration."

Now, one very ironical development accompanying the digital technology revolution, with the attendant growing importance of intellectual forms of wealth, is the rise of collaborative ownership in phenomena such as crowd-sourcing of venture capital and open-source software. It is remarkable that this has led to a renewed interest in patterns of co-ownership in small, kin-based societies. As Rishab Ghosh notes: "There are indeed similarities between collaborative production and non-monetary exchange in tribal societies and collaborative ownership in the digital economy, notably free software: both are based on the self-interested participation of individuals and communities linked by a complex web of rights and obligations" (2005: 7).

There are, indeed, which brings me to Lewis's claim that Honore's conception of property fully holds for pre-capitalist, kin-based societies. It does not, and citing a few contrarian anthropologists on the subject does not alter what are now well-established findings on the matter. What Max Gluckman wrote of land ownership in his

REVISITING SLAVERY AND PROPERTY AS A "BUNDLE OF RIGHTS"

classic studies of traditional Africa – that "there is not an individual item of land which a man owns for himself and by himself" (2012 [1965]: 294), but rather designated usufruct entitlements based on tribal membership that carried multiple obligations, has been shown to be true of all kin-based societies. (For a review of later findings, see Ward and Kingdon, 1995: 6–35.) In studies of societies as far afield as the pre-conquest Maori and Bronze Age Crete, scholars have found it best to simply ditch absolutist conceptions of property and the essentialist version of bundle-of-rights theories such as Honore's (see Jackson and Smith, 2013; Jusseret et al., 2013). In fairness to Honore, we should note that Lewis applied his conception to societies for which he never intended it. Honore repeatedly made it clear in his paper that he was speaking mainly of the modern liberal concept of property, which refers to "mature" systems such as "England, France, Russia, China and any other modern country one may care to mention." His reference to the Trobriand islanders was a cautiously qualified, speculative aside.

In *Slavery and Social Death* (1982), I deployed several of these meanings of property, depending on the context. In doing so, let me note, I was following the lead of Finley who, in 1960, was the first to draw attention to the importance of the bundle or relational concept of property to the understanding of ancient Greek slavery. When I wrote that a person has property relations in his or her spouse or that a club owner has a property relation in his athletes, not to mention the fact of someone having a property in his person, I was not only drawing on what was implicit in the bundle-of-rights view (Patterson, 2018 [1982]: 20) but rejecting what Carol Pateman (2002: 27) calls "the fiction of separability," which assumes that persons' "powers capacities, abilities, skills, and talents" are separable from their owners' bodies and, so alienated, "can become the subject of contracts and marketed as services." (Compare Karl Polanyi's discussion of the "entirely fictitious" commodification of labor, "the technical term used for human beings," which, however, was an essential organizing principle for self-regulating markets and modern society (1944: 75–6).)

2.2: Property and slavery across time and societies

In *Slavery and Social Death* (2018 [1982]: 27–32), I argued that societies may be located on a continuum between those, at one extreme, in which the basic idiom of power is personalistic, and those, at the

THE NATURE AND STUDY OF SLAVERY

other, in which power is derived from and expressed in materialistic terms. The distinction, which originated in Marx's famous observation on the transition from feudalism to capitalism, was more broadly extended by the anthropologist Marshall Sahlins as the transition from societies in which "a right to things [is] realized through a hold on persons" to those in which "a hold on persons [is] realized through a right to things" (1974: 92–3). Note, however, that these two idioms of power marked the two end points of a continuum. In extremely personalistic societies (kin-based, acephalous, tribal, and those with early state formations), I pointed out, there was no sharp distinction between the enslaved and free persons; indeed, in many of them the concept of the free person barely existed. The status of persons was conceived along a single dimension of power leading to a range of statuses. In the relational approach to property that prevailed in such societies (not called that, but this is what in fact exists, as legal anthropologists have made clear), individuals differed "in the degree of power, claims, and privileges others had in them and in the counterbalancing set of claims, powers, and privileges they had in others" (2018 [1982]: 27). The essence of natal rights (from which the enslaved were quintessentially alienated) is the experience of being embedded in the protective network of such claims or rights, however hierarchical they may be. A slave was someone who was powerless because they had to depend exclusively on a single person for protection. The non-slave was one who was able to spread their protection over a wide number of persons through a system of countervailing powers.

However – and this is critical – the fact that there was no distinction between the enslaved and free persons in such societies does not mean that there was not a fundamental distinction between the enslaved and the non-enslaved. The truth of the matter is that there was no such thing as a "free" person in most such societies. The reason why this statement may strike many as odd is the ingrained Western tendency to identify the condition of being free with that of not being a slave, but, as I argued in *Freedom in the Making of Western Culture* (1991), the idea of freedom is itself originally a Western construct that emerged from the first large-scale slave systems in the world, those of ancient Greece, especially Athens. The idea, and positive valence, of freedom is not found in non-Western societies before Western contact. We should not assume that a plurality of claims or powers over the enslaved means that the slave is any less socially dead or the quintessential, powerless and degraded outsider. Nor should we assume that the existence of persons in varying degrees of

52

dependency on others blurs the sharp social distinction between the enslaved and the non-enslaved. Indeed, the more impoverished and dependent non-enslaved were, the greater the importance of demarcating themselves from the enslaved. At the very least it established an identity with all non-slave members of their communities who belonged, who were not at the complete mercy of another, and who had some honor that could be defended; and they were not excluded from what most defined as the community. They were, as the prehistoric Indo-Europeans put it, "among the beloved."

Slavery in personalistic and mixed notions of property

The relational, non-exclusive view of property, and of the slaves' proprietary incapacity (subject to the slaveholder's whim in regard to the socio-legal fiction of the peculium where it existed) is found in nearly all tribal and many centralized non-Western, pre-capitalist societies.

In their review of tribal and other small-scale Indigenous societies of the Americas and other societies, Catherine Cameron (2017, 2018), Fernando Santos-Granero (2017), and Christina Snyder (2018) found a range of marginal statuses between the extreme of slavery, on the one hand, and the most connected and powerful, on the other. However, the slave, as a kinless person, was always viewed as socially dead. She "remained an outsider because she was not part of a kin group. Slaves ... not only created honor for their master or mistress, but also produced wealth for them; unlike state-level societies, however, wealth was not accumulated, but given away to create prestige and honor for the master" (Cameron, 2017: 211). Snyder likewise found that "all captives faced a kind of social death," and that the enslaved were distinct in three ways: "masters deemed slaves kinless, exploited them to enhance their own power, and marked them as different" (2018: 172–4).

We find something similar in the ancient Near East where, as Heather Baker (2017: 16) points out, there was a range of servile statuses: "The Mesopotamian world-view ... held that everyone, including the king himself, was subject to a higher authority and this relationship of subordination was expressed using the term for a common slave, *urdu*." As among the Ashanti, "the concept of complete individual freedom is anachronistic." Nonetheless, "cutting across these nested hierarchical relationships" there was a clear distinction between the enslaved and others. The enslaver's power over the enslaved was total. Slaves had families (as they did in all but the most brutal of systems), but "the master's domination was complete

THE NATURE AND STUDY OF SLAVERY

and he could dispose of his slaves as he wished, regardless of their family ties." That was because the enslaved had no countervailing claims and rights in others. Another factor defining the enslaved was their debasement and the parasitic dishonoring in their interaction with their enslavers. I was struck by Baker's quotation from a text describing the campaign of king Esarhaddon in 673 BCE because it is an apt example of what I mean by parasitic dishonor. The vanquished enemy is not simply described as debased, but beseeches with open hands his new enslaver, "saying 'Ahulap!' again and again to the heroic Assur, my lord, and the praise of my heroism." Baker makes the important point that very often the only data we have on the enslaved comes from surviving laws, and hence we should be very careful not to reflect this legal bias in our interpretations. Invariably, when the sources allow us to peer behind the veil of legal texts, we find the additional factors of natal alienation and parasitic dishonor, as illustrated above in the neo-Assyrian text cited by Baker.

The cases of the Thetes and debt-bondsmen in pre-Solonic Athens, and of the Helots in Sparta, also fall at this pure relational end of the continuum, although they are, as Peter Hunt (2017: 61–9) notes, complicated. In both we are faced with scanty evidence, and, in such situations, I and others have argued that recourse to a comparative strategy is likely to be the most fruitful way forward (Patterson, 2003; Scheidel, 2015: Introduction and Ch. 5). We know, as Hunt points out, that in late seventh-century Athens there was a "variety of different classes of peasants, slaves, or laborers in different relations with the wealthy few" (Hunt, 2017: 59). In other words, a range of statuses existed between the most powerful and the least, with diminishing bundles of rights in others and themselves and, apart from the special cases of classical Athens and Rome, it is a mistake to sharply differentiate between one status and another. As Finley warned his fellow historians of antiquity: "There is a fetishism about words which must be overcome" (1981: 134). The conventional wisdom (or hypothesis) is that Thetes were landless laborers, but a landless laborer would simply have been a severely indebted debt-bondsman who had lost his or her land. We know from the comparative evidence on small-scale societies that this is a precarious economic situation. It is striking that Hesiod, some five to ten decades earlier, recommended hiring males without family from the group, as well as childless women, indicating that they were readily available (Nussbaum, 1960: 215). This attests even more to their marginality. Family and kinsmen were the foundation of Hesiod's world, as was the case in all such small-scale societies. To be a man without kin, to be a childless woman wandering about the countryside looking for work in exchange for food and shelter, was to be on the margin of servitude, indeed to be on the verge of internal expulsion – what I labeled extrusive natal alienation in *Slavery and Social Death* – whatever it may have been called.

Between Hesiod's time and Solon's their condition worsened. One methodological strategy when dealing with scarce data is to search for the critical event or case. This is an observation that, if true, must hold for all others. I submit that we have such a critical case in the sale of Thetes – presumably those who had fallen hopelessly in debt – into slavery abroad. The comparative data on debt servitude, both historical and contemporary, reveal that there are always some limits, however few, on the bundle of powers or rights that a creditor had over his debt-bondsman or those working for him, however destitute; and the most important of these was restraint on the creditor's capacity to dispose of the bondsman beyond his natal community, forever denying him or his kinsmen the opportunity to redeem the debt. If this happened in a single case with impunity, it is decisive evidence that all Thetes and severely indebted bondsmen were considered people who could be treated as enslaved. Now we know that Solon bought and brought back from foreign slavery not one, but ten such cases. It doesn't matter whether he was boasting or not, as some claim. That one, much less ten members (and very likely far more, since the probability of finding and redeeming people enslaved abroad approaches zero in the vast majority of known cases) of a group could have been sold into slavery abroad is compelling evidence that the group had few rights worth respecting in the reciprocating bundles of proprietorial claims and powers that constituted the socio-legal fabric of late seventh-century Athens.

Add to this another critical bit of evidence: the fact that they were on the verge of revolt against their treatment. The comparative significance of this cannot be overstated. Landless laborers rarely, if ever, revolt, especially in small-scale societies. They are too impoverished, too lacking in organizational resources, too isolated from each other in the search for work on farms scattered over the countryside, too mentally burdened with the anxieties of daily survival, to organize or seriously threaten revolt. Consider the vast numbers of farmers thrown off the land, and wandering aimlessly around the countryside as a result of the enclosure movement of Elizabethan England. There was not a rebellious peep out of them, and this was a group whose ancestors had shown themselves quite capable of revolt, the English rising of 1492 having occurred less than a century earlier. When

Marx dismissed the possibility of revolutionary consciousness among peasants with his derisive description of them as "a sack of potatoes," he would have done better to speak of landless laborers. To conclude, landless laborers don't revolt or threaten to revolt, unless this refers to a group who found themselves treated as enslaved even though in theory and formal designation they were supposed to be accepted members of their communities – people who, however impoverished, nonetheless belonged. It is significant that they were not sold within the Greek homeland. That would have blurred unacceptably the critical social distinction between slave and impoverished non-slave, who still had some countervailing relational claims on the protection of others. They had to be sold abroad. Even so, this must have created outrage, leading up to the edge of revolt, averted only by Solon's *seisachtheia*, which not only abolished debt bondage and the *hectemoroi* or one-sixth laborers, but took the extraordinary step of finding, and manumitting and repatriating those who had been sold abroad.

In another cluster of slaveholding societies, we find a mix of the bundle-of-rights and more absolute approach to the enslaved, depending on the occupation or disposal of the enslaved and the status of their owners. This may have been the case in Europe after the collapse of the late Roman empire, no longer dark, in light of McCormick's (2001) monumental study of the period. Thanks to his work, we now know that slave trading was alive and well from the sixth century onward through Charlemagne's empire, when it surged. The slaves being traded from north of the Alps down to the Mediterranean would have been chattels in the strictest Roman sense (until they reached their mainly Islamic purchasers, where their racial features, especially if blond, would undoubtedly have determined what kind of slave they became and their ultimate fate as well as those of their children). In the traditional European societies from which they came, however, the relational approach to property rights in persons would have prevailed along with the typical range of statuses between the most powerful and the least so.

This was also the case in many of the advanced premodern slaveholding societies, in medieval and premodern Korea and Muslim South Asia. In premodern Korea, for example, the complex pattern of possession of slaves varying between public and private, resident and non-resident, elite and commoner, religious and secular, as well as the periodic intrusions of royal reforms, determined a relativistic approach to slaveholding. The ownership of military, administrative, and skilled urban slaves, especially those living away from their slaveholders, the concubines and harem slaves, and the enslaved who had borne their slaveholders' children, especially sons, can best be understood in relativistic terms (see the discussion of Korean slavery in Chapter 3).

In the Islamic world, the fundamental belief that all property belongs to God, with persons being stewards of their possessions, imposed ethical constraints on ownership, as did specific injunctions concerning who could not be enslaved, the manumission and inheritance rights of sons of enslaved women by their enslavers, as well as the mothers of such children on the death of the enslaver, and the mukataba contract permitting the enslaved to buy their manumission over time: all mediated the proprietorial powers of slaveholders in theory and, for certain categories of slaves such as the highly skilled, soldiers and administrators, domestics and concubines, in practice. We should be very careful, however, not to overemphasize the role of religion and legal doctrine in considerations of Islamic slavery, as was done in earlier studies of the role of the Catholic Church and Spanish law in interpretations of the Hispanic treatment and conception of the enslaved (see, e.g., Tannenbaum, 1946).

While there were common, distinctive features in the conception of property throughout Islamic lands – derived from their foundation in the Shari'a and the dictates of the Quran and Hadith – significant variations exist in their interpretation and application to the status and treatment of the enslaved based on regional, sociocultural, racial, and historical differences. Toledano (2017: 148–9) has usefully offered six factors accounting for variations in the treatment and status of enslaved persons in the Ottoman world:

- the task the enslaved performed – whether domestic, agricultural, menial, or kul/harem;
- the stratum of the enslavers – whether an urban elite, rural notability, small-scale cultivators, artisans, or merchants;
- location – whether at the core or the periphery;
- type of habitat – whether urban, village, or nomad;
- gender – whether male, female, or eunuch;
- ethnicity – whether African or Caucasian.

Under *task* he might have added, crucially, the occupation of soldier, and the criterion of *ethnicity* should include "mixed race" as well as "West European," since there were marked differences between the treatment of West Europeans and other Caucasians as well as between mulatto progeny and Africans. Otherwise, these factors well explain not only the treatment of the enslaved but the conception of them as more or less relational property.

Elsewhere (2018 [1982]: Ch. 11), I have discussed at some length why, in spite of their elite location and the power they wielded, the Islamic *Ghilman*, like their counterparts the *familia Caesaris* of ancient Rome and palatine eunuchs of Byzantium and China, were nonetheless enslaved. There is no need to re-argue the issue of the nature of elite slavery here. Clearly, much depends on the period one is discussing. The Janissaries of the first three centuries of the Ottoman empire were a different group from the corrupt, self-reproducing elite class increasingly engaged in nonmilitary occupations, palace coups, and landowning from the seventeenth century through to their elimination, and were slaves of the Sultan in name only. When Mamluk leaders seized power they were obviously no longer enslaved, whatever their original and persisting mode of recruitment. Before such developments, a strong case can be made that elite slaves, recruited from foreign lands precisely to retain their outsider status, forbidden from self-reproducing, faithfully serving the head of state as mere extensions of his will and person, were genuine slaves, natally alienated, and (in the eyes of the enslaver's community) socially dead. The power they exercised was not *their* power, but their slaveholder's power; what was honored in their presence was not *their* honor, not something inhering in them (a fundamental quality of honor), but in the person of their lord and master. This was only possible because they were enslaved, the complete instruments and extensions of their enslaver's will and person. Or, as John Willis (1985) puts it: "the [Muslim] slave as alter ego becomes a manifestation of the master's self: his prestige, his status and lastly, his responsibility." Furthermore, they shared with all slaves the condition of natal alienation, of not belonging. William Sersen (1985) observes that, throughout the Muslim world, "slaves were seen to lack those attachments of lineage or genealogy which an Arab-dominated society held in highest esteem: they were [considered] without honor, praise and identity." While a relational approach best describes the proprietorial view of such elite and other valued slaves, those outside this more privileged group were usually viewed and treated in less relational property terms, indeed as near brutes "outside civilised life, if not outside humanity itself" (Farias, 1985). African slave women in nineteenth-century Egypt, for example, were callously used, raped, overworked, and disposed of in lives that were nasty, brutal, and short (La Rue, 2007).

Slavery and the invention of absolute property

It was in Rome, with its far more sophisticated legal tradition, that the notion of absolute property was first fully expressed as a legal principle. How did this happen? In Rome, I have argued, the principle developed in tandem with the growth of slavery and, by this means, "the condition of slavery was transformed into a condition of powers *in rem* . . . The enslaved were above all a *res, the only human res*" (2018 [1982]: 32, emphasis in original). What this meant then, was that to become the property object of another amounted to social or, as the Roman stated it, civil death. This remarkable legal innovation was carried through with such thoroughness and sophistication that it was to remain, little changed, in Western legal thought – and legal traditions influenced by the West – right down to the present. It became the way of conceptualizing property not only in the civil law countries of continental Europe, whose legal traditions were directly inherited from Rome, but in the slave systems of France and Latin America, which simply transferred and adapted the pre-existing slave codes of Spain, France, and Portugal.

Alan Watson's fine study (1989) documents this transition. In Spain the slave laws of the Justinian *Corpus Juris Civilis* was incorporated with few changes to *Las Siete Partidas*. There was "a complete transplant of the law of Castile to the New World," and with it went the Castilian law of slavery (Watson, 1989: 47). To be sure, adaptations had to be made to the peculiar circumstances of the Americas, reflected most strikingly in the royal decree of 1789, *The Royal Decree of His Majesty on the education, treatment and occupations of slaves in all their dominions of the Indies, and the Philippine Islands, under the rules expressed.* However, the Roman conception of the enslaved as property *in rem* remained intact; the distinctive Spanish American legal tradition of *coartación* was directly influenced by Roman manumission law.

France had no counterpart to the Spanish *Las Siete Partidas* with its pre-existing slave codes, but, as was true of its traditional conception of property, it was to Roman law that it turned when the need arose to develop codes to regulate its colonial slave systems: "Roman law provided a ready-made model for slave law. Roman law was thus the inevitable model for the French law on slavery" (Watson, 1989: 85). Importantly, the Roman treatment of the enslaved as property *in rem* was adopted in its entirety, to the point where they were considered to be movables. For all the peculiarities in the governance of its Caribbean and South American colonies, the evolution of Dutch slave

THE NATURE AND STUDY OF SLAVERY

laws closely parallels that of France, especially in regard to the treatment of the enslaved as property *in rem*. Watson notes that "although it is nowhere so stated, slaves in the Dutch West India Colonies, just as slaves in Rome, had no legal personality" (1989: 112). If in doubt, the company simply turned to the Roman law of slavery when the need arose to enact codes for the regulation of its enslaved.

In the Anglo-American world, the development of the law of slavery was far more complex. In practice, slavery led to two traditions of property law. Among free persons, the common law bias toward a bundle-of-rights conception prevailed. However, in the slaveholder's relation to their slave, and, indeed, in the relation of all free persons toward the enslaved, Anglo-Americans freely borrowed from the Roman law of property. "England did not undergo a Reception," writes Watson, "but English American judges adopted the habit of using Roman law to fill gaps in the law relating to slaves" (1989: 129). The contradiction did not present much of a problem because the Roman view actually worked better in the early and even pre-advanced industrial phases of capitalist development. It also worked extremely well in the plantation slavery of the Caribbean and the US South, which is hardly surprising since, in many ways, they were simply the modern replication of the ancient Roman latifundia slave systems that had motivated the legal principle of dominium in the first place.

However, this remarkable historic synergy began to create major contradictions within the joint development of advanced industrial capitalism and equally advanced capitalistic slavery in America during the second half of the nineteenth century. How so?

Slavery, property and advanced industrial capitalism

To understand the contradiction, one has to recognize the role of legal fictions and the degree to which one crucial category of persons refused to take them seriously, namely free persons, especially the freely born who earned their living by working for others. The problem for such persons is this: if being a slave meant being owned by another, in what sense were those who survived by laboring for another not slaves? The answer, which the slaveholders and employers of free labor and their legal supporters gave, is well known: it was to develop the fiction of separability, discussed above, the fanciful, metaphysical notion of disembodied labor, and to try to persuade the "free" laborer, first, that it was only his or her disembodied labor that was being bought by the employer and that such an economic

60

exchange constituted a contractual relationship, having nothing to do with slavery. There was only one problem: for a long time the only people who believed this piece of legal metaphysics were the owners and their hired legal theoreticians. The evidence is abundant that both employed free persons in the early modern seventeenth century and advanced slave societies during the nineteenth century considered it spurious. They saw no difference between selling their labor in order to survive and selling their bodies, especially in light of the widespread practice of slaveholders hiring out the labor of their slaves to others (Martin, 2004).

During the late seventeenth and eighteenth centuries, when a large proportion of the White laboring classes were either indentured servants or their descendants, the prevailing legal paradigm for non-slave labor was the Masters and Servants Act, which retained medieval notions of the employer or enslaver having an enforceable property right in the labor of the worker or apprentice. This coexisted with a slowly emerging reconception of the relation as a contractual one between free laborer and contractor, but, in reality, it hardly mattered how it was legally defined; employees could be imprisoned for failing to meet their end of the bargain, though never employers (Steinfeld, 1991). As Edmund Morgan showed in his classic study of early Virginia (2003 [1975]), White indentured servants so identified their labor condition with that of the growing Black slave population that they united in violent conflict against the ruling class in Bacon's (himself no angel) rebellion, burning the capital of Jamestown to the ground. The response of the alarmed elite was a strategy that would become one of the formative and permanent forces of American social and cultural history: dividing the White working class from Blacks by acclaiming and sanctifying White solidarity and superiority, by restricting slavery to Blacks, and by incorporating the White poor in a vibrant *herrenvolk* democracy. In short, the joint social construction of freedom for Whites, built on the contradistinctive permanent enslavement of Blacks, what Morgan calls "the central paradox of American history . . . how a people could have developed the dedication to human liberty and dignity exhibited by the leaders of the American Revolution and at the same time have developed and maintained a system of labor that denied human liberty and dignity every hour of the day" (2003 [1975]: 4–5).

In the antebellum nineteenth century, with the growth of both industrial labor in the North and large-scale plantation slavery in the South, itself deeply intertwined with the industrial system of the US North and industrializing Britain, activist White laborers and their

THE NATURE AND STUDY OF SLAVERY

leaders increasingly identified so-called "free labor" with slavery, not to mention the fact that the spread of the slave system in the southwest was seen as antithetical to the interests of workers who considered the frontier to be the last best hope of independence and genuine freedom (Foner, 1995). Interestingly, some of the harshest indictments of the Northern labor system as a form of slavery came from racist Southern defenders of slavery, the most famous being George Fitzhugh (1857) who wrote mockingly of the Northern White laborers:

> We do not know whether free laborers ever sleep. They are fools to do so; for, whilst they sleep, the wily and watchful capitalist is devising means to ensnare and exploit them. The free laborer must work or starve. He is more of a slave than the negro, because he works longer and harder for less allowance than the slave, and has no holiday, because the cares of life with him begin when its labors end. He has no liberty, and not a single right.

There was, as is well known, an ancient antecedent of this – the first-century BCE Roman statesman and scholar Cicero's contemptuous dismissal of hired laborers whose wage "is a pledge of their slavery" (1913: 1.150). However, Cicero could well feel that he had nothing to fear from the contradictory condition of the free plebs, since he, like nearly all his ruling-class counterparts, had all their manual, technical, and business needs, and even the pedagogical needs of their children, met by the enslaved. Not so America between the seventeenth and the nineteenth centuries.

Something similar to what occurred in late seventeenth-century Virginia re-emerged in the latter half of the nineteenth century when millions of European immigrants flooded into the factories of the rapidly expanding industrial North, many of whom increasingly saw their condition as one of wage slavery, which was the main campaign slogan of the earliest labor movements going back to the 1820s (Gourevitch, 2013). So deeply rooted was the conviction – that laboring for the capitalist was a form of slavery – that the rhetoric intensified rather than abated after abolition: "Cry it out to all you meet: we are robbed, we are maltreated, we are slaves!" raged a typical editorial in the *Journal of United Labor* of May, 1881 (cited in Hallgrimsdottir and Benoit, 2007).

The notions of absolute property rights in the person of the enslaved and the legal fiction of separation having failed to distinguish free laborer from slave, the slaveholders and employers of free labor doubled down on the familiar *herrenvolk* strategy, Morgan's paradox, by intensifying the cultural markers that defined the boundary between slave and free, Black and White (Roediger, 1991). They did so by means of three cultural strategies: the intensification of natal alienation through the ideology of racism; the intensification of the parasitic dishonoring of the slave; and the further development of the shared *herrenvolk* democracy through the principle of inclusive exclusiveness and expansion of the franchise (Saxton, 1990). All greatly enhanced the cultural definition of the enslaved as someone socially dead, the permanent outsider, the "domestic enemy." None of these was new in kind; what was new was the extent to which they were ideologically developed and the enormous consequences for both the enslaved and the slaveholder class, as well as their descendants. The story of the intensification of racism, the association of African appearance with slavery, and the later nineteenth-century rise of scientific racism in which Blacks came to be seen as an inferior race incapable of integration in American society are too well known to be labored here. What it meant in sociohistorical terms – and nothing better makes the point that slavery can never be defined in exclusively legal terms – is that the culture of slavery persisted in the postbellum South long after the formal legal abolition and passage of the Thirteenth Amendment of the US Constitution. That persisting slave culture in the Jim Crow South continued to define the ex-slaves and their descendants as persons who did not belong, who had no honor that needed to be respected by White free persons, and who were so powerless that their young men could be hunted down like helots with bloodhounds, lynched and burnt alive by the thousands with impunity. For the planter elite, it was a remarkably successful strategy, "with astonishing economic results," as DuBois long ago made clear.

> The white group of laborers, while they received a low wage, were compensated in part by a sort of public and psychological wage. They were given public deference and titles of courtesy because they were white. They were admitted freely with all classes of white people to public functions, public parks, and the best schools. The police were drawn from their ranks, and the courts, dependent on their votes, treated them with such leniency as to encourage lawlessness. (1935: 700)

The economic results for the planter elite came through the sharecropping enserfment system. Throughout the neo-slavery South up to as late as the 1940s, thousands of Black youth were annually rounded up on trumped-up vagrancy charges, made into virtual state slaves, and placed at the unpaid service of major companies, such as U.S. Steel (Blackmon, 2008). However, this use of neo-slavery laws to meet the labor demand of major companies was only the tip of a much greater inequity. As indicated in the previous chapter, the Southern landowning classes arranged for the courts to release Black laborers in their charge by paying their trumped-up fines, or releasing them in their charge, thereby ensuring a compliant labor force in the neo-slavery sharecropping system (Muller, 2018, 2021; Muller and Schrage, 2021).

To conclude, in America, already the most advanced capitalistic slave system in the modern world by the late nineteenth century, the attempt to define the enslaved in neo-Roman legal terms as someone in whom there were absolute rights *in rem* faced a crisis of legitimacy with the leadership and more radical wing of its rapidly growing and supposedly free working class, which refused to recognize the fiction of disembodied labor or any meaningful difference between the absolute property in the body of the enslaved and the relative property rights in their labor. The contradiction was resolved, in two decisive moves by the post-slavery ruling classes of the South and jurists in the North, which were really revivals and reinforcements of earlier legal and social strategies. One was the move from absolute notions of property and the legal mainstreaming of property as a bundle of rights or sticks. The other was the institutionalization of Whiteness as a valued positional good held out to previously excluded European ethnics who eagerly grasped it by means of the collective dishonoring, Northern ghettoization and incarceration, and Southern enserfment of the ex-slave population and their descendants, permanently excluded from any possibility of incorporation in the American body politic, a neo-slavery condition that persisted long after the 1863 abolition of Roman rights *in rem* in the person of the Black slave (Roediger, 2018; Ignatiev, 1995; Brodkin, 1998).

— 3 —

BEYOND "SLAVE SOCIETY": THE STRUCTURAL ARTICULATIONS OF SLAVERY IN PRE-CAPITALIST AND CAPITALIST SOCIAL FORMATIONS

In the comparative study of slavery, it is commonplace to distinguish between slaveholding societies in which slavery is present but possibly of marginal significance and those where the institution became structurally significant, described by Moses Finley (1968) as "genuine" slave societies. The distinction is popular; entire volumes are devoted to it. However, problems arise in isolating the criteria by which we demarcate the one from the other. This chapter examines attempts to do so, then provides a different approach that moves away from substantivist perspectives to one in which the emphasis shifts to the dynamics of interaction between slavery and the broader social system, what I call slave formations that are determined by patterns of structural articulation of slavery.

3.1: Approaches to the study of slave societies

Marxist scholars were the first to take seriously the problem of the origins, nature, and dynamics of large-scale slavery (for a review, see Patterson, 1977). Engels's (1962) periodization view that large-scale slavery constituted an inevitable stage in the development of all human societies was merely one version of nineteenth-century evolutionism. It dominated East European thought on slavery until the de-Stalinization movement, and was the orthodox view in mainland China up to the end of the Mao period. More sophisticated, but no less problematic, have been attempts by modern Marxists to formulate a "slave mode of production." The most empirically grounded of these attempts is that of Perry Anderson (1974), who argued that "the slave mode of production was the decisive invention of the Graeco-Roman world, which provided the ultimate basis both of its accomplishments and its eclipse." There is now no longer any doubt that slavery was foundational for both Athens and Rome, and that these were the first societies in which large-scale slavery emerged. However, the concept of the "slave mode of production" overemphasizes the materialistic aspects of slavery, making it of limited value for the comparative study of slavery. The enslaved were indeed sometimes used to generate new economic systems – as in Rome and the modern plantation economies – but there are many cases where, even when used on a large scale, there was nothing innovative or distinctive about the resulting economic structure. The narrow materialist focus not only leads to a misunderstanding of the relationship between slavery and technology in the ancient world, but, more seriously, it fails to identify major differences between the Greek and Roman cases, and it is of no value in the study of slave societies in which the structurally important role of the enslaved was noneconomic, as was true of most of the Islamic slave systems.

Several non-Marxist historical sociologists, drawing also on the experience of ancient Europe, have made important contributions to our understanding of the relation between slavery and society. According to Max Weber (1964) slavery on a large scale was possible only under three conditions: "(1) where it has been possible to maintain slaves very cheaply; (2) where there has been an opportunity for regular recruitment through a well-supplied slave market; (3) in agricultural production on a large scale of the plantation type, or in very simple industrial processes." However suggestive, there is little support for these generalizations from the comparative data. Medieval Korea (Salem, 1978) and the US South (Fogel and Engerman, 1974) disprove (1) and (2). And work on urban slavery in the modern world as well as the relationship between slavery and technology in the ancient world disprove (3) (Finley, 1973).

Finley (1960, 1973, 1981) was the first non-Marxist scholar to grapple seriously with the problem of defining what he called "genuine slave societies." His emphasis on the enslaved as a deracinated outsider led him to the conclusion that what was most advantageous about the enslaved was their flexibility, and their potential as tools of change for the slaveholder class. He also offered valuable pointers in his analyses of the relationship between slave and other forms of involuntary labor. And in criticizing Keith Hopkins's (1978) conquest theory of the emergence of genuine slave societies, Finley encouraged an emphasis on demand, as opposed to supply factors in the rise of slave society. Romans, he argued, captured many thousands of slaves during the Italian and Punic wars because a demand for them already existed and "not the other way around." He postulated three conditions for the existence of this demand: private ownership of land, and some concentration of holdings; "a sufficient development of commodity production of markets"; and "the unavailability of an internal labor supply." In another work, Finley proposed three criteria for the development of genuine slave societies: that the enslaved make up a significant proportion of the total population, roughly at least 20 percent; that they contribute significantly to surplus production; and that they "exercise a pervasive cultural influence" on the society as a whole (1980: 79–82).

Although very influential, especially among historians of the ancient world, Finley makes several assumptions and claims that are problematic. The first is the Western bias. Finley confined the set of genuine slave societies to the Western world. While it is correct that slavery has played a major role in the development of Western civilization, it is simply not the case that it has not been of major significance elsewhere, especially in Islamic lands. Second, Finley's claim that there have only been five genuine slave societies, a view repeated by other classical historians, notably Keith Hopkins, is wildly inaccurate. Even if we confine our attention to Western societies, it is odd that Finley and others chose to count all the Caribbean slave societies as a single case. These societies differed strikingly in imperial origin, in language and culture, and in important structural features. This is the equivalent of counting all West European societies as a single case of advanced welfare states, or all of Latin America as a single case of developing economies. Using the percentage of the enslaved as an important criterion is also problematic. It is possible for a small number of persons – well below 20 percent – to play a major role in the economic and social life of a society. America is a high-technology economy, the sector generating nearly a quarter of national output and of major importance to the entire economy, but it employs only 17 million workers who constitute a mere 12 percent of the entire workforce. Further, the emphasis on the economy neglects the fact that the enslaved can have major impact on other areas of society while being of minor economic significance, as we will argue below. Finally, it is not always the case that where the enslaved were important they also had pervasive cultural influence. As we will see in the case of Korea, discussed later, the enslaved may occupy a major place in the economy without any significant influence on the broader culture and society.

Noel Lenski is also highly critical of Finley's slave society model, which he found "extremely ... outdated in its methodology, ethnocentric in its scope, and deceptive in its generalizations" (Lenski and Cameron, 2018: 46–7, and Ch. 4); his own model is unquestionably the most imaginative and potentially useful approach to this problem (see Lenski and Cameron, 2018: Ch. 1). It compares slaveholding societies on a series of scales, termed vectors of intensification, that measure the degree to which a given society approximates aspects of an ideal-type slave society. One set of four components assesses the value of the slave, and hence benefit to the slaveholder; these include community use and exchange value, as well as labor product use and exchange value. A second set of components measures the degree to which the enslaved are dominated, or the disadvantage of the system to them, and includes the permanence of their status, the degree of violence against them, and the extent of their natal alienation and dishonor. The (estimated) benefit of the system to the slaveholder when plotted against the extent of disadvantage to the enslaved defines a two-dimensional graph that charts the intensity of benefit to the slaveholder against the disadvantage to the enslaved for any given slaveholding society. This is, theoretically, an elegant procedure that avoids the simple binaries of Finley's model, emphasizing instead the degree of intensity on the different components of slave societies. The problem, as Lenski is himself aware, is that it makes more demands on data than is available for most slaveholding societies, especially non-Western ones. Nonetheless, it encourages historians to make informed guesses about the different dimensions of slavery's role in society. Lenski's comparison of the US South and ancient Rome, for example, is highly suggestive and indicates that the former was far more beneficial to slaveholders and far more exploitative of the enslaved than the Roman system. However, it neglects what is a critical dimension of slave societies – the extent to which the system as a whole, not simply the slaveholders, was functionally dependent on the institution. On this dimension, the ancient Roman slave system stands in a class by itself in the pervasiveness of slavery and structural dependence of the entire system on the institution, far more so than the antebellum South, whose socioeconomic order after abolition and the turmoil of reconstruction was able to reconstitute itself in a neo-slavery Jim Crow order that continued to benefit the ruling class of previous slaveholders, and to brutally exploit the previous slaves and their descendants. In contrast, as Kyle Harper (2011) has brilliantly shown, the end of slavery in ancient Rome marked a profound divide between its social order and the early medieval system that followed.

Ancient Rome was the ultimate slave society in the totality of its dependence – economically, socially, demographically, and culturally – on the institution.

3.2: An alternative framework for the study of slave societies

It is useful to approach the comparative study of slave society with an understanding of what structural dependence means. There are three fundamental questions. First, what was the *nature* of the dependence on slavery? Second, what was the *degree* of dependence? And third, what was the *direction* of dependence? Answers to these three questions together determine what may be called the modes or patterns of articulation of slavery, leading to different slave formations.

The nature of dependence on slavery may have been primarily economic or social, political or militaristic, or a combination of these. Economic dependence was sometimes the case, especially in ancient Rome and in the modern capitalistic slave systems. Here the critical question is: what were the costs and benefits of imposing and maintaining an economy based on slave labor? Stanley Engerman (1973) has written authoritatively on this subject. He distinguishes between the costs of imposition, of enforcement, and of worker productivity. Lower maintenance costs, more constant supply of labor, greater output due to the neglect of the nonpecuniary costs of labor, higher participation rates and greater labor intensity, and economies of scale are the main factors proposed by Engerman in explaining the shift to slave labor. They apply as much to ancient Rome as they do to the modern capitalistic slave systems of America, Brazil, and the Caribbean.

Military and bureaucratic dependence were the main noneconomic forms, and they could be as decisive for societies as was economic dependence. This was particularly true of the early Islamic social formations. Military slavery was the essential foundation of the rise and spread of Islam. The political might and administrative structures of the great empires were inconceivable without this all-important institution (see Pipes, 1981; Crone, 1980; Marmon, 1999). "The practice of using purchased slaves as the mainstay of the military forces of various Muslim dynasties," writes Paul Forand (1962), "is one which was characteristic of the Islamic Near East from the early ninth century CE until the end of the Mamluk period in Egypt." Not just the political structure, but the very style and character of Islamic civilization during the Middle Ages were based on slavery. As Samuel

THE NATURE AND STUDY OF SLAVERY

Haas has written: "When the brilliance of the culture of Islam from the ninth to the fourteenth centuries is compared with its desert simplicity in the time of Muhammad the contrast is striking. The cause is not hard to find. The leading elements in this cultural transformation were derived from the peoples conquered by the armies of Islam." From its inception to the end of the Umayyad period, "slaves made important contributions and exerted strong influences in the realm of politics and public administration, warfare, religion, arts and crafts, music, poetry, grammar and learning in general." Further, he continues, "the downfall of the Umayyad caliphate and the rise of the Abbasid regime was mainly brought about through the untiring efforts of the slaves who had enlisted in the latter's cause" (1977: 1, ii).

Finally, slavery may become indispensable for a social formation in purely ritual ways. Although the slave population of precolonial Maori was estimated to reach proportions as high as 15 per cent, the economic role of the enslaved was marginal. Maori men, however, had strong taboos against performing certain kinds of tasks – tasks that were nonetheless vital, such as carrying water and handling food. The whole ideological structure of this social formation was predicated on the avoidance of vital tasks that endangered a man's taboo. The enslaved and women solved the problem. It has not gone unnoticed that the taboos might well have been developed to rationalize the exploitation of women and the enslaved, but Raymond Firth (1959) stoutly rejects this view, and we cannot lightly dismiss the objections of such an authority. Among the Northwest Coast Indians of America, where the enslaved constituted between 15 and 25 percent of the population, they were mainly prestige items for their enslavers (Cameron, 2017: 214–15).

The degree of dependence refers simply to the size of the slave population and the extent to which the non-enslaved were dependent on them. As indicated earlier, Finley made this one of his three determinants of slave society. Its importance, we also noted, can be overstated. At the same time, we should be careful not to underestimate absolute numbers. Slavery, it cannot be too often repeated, is the most extreme form of dehumanization known to mankind, and the number of human beings suffering under its yoke in a given society is of importance in itself, regardless of their structural significance. In *Slavery and Social Death* (1982) I listed the sixty-six slaveholding societies in the Murdock sample of 186 world societies that provided the database for my statistical analysis (Appendix B, pp. 350–2). I also provided estimates of the proportion of the enslaved in what

I called the "large-scale" slave societies in world history known to me then (Appendix C, pp. 354–64). Since its publication, several societies with large numbers of slaves have been identified, a few in surprising places such as medieval Bavaria, where the slave population was well over 33 percent, approaching 100 per cent in some regions (Hammer, 2002: 45–56, 65–7), and slave ownership was ubiquitous, the majority owned by free peasants, burghers, craftsmen and even serfs (Sutherland, 2017: 75–7). Significant proportions of the enslaved, ranging between 11 and 25 percent, have also been identified in the late nineteenth- and early twentieth-century Persian Gulf states (Hopper, 2018: 317–18), although whether this made them "slave societies" has been explicitly contested (Turley, 2000: 76). Nearly all my estimates for the premodern slaveholding societies were, admittedly at best, "educated." Those for the modern world relied on contemporary observers, but two caveats are to be noted. The first is that, before the latter third of the eighteenth century, nearly all contemporary census counts were informed guesses. The second is that point-in-time estimates, even when moderately accurate, may give a misleading account of the total number of persons *ever* enslaved. This is especially true of slave societies such as ancient Rome with relatively high rates of manumission.

Finally, there is the *direction of dependence*. I distinguish between active and passive articulation. Even where a society had a high functional dependence on slavery it was not necessarily the case that slavery played an active, causal role in the development of its distinctive character. The institution, though important, was not structurally or culturally transformative. In medieval Bavaria during the eight and ninth centuries, as Hammer (2002) has shown, slavery was "large-scale," and clearly actively articulated in its "decisive" impact on the broader society and culture; but between 975 and 1225, the period studied by Sutherland (2017), while slaves and slavery remained ubiquitous, the institution's role had drifted toward structural and cultural passivity. The classic instance of large-scale passive articulation was Korea during the Koryo and Yi periods (discussed below), where, although a majority of the rural population were at times enslaved, there was no significant transformation of the economy, and no impact on the regime's government and culture. The same was true of several of the modern Spanish colonies of Central and South America. During the sixteenth and seventeenth centuries there was marked functional dependence on slavery in Mexico and Central America, as well as Peru and the urban areas of Chile and Argentina, but the institution was not determinative in the course

THE NATURE AND STUDY OF SLAVERY

of development of these societies and, as in Korea, when slavery ended it left hardly a trace, either cultural or social (Mellafe, 1975; Palmer, 1976; Klein, 1986; Blackburn, 2010 [1997]). In the Spanish Caribbean, the direction of change, unlike medieval Bavaria, moved from passive articulation between the European conquest of the late fifteenth century and the late eighteenth century, to that of rapid, near-explosive active structural articulation with the growth of the sugar and coffee plantation systems between the early nineteenth century and its abolition in 1886 (de la Fuente, 2004; Knight 1970; Bergad, 2017).

These three factors together determined the modes of articulation of slavery in society, or the nature of the slave formation, that is a sociologically more useful construct than that of the so-called slave mode of production or genuine slave society. Space permits only the most cursory mention of some of the most important such modes of articulation.

The lineage mode of articulation refers to those kin-based socie-ties in which large-scale slavery was related critically to the rise to dominance of certain lineages in the process of class and state for-mation. In some cases, slavery originally served primarily economic ends; in others, mainly social and political ones; but in the majority the institution became multifunctional. This kind of slave formation was most commonly found in western and west-central Africa as well as all regions of the pre-Columbian Americas, especially the northwest coast of North America, the southern plains where the Comanche held up to a quarter of their populations in slavery, and in tropical South America from what is now southern Florida down to the upper Amazon (Wilks, 1975; Klein, 1981; Lovejoy, 2000, 2018; Cameron, 2018; Snyder, 2018; Santos-Granero, 2017). Not only did the enslaved engage in production but they were themselves "high value objects that often circulated in a 'prestige goods' economy or as gifts in intergroup interactions" (Cameron, 2018: 166). Warfare, combined with some critical internal factor such as demographic change, accounted for the rise of slavery (for the Kongo kingdom, see Miller, 1977). The ideal case of this mode of articulation was the Asante state (Wilks, 1975; Klein, 1981). The enslaved were originally incorporated as a means of expanding the number of dependents, a tendency reinforced by the matrilineal principle of descent. The grow-ing number of slaves enhanced the lineage heads who owned them, and facilitated the process of lineage hierarchy and state formation. Later, the role of the enslaved was greatly expanded to include a wide range of economic activities, including mining.

72

BEYOND "SLAVE SOCIETY"

The *predatory circulation* mode refers to those slave societies in which warfare and raiding mainly to enslave people were the chief occupations of a highly predatory elite. The warrior class was usually assisted by a commercial class that traded heavily in slaves. There was usually a high rate of manumission of the enslaved, who not only contributed to the production of goods, but, in their role as freedmen soldiers, helped the ruling class to produce more slaves. Thus there was a continuous circulation of persons in and out of slave status as outsiders were incorporated as loyal freedmen retainers, creating a constant need for more enslaved outsiders. The enslaved and freedmen often played key roles in, and sometimes even dominated, the palatine service and elite executive jobs.

The contiguous existence of pastoral and sedentary agricultural peoples with different levels of military might was the major factor in the development of this mode of articulation of slavery. The mode is strongly associated with Islam, and there are many examples of it in the Sahel and North Africa. The west–east spread of the Fulani over an area of some three thousand miles over a period of eight hundred years provides one of the best cases of this mode, on which there is an abundance of historical and anthropological data (Lovejoy, 2000; Pipes, 1981; Meillassoux, 1975, 1991). The Tuareg of Mali and Niger are another classic pastoral group in which slavery became "a central component in social organization," the enslaved making up over 70 percent of most groups by the late nineteenth and early twentieth centuries (Winter, 1984: 4, 8). Unlike in other Islamic groups, there was relatively little concubinage with slave women and no recognition of slave children of slaveholders. The *eklan*, or slave class, were excluded from ownership of cattle, the main means of production and subsistence. It was thus a closed system of slavery in which rigid endogamy among the slaveholder class prevented any movement of the all-important means of subsistence – cattle – to the slave class.

The *embedded demesne* mode embraces those patrimonial systems dominated by large landed estates in which the enslaved were incorporated on a substantial scale to cultivate the demesne land of the lords. Serf or tenant laborers continued, in most cases, to be the primary producers of food for the society, and their rents or appropriated surpluses remained a major source of wealth for the ruling class. However, the enslaved were found to be a more productive form of labor on the home farms of the lords for the cost–benefit reasons analyzed by Engerman, mentioned above. The landowners got the best of both types of labor exploitation. This was a particularly valuable arrangement, where a landed aristocracy needed to change to a new crop but was not prepared to contest the technical conservatism of serfs, where there was a supply of cheap labor across the border, or where there was a high level of internal absenteeism among the landed aristocracy.

This is the least understood or recognized form of advanced slave systems, perhaps because its mode of articulation was usually passive. Many of them were to be found in medieval Europe, especially in France, Spain, and parts of Scandinavia and early medieval Bavaria (Dockes, 1982; Verlinden, 1995; Bonassie, 1985; Anderson, 1974; Hammer, 2002; Pelteret, 1995). The slave systems of the western "states" of eleventh-century England, where slave populations in some regions were as high as 20 percent of the total, are likely examples. So, possibly, was Viking Iceland, which may well have had similar proportions of slaves (Williams, 1937; Foote and Wilson, 1970). This may be what Alice Rio has in mind in her discussion of the "bi-partite estate, characterized by a much higher level of articulation and inter-dependence between tenancies and the lord's own directly exploited reserve," which emerged in northern Francia and northern Italy from about 800 and was widespread in most of manorial Western Europe by the eleventh and twelfth centuries (2017: 176–7, Ch. 5 *passim*). However, the ideal case of embedded demesne slavery was to be found in Korea, especially during the Koryo and early Yi periods. Here, the slave population sometimes exceeded that of other forms of bonded labor (Salem, 1978; Wagner, 1974; Hong, 1979). I discuss this large-scale mode of passive articulation at greater length below.

The *urban-industrial* mode of articulation was that in which the urban elites came to rely heavily on the enslaved for support. The enslaved played a relatively minor role in agriculture, although they may well have dominated the "home farms" of certain segments of the ruling urban elites. Slave labor was concentrated in urban craft industries that produced goods for local consumption and exports, as well as the mining sector where it existed. Slavery emerged on a large scale in such systems as a result of a combination of factors, among which were the changing nature and frequency of warfare, conquest of foreign lands, the changing tastes of the ruling class, crises in the internal supply of labor, shifts in food staples, growing commercial links with the outside world, and demographic changes.

This mode of articulation could be either passive or active. To the extent that the character of the civilization depended on its urban economy, and to the extent that the economy depended on slave laborers, both manual and technical, these slave formations were active in their articulation. The classic case of the active mode of

74

slave articulation was the ancient Greek slave systems, especially Athens of the fifth and fourth centuries BCE (Finley, 1981; Garlan, 1982; de Ste. Croix, 1981; Ismard, 2017; see also section 5.2 in this volume). Typical of the passive mode of urban-industrial articulation were several of the Spanish slave systems of Central and South America during the sixteenth, seventeenth, and eighteenth centuries (Andrews, 2004). For its first half century, Buenos Aires was primarily a slave-trading port, supplying the vast majority of slaves to South America. The enslaved later performed important economic roles not only in the cities but in mining and agriculture, constituting some 37 percent of the total population in 1778, and in some provinces and towns over 50 percent (Andrews, 1980; Galvan, 2002). The erasure of the Black presence in Argentina's demography and history has been the subject of more recent studies (Goni, 2021). The fact that this erasure was possible is the best indication of the passivity of slavery in the region, in spite of its long period of economic and social significance.

The Roman or *urban-latifundic* mode: ancient Roman slavery stands in a class by itself, having no real parallel in the ancient, medieval, or modern worlds. It was unique, less in the totality of slavery – which is more true of the Caribbean – than in the pervasiveness of the institution, which reached into nearly all regions of the social system: economic, social, administrative, and governance. It was distinctive, first, in the sheer magnitude of its imperial power and the degree of dependence on slavery, both at the imperial center and in its major colonial sectors. As Kyle Harper and Walter Scheidel (2018: 104) note: "In terms of its intrinsic character and its structural location, slavery occupied a central position in the Roman economy. By nature, empire and chattel slavery were very much alike, constituting analogous systems of violent and asymmetric domination and predatory appropriation that mobilized and located resources and created, sustained, and reinforced inequality and hierarchy." Second, Rome was unique in the extent of its reliance on slavery in both its rural and urban-industrial sectors. In this regard, it has no parallel in the modern world, where urban economies and governments were dominated, often exclusively, by free persons. Third, the articulation of slavery was more actively transformative than in any other system, entailing what Hopkins (2010 [1978]) called an "extrusion" of free, small farmers and their replacement by slaves organized in gangs on large latifundi. It was truly "a driving force of political and economic development" (Harper and Scheidel, 2018: 104). Rome was unusual too, not only for its relatively high levels of manumission, but for the extent to which slaves and slavery came to influence all aspects of its culture (Scheidel, 2012; Harper, 2011; Harper and Scheidel, 2018).

The *capitalist plantation* modes: contrary to the views of early economic theorists such as Adam Smith, and of Marxist scholars until fairly recently (Genovese, 1965), modern plantation slavery was in no way incompatible with capitalism. Indeed, the rise of capitalism was intimately bound up with this mode of articulation of slavery, and at its height in nineteenth-century America was as profitable as the most advanced industrial factories of Europe or the Northern United States (Fogel and Engerman, 1974). Plantation slavery constituted one version of the worldwide systemic spread of capitalism, in which capital accumulation was advanced through the use of the enslaved in the peripheral colonial regions, complementing the use of so-called free labor in the metropolitan centers, and of serf and other forms of dependent labor in the semi-peripheral areas of Eastern Europe and Latin America (Wallerstein, 1974; Blackburn, 2010 [1997]; Beckert and Rockman, 2016).

While plantation slavery bore some organizational resemblance to the ancient slave latifundia, and indeed can be traced historically to late medieval and early modern variants of the ancient model (see Verlinden, 1995; Solow, 1991), it was distinctive in its complex, transnational system of financial support, in its production for international export, in its heavy reliance on a single crop, in its advanced organizational structure– which in the case of sugar involved innovative agri-industrial farms – in the vast distances from which slaves were imported, entailing a complex transoceanic slave-trading system, and in its reliance on the enslaved from one major geographic region who differed sharply from the slaveholding class in ethnosomatic terms.

However, in spite of these common attributes of the mutual constitution of capitalism and modern slavery, or "racial capitalism," as Robinson (1983) called it, there were important differences in the articulation of slavery in the capitalist social formations. At one extreme are what may be called pure plantation slave systems. These emerged only in the Caribbean. Essentially, slavery was not simply the most important institution in these societies; it permeated all areas of the system. Unlike in ancient Rome, slavery was all-pervasive. In ancient Rome, the military excluded slaves. In the West Indies, there were major slave regiments upholding the system. Ancient Rome also had a large working class – the Plebs – that constituted the majority of laboring persons; and most free persons did not own slaves. Not so the West Indian systems, where all laborers were enslaved, and nearly all free persons either owned slaves or were supervisors of slaves.

In these respects the West Indian slave systems also differed from the US South and northeastern Brazil. In the West Indies, the enslaved constituted between 80 and 90 percent of the populations. In the US South, the enslaved constituted on average a third of the population: in 1840, at the height of the antebellum, capitalistic slave economy, 47 percent of the population in the Lower South were enslaved, 29 percent of the Upper South, and only 13 percent of the border slave states (Fogel and Engerman, 1974; Higman, 2017). Also, less than a third of Southern Whites owned slaves and most were involved in economic activities not directly related to the plantation system, although many were engaged in farming that partly supplied produce to the plantations. The average size of units was also much smaller in the United States and Brazil than the West Indies. In early nineteenth-century Jamaica, nearly three-quarters of the slave population were in units owned by slaveholders owning fifty or more slaves, compared with less than a quarter in the antebellum United States (Engerman, 1976: 265). Most important of all, the elites of the West Indian slave system were not simply economically integrated with the British economy but were also socially integrated, in that a substantial proportion of the most successful planters resided in the imperial center (Patterson, 2022 [1967]: Ch. 1; Hall et al., 2014). In the US South and South America slaveowners resided in the plantation areas, reinvested their wealth there, and were devoted to the development of a distinct settler culture and social order (Genovese, 1969). What emerged from the West Indian slave systems, and shaped the post-emancipation socioeconomic order in the Caribbean, were what the New World group of West Indian social scientists called the "pure plantation economy" (Best, 1968). In their classic statement of the model, they emphasized

> that all plantation economies are not the same and that there are different modes of engagement with global capitalism, with different distributional effects between the metropoles and the hinterlands as well as within the hinterlands, depending on whether it is a colony of conquest, a colony of exploitation, or a colony of settlement . . . [and] is relatively original and independent given its emphasis on the inherent rigidities of "small size" and "islandness," and the socio-cultural dimensions of plantation systems such as social stratification based on "race." (Nurse and Crichlow, 2011: 203)

This contrast with the US South, and large-scale South American slaveholding regimes such as northeastern Brazil, already indicates what was distinctive about this mode of articulation, which we designate

THE NATURE AND STUDY OF SLAVERY

as "pure plantocratic slave systems." Although the slave plantation was the most important sector of such systems and the owners of the large plantations leveraged their wealth and socioeconomic status to dominate the entire order politically, socially, and even culturally, the non-slave sector to this plantocratic mode of articulation engaged the majority of the population.

3.3: Large-scale passive articulation: The case of Korea

Of the three factors determining the mode of articulation, that between the active and the passive modes may be the most unfamiliar. But it most reveals the strength of our approach, so let us now look more closely at the very remarkable case of the articulation of slavery in a large-scale yet passive fashion: premodern Korea. The institution persisted in this society on a significant scale and for a longer period of time than in most other parts of the world. For all of the Koryŏ (935–1392) and most of the Chosŏn (1392–1910) periods, the enslaved constituted, on average, 30 percent of the total population, and at its peak in the late fifteenth century amounted to 40 percent, far higher than at any time in ancient Greece or the US South (Bok-rae, 2003: 167). There is general agreement that the enslaved were not only ubiquitous, but performed important economic and social roles, as well as lower-level public service (Salem, 1978; Palais, 1984; Kye, 2021; Kim, 2023). And yet, the influence of slavery on the broader economy and social structure was never determinative. It would seem, rather, that slavery on a large scale was embedded in the Korean social formation. This seems to be what Bok-rae was getting at in her description of the system at its zenith between the fifteenth and seventeenth centuries, as "a serfdom developed under slavery" (2003: 159).

A comparison of the five centuries of the Yi dynasty with the rise of slavery during the centuries following the Solonic reforms in Athens is revealing. At no time can one detect in Korea the same close association between the rise of slavery and the sectoralization of the economy, the shift to commodity production for trade, the rise of an urban elite and the general urbanization of the population. I am not suggesting that some such changes did not take place in Korea; rather, slavery was in no way the cause of any structural changes that occurred during this period. Instead, slavery passively adapted to such changes. Unlike the Solonic reforms, those of Yi Sung-gye, the founder of Chosŏn, took place quite independently

78

of the institution of slavery. More telling were the effects of the drastic changes introduced during the reign of T'aejong (1401–18). The official shift in favor of Confucianism, the restriction on the number of Buddhist temples and on the number of slaves and land each priest could own, resulted in the expropriation of some eighty thousand slaves. These, as well as the lands seized, were then given to favored royalists, in this way increasing the concentration of owner-ship in land and the enslaved. Note, however, that slavery was in no way the cause of the concentration of proprietorial powers, but its consequence, and this major shift in ownership had no significant changes in the means of production or overall volume of wealth (Henderson, 1968).

The answer to the puzzle of the passivity of slavery in the social formation of premodern Korea is to be found in the centralities of its peculiar mode of production and sociopolitical development. In his critique of that Marxian shibboleth, the "Asiatic mode of produc-tion," Perry Anderson (1974) has rightly observed that "the modes of production of any pre-capitalist social formation are always specified by the politico-juridical apparatus of class rule which enforces the extra-economic coercion peculiar to it." Of few formations is this more true than premodern Korea. "Smallness of dimension (in Asian terms), stability of boundaries, ethnic and religious homogeneity, and exceptional continuity mark Korea," writes Henderson (1968). Within this context emerged a political system that was exceptional for its centralism, for the control of the military by the bureaucratic and royal elite, and for the dominance of authoritarianism in almost all social relationships. There were few marked regional differences in either cultural or economic terms. In this system, the economy was totally subordinate to the polity and official interests and reflected the highly centralized nature of the formation. "There was no real theory of private property." Land was, in theory, owned by the state, but was in practice monopolized by the bureaucratic and aristocratic classes. Henderson adds: "Economic status was based exclusively on political power. The monarch and his officials had first claims on all and could, in theory, distribute and redistribute as they saw fit. Bureaucracy was increasingly a self-serving, not a public-serving, instrument, seeing the state and its population largely as a farm to be 'eaten' and exploited."

And yet, in marked contrast to the arrested growth of slavery in China, we find a remarkable growth and economic utilization of the enslaved throughout Korean history. Why, then, did the institu-tion develop to the degree that it did in Korea? The answer, in the

THE NATURE AND STUDY OF SLAVERY

broadest terms, is that Korean slavery was a compatible means of temporarily solving some of the contradictions inherent in its social formation. The excessive demands of an overcentralized, top-heavy, and often corrupt state apparatus on the work force in the forms of taxes, tribute, corvée, and military draft led to disruptions in the production of wealth, which sections of the ruling class itself, not to mention the peasants, resented. Slavery papered over and delayed the full implications of these problems because the enslaved were exempt from such taxes and compulsory services, so much so that, occasionally, commoners, in extreme circumstances, found it convenient to falsely claim that they were enslaved (Bok-rae, 2018). Slavery was a means of privatizing property, in a system where an unusual degree of state control of land undermined the production of wealth; it was a means of extracting more surplus from the worker using the same mode of production. The unusual system in which most of the enslaved lived away from their owners (between 48 and 72 percent, according to Kim, 2023) meant that they were, in economic terms, more like bond-tenants and bond-debtors who were left to their own traditional devices as long as they paid the tribute or the produce from the slaveholder's portion of allocated land (the "chak-kae" system) due from them (Kye, 2021: Ch. 12). However, their social death was never in doubt, since they could always be sold, no matter how far away, arbitrarily punished, sexually violated, and even killed with impunity; lacking family names, they were instead given names such as "yellow dog" and "human excrement" (Kim, 2023: 325–6). Slavery was also sometimes the means by which one section of the ruling class could seize power from another without running the revolutionary risk of involving the peasants, and of consolidating control over the traditional means of production and the state machinery. It is noteworthy that during the Mongol domination (*c.* 1270–1360), the one period in which the enslaved held influential positions as soldiers, politicians, palace eunuchs, and confidants of kings – outwardly similar to the *familia Caesaris* of early imperial Rome and the Islamic *Ghilman* (Patterson, 2018 [1982]: Ch. 11) – their role was largely that of preserving the old order rather than creating a radically new system, as happened with the rise of the Abbasid caliphate or Egyptian Mamluks. Thus, the *coup d'état* of 1258 against Ch'pe Ui (the last Choe dictator of the Ubong Choe military regime), led by Kim Jun (the son of Kim Yun-seong, a house slave of the Choe family) in a cabal of several slave retainers and officials, resulted in the formal *restoration* of the Korean monarchy with the ascension of Wonjong in 1260.

BEYOND "SLAVE SOCIETY"

All in all, slavery gave the traditional system a measure of suppleness and structural flexibility that permitted its survival and extension. Korea, then, fully exemplifies the large-scale articulation of slavery in an entirely passive way and is a classic illustration of embedded slave formations. When this slave formation slowly drew to a close in the nineteenth century, it is significant that its demise entailed no social disruption. Its economic role was quietly replaced by independent peasants. "The eventual abolition of slavery," Kim writes (2023), "was not the result of any radical or persistent abolitionist movement." There is no better indication of the passive articulation of slavery in the embedded Korean slave formation than the fact that, after more than one thousand years of existence, it simply passed away – not with a bang, but with a whimper.

Conclusion

The case of Korea reveals why our analytic focus should shift from "slave society," not to mention the "slave mode of production," to the dynamics of the *relationship* between slavery and society. It is the structural articulation of the institution that should be the focus of our study, not undue preoccupation with the size and proportion of the slave population, although this is not unimportant. Each mode of structural articulation of slavery will be a special ordering of the three basic processes I have discussed above, leading to an indeterminate set of slave formations, in some of which, like the Mamluk Sultanate (Ayalon, 1951), the proportion of the enslaved may be well below 10 percent, though of major structural significance.

Angus Walker (1978), a bourgeois critic of Marx, in his discussion of Marx's response to Mikhailovsky's mistaken interpretation of his theory of history, cites the closing passage in Marx's rejoinder that he (Walker) found "somewhat obscure." The passage by Marx runs as follows:

> Events of striking similarity, but which are played out in different historical circumstances, thus lead to quite different results. If these developments are studied for themselves and then compared with each other the key to these phenomena is easily found, but not by using the universal key of a general historiosophical theory of which the chief virtue lies in its suprahistoricity. (Cited in Walker, 1978: 20; see Marx's entire letter at Marx, 1934; see also Anderson, 2007)

THE NATURE AND STUDY OF SLAVERY

Unlike Walker, I do not find this passage by Marx in the least bit "obscure." Any approach to history that compares societies as static entities, or rejects the bold, worldwide comparativism that Marx advocated in favor of an overemphasis on the particularism of given social formations as end-states, will indeed find the above-cited passage obscure. What Marx had in mind, I submit, is the approach to comparative sociohistorical analysis I have sought to follow in this chapter. It is an approach that rejects the vain search for general laws of static social orders as well as the particularism which the "pure history" school of bourgeois scholarship has always embraced, and which an increasing number of misguided Marxists are now finding attractive. The "striking similarity" of the event of slavery in "different historical circumstances," we have seen, "lead[s] to quite different results." By studying these *developments* (in our case, these articulations) in themselves, and then by comparing these *articulations* with each other, we will eventually understand "the key" to the social formations of slavery.

— 4 —

THE DENIAL OF SLAVERY IN CONTEMPORARY AMERICAN SOCIOLOGY

Introduction

Consider the following five preliminary observations:

1 Slavery is one of the most foundational institutions in the history of the West. (See Davis, 1966, 1986; Piketty, 2014: 158–63; Patterson, 1991, 1999; Engerman et al., 2001; Rio, 2017; Eltis et al., 2004; Williams, 2021 [1944]; Blackburn, 2010 [1997].)
2 Of all Western societies, the United States has been most profoundly influenced by slavery, economically, socially, politically, and culturally, its centrality emphasized in numerous classic works and in a spate of more recent ones. (Classic works include: DuBois, 1935; Morgan, 2003 [1975]; Stampp, 1989 [1956]; Kolchin, 1993; Fogel and Engerman, 1974; Berlin, 1998. More recent works include: van Cleve, 2010; Johnson, 2013; Rothman, 2012; O'Malley, 2012; Lott, 2013; Roediger and Esch, 2012; Lepore, 2018.)
3 One of the most, if not *the* most, important social problem in the United States today is the persistence of racial inequality and chronic racism, exacerbated in recent years when an openly racist president led the backlash against the nation's first Black president. (See Jordan, 1968; Smedley and Smedley, 2011.)
4 It is generally agreed that this problem originated in the nation's long history of slavery and the succeeding neo-slavery of Jim Crow. For this reason, academic work on slavery is flourishing in history, European classical and medieval studies, economics, and

83

THE NATURE AND STUDY OF SLAVERY

all but one of the social sciences. (These works are too numerous to mention, but see Beckert, 2014; Beckert and Rockman, 2016; Schermerhorn, 2015; Ruef, 2014; Johnson, 2013; Baptist, 2014; Rockman, 2009; Acharya et al., 2018. For a review of this literature, see Rockman, 2012. See also Inikori and Engerman, 1992.)

5 Sociology is the academic discipline that is most involved with the problem of race and inequality. And yet, paradoxically, sociology is the discipline least concerned with the subject of slavery, a neglect that verges on disdain. Works on slavery rarely, if ever, appear in the pages of its leading journals. Graduate students steer clear of the subject.

Other than myself, a Jamaican, I know of only six professional sociologists in America (at the time of writing) who currently work either directly or indirectly on American slavery, its legacies, or its critical role in the development of capitalism: Martin Ruef at Duke; John Clegg, formerly at the University of Chicago who is an Englishman; Fiona Greenland at the University of Virginia; Chris Muller at Berkeley; Robert Reece at the University of Texas at Austin; and Heather O'Connell at Louisiana State University. Of the six, only Clegg currently works primarily on slavery. Ruef has so far published a major book-length study on the subject – the only living American-born sociologist to have done so – but is increasingly focused on contemporary issues. Reece's dissertation (2017), and subsequent work, on the post-emancipation consequences of slavery, especially for segregation, inequality, and colorism, are important contributions (Reece and O'Connell, 2016), as is the work of Heather O'Connell (2012) on the effects of slavery on poverty and the spatial dimension of racial inequality. Muller's work on convict-leasing during the Jim Crow era, and, with Deirdre Bloome, on tenancy and African American marriage in the postbellum South, as well as his current work on the historical origins of the Black–White wealth gap, are path-breaking studies on the consequences of slavery (Muller, 2018; Bloome and Muller, 2015). Fiona Greenland's current work on the persistence of slavery in European history from ancient to modern times, with special emphasis on the gender dimension of this civilizational continuity, is remarkable for its comparative methodology and theoretical sophistication. Her problematizing and extension of the role of parasitism in relations of domination has implications for the study of power and subjection at the micro, meso and macro levels of human exploitation.

THE DENIAL OF SLAVERY IN CONTEMPORARY AMERICAN SOCIOLOGY

While his focus is on colonial and postcolonial studies, George Steinmetz's (2013) work on the entanglement of sociology with imperialism is one indication of the reasons for the discipline's aversion to the study of slavery (see also Steinmetz, 2019). Although she has moved away from an earlier, more direct interest in slavery, Zine Magubane's (2016, 2017) critique of the compartmentalization of the study of "race relations" in American sociology away from broader concerns of the discipline, its insistent presentism, and failure to acknowledge the roots of the discipline in the defense of slavery and colonialism, complements the work of Steinmetz and also goes some way in explaining why sociology shuns the study of slavery. Berkeley sociologist Loïc Wacquant (2002) certainly takes the subject of American slavery seriously, but like Clegg, he is a European. It is noteworthy that the great sociologist W. E. B. DuBois's foundational role in the discipline was, until very recently, shamefully neglected (see Morris, 2015), along with his monumental work of historical sociology, *Black Reconstruction in America, 1860–1880*, published in 1935, one of the most important studies in the historical sociology of slavery and its afterlife.

Race, let me hasten to add, has little to do with this strange disciplinary aversion. American sociologists of all ethnicities share this strange disciplinary blindness to slavery. I do not know of a single Black sociologist who works *primarily* on the subject, although nearly all attest to its importance.

The remainder of this chapter briefly expands on these preliminary observations.

4.1: The historical significance of slavery

It is becoming increasingly evident to historians that slavery was one of the foundational institutions of Western civilization. Not only did the institution play a critical role in the Greco-Roman origin of the West, but at all the subsequent high points of its development (Patterson, 2016). Long resisted by classical historians, a turning point came in the 1960s with the work of the great classical scholar and historical sociologist Sir Moses Finley (1960; see also Finley, 1973). It is now the established view that the answer to the title of his famous essay, "Was Greek Civilization Based on Slave Labor?" is a resounding "Yes!" Not only was slavery essential to all aspects of the Athenian economy, but it was important too for the rise of freedom as central value and the attendant emergence of democracy (Pohlenz, 1966; Patterson, 1991; Raaflaub, 2004; Meier, 2011).

Slavery rose to even greater importance in all periods of Roman history, from the era of the Twelve Tables right down to the collapse of the Western empire in the late fifth century, and remained important in Byzantium down to its demise in 1453. Slavery permeated all aspects of Rome except its military – its economy, bureaucracy, educational system, popular and elite culture, and religion (see Scheidel, 2012; Bradley, 1987).

It was within the context of Roman slave society that emerged the institution that was later to dominate and fashion Western civilization: Christianity. This institution was not only critically dependent on the enslaved and freedmen in its formation, but was profoundly influenced in its theology by the metaphor of slavery, Pauline Christological soteriology being largely an introjection of the experience of manumission from the social death of slavery, while Jesus' crucifixion was symbolically reinterpreted as the redemption fee (from Latin *redemptio*: to purchase out of slavery), which paid for a Christian rebirth into spiritual freedom (see Chapter 6, pp. 151–3).

The traditional historiography of the post-Roman death of slavery and its early replacement by serfdom has been demolished. Early medieval Europe is no longer a dark age, its history lit up by remarkable methodological advances in the new science of the human past (see McCormick, 2001). Wherever that light shines, we find the brutal face of slavery: in Carolinian Europe (McCormick, 2002), medieval Bavaria (Hammer, 2002; Sutherland, 2017), medieval Scandinavia (Karras, 1988), Anglo-Saxon and Norman England and eleventh-century Ireland (Pelteret, 1995; Wyatt, 2009); in the rise of the late medieval city-states (Williams, 1995; McKee, 2004); and in Europe generally (Rio, 2017), especially with regard to the persistent enslavement of women (Stuard, 1995; Greenland, 2019; McKee, 2016). The slave trade was a major economic source for several of the great Renaissance states, especially Genoa and Venice, the latter running large slave plantations producing sugar in the Mediterranean islands that were the models for the slave systems that later emerged in the New World (Verlinden, 1970). Even where, as in Renaissance Florence, slavery was of only domestic significance, it nonetheless loomed large in the consciousness and thought of elite Florentines, as I have argued elsewhere (Patterson, 2018; see also Epstein, 2001).

The rise of the modern West, based on the Atlantic system, was largely made possible by the enslavement and sustained holocaust of at least 12 million Africans. Early capitalism depended heavily on the

THE DENIAL OF SLAVERY IN CONTEMPORARY AMERICAN SOCIOLOGY

profits of the slave trade and New World sugar plantation slavery; later, industrial capitalism, right down to the latter half of the nineteenth century, was integrally involved with slave-produced cotton (see Williams, 2021 [1944]; Morgan, 2000; Acemoglu et al. 2005). It is remarkable that "grand historical sociology," though largely preoccupied with the rise of modern Europe, almost completely missed the mark with regard to the centrality of slavery in its development, in sharp contrast with European historical sociologists.

Slavery in the United States, it is increasingly established, was critical not just for the development of its economy; the institution was also a vital factor in the rise of American democracy. It shaped the character of freedom as a central value in America, and defined Blacks as permanent internal outsiders, an inferior race whose Blackness defined Whiteness as a unifying cultural force (Morgan, 2003 [1975]; Patterson, 1987). What ended in 1865 was individual, legally based slavery. After the radical interlude of Reconstruction, it was followed by the collective post-juridical system of slavery known as Jim Crow, which DuBois long ago showed to be slavery by another name. This system formally came to an end only with the dismantlement of Jim Crow laws in 1965. The permeation of slavery in American history, society, and culture was therefore deep, broad, foundational, and lasting. American historical sociology is also completely in the dark about these fundamental developments. There is now a lively and growing body of scholarship on the social, political, and economic legacies of slavery in modern American society and elsewhere, but, with the noteworthy exception of the few sociologists mentioned earlier (Ruef, Clegg, Muller, Reece, and O'Connell) almost all scholars working in this important area are from economics, political science, and other disciplines (see, e.g., Acharya et al. 2018; Bertocchi and Dimico, 2014; Sacerdote, 2005; Soares et al., 2010; also this volume, pp. 36–40).

Why then the resounding silence of sociology, compounded by its deliberate academic banishment of the few who have dared to study the institution of slavery and its persisting lineaments?

4.2: The silence of the sociological clan

First, it is important to note that this neglect and censorship of the subject are true only of American sociologists. In Europe, the study of slavery has long been taken very seriously. One of my mentors, C. L. R. James, the great Caribbean Marxist counterpart and contemporary of DuBois, holds a revered place among British and French

THE NATURE AND STUDY OF SLAVERY

sociologists. His classic work, *The Black Jacobins* (1938), on the Haitian slave revolt and its imbrication with the French Revolution, is still widely cited and taught. This is especially true of, though not confined to, Marxist and neo-Marxian sociologists, in view of the importance Marx attributed to slavery in his own historical sociology. It is reflected in the works of historical sociologists such as Keith Hopkins (my former colleague in sociology at the London School of Economics, later professor of ancient history at the University of Cambridge), Perry Anderson, and Robin Blackburn. My own works on slavery have received far greater attention in Europe than in America, starting with my first book about slavery in Jamaica, *The Sociology of Slavery*. It is striking that, when it was first published in 1967, although written by a then relatively unknown young scholar just out of graduate school, the work was widely reviewed in both the academic and mass circulation British press, including a favorable one by the eminent British historian Eric Hobsbawm in the *Manchester Guardian*. Very few American sociologists read, or even know of the existence of, *The Sociology of Slavery*. So it is hardly surprising, though galling, that several *American* scholars have criticized me for not doing what I was among the first postcolonial scholars of any discipline to do: write a detailed, archival-based study of the lived experience of the enslaved – their social and cultural lives, psychological reactions, hopes, fears, and widespread resistance.

Why have American sociologists, in spite of their deep engagement with the problem of racism and racial inequality, disdained the study of slavery? One reason is disciplinary parochialism: plain ignorance of developments in ancient, modern, and economic history, including that of America, and of the remarkable new methodological breakthroughs that are revolutionizing our knowledge of the past.

Closely related is what George Steinmetz (2018) has called the "pervasive presentism of American sociology," reflected in the temporal and regional parochialism of the papers published in the discipline's leading journals, the vast majority of which "usually do not indicate any era, period, or time frame, and are written in the sociological present tense," which "conveys an image of the social world as being governed by unchanging universal laws and logics of necessity . . . the message is that the present is the same as the past, or that the past is simply not interesting" (2018: 3). (For my critique of such presentism and the related neglect of the problem of continuity, see Patterson, 2004.)

An important further reason is that slavery became entangled with changing ideological fads and fashions in sociology. Up to the 1960s, slavery was, indeed, considered an essential factor in explaining racism and the plight of Black Americans. DuBois's work was still influential and Black sociologists such as E. Franklin Frazier and Kenneth Clark, as well as White scholars, took the subject seriously in their work, as did Gunnar Myrdal in his influential magnum opus, *An American Dilemma* (1944). This all came to a screeching academic halt with the now notorious leaked pamphlet by Daniel Patrick Moynihan in 1964, who did no more than summarize what was then common knowledge: that slavery had a devastating impact on Blacks both externally in its generation of racism, Jim Crow and segregation, and internally in its effects on Black marital and familial relations. Nor was his language, which we now cringe at, any different from that used by sociologists, Black and White, at the time. This was the heyday of functionalism and terms such as "deviance," "dysfunction," and "pathology" were commonly invoked by both White and Black sociologists and policy advocates on both the right and the left when describing problems of the lower classes of all ethnicities. However, the document came at the wrong time and was written by the wrong person (only a year earlier Kenneth Clark, whose work played a critical role in the Supreme Court's outlawing of school segregation, had used exactly similar terms in his book *Dark Ghetto: Dilemmas of Social Power* (1965), chapter 5 of which was entitled "The Pathology of the Ghetto"). The intellectual tide, however, had suddenly turned sharply away from Parsonian functionalism, and from historical and cultural explanations of social life. To complicate matters, Oscar Lewis's culture of poverty theory, first published in 1959, which had initially gained currency, was, by the mid-1960s, being denounced, along with Moynihan, as academic attempts to blame the victim. (It is worth noting that Lewis was a Marxist anthropologist who died while working in revolutionary Cuba, in violation of American laws.) Thus culture became suspect among sociologists, and the subject was largely dropped from sociological work on race and poverty from the mid-1960s to its revival, on strictly enforced academic norms that exclude it as an explanatory factor in the study of race (for more on this development, see Patterson, 2014).

Alas, the study of slavery became smeared through a kind of intellectual guilt by association among sociologists, especially in light of Moynihan's rather heavy-handed attribution of Black familial "pathology" to the direct effects of slavery, without sufficient consideration of the nuances of continuity and the importance of interacting structural forces. This banishment of slavery from the explanatory tool-kit of sociologists was reinforced by parallel developments among

THE NATURE AND STUDY OF SLAVERY

historians studying slavery during this period. Partly motivated by the uproar over the Moynihan report, historians went on a massive revision of the, until then, common view that slavery had devastating consequences for Black life. Very soon, a new romanticized orthodoxy emerged that emphasized the wondrous ways in which Black slaves, in spite of two and a half centuries of enslavement, the last fifty of which saw the brutal separation of couples from each other and of parents from their children, and the inhuman breeding of Black bodies to meet the demands of the internal slave trade from the Old South to the new cotton belt (a subject on which DuBois wrote forcefully), nonetheless created harmonious communities on the slave plantation sustained by nuclear, god-fearing families that rivaled modern suburban families in their stability and loving unity. The Black historian John Blassingame's book *The Slave Community* (1972) became a bestseller. Among White historians, Herbert Gutman's 1976 book, *The Black Family in Slavery and Freedom*, became the *locus classicus* for those seeking support for the view that slavery left the Black family unscathed. Indeed, Gutman left a portrait of Black slave women as models of Victorian primness. Fogel and Engerman's *Time on the Cross* (1974), although pathbreaking in its cliometric methodology and macro-economic reinterpretation of the capitalistic nature of Southern slavery, also reinforced the view that slavery was nondestructive of the social lives of the enslaved. The unintended effect of this new historiography, as one skeptic has noted, was to write the role of the enslaver and the sexual horrors of slavery, the double burden of female slaves as overworked laborers and rape victims, clean out of the accounts of Southern slavery. Nonetheless, it fitted squarely with the sharp structural, anticultural turn in the sociology of Black life and poverty. Every sociologist of race now assumed that there was no need to consider slavery in the study of race and poverty; on the contrary, any such consideration immediately raised suspicion and the risk of being flattened with the trigger-ready charge: blaming the victim. One sociologist, Frank Furstenberg Jr., after peeking into the new historiography, confidently informed the sociological community that slavery had nothing to do with the high rate of single parenting among the Black poor. It was all about the present urban experience (see Furstenberg et al., 1975). It took a professional historian, Steve Ruggles (1994), to demolish this presentist manifesto, in a paper that is now a classic study in the historical sociology of the Black family.

It is very likely that this view of the irrelevance of slavery carried over to the generation of scholars who ushered in the new wave of

THE DENIAL OF SLAVERY IN CONTEMPORARY AMERICAN SOCIOLOGY

what John Goldthorpe has called "grand historical sociology," which emerged in the mid- to late 1970s and early 1980s, led by scholars such as Theda Skocpol, Dietrich Rueschemeyer, Peter B. Evans, Fred Bloc, Margaret Somers, and others, under the inspiration of Barrington Moore's seminal 1966 book, *The Social Origins of Dictatorship and Democracy*. Their manifesto, *Vision and Method in Historical Sociology*, edited by Skocpol, was published in 1984, two years after my *Slavery and Social Death*, seventeen years after my *The Sociology of Slavery*, and I was immediately left in no doubt about the fate of slavery, not to mention my own works, in this then hot new school of American historical sociology. On the rare occasion when the subject was mentioned, as in Immanuel Wallerstein's first volume of his *The Modern World System* (1974), it was from forty thousand theoretical feet above the slow-motion genocidal horrors and grounded socio-logical terrain in which I worked – one mode of labor production, along with East European serfdom and Western wage labor, in the magnificent emergence of the modern world system. My own intel-lectual trajectory was completely at variance with this "grand" new vision. *Slavery and Social Death* was, of course, a very comparative work. But there all similarity ended, substantively, methodologically, and theoretically, as George Steinmetz (2019) has pointed out.

The fundamental issue at stake here is the misguided pseudo-liberal failure of sociologists, both those who work on present problems and those who work on historically oriented ones, to recognize one of the most tragic complexities of oppression. This is the fact that oppres-sion works both externally and internally, a commonplace among European Marxist and non-Marxist scholars such as Paul Willis (1981). If a person is brutally abused as a child, the injuries linger not only in the scars on her flesh and the persisting presence of her abusers, but in the psychological wounds that often result in her own self-inflicted cuttings and suicidal urges. What is true of individuals holds equally true for groups. If a people is brutally oppressed for several centuries, it is inevitable that their hurt, their rage, and their degradation are partly turned on themselves, in the tendency of those with some little power to turn upon those even more vulnerable. The abuse of children by their parents, which I observed every day in my fieldwork among the slum-dwellers of Kingston, and experienced myself from my sadistic teachers at elementary school in rural, colo-nial Jamaica, are direct reflections of a system in which for centuries the lash was the primary motivation to work. The daily degradation that men experienced, under slavery, in the post-emancipation cane-fields, as yard-boys and fast-food workers in the postcolonial and postindustrial economies, inevitably corrodes to a perverse masculinity in which men assuage their socioeconomic impotence through the physical and sexual abuse of women and children. Among the Jamaican working classes, the favored male synonyms for fucking a woman is to "beat" and to "lash" her. In the ghettos of America, "running train" (gang-raping) young girls is the height of masculinity. In Jamaica, more than 80 percent of children are being brought up by impoverished women. In America, it is more than 70 percent and rising. Intergenerational trauma is real and tragic in its self-inflicted wounds (on Jamaica, see Patterson, 2019: Ch. 2; on the US, see Patterson, 1998c: Chs. 1 and 2). Bourgeois historians and sociologists cannot bear to face such horrors of self-injury. Instead, we are presented with the romantic ennobling of the slave condition in which slavery is reinterpreted as a mere "predicament" nobly negotiated by the slave (see Brown, 2009). Bourgeois sociologists observe the homicidal, sexual, and familial tragedies in the ghettos of Kingston, Montego Bay, Rio de Janeiro, Baltimore, Philadelphia, and Chicago, and proclaim that it is *only* structural and external. It is indeed structural. Monstrously so. But history matters, as does culture, the mouth of history's flow, which interactively bears down on the oppressed, both externally and internally, like a disgorging amazon.

II

Slavery in the Premodern and Early Christian Worlds

— 5 —

THE ORIGINS OF SLAVERY AND SLAVE SOCIETY: A CRITIQUE OF THE NIEBOER-DOMAR HYPOTHESIS AND CASE STUDY OF ANCIENT ATHENS

This chapter examines the origins of slavery as an institution and of slave society. The first section focuses on the best-known attempts to explain the origins of the institution, especially the hypothesis of the comparative ethnographer H. J. Nieboer and the economist E. D. Domar, my critique of this hypothesis, and my own alternative explanation. The second section examines the case of ancient Athens, which both serves as a historical critique of the hypothesis and also provides a brief account of the first known large-scale slave society in human history.

5.1: The origins of slavery as institution

Over the past century or so a curious hypothesis has recurred among some scholars engaged in the comparative study of slavery. It is the view that slavery, indeed bondage in general, is only possible where there is an abundance of resources relative to population, this being so because human beings can be induced to work for others under such conditions only through force. Where land is the dominant resource, as is true of the vast majority of human societies, the hypothesis may be more simply stated as follows: bondage and, in particular, slavery will only arise where the ratio of people to land (man/land ratio) is low and, conversely, will tend to die out when that ratio is high.

As early as 1849, E. G. Wakefield published a version of the hypothesis (1849: 126–4, 326) in which he argued that the cheapness of land was the main cause of the scarcity of labor for hire in the colonies. Forty-four years later, Achille Loria (1893: 2–6) formulated the hypothesis in a more precise way, arguing that wherever land is abundant and can be cultivated without much capital input, slavery or serfdom will be the only means of securing a work force other than the labor of the landowner's family. When all land has been taken up, those who own no land will be at the mercy of the landowners, so the political force of slavery or serfdom becomes unnecessary.

It was the Dutch comparative ethnologist, H. J. Nieboer (1900: Ch. 4), however, who first advanced what may be called the strong version of the hypothesis and attempted to test it empirically. In writing that "when all land fit for cultivation has been appropriated, slavery is not likely to exist," he was presenting the weaker version of the hypothesis; but forty-one pages later, when he comes back to it, we are presented with the strong version: "Oceania fully justifies our theory that slavery is inconsistent with a state of scarcity in which all land is held as property." Conversely, we are told that "slavery as an industrial system can only exist where there is still free land" (1900: 306, 347, 348).

The hypothesis was generally neglected by historians of slavery (although not by anthropologists) for more than a half a century, and seemed to have died a natural death when E. D. Domar, an MIT economic historian, independently revived it. Domar made it clear that he was explaining the origins of both slavery and serfdom, "used here interchangeably" (1970: 18). He developed the hypothesis in light of Russian economic history during the seventeenth and eighteenth centuries, when the availability of cheap land in the newly conquered areas led to a mass migration of peasants away from the traditional large estates, creating a labor crisis for the large landowners. To solve the problem, Domar argued, two things were necessary: the ruling classes were given sole rights of ownership of land and the rights of the peasants to migrate were abolished.

Domar was quick to point out that, due to a combination of economic and political factors, his hypothesis was neither necessary nor sufficient. It was not necessary because, as he saw, even where land was no longer free, it was possible for the marginal productivity of labor to be so high that serfdom would still have been necessary to secure labor; and it was not sufficient because political force had to be brought into play to reinforce what was supposed to have been an economic necessity. This indeed had been the thrust of Bernard Siegel's (1945) critique of Nieboer, a critique of which Domar seemed to have been unaware: that it was too crudely deterministic, not to mention monocausal. Economic feasibility does not warrant a hypothesis, especially when, on the basis of Nieboer's own data, some 40 percent of the cases meeting his criteria failed to exhibit slavery.

In spite of the unpromising results of his somewhat cursory review of relevant data from the economic history of Europe, Domar ends his paper on an optimistic note. The man/land ratio, he claims, is at least quantifiable and, as such, is subject to empirical testing. Furthermore, he writes, "I would still expect to find a positive statistical correlation between free land and serfdom (or slavery)" (1970: 21).

Before attempting to lay the ghost of the hypothesis, however, it is necessary to take note of two other restatements of it and a more recent comment: those of Folke Dovring and Ester Boserup, as well as Stanley Engerman's intervention. Interestingly, Dovring's (1965: 6) statement of the hypothesis was also prompted by the Russian experience, but his interpretation is far more subtle. His basic thesis is that a *perceived* labor shortage – whether real or imagined – is what induces a ruling class to impose bondage on the subject population. Second, drawing on the work of Michael Confino (1963), Dovring attempts to show that the Russian servile system cannot be entirely explained in economic terms, but was due to a combination of factors, some economic, some political, and some cultural. The Russian lords, for example, were forced back on the land by Catherine ("the Great"); they seemed to have had no conception of opportunity costs, and even less of estate management; and they had an overriding need to feel that they were somehow relevant to the productive process. Dovring's most intriguing idea, however, is that the servile system may itself have created the labor problem that it largely "imagined" into existence. Culturally determined attitudes toward the level of living appropriate to peasants created a situation in which rent was artificially increased whenever the peasant, by his extra effort, increased his income. Thus, there was no motivation to improve his condition and the peasant was driven to migrate.

Dovring, then, while basically restating the view that labor scarcity is a condition of bondage, and an abundant labor supply a condition of freedom, makes this an intermediary variable by adding that the perception of economic pressures as well as political and cultural practices will influence the relationship. He merely illustrates the point and does not say how these different primary factors interact with each other or influence the intermediary variable. Furthermore, he assumes that bondage will always be inefficient and lead to an economic "dead end," a fallacy initiated by Adam Smith in his *Wealth of Nations*. His problem, then, which he leaves unanswered, is to explain why the "dead end" inefficiency of bondage is always accepted. Furthermore, it never occurs to him that there are conditions under which bondage, not to mention slavery, might work well for elites.

Dovring, like Domar, also fails to distinguish between slavery and serfdom in attempting to explain their origins and decline. He assumes that the same set of factors explaining the rise and fall of one will explain those of the other. Because of this major deficiency in his thinking, Dovring, again like Domar, backs himself into the most untenable historical corner when trying to explain the rise of the colonate and serfdom in late imperial Rome in view of the fact that the colonate developed as a replacement of large-scale slavery (on which, see Bloch, 1966).

Although she never mentions either Nieboer or Domar, Ester Boserup's two best-known works directly address the hypothesis and, in some respects, appear to support it. In *The Conditions of Agricultural Growth* (2017 [2005]) Boserup famously attempts to turn Malthus on his head by arguing that the prime motive for change in pre-industrial societies was population change, which induced humans to develop modes of agricultural intensification and other horticultural improvements such as short fallow, as well as technological changes, such as the shift from digging stick to hoe to the plow. Such innovations, after a period of difficult adjustment, then led to growing population density, urbanization, further technical improvements, and an advance in civilization. However, most small populations operating under conditions of low population density resist such changes because they initially entail lower output per man hour, more work, and less leisure. Instead, they stick to long-fallow and shifting agriculture, which meets their basic needs without much effort. There are only two ways cultivators operating under such leisurely conditions can be induced to change to more intensive agriculture with all its long-term advantages: population pressure and/or slavery. Boserup writes:

> Where population is sparse and fertile land abundant and uncontrolled, a social hierarchy can be maintained only by direct, personal control over the members of the lower class. In such communities therefore, both subjugated peoples and individual captives of war are kept in personal bondage. Bonded labour is a characteristic feature of communities with a hierarchic structure, but surrounded by so much uncontrolled land suitable for cultivation by long-fallow methods that it is impossible to prevent the members of the lower class from finding alternative means of subsistence unless they are made personally unfree. When population becomes so dense that the land can be controlled, it becomes unnecessary to keep the lower class in personal bondage; it is sufficient to deprive the working classes of the right to be independent cultivators. (2017 [2005]: 73)

THE ORIGINS OF SLAVERY AND SLAVE SOCIETY

Boserup draws heavily on the experience of traditional African farmers in developing her theory of the causal force of population growth as the primary engine of pre-industrial development, with the enslavement of more backward tribes hanging on to their low-population density and long-fallow farming by more "progressive" tribes who practiced short-fallow farming using better techniques. In a direct swipe at Malthus, Boserup summarized her theory of growth as follows:

> A tribe which *for some reason* had a more rapid rate of growth than its neighbors, was not faced with the choice between starvation and conquest by territory, as those following a Malthusian line of thought might expect. Instead, the young men of the tribe would set out to capture additional labour outside their own territory and put them to agricultural work. In this way, taking advantage of their larger numbers by enslaving members of neighboring tribes, a tribe with rapid growth of population could secure for itself the advantages of dense and permanent settlement while avoiding the burden of additional hard work in agriculture. Thus, a beginning of economic development would be achieved by the method of increasing the population through imports of slave labour. In fact, population increase is a condition for economic development in its first stages. (2017 [2005]: 74)

This second statement on the rise of slavery differs significantly from the first in that the factor determining slavery is not low population density but, on the contrary, population growth. Defenders of Malthus might certainly differ, but here we are in agreement with Boserup that population growth and growing density can be an inducement to the enslavement of others, as we will see in the case study of ancient Athens discussed later. (Indeed, I rather suspect that Boserup had precisely the case of ancient Athens in mind in arriving at this generalization.)

The Nieboer-Domar hypothesis has not gone entirely unchallenged by modern economic historians. In 1973, Stanley Engerman restated more forcefully the major criticisms that Domar had himself anticipated (but then promptly neglected) – that free land was neither necessary nor sufficient in explaining the rise of slavery, and that the political variable cannot be treated exogenously – and added an important contribution of his own, namely, that it is "possible to distinguish those features which lead to the imposition of the slave system from those which make for its continuation" (1973: 60). Engerman then isolated the major costs of slavery – those of imposing the system and of enforcing it, and those incurred "by the slave condition upon worker productivity" – and claimed, rightly, that "important as the

99

SLAVERY IN THE PREMODERN AND EARLY CHRISTIAN WORLDS

land–labor ratio may seem, much more must be considered before we can satisfactorily develop a theory of the causes of slavery" (1973: 62). Although valuable, Engerman's contribution was largely theoretical and was based mainly on his work on modern slavery. It conceded some significance to the man/land ratio, but does not explore the degree of this significance, something that would only have been possible had he drawn on the comparative data on slavery. And while he concludes his analysis by asserting, correctly in my view, that "more complicated models drawing upon social, political and moral, in addition to economic, consideration are necessary before we can develop a more complete explanation of the rise and fall of slavery," he does not indicate in specific terms what these considerations might be. This is precisely what we will attempt to do in this chapter.

In 2003, the Nobel economist Paul Krugman (2003) took a brief shot at the weakest point of the hypothesis, its contradiction by well-known facts of European history, by noting that after 1348 the European population decreased dramatically by more than one-third as a result of the Black Death, yet serfdom was not reimposed. Other economists have taken issue with the theory, although in largely theoretical terms such as Jean-Jacques Rosa's (2011) argument that the two interacting conditions of serfdom are "oligopsony power in labor demand, sustained by . . . an oligopsolistic supply of violence by large land owners" – in other words, where land is cheap because there are relatively few buyers combined with the monopoly of the instruments of violence by landowners, or, in simple terms, hierarchy and naked political power. Rosa, while praising Domar's "scientific integrity" in admitting that the conditions specified by his theory were neither necessary nor sufficient and had to be supplemented by an exogenous political explanation, went on to question why all states did not choose to "enforce a legal status of serfdom everywhere." He correctly insisted on the important differences between slavery and serfdom, neglected by Domar (and other theorists on the subject), a point with which I agree, but then made the stronger, untenable claim that the two institutions are "mutually exclusive phenomena," which finds no support in the facts of Western and broader global histories of the two institutions. In ancient Sparta, the Laconians were public slaves assigned to individual slaveholders, while the Messenian helots were more like serfs until their revolt in 370 BCE (Patterson, 2003); the two institutions coexisted in Athens and other parts of Greece for much of the late eighth and seventh centuries BCE until the abolition of serfdom for Athenian citizens by Solon in the early sixth century BCE. Serfdom and slavery also coexisted in England from the

100

THE ORIGINS OF SLAVERY AND SLAVE SOCIETY

tenth to the fourteenth centuries CE and in many areas of Europe, especially Bavaria. A larger problem for Rosa is that, like Domar, he is really attempting to explain the origins of slave societies, rather than the institution of slavery, his explanatory variables being a large market economy, the price mechanism, extensive landownership, and advanced state structures. For most of human history, humans lived in small-scale societies, many of which harbored slavery. Hence, a theory of the origins of slavery cannot be confined to advanced premodern systems with centralized states, price mechanisms, large international markets, and mobile labor.

Erik Green (2012), the Swedish economic historian, tests the hypothesis with the case of eighteenth-century Cape Colony. He claims to find partial support, but most of what he presents is actually highly critical. He follows Engerman in distinguishing between the factors determining the rise of slavery and those accounting for its persistence. Slavery first emerged not in response to the labor demands of settler farmers in the rural parts of the Colony where the hypothesis suggests it should have done, but in the urban areas. Only after they were well established and had the means to generate a surplus did the farmers turn to slavery, and even then along with other kinds of labor: "It was the VOC's (Dutch East India Company) demand for labour that led to slaves being imported to the Cape . . . the rise, role, and profitability of slave labor can be understood only in relation to the various forms of labor contract used in the settler farms" (2012: 67).

Let me repeat that, in this chapter, I will be concerned mainly with the origins of slavery in early and premodern societies. The introduction and growth of slavery in the modern world, especially large-scale plantation slavery in the Americas, will not directly concern me because of the many special issues raised by the close relationship of the institution and the rise of European imperialism as well as capitalism itself, what has come to be called "racial capitalism," the view that there is a two-way relationship between the rise of plantation slavery and this most important institution in the emergence of the economic foundation of the modern world. Domar did attempt to relate the hypothesis to the modern Americas, especially North America, but this was the least satisfactory part of his analysis because, as he himself saw, North American history presented just as much apparent support for the hypothesis, for example the US South, as disconfirmation of it, as exemplified by the American West and North, as well as the wide open spaces of Canada.

* * *

Ideally, comparative analysis should always proceed on two fronts. One employs the method of cross-cultural analysis in which the dependent variable in question is examined across a representative sample of social units. The great advantage of this approach, as George Murdock and his school have shown, is that it lends itself to statistical analysis (see Murdock and White, 1969: Ch. 2; for an appraisal of the Murdock school, see Naroll, 1970). Its great disadvantage is that any attempt to derive patterns of change from it presents enormous problems. These problems can be solved in only two ways, one theoretical, the other empirical. The theoretical solution involves making evolutionary assumptions about the societal units being studied. We have not found this to be a very fruitful path. The second is to collect time-series data on the units in one's sample and then apply techniques such as panel analysis. The problem with this approach is that it makes enormous demands on the data. In the case of the comparative study of slavery, such data is usually not available, except for certain modern slave societies and a few ancient ones. These problems therefore make it all the more necessary to employ the second, complementary approach, namely, the diachronic or sociohistorical analysis of a representative number of cases. This second approach presents one problem: it cannot satisfactorily be undertaken within the confines of a single paper or chapter. It is for this reason that we shall restrict ourselves to an examination of the history of slavery in one critical case, that of Greece, especially Athens, the world's first large-scale slave society, between the beginning of its archaic period and the end of the classical age, roughly 800–300 BCE.

The sample used in the statistical analysis is Murdock and White's (1969) world sample of 186 societies, selected for being relatively independent of each other, having weak or no cultural diffusion and phylogenic relationships (for the list of societies and variables in the Murdock sample, see Standard Cross Cultural Sample, 2004). The sample includes the full range of known human societies, from hunter-gatherers and early historic states to modern cases. Based on the coded studies of numerous scholars, there is now a repository of some two thousand variables on the sampled 186 societies. Although traditional cultural anthropologists, committed to in-depth, sample-of-one studies, have expressed skepticism about the sample and the *Ethnographic Atlas* database from which it was originally derived, it is striking that a rigorous assessment of the *Atlas*'s validity by three distinguished social scientists found that "accounts of ethnographers about life in pre-industrial societies as captured in the

102

THE ORIGINS OF SLAVERY AND SLAVE SOCIETY

Table 5.1 Population density: numeric label and frequency

Numeric label (v1130)	Frequency
1 Less than 1 person / sq. mile	51
2 1 to under 5 persons / sq. mile	28
3 5 to fewer than 25 persons / sq. mile	35
4 25 to fewer than 100 persons / sq. mile	37
5 100 to fewer than 500 persons / sq. mile	24
6 500 or more persons / sq. mile	11

Atlas are informative" and that "the *Atlas* is a meaningful source of information about diverse human societies" (Bahrami-Rad et al., 2021).

A total of eighty societies in the sample are reported to have had some kind of slavery at the time of observation, of which twenty-seven are classified as incipient and nonhereditary, forty-four institutionalized and hereditary, and nine unclassified. These were recoded to generate three new variables:

1   "slavery1," a two-category variable with 0 = absent or incipient, 1 = present and hereditary, with all others, including the unclassified, excluded;
2   "slavery2," a three-category variable with 0 = absent, 1 = incipient and nonhereditary, and 2 = hereditary; and
3   "slavery234," a two-category variable with 0 = absent and 1 = all other kinds of slavery, including unclassified cases.

The analysis mainly uses the "slavery1" variable, since my primary interest in this chapter is with hereditary and institutionalized slavery.

The main independent variable used in appraising the hypothesis is "population density," (v1130), a six-category variable ranging from less than one person per square mile to more than five hundred persons per square mile, as shown in Table 5.1. All 186 societies were coded for this variable. A related variable, the Cropping Index (v1128), which measures the percentage of land used each year in farming, was also used. The nature and value labels of the other variables used will be made clear from the tables. To avoid tabular and statistical clutter in the text I will place all the tables of the logistic regression models in the Appendix at the end of this chapter. The title of these appended tables will be preceded by "A." The figures showing the transformations of the odds ratio output from the logistic models into more interpretable probability graphs will be included in the text.

* * *

In the simplest terms, what the Nieboer-Domar hypothesis predicts is an inverse relationship between the presence of slavery and population density, what they called the man/land ratio. There is, indeed, a strong and significant association between population density and hereditary slavery, but it is close to the opposite of what is predicted, as the logistic regression output shown in Table A1 indicates.

Using the lowest population density as the reference category (under 1 person per square mile), where the Nieboer-Domar hypothesis predicts the highest likelihood of slavery, we find that the odds of slavery are substantially greater, and increasing, at higher population densities. As Table A1 shows, the odds are three and a half times greater at between one and under five persons per square mile and rise to six times greater at between one hundred and five hundred persons per square mile. The odds dip to being no greater than the reference category at the highest category (five hundred or more persons), but at this population density the prediction is not significant.

Figure 5.1 graphs the predicted probabilities of slavery from the odds ratios, which more intuitively expresses the association with population density. The graph is based on the logistics model reported in Table A1. It demonstrates, even more vividly, the failure of the Nieboer-Domar hypothesis. The likelihood of slavery is lowest at the lowest population densities and is most likely at between one hundred and under five hundred persons per square mile. Even so, population density remains a weak predictor of slavery at any level. As a predictor of slavery it barely rises above a 30 percent likelihood at the highest population densities. This hypothesis is a dud.

One defense of the Nieboer-Domar hypothesis is that it should apply only to agricultural societies. This is questionable since the argument was meant to apply to all societies except the simplest hunter-gathering groups, which Nieboer explicitly excluded. However, for the sake of the argument, let us probe the hypothesis for agricultural societies only. The overall association between slavery and agriculture is, as we will see later, complicated, depending on the intensity of cultivation. A better approach at this point is simply to examine the association between the cropping index of societies – i.e. the percentage of available land used each year in farming – and slavery. The logistic model that examines this association (see Table A2) is quite significant, but

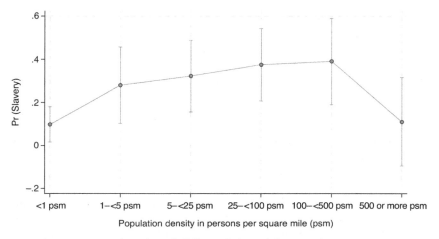

Figure 5.1 Predicted Probability of Slavery by Population Density, with 95% CI

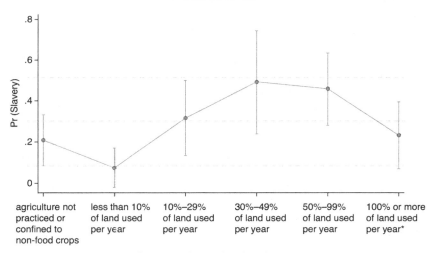

Figure 5.2 Predicted Probability of Slavery by Cropping Index, with 95% CI

the association holds only where between 50 and 99 percent of land is being farmed. It is insignificant at levels where less than 50 percent of land is in farming. The predicted probability of slavery from the cropping index, shown in Figure 5.2, indicates that, even at the highest association category, the chance of slavery as a result of cropping is still below 50 percent, or less than even.

So, what factors might have explained the origins of slavery in the premodern world? First, no single variable explains the presence of slavery and there was no unilineal emergence of the institution. Rather, it resulted from the interaction of fortuitous supply and demand factors. The process was largely supply-driven. Slavery is such an extreme case of inhumanity that it is hard to imagine someone in the premodern world suddenly harboring the idea that it would be to their advantage to enslave a fellow human, in their own community or another. Instead, the inclination to enslave came when confronted with the extreme vulnerability of others. It was when people were confronted with utterly helpless and/or defeated others that slavery was imagined as one way of dealing with them. Such situations occurred both externally and internally although, in all likelihood, the external stimulus came first.

The classic external vulnerability was defeat in warfare and it is very likely that this was what first prompted slavery, depending on its feasibility in the victor's community. Contrary to common opinion, tribal and more advanced premodern peoples were far more violent and warlike than modern ones (Pinker, 2011). Lawrence Keeley (1997) estimates that up to 90–95 percent of premodern societies engaged in warfare, and that among Indigenous Americans only 13 percent were not at war with their neighbors at least once per year. However, it is important to be clear that defeat in warfare does not automatically lead to enslavement of the defeated warrior; indeed, in the great majority of cases it did not, for the simple reason that captors saw little need to burden themselves with the defeated, since this incurred the costs of transporting them back home and of finding ways of making their enslavement worthwhile, a burden which, on calculation, struck many captors as not worth the effort. In most cases it made more sense to simply kill the male captives and, where convenient, take women and children. Casualty rates in tribal societies have been estimated at 60 percent, and the mass destruction of entire groups occurred among peoples as varied as the Dogrib Indians of North America, who exterminated neighboring Indigenous tribes, and the ancient Athenians, who frequently committed urbicide or the genocidal elimination of entire urban populations (Cartledge, 2023). Internecine warfare was "an ever recurring phenomenon" in early Anglo-Saxon England, both between the invading Germanic tribes and the native Celtic populations, and among the invaders themselves, and was a major source of slavery (Pelteret, 1995: 34, 423). However, the slaughter of conquered

THE ORIGINS OF SLAVERY AND SLAVE SOCIETY

males and enslavement of women and children was sometimes the main point of warfare, especially where a culture of violence was highly institutionalized among young warriors, as was true of Anglo-Saxon and Celtic Britain between the eight and eleventh centuries (Wyatt, 2002). Viking age slave traders overwhelmingly favored women and children (Delvaux, 2019: 50). Sometimes, captives were sold to traders who specialized in trailing armies for the express purpose of buying the defeated. But this occurred only among more advanced peoples with international slave-trading systems, and leads to the question of how the decision to enslave was made in the first place, which is our concern here. Where captives were of high rank, demanding a ransom for their release was often the most lucrative option, a classic case of which was the capture of the Northumbrian *thegn* during the battle of the Trent between the victorious Northumbrians and the Mercians. He was sold to a Frisian merchant who, upon discovering his noble identity, ransomed him to a king of Kent (Pelteret, 1995: 34). Often it was more efficient to reduce the defeated to the status of a subjected people in their own homeland who then paid tribute to the victors. Even when victors or their leaders took captives with them in chains, they often found it more profitable to simply resettle them on available idle land on condition that they paid an internal tribute as a subjected people. This was common in the ancient Near East. Other ways to treat captives after warfare included prisoner exchange, impressment in the victor's army, colonization, human sacrifice, and cannibalism. Enslavement, then, was simply one of many fates faced by the defeated and depended on whether a demand existed for their use in the victor's homeland, which we get to below. In the case of Europe, John Gillingham (2012) has argued that there were two phases in the history of warfare: a first phase during the earliest medieval centuries when women and children were the intended victims of warfare, and a later post-chivalric phase when, for the first time in history, a new norm emerged in which the doctrine of "noncombatant immunity" prevailed and victors did not go out of their way to kill or enslave civilians.

In light of all this, it is useful to examine the logistic regression output (Table A3) and the probability chart derived from it (Figure 5.3). The model indicates that, all else being equal, frequent warfare is associated with a higher likelihood of slavery: the odds of slavery are 2.2 times higher in scenarios with occasional warfare (though of questionable significance), and 2.8 times higher with frequent warfare, than in the absence of warfare. However, as the probability graph shows, even where there is frequent warfare, there is only a

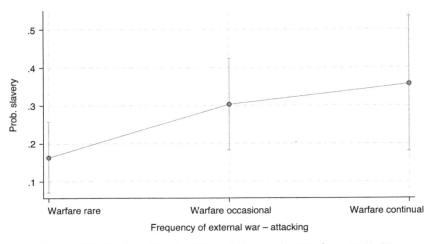

Figure 5.3 Predicted Probability of Slavery by Warfare, 95% CI

35 percent probability of slavery (with occasional warfare the coefficient is barely significant). In other words, there is a moderate but less than even chance of slavery occurring in societies that go to war frequently. This is consistent with all the alternate options, mentioned above, that are open to victors.

It seems likely that societies whose boundaries and populations expanded as a result of success in warfare were more likely to enslave their captives, and this is clearly indicated by the relevant variable in the Murdock sample. The logistic model (Table A4) indicates that the odds of slavery among warring societies whose boundaries and population expanded as a result of their victories are more than 2.6 times more likely than in societies whose boundaries and population were shrinking. For example, in tenth-century Viking Sweden, according to Ben Raffield, "at a time when expansionist raiding, colonisation, and trade were taking place, farms needed to produce additional materials to those that they would have normally required for daily subsistence, and slave labour might have been used to meet these demands" (2018: 33). One major exception to the norm of taking women and children rather than men occurred during the colonization of Iceland between c. 870 and 930 CE. Isotype analyses now indicate that most of the first wave of colonists were enslaved and other unfree persons – very likely from the British Isles and Norway – under the supervision of Norse overseers (Vésteinsson and Gestsdóttir, 2014).

Another factor that may have induced enslavement was food insecurity, or outright risk of starvation. This factor, however, was likely

THE ORIGINS OF SLAVERY AND SLAVE SOCIETY

to prompt slavery both externally and internally. Interestingly, short-term starvation, ordinary nutritional challenges, as well as endemic starvation are not associated with slavery. Instead, it was the occurrence of seasonal starvation, for example between harvests, that led to enslavement, though only when the risk of this happening was *very* high. Table A5 indicates that the odds of enslavement were 5.6 times higher under conditions of *very* high seasonal starvation than in societies where such risks were low or only moderate The odds of slavery were *not* any higher even where the risks of such seasonal starvation were high.

We surmise that very high food insecurity may have led those on the verge of starvation to commend themselves as enslaved to those who were better off, simply to survive. This was not uncommon, for example, in medieval Korea during periods of food insecurity, as we saw in Chapter 3, and in Anglo-Saxon England (Oliver, 2002: 93–4). Among the Tlingit tribe of the American northwest coast, those who fell on hard times and were unable to support themselves were called "friedfish slaves," suggesting that they were on the verge of falling into this status, though not quite "socially dead" (Cameron, 2017: 214) And, as we will see in the next section, it was likely a factor in the reduction of the Thetes to the condition of slavery in pre-Solonic Greece. However, food insecurity may also have induced slavery externally, in that it increased the odds of war, and with it the taking of prisoners who were reduced to slavery. An interesting question is whether it is those at risk of seasonal starvation who go to war in order to grab the food of those with surpluses, or whether it is those societies that were experiencing food insecurity who were attacked because of their obvious vulnerability. We suspect that both scenarios were likely, but more the case of the vulnerable being attacked. The logistic model reported in Table A6 indicates that, holding warfare at the mean, the odds of slavery were substantially greater at most levels of seasonal starvation, although some fifteen times higher where the risks of starvation were greatest. Results are similar when we examine the risks of slavery from the recurrence of famine.

The most important purely internal factor that presented the opportunity to enslave others was punishment for crimes. All over the world, capital and other serious offenses were sometimes commuted to slavery. Where a central authority existed, this often resulted in enslavement to the state or local authorities. In China it has been estimated that punishment for crimes was the main source of slaves, especially during the Han period (Pulleyblank, 1958). Much the same was true of Korea. In Anglo-Saxon and later medieval England, punishment was a major source of enslavement, especially after the earlier period of rampant intertribal warfare had subsided; the term 'witepeowas' was used to describe those in penal slavery, which was especially common among the West Saxons (Pelteret, 1995: 32). Even chronic idleness could result in enslavement in medieval England. Indeed, as late as 1547 a statute of Edward VI mandated that a person found guilty of vagabondage for the third time should be "condemned as a slave to the person who had denounced him as an idler" and his enslaver could "force him to do any work, no matter how disgusting, with whips and chains," and could "sell him, bequeath him, let him out to hire as a slave, just as he can any other personal chattel or cattle" (cited in Blanton, 2016: 32). This brutal punishment, coming near the end of the Middle Ages, was short-lived, but it attests to the antiquity and importance of this mode of enslavement in England.

In many premodern societies, malevolent sorcery and witchcraft were capital offences that were sometimes commuted to enslavement and sale out of the community. Sometimes, the desire to enslave may well have increased the accusations of capital offenses. During the period of the Atlantic slave trade, a substantial number of persons accused of witchcraft and malevolent sorcery in West Africa were diverted to the European traders. Although many were no doubt falsely accused in order to enrich the tribal authorities, others who were genuine sorcerers were banished from their communities instead of being locally enslaved or killed. This partly explains why slave-receiving countries such as eighteenth-century Jamaica, St. Domingue, New Grenada (presently Colombia), and Brazil witnessed an unusual number of sorcerers (called obeah-men in Jamaica) and why this aspect of West African culture was among the most widely transmitted to the New World (Gershman, 2020; Patterson, 2022 [1967]: 184–95). It should also be noted, however, that there existed in Europe, especially Spain, "popular apprehensions of the dangerous spiritual power of African peoples and their descendants" (White, 2005: 12), and Europeans' own experience of witchcraft going back to the Black Death strongly influenced how French and British planters interpreted such beliefs among their slaves (Paton, 2012).

Statistically, we found a strong association between witchcraft and slavery. Only 16 percent of societies without witchcraft beliefs in the Murdock sample had slavery, compared with 44 percent of those holding such beliefs. The odds of inherited slavery where witchcraft was the predominant explanation of illnesses was 4.3 times greater than in those without such beliefs (see Table A7). However, it is striking that there is no association in the Murdock sample between

THE ORIGINS OF SLAVERY AND SLAVE SOCIETY

slavery and sorcery beliefs. One explanation might be that sorcery in most societies can be used for both good and evil, and sorcerers were as much healers and "medicine men" as they were agents hired to do harm. Sorcery practiced for medicinal purposes, then, was not a crime in most small-scale societies even though it was so defined by European colonizers and slaveholders in the Americas.

Focusing now mainly on the demand side, it may be asked just what factors were most favorable to the keeping of slaves and institutionalization of the institution. Two structural features stand out: the mode of subsistence, including the level of development, and the sexual, social, and economic role of women. Two others come to mind but are best avoided: the level of stratification and the degree of political organization. Both are highly correlated with the presence of slavery, but we avoid them because of likely simultaneity bias. Thus, while we found that higher levels of stratification are strongly associated with slavery, it is very likely that slavery was one of the main causes of higher stratification; and much the same goes for higher levels of political organization, especially in small-scale societies where warriors and raiders may use their captive slaves and the children produced by secondary slave wives and concubines, to assert and monopolize political power. Indeed, Catherine Cameron (2016) has made precisely this argument in her comparative study of small-scale societies.

By the mode of subsistence, I mean the primary means by which the members of a society interact with their environment in order to survive and make their living. We may distinguish four dominant modes in the premodern world: hunter-gathering, fishing, farming, and pastoralism. A fifth, mixed mode, employs strategies from several of the dominant modes, although this is more the case in modern societies. Slavery is found in all modes of subsistence, but there is substantial variation in the degree to which it exists and whether the main form is incipient and nonhereditary or hereditary and highly institutionalized. Figure 5.4 shows the distribution and association of the different types of slavery among the different modes.

Slavery is least present in hunter-gathering societies, although, historically, it was in this mode that it would first have arisen. Only 14 percent of those in the Murdock sample had slavery, all but one nonhereditary. The absence of slavery was not necessarily because foragers lived on the margin of existence, for, as Sahlins famously argued (1968), many constituted the "original affluent society" given the limited nature of their wants, their relatively successful food quests, and their abundant leisure time. Marshall Sahlins, however,

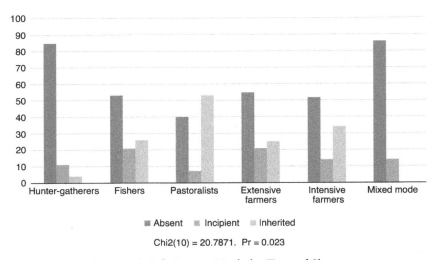

Figure 5.4 Subsistence Mode by Type of Slavery

rather overstated his argument; we are inclined to agree with David Kaplan that it makes little sense to describe societies with 50 percent infant mortality rates and life expectancies of 30 years as "affluent" (2000: 314). There was wide variation in the degree to which their basic needs were met and, in general, little room for extra mouths. However, due to the frequency of wars, captives were often taken. In most cases males were slaughtered, sometimes after being held for a period of time during which they were treated well. Two classic cases were the Tupinamba and the Maoris (see Neubauer and Kim, 2022; Métraux, 1948; Tregear, 1904), who also ate the most prized captives. A minority did have room for a few slaves, nearly all women, whose children were free, accounting for the very small proportion of such societies with inherited slavery. The warlike Calinago Caribs are among the best-known (and most maligned) cases of considerable level of slavery among a hunter-gathering group, a substantial proportion of their wives being captive women (Santos-Granero, 2017).

A surprising proportion of fishing communities had slavery, some 47 percent, the institution being hereditary in more than 26 percent of them. One reason is that fishing communities more closely approximated Sahlins's idea of Stone Age affluence, especially where their main staple was abundant, as was true, for example, of the Indigenous populations of the northwest coast of America. This is the case, in spite of having the lowest rate of warfare (33 percent), which indicates that the capacity to sustain the enslaved was more important

THE ORIGINS OF SLAVERY AND SLAVE SOCIETY

in explaining the presence of slavery than their captivity in warfare. With abundant food, there was relatively less economic demand for slaves. Instead, they were usually used more for prestige, sexual, and sacrificial purposes. The logistic model that examines the relationship between subsistence types and slavery (Table A8) shows that, where fishing was dominant in premodern societies, the odds of slavery were nearly two hundred times greater than where it was absent or sporadic.

Slavery was most prevalent among pastoralists (societies in which more than 50 percent were dependent on pastoralism), occurring among 60 percent of those in the sample. Furthermore, over a half (53 percent) of all pastoralists had hereditary slavery, twice that of all the other subsistence types except intensive agriculturalists. In the case of pastoralists, warfare was a very important factor explaining slavery, 80 percent of them engaging in occasional or chronic attacks on other groups. Historians of ancient Greece will be familiar with this from their reading of the Homeric epics, which described the endless warring of the Dark Age pastoral heroes. Nonetheless, it was not necessarily the most important cause of slavery. The demand for slaves among them sprang from their need, but disdain, for agricultural products. Although, as we have seen, slavery is found in most pastoral societies, the institution is most pronounced where there is high but not complete dependence on herding. Table A8 indicates that the odds of slavery are some one hundred times greater where pastoralism was co-dominant – meaning between 66 and 75 percent dependence on pasturing – than where it was absent. This suggests that it is where pastoral societies engage in a substantial degree of planting and foraging that they were most likely to resort to slavery, using the enslaved to perform these necessary but disdained tasks. This is typical of the pattern found in the Fulani slave systems across the Sahel. It is striking that none of the other levels of pastoralism is significantly associated with slavery.

Table A8 indicates that slavery is strongly predicted by the highest level of agricultural subsistence, but that, unlike pastoralism, there is no significant association where agriculture is co-dominant with other modes of subsistence. One possible explanation for this is that it is where agriculture is co-dominant that non-slave women are most involved with production, not only in agriculture but in other productive activities such as crafts or foraging. Where agriculture is dominant, it is important to distinguish between extensive and intensive farmers, which we do below when we come to examine the intermediary role of women in explaining slavery. Extensive farming uses relatively fewer persons per acre and practices long fallow, when the land is left unplanted for several years before being replanted and new fields are cleared annually. In premodern systems the hoe or even digging sticks were typically used. With intensive agriculture there is short fallow, sometimes even more than one crop per year. The land is fertilized and the plow is the typical instrument for tilling the soil. There is more labor input per acre, and higher productivity. Slavery is found to a substantial degree in both systems, with hereditary slavery more established among intensive farmers. The horticultural revolution clearly began with extensive farming, so it is reasonable to assume that slavery occurred first in this system, before appearing in intensive agricultural systems, even though this was after it made its appearance among hunter-gatherers. There is, typically, more use for labor among extensive farmers whose primary means of increasing production and adding to surplus was by the use of additional hands.

We come, finally, to what may well have been the most important demand factor in the emergence of slavery: gender. Not only were women more vulnerable to captivity – in warfare, but also in simple raiding and kidnapping – but they were far more useful to men in premodern societies. They could immediately satisfy sexual needs; they could become wives and reproducers, especially for younger and lower status men who were outcompeted for local women by older and more prestigious men; and they could become efficient producers and gatherers of local food. Cameron (2016) has also shown that they were major transmitters of craft technology and useful foreign cultural practices. In short, even among the most rudimentary social systems, women could easily be worth their keep, and more. It has long been shown that women gathered as much as, if not more than, men in foraging societies. And recent work has found that, contrary to long-established masculinist views, women in the majority of foraging societies contributed as much as men in the hunting of wild animals from as early as the Holocene, all the way up to the last century (Anderson et al., 2023).

An understanding of how gender contributed to the structural origins of slavery requires an analysis of four interrelated variables: the sexual division of labor or women's contribution to the labor force; polygamy; the established mode of marriage, more particularly the operation of brideprice (or bridewealth) in the formalization of marriages; and the mode of subsistence.

Let us begin by asking the most basic question: what is the association between the dominant mode of subsistence and women's share of work in producing the dominant source of sustenance? We used a simple three-category code for assessing women's contribution to

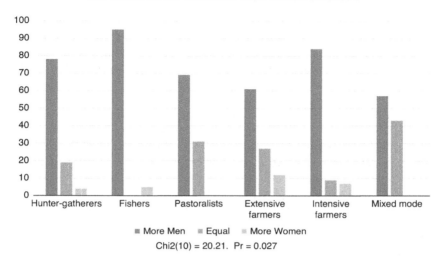

Figure 5.5 Subsistence Mode by Women's Workshare

subsistence: whether women produced less than men, equal amounts as men, or more than men. Figure 5.5 indicates significant variation between the subsistence types in the sexual division of labor. It is among extensive farmers and the small number of mixed mode societies that we find the highest proportion of societies where women contribute a greater share of work than men. Indeed, in 39 percent of extensive farming communities in the sample, women either contributed equally or were the primary producers. According to Boserup's findings (2007 [1970]: Ch. 1), in the great majority of intensive farming communities, men dominated production, which she attributed to the use of the plow and draft animals and the digging and upkeep of irrigation ditches. However, as she herself noted, a non-negligible number of intensive farming communities existed where women worked equally or were the dominant producers (15 percent).

We strongly suspect that the Murdock sample underestimated women's contribution to subsistence. Recent work suggests that their contribution was normally equal to and often greater than men's. We found no evidence of equal share of work among fishers in the sample, for example. In almost all cases, men appeared to be exclusively involved with fishing. However, here again, recent work leads us to think that women's role was underestimated in this mode of subsistence. There is a strong gender bias regarding the role of women in fishing, both in the activity itself and in official attitudes and reports by ethnographers and other observers. Overwhelmingly, the tendency has been to focus on the harvesting of fish, especially at sea, while neglecting the equally important role of the preparation and marketing of the fish, which tended to be done by women whose engagement was often far more heterogeneous and just as important. One study noted that: "In Melanesia, women dominate in reef fin fishing, while Indian women net prawns, Laotian women fish in rivers and canals, and Filipino women fish from canoes and coastal waters" (Thorpe et al., 2014: 55). More important is women's role in the post-harvest sector: "Here women predominate, whether at the processing or retail distribution level. In India, for example, 73.6 percent of those involved in distribution are women . . . and women dominate local fish markets in much of Africa" (2014: 55–6).

There are no pastoral societies in which women are the dominant producers. The same is true of mixed mode societies, but for entirely different reasons. Premodern pastoral communities considered herding, especially of larger animals, too prestigious a task for women, who were relegated to low-status work such as gathering and farming; conversely, we find men and women sharing work equally in a high proportion of mixed mode societies. The proportion of sharing may seem relatively high among pastoralists, but, as we will see, that is because the men involved are invariably low status, often enslaved.

The relationship between slavery, mode of subsistence, and the sexual division of labor is complex. At the simple bivariate level, slavery and female participation in subsistence are not significantly associated. Explaining why this is so will be an important part of our concluding argument. Among hunter-gathering communities, female captives tended to be absorbed as secondary wives. In the few cases where women participated equally, the odds of slavery were greatly reduced since captured women were of no use and there may not have been enough surplus to simply keep them as concubines. Although slavery was more pronounced among fishers, there was usually little economic use for male slaves, who were often slaughtered or cruelly treated. As among hunter-gatherers, in those cases where women engaged equally in fishing, instances of slavery were greatly reduced.

The association between pastoralism, slavery, and female participation in pastoral work is more complex. The model (not shown) regressing slavery on pastoralism and female participation indicates that, controlling for female participation, slavery is most predicted where pastoralism is between a quarter and a third of total subsistence: the odds of slavery at that level are nearly fifteen times greater than where there is little or no pastoralism in the subsistence mode. Above a 36 percent level of pastoralism, there is no slavery. At the

THE ORIGINS OF SLAVERY AND SLAVE SOCIETY

same time, every pastoral society in which women participated in farming had some level of institutional slavery. The high prestige of animal husbandry among pastoralists accounts for this outcome. Where women were incorporated as slaves they tended to do the most menial kinds of pastoral tasks, usually involving smaller animals such as goats, and/or engage in agriculture. As indicated earlier, the pastoral societies of the Sahel fully exemplify this pattern.

Boserup (2007 [1970]: Ch. 2) devoted an entire chapter to the interacting role of the polygyny mode of marriage and women's role in subsistence, and their relation to slavery, and it is useful to see how these play out in our sample. Table A9 shows that women contributed to subsistence to a greater degree, at both equal and more than male levels, in polygynous societies than in those where there was no polygamy. Further, it is where polygamy was most advanced, with more than 20 percent of marriages polygynous, that we find the strongest associations with women's contribution. In almost 40 percent of such societies, we find that women either shared subsistence work equally or did more than men. The implication is clear that polygynous men were using their secondary wives to supplement their work force. Slavery and polygyny are also associated, though only when we consider incipient or nonhereditary slavery. The model shows that the odds of polygyny are more than three times higher where there was incipient slavery than where there was no slavery, and greater than the odds of hereditary slavery which does not significantly predict polygamy. One likely explanation is that in highly polygynous societies enslaved women were incorporated as secondary wives and they and their children were eventually manumitted.

Bridewealth or brideprice usually refers to the payment of property and/or services by the kin of the groom-to-be to the family of the betrothed (Goody, 1973: 1–3; for an illuminating case study, see Harris, 1972). Goody has pointed out that, with true bridewealth, the property goes to the bride's kinsmen, usually her father, who often uses it to acquire wives for her brothers. In such cases it functions largely as a means of regulating marriages and legitimizing the children of the bride. Where the bridewealth goes directly to the bride and her husband, as is often the case in Eurasia, Goody suggests that it is a form of "indirect dowry." Bridewealth payments vary across cultures. Whatever their symbolic and regulatory role, however, they invariably have an important economic dimension and are closely related to female participation in production. Bride payments tend to be high where women's economic and social roles are highly valued. They are a measure of a woman's value "determined by the qualities of physical

117

SLAVERY IN THE PREMODERN AND EARLY CHRISTIAN WORLDS

appearance, character and social standing which she possesses." And it is also closely related to polygyny. "The two institutions," writes Goody (1973: 10–11), "appear to reinforce one another." Fully 90 percent of societies with bridewealth have some level of polygyny. As one would suspect, bridewealth is also strongly related to female contribution to subsistence. In the great majority of societies with no bridewealth, men are the main producers (84 percent) of subsistence, while women are found working equally or more than men in only 16 percent of societies. On the other hand, in 36 percent of societies with bridewealth, women contribute equally or more than men.

It is common knowledge among anthropologists and other social scientists that the distinction between intensive and extensive farming systems is closely associated with polygyny and female participation. As Russian anthropologist Andrey Korotayev (2003: 73) observed:

> An average intensive plow agriculturalist in a culture with a very low female contribution to subsistence would never even consider seriously the possibility of having five wives (as he would not be able to feed all of them). Yet, this would not constitute a serious problem for a hoe horticulturalist within a culture with a very high female contribution to subsistence . . . [because] getting five wives, first of all acquires 10 hands that may help feed the horticulturalist himself.

Table A9 strongly supports this assertion. In societies where women were the dominant or exclusive producers of agricultural goods, the odds of major polygyny (more than 20 percent of marriages involve multiple wives) were 3.6 times greater than where men dominated or were the exclusive producers. The table also nicely brings together and supports the main threads of our argument. It shows that Boserup was basically correct in seeing the presence and absence of polygyny as pivotal in consideration of women's economic role in premodern societies. In extensive agricultural societies, where women were in great demand as producers, polygyny enhanced the wealth and power of men who could afford additional wives. The model shows that the odds of major polygyny are five times greater where there are extensive agricultural systems than in intensive ones, holding the other covariates at their mean. Societies where women shared equally or were the dominant producers of the primary mode of subsistence were over 3.5 times as likely to have full polygyny as those where men were the dominant producers (see also Jacoby, 1995).

Warfare is importantly related to all this, although it is interesting that it is societies that engage in frequent rather than continuous warfare that are more polygynous than those where warfare is infrequent.

118

THE ORIGINS OF SLAVERY AND SLAVE SOCIETY

One reason may be that a disproportionate number of societies engaging in chronic warfare were pure pastoral systems, which rarely used women as dominant producers. As indicated earlier, it is nonhereditary slavery that most predicts full polygyny. Captured or bought women were both used as extra hands, as concubines, and, if attractive, as wives, their roles as both producers and reproducers being very important among extensive agriculturalists who usually had a lot of land, especially in sub-Saharan Africa and the more tribal areas of Asia, and who practiced long fallow, which usually only increases wealth by cropping more land.

But now we face a puzzle. The associations indicated in Table A8 would suggest that there should be a direct association between female participation and slavery. However, this is not reflected in any of our logistic regressions probing the association of female participation with slavery, all of which were completely insignificant. Furthermore, when we added warfare to these models, although warfare shows a significant prediction of hereditary slavery, the female participation variable not only remained insignificant, but showed a substantial *reduction* in the odds of slavery. How is this puzzle to be explained?

I offer two explanations: one for extensive farming communities, the other for societies that practiced intensive farming. My explanation for the absence of a significant association between female participation and slavery among extensive farming communities requires a dynamic rather than purely static or cross-sectional perspective. Let us consider, first, situations where men outnumber women in the dominant mode of subsistence. Where there is warfare, both male prisoners of war, if not killed, and captured women are reduced to slavery. Male slaves reinforce the male predominance in the work force, but captured women would have the opposite effect. And in the absence of warfare, we know that most of the enslaved bought in the premodern world would be women. So why doesn't slavery tilt the participation rate in favor of more women? The answer is the role of polygyny and the differential assimilation of male and female slaves. Goody (1980: 41) has observed that "there was a constant drift of the offspring of slave women into non-slave status" and that male slaves had less opportunity to reproduce themselves. This is partly reflected in the logistic results reported in Table A9: it is only nonhereditary slavery that is significant, increasing the odds of polygyny fourfold compared with societies without slavery. This results in the constant natural decline of the enslaved unless replenished through external slave-trading and/or warfare and raiding. However, as indicated earlier, there would also be a gender bias in this drift, with female slave

119

mothers and the female children of the enslaved moving into manumitted and non-slave status to a far greater degree than male slaves and their male children. As secondary wives or concubines, most were eventually manumitted. Among the Marghi of northern Nigeria, for example, women were the main captives in their frequent intercommunal wars; but most were soon absorbed as wives, and their status was similar to that of "a wife acquired without benefit of bridewealth" (Vaughn, 1977: 89). Male slaves, on the other hand, who were usually purchased, tended to remain enslaved for life. They were bought to be workers and to "found a line of mafa (slaves)" (Vaughn, 1977: 91). In Islamic slaveholding societies, as previously noted, the Quran explicitly encourages younger men to solve the problem of a shortage of marriageable women in polygamous societies – most women being monopolized by older and more powerful men – as well as the temptations of adultery, by taking the enslaved as wives (Gordon, 1990: Chs. 2 and 4). Yet another factor that accounted for the retention of male slaves among less advanced premodern societies is what I have called the "honorific trap" that captured males faced (Patterson, 1991: 51). Having experienced the devastating loss of honor in their enslavement, there was no place for them among the free men, especially where honor was prized, as was usually the case in small-scale societies engaged in warfare. Among the Maori, slave men were constantly insulted with the taunt that they were "remnants of the feast" (lit. *toenga kainga*, not worth cooking), meaning that they not only lost their manhood by their defeat in warfare, but that they were not even considered worthy of being eaten in the honorific cannibal feast after the victory, and, were they to escape and return to their group, they would be rejected and subject to even greater taunts for bearing the taint of slavery (Tregear, 1904: 155). Women did not face this honorific trap. Even if women had been sexually violated, enslavement did not preclude them from entering the role of concubine and even of secondary wives. As Ruth Karras has pointed out: "Men could be dishonored by enslavement. But the ownership of slave women, because it fit into the whole system of masculine purchase of control over women's sexuality, was of greater ideological significance" (1994: 24). In the long run, then, slavery in polygynous extensive farming societies resulted in a selective bias in favor of the retention of males as slaves and the manumission of females. To be sure, not all female slaves were absorbed and manumitted, especially those who were considered unattractive, but, at best, what we find is a shift toward more equalization of the genders in the dominant subsistence mode.

120

THE ORIGINS OF SLAVERY AND SLAVE SOCIETY

Now consider societies where free women were the primary producers. As in all societies, the fact that women dominate an occupation usually means that it has lower status among men. Where women are the primary producers, in fact, men are often engaged in warfare or struggling over status. To do women's work would be dishonoring. But, as we have shown, the enslaved are quintessentially people without honor. Hence male slaves in such societies would be incorporated as workers alongside women, in this way tilting the work force toward a greater number and proportion of men. This male bias would also be reinforced by the reproductive process. With the exception of some of the more advanced Islamic societies, the male children of both male and female slaves tended to remain in slavery to a far greater degree than the female children of both. In polygynous societies, such second-generation slave girls and young women would become prime targets for sex- and wife-deprived younger and poorer men, especially in societies with high bride prices and full polygyny.

Another factor that shifts the slave gender ratio in favor of men, even though women are typically captured and brought home at greater rates, is the re-sale of the enslaved. This would have been common in Viking-era Scandinavia, given the much greater demand for women among the Arab buyers of the South as well as the demand for concubines in the societies of the North Atlantic. The same was also true of domestic slave raiding in medieval Bavaria between the late tenth and early thirteenth centuries, when domestic slave raiding by predatory lords targeted women for local enslavement (Sutherland, 2017: 73), unlike the early medieval period, when captured women were nearly all exported south to the more profitable Arab markets (Hammer, 2002: 45–56). In the Sahel, like most other parts of Africa, female slaves were worth more than male slaves, and in many cases it was more profitable for the owners of captive females to resell them and keep the males for their own uses. Thus, according to Manning, slave captors in the Savanna sold "two-thirds of the female captives and one-third of the males" across the Sahara. However, they further removed a significant number of women from slavery to become wives and concubines and reproducers in polygynous unions. At the same time, slave men suffered a severe shortage of spouses and many ended up in "nearly all male barracks" (Manning, 1990: 45–6). In the long run, then, the processes of enslavement would eventually lead to growing numbers of men in the labor force, even if the initial effect of warfare and raiding was to increase the number of women; hence, the lack of association we observe between slavery and female participation in the labor force.

Let us turn now to systems of intensive farming. We have seen that slavery occurred just as frequently in such systems as in extensive farming systems. Indeed, inherited slavery was more institutionalized in such systems: 33 percent compared with less than a quarter among extensive farmers in the Murdock world sample. Further, in these systems, women were not only captured but even more disproportionately incorporated into the victors' and raiders' communities. So why is there no association between slavery and female labor force participation? Part of the answer is to be found in the bias of ethnographers, historians, and analysts in their definition of what constitutes productive labor, as mentioned earlier, and the erroneous tendency to assume that most prisoners of war were men (Gillingham, 2012: 68). We already came across this bias in our discussion of fishing communities, but the same holds for intensive farming systems for all historical periods, including medieval Britain, as Susan Stuard (1995) has persuasively argued. The fact that women were not plowing in the fields or leading pack animals – the *apparently* typical labor activity among intensive farmers – does not mean that they were not very productive. Boserup has been criticized for underestimating the amount of productive work women did in *all* intensive farming systems, both in and out of the household, not to mention their role as reproducers (Beneria and Sen, 1981; but in Boserup's defense, see the more recent study by Alesina et al., 2011).

Cameron's innovative comparative work has shown that women, and especially women captives, were a major factor in the economic life and advancement of their captors' societies, especially in the diffusion of craft skills and broader cultural practices; they were greatly preferred to male captives because they were the major producers in small-scale societies (2016: Ch. 3). However, of even greater importance here is Cameron's analysis of the extraordinary role of women in the dynamics of power in small-scale systems (2016: Ch. 4). The capture and incorporation of women from other groups was an essential aspect of male expression of power, as much as the slaughter of male captives. Furthermore, because wealth and prestige in small-scale societies was achieved mainly through control of people, women's role as concubines, secondary wives, sex objects, and additional hands greatly enhanced the power of their captors. They also generated surplus for their captors and, as noted earlier, Cameron argues that the social distinction created by the presence of captives, and the disproportionate wealth they generated for their enslavers, may have marked the beginning of stratification in early human societies.

THE ORIGINS OF SLAVERY AND SLAVE SOCIETY

Cameron persuasively illustrates her argument with examples from small-scale societies from around the world, but especially from the Indigenous cultures of North America, the equestrian, warfaring Comanche of the southern Great Plains of North America being the ideal-type case. However, the pattern of male power expressed in extreme violence that was focused on the institutionalized violation and control of captive women was exemplified in its most extreme form among the British and Scandinavian peoples of the early Middle Ages. David Wyatt's brilliant study of slavery, patriarchy, and power in medieval Britain and Ireland documents in vivid detail how warfare, raiding, and enslavement constituted a "powerfully symbolic activity that was closely associated with sexual rapine and female abduction" (2002: 44). Violence against other groups was an essential rite of passage of males from childhood to adulthood. Women were forced into marriage through the *raubehe*, or abduction and rape, by the male warrior. (The old English term for marriage, *brydhlop*, literally meant "bride-running" or marriage instigated by rape.) The *fian*, found throughout the British Isles, "was a ritualized institution devoted to male violence, age initiation and the establishment of gender identities" (2002: 58). The transitional status of the young male warrior was a kind of "ritual death" akin to the "social death" of the slave, and, free from the cultural constraints of his group, he "had free license to kill, rape and enslave" (2002: 55). Rape and enslavement were also the means by which exiled men could reassert themselves, as Wyatt writes:

> Sexual possession and enslavement were, thereby, methods by which an individual might reassert his position in the masculine hierarchy. Furthermore, the rampant sexual license of such transitional males fostered a pool of illegitimate, often unacknowledged sons, who would eventually join war-bands themselves. The institution of the male warrior fraternity was, therefore, self-perpetuating. Moreover, violent sexual activity was fundamentally significant for the construction of masculine gender identity in the societies of medieval Britain. (2002: 95)

Polygyny also played a critical role in this system. Wyatt finds a pattern of what anthropologists call "resource polygyny" in medieval Britain right up to the late eleventh century, in which "women might be accumulated in various ways, for example: through marriage, concubinage, paternity, fosterage, guardianship, service and slavery" (2002: 95).

This interrelation of slavery, male violence, power, and the enslavement of women was also found in medieval Scandinavia. Indeed, the

123

SLAVERY IN THE PREMODERN AND EARLY CHRISTIAN WORLDS

British and Scandinavian systems were closely interlinked through Viking raiding and slave-trading between the eighth and eleventh centuries (Wyatt, 2002: 276). While the emphasis on Viking marauding has been largely associated with the capture and trading of West and East European women south to the Muslim Mediterranean (on which see Delvaux, 2019), it has now been well established that medieval Scandinavian societies were highly developed slaveholding systems (some, like early Icelandic large-scale, actively articulated slave societies), in which warrior fraternities captured women from neighboring communities not only to exert their power over them, but also to enhance their power within their own societies through the subordination of captive women as concubines and laborers. Polygyny was common in pre-Christian Scandinavia, although Ruth Karras (1990: 144) suggests that the term "polycoity" may have been more appropriate. Concubinage, which originated in enslavement, was well established, being one of the three recognized kinds of carnal relations – legal marriage, open liaisons with free women, and servile concubinage – and men had the option of acknowledging or keeping as slaves the sons of their concubines. Sutherland (2017: 119–35) also documented a pattern of extensive "servile concubinage" among medieval Bavarians between the late tenth and early thirteenth centuries.

What all this amounted to was that, however violent the process, the great majority of captives taken into slavery were women. Over time, however, most of them were incorporated as concubines, or out-of-sight servants within the household, or craftswomen in the workshops, gifts to friends or religious organizations, or sometimes resold to distant lands when their owners grew tired of them or fell on hard times. Sometimes, women were even sacrificed on the death of their enslavers to keep them company in the afterlife. In all cases, women were still victims, but rarely enslaved.

For all the above reasons, the typical slave population in most premodern slaveholding societies ended up consisting mainly of males. One alternative explanation for why the sources indicate that the typical slave population was male, especially by more recent students of medieval European slavery, is that both the sources and the biases of earlier historians have tended to emphasize male slaves, in part because of the simple, erroneous conviction that most captives must have been males, and the fact that women slaves were not working in occupations considered to be "real" work, or else were hidden in the households of their enslavers. While there is some truth to these explanations, we think that it may well be the case that both the

124

THE ORIGINS OF SLAVERY AND SLAVE SOCIETY

sources indicating more male slaves in the typical slave population and the skeptics emphasizing the greater proportion of female enslaved persons are correct. In the course of human history, the earliest slaves, and the great majority of captives enslaved, up to the Atlantic slave trade (when, indeed, most slaves taken from Africa were male), were women and children. However, in nearly all premodern slave systems, I have argued, the weight of the comparative evidence and the simple statistical absence of any significant association between slavery and female participation in the dominant mode of subsistence indicate that women were rapidly incorporated into non-slave statuses, while men remained enslaved throughout their lives; the male children of slave women disproportionately inherited the former slave status of their mothers, while those of their slave fathers remained enslaved. In this way, the typical slave population, in both kinds of farming systems, experienced an inexorable drift toward maleness.

To sum up, I have shown that there is no merit to the view that slavery emerged in response to low-density populations. Instead, we can see that the means by which slavery came into the world were complex and nonlinear. A combination of supply or push factors, some external, others internal – notably warfare, raiding, starvation, punishment for crimes – combined with suitable demand factors such as the mode of subsistence, male violence and a striving for dominance, sexual desire, the demand for foreign skills, the need for extra labor to expand production or colonize new regions (which often coexisted with dense or growing populations in the expanding societies) account for the emergence and rise of slavery. What we can say with some confidence is that, although the typical slave population in early times was mainly male, the first people to be enslaved, and the majority of those torn from their homes – their children and their kinsfolk – were females. That most may have ended up in statuses other than slavery in no way assuaged the tragedy of their deracination and violation. Women were the first slaves, but the conditions into which they transitioned may have been no better, and would have involved a greater daily violation, than those of a largely unmolested plowman or swineherd toiling in the fields.

* * *

Our critique of the Nieboer-Domar hypothesis has relied primarily on cross-sectional statistical data supplemented by comparative ethnographic and historical materials. What is needed now is an historical case study that will demonstrate in dynamic terms the fallacy of this theory. The case study of ancient Athens, which follows, will do just that. However, it will also serve another purpose. We do not, of course, know when slavery as an institution began. This is lost in the mists of prehistory and, given the global distribution of the institution, it must have originated numerous times. However, it is an entirely different story with the invention of what Finley called "genuine" slave society in which the institution was first actively articulated in a structurally transformative way, leading to an entirely new social formation. This came relatively late in the evolution of mankind, well after the invention of writing and civilization. The social system we call, more simply, large-scale slave society, the theoretical basis of which we discussed in Chapter 3, emerged for the first time with that seedbed of Western civilization, ancient Athens, over the course of the half-millennium between 800 and 300 BCE. To a brief account of this remarkable episode in the history of slavery, slave society, and Western civilization we now turn.

5.2: The origin of slave society: Athens 800–300 BCE

The collapse of Mycenaean civilization in the twelfth century BCE, and the presumed Dorian invasions, ushered in a new era in Greece, the period that classical historians call the Greek Dark Age (c. 1050 to c. 800 BCE). The communities that existed in Greece during this period were primitive, nonliterate, small-scale pastoral societies characterized by simple geometric pottery designs. The only certain data we have on this period are material remains, but what they tell us about slaves and slavery is, in the view of one archeologist, "so slight as to be almost negligible" (Thompson, 2003: 51). There has, however, been a long tradition of scholars who have argued that the Homeric poems can be taken as literary evidence of this period, allowing, of course, for the distortions of poetic license, the inaccuracies of oral tradition, and the time-lag between the heroic age and its transcription. Moses Finley (1956) is perhaps the most persuasive student in this tradition. Unfortunately for those who must rely on specialists in these matters, there is sharp disagreement on this point between archaeologists and the literary historians. Thus Anthony Snodgrass (1971), in his review of the archeological evidence up to the early 1970s, strongly disputes Finley's interpretation. He argues that the Homeric poems could not possibly refer to any period of Greek history between the collapse of Mycenaean civilization and the end of the ninth century; that Homer got his archeological ages

THE ORIGINS OF SLAVERY AND SLAVE SOCIETY

all mixed up (Bronze Age weapons, for example, along with Iron Age implements); and that the most likely explanation of the material background of the Homeric poems is that they constituted a deliberate and "artificial amalgam of widely separated historical stages" put together mainly to impress (1971: 388). Snodgrass allows, however, that a careful reading of the epics could throw much valuable light on Homer's own period. In this respect, then, we can still use Finley's and other more recent analyses of the literary evidence.

Dark Age Greece, if we are to follow Snodgrass and other archeologists (e.g., Thompson, 2003; Morris, 2011), was a thoroughly primitive society. It was a grazing economy with a meat-based diet (Lencman et al., 1967: 378), provided by cattle, swine, sheep, and goats. Politically, it consisted of kin-based units in which a royal clan formed the nexus of the social order. The situation reminds one very much of certain pre-European African kingdoms. Increasingly, the royal clan seems to have become the first among equals with respect to the other aristocratic clans, and, while kingship persisted until well into the ninth century, the authority of the monarch had, by that time, been largely usurped by other aristocratic clans. As in all such systems, it is dangerous to speak of class distinctions: "Even such apparently clear-cut issues as those of freedom, serfdom and slavery, or the ownership of the land, may have been far from straightforward in contemporary eyes" (Snodgrass, 1971: 387). Although there was a good deal of external warfare, we must certainly agree with Vincent Desborough that there is no evidence whatever for the existence of a warrior class, the communities being too small to support such a distinct group (1972: 311–12). Vertical kinship divisions were far more important. There was little or no room for slavery in these dirt-poor communities, where almost everyone lived in mud huts and tended their sheep and cattle. At the very most, "a few slaves no doubt remained in the possession of the better off" (Snodgrass, 1971: 394), but they were of little economic significance. As is true of all herding communities, there was a low ratio of people to land, but this bears no relationship, one way or the other, to the presence or absence of servile labor. The important point here is the near complete absence of surpluses and the prevailing poverty of all classes, as the paucity of the remains in excavated tombs suggests (Snodgrass, 1971: 394). Summing up more recent work based on a greater variety of data, Josiah Ober finds that the Greek population had declined to its nadir during the Dark or early Iron Age – estimated at 330,000 for the entire region in 1000 BCE, a staggering decline from the Mycenaean period estimate of about 600,000 (see Figure 5.6) – and that the entire

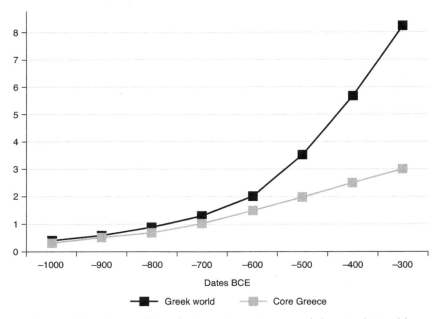

Figure 5.6 Estimated Populations, Core Greece and the Greek World, 1000–300 BCE

Source: J. Ober, *The Rise and Fall of Classical Greece* (Princeton University Press, 2015), p. 22.

Ober adds the following notes on this graph: "The data points at the far left (1000 BCE) and far right (300 BCE) of the chart are based on evidence discussed in Chapters 2, 4, and 6. Points in between (900–400 BCE) are interpolated. Core Greece = the territory controlled by the Greek state in 1881–1912 (mainland from Thessaly south, Ionian islands, Cycladic islands). Core Greece figures after 800 BCE are reduced at least marginally by migration to other parts of the Greek (and non-Greek) world. Greek world figures include Hellenized populations, per discussion in Chapter 4."

era was "exceptionally poor" (2015: 73–4, 81; see also Morris, 2011: 211–35).

When we move to the early archaic period (beginning around 800 BCE, during the early part of which Homer wrote) several things immediately impress us. In material culture, we find the beginnings of a shift away from a livestock-based economy to arable farming. It was, however, a slow process, lasting for at least a century and a half. As late as 700 BCE, "Greeks still needed exhortation on elementary instruction in arable farming" (Snodgrass, 1971: 379). Using Greek house plans as a proxy of living standard, the archeologist and historian Ian Morris found that the median Greek house in the ninth century was still "small and squalid" (2011: 227; see also Ober, 2015: 82). It was essentially a mixed system with communal access to pasture and, to a declining degree, farmland. Closely related to this change in economic base was a rapid increase in population. Ober estimates that the population of the greater Greek world expanded from a little under 1 million in 800 BCE to about 1.3 million by 700 BCE, before surging to approximately 2 million by around 600 BCE (Ober, 2015: 23, fig. 2.1). One explanation of the rapid economic growth was a major climate shift in the Mediterranean from the dry Subboreal phase to the cooler and wetter Subatlantic phase (Morris, 2011: 236). Modern demographic theory would also support the assumption that the changeover to arable farming was a determining factor in the increased rate of population growth, but the two variables were undoubtedly mutually reinforcing. Land-hunger in the grazing economy may have initiated the changeover to arable farming, which then had a dramatic effect on fertility, leading to a surge in the population. So, in true Malthusian fashion, land-hunger may then have returned. Antony Andrews is somewhat emphatic in his observation: "We have no hesitation in believing that land hunger was the main stimulus to the colonizing movement which began in the latter part of the 8th century, under very different conditions from those of the older migration" (1967: 99). While population growth and the subsequent land shortage were the major causes of the migrations (Bérard, 1960: 60–2), we also take note of Snodgrass's thesis that an acute shortage of metal during this and earlier periods may have played a part. This conclusion is based on the absence of weapons in the tombs of the periods under review and seems quite persuasive: however, it carries the risk of all *argumenta e silentio*, and Desborough, for one, finds some "hesitation in accepting" it, although he does not rule it out completely (1972: 317–18). That there was a marked increase in the population, however, no one disputes.

To this we should add one important caveat. We know from modern demographic studies that emigration, other than forced mass movements such as the Atlantic slave trade, tends to have negligible impact on the growth of the sending population, and is of far less importance than fertility and mortality rates in accounting for population stability or growth (United Nations Population Division, 2017). The same was likely true of Greece during and after the colonial movements. According to Finley, in the mid-eighth century, Hesiod was advising his fellow farmers in Boeotia (located in central Greece) to control the size of their families by having only one son, which would have been a most extraordinary position for a conservative

SLAVERY IN THE PREMODERN AND EARLY CHRISTIAN WORLDS

yeoman farmer to take in a still natural economy. However, Gregory Papanikos (2022: 19–20), among others, has strongly contested this interpretation, claiming that Finley mistranslated the relevant passage in Hesiod, who, to the contrary, considered it a curse if women could not bear children, which is more in line with fertility views in societies at Boeotia's level of development. In any case, emigration decreased sharply by the middle of the sixth century and virtually came to an end by the start of the fifth century (Bérard, 1960: Ch. 5), except for what Claude Mossé called "imperial colonization," which carried on through to the latter half of the fourth century BCE (1970: Ch. 2).

In the nonmaterial areas of culture, we find the emergence of a stratified society with a rudimentary state system. There was still a natural economy, but one now capable of generating sufficient surplus to support a ruling class in some modest style. A three-class society now emerged, consisting of the ruling aristocracy; the *demos* or "mass of small free landowning peasants who had approximately equal shares of land after regulated field grass economy had been given up for good and the tribal area had been finally distributed" (Heichelheim, 1958, vol. 1: 274); and the *thetai*, "free people who owned no land, and were instead traders, craftsmen, agricultural laborers, and the personal servants of the upper class, a group which fluctuated between wide extremes" (Desborough, 1972: 275). Below this group, and in one sense almost outside it, were the serfs and slaves.

With respect to the enslaved, it would not be unreasonable to say that there was a marked increase in their numbers, especially when we consider the growing militarism of the aristocratic clans during this period. Finley's interpretation of slavery in the world of Odysseus would seem to be relevant here:

> Slaves existed in number; they were property, disposable at will. More precisely, there were slave women, for wars and raids were the main source of supply, and there was little ground, economic or moral, for sparing the lives of the defeated men. The heroes as a rule killed the males and carried off the females, regardless of rank. (1962: 61)

Enslaved women were used as household help in the *oikos* and as concubines, and their illegitimate offspring were assimilated, even by the aristocrats (Finley, 1962: 67–8). Because status was determined by the father, and not the mother, slaves' children were constantly assimilated into the free group and, in the absence of male slaves, this meant that the enslaved could only be recruited from outside. This situation is similar to that which we described in the previous section.

THE ORIGINS OF SLAVERY AND SLAVE SOCIETY

The rudimentary state structure was physically represented in the growing tendency of town-like habitations to emerge as the aristocrats built their homes around the home of the basileus. At the same time, this encirclement of the basileus' domain reflected, in perhaps more than symbolic terms, the growing encroachment of the aristocracy on his authority. Increasingly, the latter lost his powers as the aristocrats became more and more independent, leading, for example, their own war parties in raids on other societies (Desborough, 1972: 79). This relative mobility of the aristocracy had its counterpart in the emergence of a more prosperous group of peasants. The growth in surplus, growing pressure on land, and emigration are all ideal conditions for some degree of upward mobility, and it was not only the aristocrats who benefited. One critical development that enhanced the mobility of this prosperous segment of the peasantry was the radical change in techniques of warfare during this period. The growing significance of the hoplite now shifted the fortunes of war in favor of the infantry. It was no longer the heavily armed aristocrat with his prohibitively expensive armor that decided the outcome of a battle, but the disciplined, swift-moving phalanx. The horse gave way to the ambitious peasant (Lorimer, 1947; Greenhalgh, 1973: Chs. 4 and 7; Burn, 1966 [1936]: 105). More wars and more successes in them meant, of course, more prisoners of war and, as such, more slaves. Furthermore, the increasing role of the peasant in warfare meant that, for the first time, the prosperous peasant could hope for the prestige and labor support of owning one or two slaves, most likely females.

Moving now to the Hesiodic or late eighth- and seventh-century Greece, we find a striking combination of factors leading to certain basic changes in the structure of the society. A natural economy still prevails, but population growth is now in full swing, in no way abated by the colonizing movements. Land-hunger increased among the peasants and reached the point where, on the one hand, a substantial number of lower-class persons became landless, and, on the other, the peasants became increasingly indebted to the aristocrats. These developments require some elaboration. "The prevailing impression" of the world of Hesiod, A. W. Burn tells us, "is one of hard and unremitting work with a few stark seasons . . . with hunger a familiar acquaintance and sheer starvation a very present possibility" (1966 [1936]: 36). All land was now held in private property and could be sold on the market. From the latter half of the eighth century, we find Hesiod complaining bitterly about the rapacious aristocrats. Land was obviously changing hands rapidly, although we should bear in mind N. G. L. Hammond's qualification that, down to as late as 431

131

SLAVERY IN THE PREMODERN AND EARLY CHRISTIAN WORLDS

BCE, certain kinds of land, especially familial, corporate property, remained inalienable and as such immune from the impact of the new money economy (introduced during the late seventh century with major commercial consequences), or, later, from the reforms of the politicians (1973: 137; see also Burford, 1993: 24; Schaps, 2004).

More important is the fact that we should distinguish between the debt-ridden peasants and the landless *hektemoroi*. W. J. Woodhouse thinks that the growing indebtedness was due primarily to a "vicious land system." His vivid description is consistent with later work: "Society as a whole was bursting its archaic swaddling bands and evolving into a more complex economic structure and greater differentiation of types of life, with corresponding shift in social values, both yielding place to wealth, and wealth itself receiving new definition" (1938: 32). Population growth and land fragmentation, due partly to the *gavelkind* system of inheritance, led to the growth of debt bondage and the accumulation of ownership of peasant lands in the hands of the aristocracy. Thus, a modified form of quit-rent serfdom emerged. The serfs, however, must not be confused with the *hektemoroi*. Woodhouse's argument still holds: that it was not possible for them to become indebted, since the rent they paid was a ratio, "not a competitive quantum" of their produce (1938: 33). They were, instead, mainly "ruined men" who "voluntarily surrendered" themselves and their families to others. This, Woodhouse argued, was deliberately fostered by the nobles, who were more interested in getting a flexible labor force that could be used to exploit the land in producing crops aimed at the foreign market than in getting tenants. By this means, "a primitive domestic economy gave place to production on a considerable scale, for export" (1938: 64–5). I still find this to be one of the best explanations of what was going on, and it is consistent with Bresson's more recent and widely accepted analysis.

What, indeed, had taken place was the emergence of new tastes among the all-important elite whose demands and consumption patterns were being increasingly influenced by their eastern neighbors. To get the luxury goods they needed, and to live the new style of life they coveted, they had to produce goods that could generate some kind of foreign exchange. As Chester Starr pointed out, the seventh century saw the "creation of consciously aristocratic patterns" corresponding to "new modes of artistic and poetic thought" (1961: 303). A more urbane way of life, a more centralized political structure, a change in the underlying economic base to a more diversified and specialized economy both in the agricultural and nonfarm sectors, and a totally ruthless exploitation of the lower classes: these constituted the new order of the day (Bresson, 2015: 109–10).

THE ORIGINS OF SLAVERY AND SLAVE SOCIETY

Some scholars hold that slaveholding substantially increased during the late eighth and seventh centuries BCE before the reforms of Solon, to the point where Greece may be called a slave society. Edward Harris wrote: "The communities of the Greek world did not become societies in which slavery played a large role in the production of wealth for the elite only in the sixth century BCE and later. Slavery was already widespread in the society depicted by the Homeric poems" (2020: 389; see also Harris, 2012). Not everyone agrees (see, for example, Papanikos, 2022). Greece, especially what Ober (2015) called the "core" regions, may not yet have been a Finley-type "genuine" slave society, but that was clearly on the way.

Now, while Solon's abolition of all debts in the *seisachtheia* law and his prohibition of debt-slavery have become justly famous, it is important to realize that he was no revolutionary from above. The condition of the peasants, and that of the lower classes generally, were certainly stabilized, but their land-hunger continued, and while some elements of the upper classes suffered, overall there can be no doubt that the net effect of the reforms worked in favor of the aristocrats. One is obliged to agree with Kathleen Freeman's judgments that the benefits of these reforms to the mass of poor Greeks were mainly of a temporary nature, for, to take one example, the change in the standard of measurements created benefits that were soon wiped out by the inflationary impact of Solon's fiscal policies (2014 [1926]: 111). Harris (2020: 389) also reminds us that what Solon abolished was the practice of enslavement for debt, not debt bondage itself, which persisted down to Classical times. However, the long-held view of Heichelheim that, apart from a brief period during the Periclean age, there was no general improvement in the standard of living of the mass of Greek people throughout all the periods of antiquity (Heichelheim, 1958, vol. 2: 33) has been stoutly challenged. Ober estimated that unskilled and skilled laborers "were paid wages sufficient to elevate them to a decent, middling premodern standard of living," which, he admits, was rare in human history prior to the nineteenth century (2015: 89–98, esp. 90, 95, and Table 4.4). This, however, refers to free-wage workers. Farmers on marginal lands, indebted farmers, and landless farmworkers, who still constituted a substantial part of the population of Attica, were likely no better off than their counterparts in Hesiod's day, not to mention the 20–30 percent of the population who were enslaved in the classical period. But we have gone too far ahead.

What the reforms of Solon set in train was an even greater pace of change in the Athenian economy. A larger commercial class now emerged whose interests were identical to those of the aristocracy. It was they who provided the financial and commercial infrastructure that made the good life in the city possible for the elites and enhanced the changing agricultural practices of the large landowners. In the agricultural sector, the vast majority of Greeks remained independent smallholders until the Peloponnesian War, when hostilities brought disaster to many of them, resulting in a new accumulation of land in the hands of the upwardly mobile commercial classes anxious to join the ranks of the landowning classes. The elites continued to move into more specialized types of farming aimed at the foreign market (Pečirka, 1973: 120–1; Bresson, 2015: Chs. 5–7). And in the non-farming sector we find a rapid escalation of urban craft industries, as well as mining in southeast Attica.

Before going further, let us take stock of how the development of Greek society as we have sketched it so far relates to the rise of slavery. First, we saw how Homeric society changed into a largely quit-rent serf economy, in spite of growing population density during the eighth and seventh centuries. Why did the Greek ruling class reduce a significant part of its population to servility at a time when there was an increase in the supply of labor? According to the Nieboer-Domar hypothesis, lower-class Greeks of Hesiod's time and the late seventh century should have been knocking down the doors of their lords begging for work. The case of the *hektemoroi* may be cited in defense of the hypothesis, but apart from the fact that they did not meet anything like the complete labor demands of the aristocrats, there is sufficient evidence to suggest that the threat of complete enslavement was necessary to keep them in line once they had survived the threat of starvation. This threat was indeed carried out in quite a number of cases, for one of Solon's reforms was to buy back the freedom of Greeks who had been sold abroad. The Greek experience totally defies the Nieboer-Domar hypothesis, for even during the sixth century, when there was overcrowding in the rural areas, jobs went begging, both on the fruit farms of the aristocrats and in the urban areas. Indeed, the situation became so critical that Solon had to pass a law requiring Greeks to work, not as slaves, or serfs, or any other kind of bondsmen, but simply as honest paid laborers. What, in this now thriving money economy, we want to know, became of economic man? To answer this question, we must turn to Greek attitudes toward manual labor, and in doing so we leave immediately the simplicities of vulgar demographic determinism.

The ancient Greek attitude toward manual labor was both complex and changing during the half millennium under review (800–300 BCE). The general impression, based on the classical period, is that the Greeks despised all forms of manual work. But, as Rodolfo Mondolfo and D. S. Duncan pointed out long ago, this was true only after the

THE ORIGINS OF SLAVERY AND SLAVE SOCIETY

fifth century BCE. Archaic Greece had a healthy respect for agricultural labor, and "recognized the threefold value of labor: economic, moral and intellectual" (Mondolfo and Duncan, 1954: 5). However, by the fifth century a growing contempt for all forms of manual work developed. Some ambivalence remained with respect to agricultural work, a good deal of which can be explained by the conservative yearning for the "good old days," not to mention the time-old patronizing hypocrisies of all intellectuals for "the good earth" (Dodds, 1973: 24), but there can be no doubt from the writings of Plato, Xenophon, and Aristotle that the prevailing Greek view was one of utter contempt for manual labor. To this, however, we must add Finley's point that the Greeks made an important distinction between manual labor, as such, and independent labor (1964: 239). It was the lack of independence, Finley argues, that the Greeks detested, rather than manual labor as such. Finley's observation must, however, be qualified. In the same way that, as Mondolfo and Duncan plead, it is wrong to see the post-Socratic contempt for manual labor as something typical of all Greek history, so, I think, it is equally wrong to see the nice distinction that Finley makes as something true of all periods. The distinction, it would seem, holds until about the late sixth century, after which there can be no doubt that it was lost with the growing contempt for all manual work and its association with slave labor.

Nowhere was this more evident than in the extraordinary attitude of the Greeks toward the artists and craftsmen who were producing the very objects of beauty that they prized so much. Thus Alison Burford, in her study of craftsmen in antiquity, tells us that the Greeks had nothing but contempt for the "men to whom the nature of their employment denied all possibility of moral or political virtue" (1972: 12). This included every category of artist and craftsman, from miner to goldsmith, from shoemaker to potter to architect. A sharp, and what can only be called intellectually strange, distinction was made between making (*poiesis*) and doing (*praxis*). When a thing was made, it was alienated from the act of making and from the maker; but no such alienation took place with respect to doing (Burford, 1972: 185). Needless to say, what the intellectuals and other members of the ruling classes did was "doing," while what the craftsmen and artists did was "making." My reaction to Burford's interpretation was that this was not only a rationalization by the Greeks of an elitist view of the world, but a silly one. However, Paulin Ismard's brilliant recent study of the "astonishing institution of public slavery" among the ancient Greeks has greatly clarified this complex cultural phenomenon:

135

Even while entrusting posts that granted de facto power and expertise to slaves, the cities tainted these functions with an irrevocable stigma attached to the status of those who performed them. The use of slaves, "living instruments" in the hands of the people, theoretically guaranteed that no administrative apparatus could erect an obstacle to the will of the demos. The city, in making invisible those in charge of its administration, warded off the danger of a state that could constitute itself as an autonomous agency and, if need be, turn against the city itself. (2017: 111)

This sounds like an ancient version of far right American Republicans' suspicion of the deep state.

Now, the relationship of all this to slavery is direct and critical. In the early period, when Finley's point holds, the shortage of labor in the midst of growing population densities is to be explained by the refusal of the average Greek peasant to give up his independence under any terms except the imminent threat of starvation. The abolition of debts and the reluctance of the Greeks to work for others (except as a favor) were partly responsible for creating the labor crisis that the upper classes faced from the early sixth century. But only partly, for the crisis had both a demand and a supply side. After the start of the sixth century, the increased shift to cultivation of olives and figs and to viticulture was no longer optional, but essential, in view of what must have been, by then, a state of increasing failure of local production to meet domestic demand for grain in Athens. It therefore had to move, on the one hand, into industrial and commercial activities, including seafaring, and, on the other hand, into the agricultural crops in which it had the greatest comparative advantage, namely grapes, olives, and barley, for which the soil of Attica is ideally suited. By the end of the fifth century, according to Jameson (1977–8: 130), Attica was producing ten times as much barley as wheat. However, barley was the poor man's food. It was largely sold abroad and the much preferred wheat was increasingly imported to supplement local supply. Olive and grape production, two other crops for which Attica had a comparative advantage, also greatly increased. More land, including what was formerly marginal, had to be brought into production. There was, in a nutshell, a massive intensification of agricultural production. In addition, as Jules Toutain noted long ago: "There was an insatiable demand for wood . . . for building the expanding towns, for shipbuilding, to facilitate the expanding trade and for carpentry" (1968: 33). Greece became rapidly deforested during this period. This all entailed growing demand for labor.

But it was not forthcoming internally. There were factors other than the Greek attitude toward labor that accounted for this. We

THE ORIGINS OF SLAVERY AND SLAVE SOCIETY

have already been led by our earlier comparative analysis to expect a higher likelihood of slavery where there is an increase in agricultural intensification. Furthermore, fruit farms often require heavy capital expenditure and there is a long wait before returns. Olives have to be irrigated; vines are notoriously labor-intensive. If native free laborers were not forthcoming in sufficient numbers, there was only one alternative – imported labor, and in the premodern world that meant slaves.

However, it was not only on the farms of the elite that the demand for slave labor grew. The intensification of agriculture on the farms of small farmers also led to an increased demand for labor beyond the resources of the family. The model Athenian citizen, as Jameson (1977–8: 124) has pointed out, was a man who owned farmland, and all but the richest worked the land themselves, a view more recently strongly emphasized by Robin Osborne (2010: Ch. 7). Increasingly, it was to imported slaves that ordinary citizen-farmers also turned to meet their increased labor needs. They could do so because the enslaved were relatively cheap, and increasingly so throughout the fifth century, compared to the alternatives, these being mainly mules, given the unavailability of free farm labor. At the end of the fifth century, a typical farm slave cost 150–200 drachmas, as opposed to a pair of mules, which cost between 450 and 800 drachmas (Jameson, 1977–8: 139). There were also what Jameson calls "social gains" in this increasing reliance on slave labor, since it enabled the ordinary farmer to meet and enjoy his civic obligations:

> The slave, minding the farm, permits the farmer to serve as hoplite or as juryman or to exercise his other civic rights. Under the most favorable circumstances, slaveholding enabled the Athenian to be a participant in a democracy. The public pay available through a democracy might not enable him to support his family but at least he could feed his slave. Under less favorable circumstances he dropped out of his society. (1978: 140; see also Osborne, 2010: Ch. 5)

Similar developments took place in both the urban-commercial sector and in mining, where, from the early fifth century onward, as we indicated earlier, slavery became the dominant form of labor. Again, it was not the shortage of bodies as such that led to the dominance of the enslaved in the mining workforce, but the absolute refusal of Greeks to even think of working there, unless, of course, they were small-scale contractors (Lauffer, 1979: 10). Nor could the demand for skilled labor be met by the native Greek population.

137

SLAVERY IN THE PREMODERN AND EARLY CHRISTIAN WORLDS

According to Burford, this shortage was "one of the most important limiting factors in the ancient economy, and one which was partly responsible for the institution of slavery" (1972: 58–9).

By the late fifth century, all these changes culminated in the highly successful socioeconomic order that underlay the classical city-states. According to Bresson (2015), an enormous Aegean-wide division of labor occurred, resulting in productivity gains that generated the relatively high level of development seen in classical Greece. Accompanying all this was a tremendous increase in the number and proportion of the enslaved. They were employed in every kind of activity except political and military affairs and, in emergencies, even in the military (Sargent, 1927). The enslaved were not only the main source of labor on the home farms of the elite but, it is now believed, they also played important roles in the farms of modest citizens, allowing them to not only increase the productivity of their farms but participate in public life. The question of their numbers will always remain contentious (Vujcic, 2012) but there is growing consensus that playing the numbers game with the sparse available data is meaningless. More meaningful is the fact that we know enough to be certain that their role was economically critical for the classical economy. Bresson admits as much in his discussion of the number of slaves, but he somewhat underplayed the role of slavery in the emergence of classical Greece when he wrote: "This fundamental reorientation of their economies supposed also reorganizing production structures and resorting massively to slave labor" (2015: 347). This suggests far too passive a role for the enslaved and slavery in the economic revolution he so well describes. The enslaved were not simply passively exploited bodies, but active and creative agents in the emergence and workings of this leading edge of the ancient economy, and nowhere more so than in the crafts and beautiful works of art and architecture that they were primarily instrumental in creating.

But they did more. As another French classicist has shown, the enslaved *demosios* not only maintained order as the city's law enforcement officers and ran its bureaucracy at all levels of technical expertise and supervision; it was their presence and performance that made possible that crown jewel of classical Athens, and the Western world's greatest inheritance: democracy. The state, as Ismard has shown, "never existed in the Greek city, except in the purely negative form of its public slaves; the *demosioi* therefore constituted the 'secret hero' of the Greek state" (2017: 132). And also, we might add, the genocidally used workers of the Laurion mines, who generated the wealth that largely supported Athenian democracy and empire;

THE ORIGINS OF SLAVERY AND SLAVE SOCIETY

the enslaved on the home farms, who supported the leisure class of intellectuals; the resident aliens, metics *(metoikoi)*, many of them former slaves, and not a few who contributed directly to Athens's greatest glory, its philosophy: Phaedo, Diogenes, Menippus. From Hesiod to Aristotle, the enslaved and slavery pervaded the economic, social, and cultural life of Athens, *un peu partout*.

* * *

This brief review of the relationship between the development of ancient Greek society, especially Athens, and the various forms of servile labor in it, has fully confirmed our conclusions concerning the spuriousness of the Nieboer-Domar hypothesis. But more important perhaps, it has given an ounce or two of humanistic flesh to the bare bones of our statistical analysis, as well as a dynamic perspective, and, in so doing, has illustrated the kinds of factors that come into play, over time, in the complex processes whereby a society adopts a dulotic labor system. We have seen that in the five hundred years between the primitive economy of the early ninth century BCE and the complex urban civilization of the late fourth, serfdom was to rise and fall, and slavery was to rise from a position of minor economic significance to one of central importance in the economy and social life of Greece, and the foundation of its civic culture.

At the same time, the Greek population kept rising, at first steadily, then rapidly, increasing tenfold between 800 and 300 BCE. We are not saying that there is no relationship between population densities and patterns of servile labor. What we are saying is that we have detected no inverse causal relationship, and where meaningful relationships have been found to exist, they have not only usually been strongly positive, but also complex and subject to other causal factors. Of these other factors, we have identified the changing tastes and habits of the elites, the attitude of free persons toward manual labor for others, the changing patterns of warfare and the effects of warfare itself, the degree of scarcity and threat of hunger, the working of mines, the changing structure of the economy, including its mode of subsistence, the kinds of crops and commodities produced, the degree of intensification and diversification in agriculture, the extent of urbanization, and the growing commercialization of the economy and reliance on external trade. It is the interaction of these factors both with each other and with increasing population growth and densities, in ways that we could only hint at here, that accounts for the development of slavery in ancient Greece.

SLAVERY IN THE PREMODERN AND EARLY CHRISTIAN WORLDS

And it is also these factors that accounted for the first large-scale slave society, with consequences for human culture, the cherishment of freedom as supreme value, and the birthing of Western civilization, that were to change the world forever (Patterson, 1991; Raaflaub, 2004).

Appendix

I constructed the following tables of logistic models with the coded data from the Murdock World Sample, using STATA software. The reference category for the odds ratios of the categorical dependent variables is indicated by "Ref." and is generally the lowest or absent category. From five of these logistic models, I also derived the predicted probability estimates included in the text. Most people find probability values more intuitively understandable, but bear in mind that these are not the same as, or even counterparts of, the odds ratios.

(For the Standard Murdock World sample and complete list of variables used in the analysis see: https://www.academia.edu/5900 83/Standard_Cross_Cultural_Sample_Codebook_variables_1_to _2000.)

Table A1. Logistic model predicting slavery by population density

Persons per sq. mile	Odds ratio	Std err	P-value	[95% conf. interval]	
<1 person/sq. mile	Ref.	Ref.	Ref.	Ref.	Ref.
1–5 persons/sq. mile	3	1.92	0.087	0.852	10.55
>5–25 persons/sq. mile	7.22	4.39	0.001	2.24	23.08
26–100 persons/sq. mile	5.4	3.04	0.003	1.76	16.33
>100 persons/sq. mile	2.8	1.64	0.072	0.912	8.80
Cons	0.12	0.05	0.000	0.050	0.274

# Obs. = 171; LR chi2 = 15.28; Prob > chi2 = 0.0042; Log likelihood = –89.867.
Ref. = Reference category

140

THE ORIGINS OF SLAVERY AND SLAVE SOCIETY

Table A2. Logistic model predicting slavery by the cropping index

Cropping index	Odds ratio	Std err	P-value	[95% conf. interval]	
Agriculture absent	Ref.	Ref.	Ref.	Ref.	Ref.
<10% land used per year	2.233	0.258	0.189	0.0265	2.044
10–29% of land used per year	1.823	1.119	0.328	0.547	6.073
30–49% of land used per year	3.875	2.579	0.042	1.051	14.282
50–99% of land used per year	3.386	1.888	0.029	1.135	10.100
100% or more of land used per year	1.165	0.762	0.815	0.323	4.199
Cons	0.225	0.094	0.000	0.099	0.512

Obs. = 151. LR chi2(5) = 15.03. Prob > chi2 = 0.010 3. Log likelihood = –79.783
Note: more than 100% land used refers to double cropping). Ref. = Reference category

Table A3. Logistic model predicting slavery by frequency of warfare

Frequency of warfare	Odds ratio	Std err	P-value	[95% conf. interval]	
Warfare rare	Ref.	Ref.	Ref.	Ref.	
Occasional warfare	2.223	1.004	0.077	0.917	5.388
Frequent warfare or endemic	2.833	1.486	0.047	1.013	7.921
Cons	0.196	0.067	0.000	0.099	0.386

No. of Obs. = 145. Log likelihood = 79.8. Prob > chi2 = 0.08. Ref. = Reference category

Table A4. Logistic model predicting slavery by warfare if boundaries of populaton expanding

Warfare with boundaries expanding	Odds ratio	Std err	P-value	[95% conf. interval]	
Not expanding	Ref.	Ref.	Ref.	Ref.	
2	1.490	1.346	0.658	0.254	8.750
3	0.573	0.292	0.275	0.211	1.556
4	2.640	1.226	0.037	1.062	6.562
Cons	0.268	0.091	0.000	0.137	0.521

No. of Obs. = 160. Log likelihood = –82.39. LR chi2(3) = 10.62. Prob > chi2 = 0.014.
Ref. = Reference category

Table A5. Logistic model predicting slavery by the occurrence of seasonal starvation

Occurrence of seasonal starvation	Odds ratio	Std err	P-value	[95% conf. interval]	
Very low or absent	Ref.	Ref.	Ref.	Ref.	
Low	5.166	7.056	0.229	0.355	75.13
High	4.536	3.028	0.023	1.226	16.783
Very high	2.695	2.045	0.191	0.609	11.927
Chronic	5.683	4.044	0.015	1.408	22.929
Cons	0.0967	0.0585	0.000	0.029	0.316

No. of Obs. = 156. Log likelihood = –83.29. LR chi2(4) = 8.86. Prob > chi2 = 0.064.
Ref. = Reference category

Table A6. Logistic model predicting slavery by starvation levels, controlling for warfare

Covariates	Odds ratio	Std err	P-value	[95% conf. interval]	
Starvation level					
Very low/absent	Ref.	Ref.	Ref.	Ref.	Ref.
Low	5.112	7.437	0.262	0.295	88.498
High	4.268	3.453	0.073	0.874	20.845
Very high	1.624	1.583	0.619	0.240	10.979
5	6.179	5.172	0.030	1.197	31.880
Frequency of warfare					
Rare	Ref.	Ref.	Ref.	Ref.	Ref.
Occasional	2.425	1.218	0.078	0.906	6.489
Continual	2.707	1.586	0.089	0.585	8.539
Cons					

No. of Obs. = 135. Log likelihood = –67.86. LR chi2(5) = 14.43. Ref. = Reference category

THE ORIGINS OF SLAVERY AND SLAVE SOCIETY

Table A7. Logistic model predicting slavery by degree of witchcraft beliefs

Belief in witchcraft as cause of illness	Odds ratio	Std err	P-value	[95% conf. interval]	
Absence of such a cause	Ref.	Ref.	Ref.	Ref.	Ref.
Minor or unimportant cause	4.924	2.650	0.003	1.714	14.139
Important auxiliary cause	3.611	2.215	0.036	1.084	12.020
Predominant cause	4.333	3.209	0.048	1.014	18.507
Cons	0.184	0.058	0.000	0.099	0.341

No. of Obs. = 116. Log likelihood = –58.559. LR chi2(5) = 15.49. Prob > chi2 = 0.008.
Ref. = Reference category

Table A8. Logistic model predicting hereditary slavery by degrees of agriculture, fishing, and pastoralism in subsistence

Covariate	Odds ratio	P-value	95% conf. interval
Agriculture			
Absent, sporadic	(Ref.)	(Ref.)	(Ref.)
Present, unimportant	1	(empty)	(empty)
Important, not major	15.23	0.073	[0.772, 300.4]
Co-dominant	0.720	0.833	[0.034, 15.06]
Dominant activity	37.94	0.029	[1.46, 982]
Fishing			
Absent, sporadic	(Ref.)	(Ref.)	(Ref.)
Present, unimportant	0.421	0.318	[0.077, 2.29]
Important, not major	0.947	0.942	[0.225, 3.98]
Co-dominant	1.31	0.875	[0.043, 40.16]
Dominant activity	199.0	0.009	[3.67, 1077]
Pastoralism			
Absent, sporadic	(Ref.)	(Ref.)	(Ref.)
Present, unimportant	0.259	0.206	[0.031, 2.10]
Important, not major	0.869	0.880	[0.142, 5.31]
Co-dominant	105.1	0.011	[2.84, 3879]
Dominant activity	12.46	0.142	[0.429, 361]
Cons	0.022	0.020	[0.0009, 556]

No. of Obs. = 82. Log likelihood = 36.65. Pr chi2 = 0.003. Ref. = Reference category

Table A9. Logistic model predicting polygyny >20% by agriculture type, female workload, warfare, slavery, and bridewealth

Covariate	Odds ratio	P-value	95% conf. interval
Agriculture type			
Intensive	(Ref.)	(Ref.)	(Ref.)
Extensive	5.20	0.005	[1.00, 13.31]
Female workload			
Less than men	(Ref.)	(Ref.)	(Ref.)
Equal or more	3.66	0.049	[1.00, 13.31]
Warfare			
Infrequent	(Ref.)	(Ref.)	(Ref.)
Frequent	4.39	0.030	[1.15, 16.72]
Continuous	1.01	0.981	[0.221, 4.68]
Slavery			
Absent	(Ref.)	(Ref.)	(Ref.)
Non-hereditary	4.39	0.060	[0.94, 20.5]
Hereditary	1.39	0.236	[0.60, 7.68]
Bridewealth			
Absent	(Ref.)	(Ref.)	(Ref.)
Norm	4.41	0.012	[1.38, 14.07]
Cons	0.028	0.000	[0.005, 0.147]

No. of Obs. = 84. Log likelihood = 40.56. Pr chi2 = 0.000. Ref. = Reference category

— 6 —

THE SOCIAL AND SYMBOLIC USES OF SLAVERY IN ANCIENT ROME AND EARLY CHRISTIANITY

Distinguished classical historian John Bodel (2017) has raised several important issues concerning the concept of social death and the way it was treated by me in *Slavery and Social Death* (1982). I am happy and thankful that he did so, since it offers me an opportunity to return to the concept and clarify aspects of it that were in need of elaboration. Bodel makes two arguments about the concept of social death. He notes, first, that there was an apparent shift in my analysis between the earlier discussion of slavery as a condition of social death and my later analysis of slavery as a process involving the transition from a state of freedom, to enslavement, to social death, and eventually to rebirth into social life or freedom. When viewed as a process culminating in freedom, Bodel argues, slavery becomes simply one state in a process and hence the metaphor of social death becomes inapt: "The latter [processual] view, if correct, calls into question the applicability, regardless of its emotive power, of the metaphor of death, a static and final state (as far as we know), to describe a situation represented by Patterson as 'liminal' and figured by him as the middle stage of a three-part process." Drawing on the monumental inscriptions of Roman freedmen, he argues that the attitude of the enslaved to real death serves as a way of "defying the forces of natal alienation and dishonor. Representing themselves and their kin as triumphing over death, like gods, was for the slaves an existential parting shot" (2017: 84).

Bodel's second argument is really a reinforcement of the first, using not the cultural evidence implied by the inscriptions, but the presumed sociological realities of Roman slavery, to wit, that "there is abundant evidence that slavery was regarded by Roman slaves and slave owners as a temporary rather than a permanent condition"

(2017: 89). Assuming this to be the case, he wonders how this could be reconciled with my "conception of social death as the central element, a place of 'institutionalized liminality' within a process that in an ideal state maintains an equilibrium, of slaves moving into and out of the system" (2017: 90). These are very interesting and insightful arguments which, as Bodel gracefully concludes, pose issues that are matters for discussion, one that I welcome, especially because it allows me to relate the discussion of death in *Slavery and Social Death* to my later study of freedom (Patterson, 1991: Part 4).

My first response is to the sociohistorical claim that there is abundant evidence that Roman slavery was a temporary condition, and was regarded as such by enslavers and the enslaved alike. This is what the literary evidence suggests, and Bodel's claim is consistent with what has long been the consensus view. However, this view has now been seriously challenged. Recent studies based on a more rigorous analysis of available data on manumission rates, the numbers of the enslaved, their natural reproduction, the longevity of the system of slavery, the diminishing supply of the enslaved from external sources, the centrality of the enslaved to the Roman economy, the relative prices of male and female slaves, and inferences from comparative studies of manumission's role in the incentive structure of Roman slavery as well as from demographic theory: all, as Walter Scheidel compellingly argues, lead to "the notion of a Roman imperial slave system that was sufficiently large in scale for natural reproduction to have been its most important means of maintenance and *manumission to have been fairly limited*" (2012: 95).

Now, this does not mean that manumission was not highly desired and relatively frequent in Rome. It is a well-established fact that the rate was higher than in most other slaveholding societies, and the granting of citizenship upon manumission was considered by contemporaries to have been quite remarkable. In an exhaustive study of freedmen in Roman society, Henrik Mouritsen shows that every slave was encouraged to believe that freedom was a realistic possibility, made credible by the not insubstantial minority who in fact became free. This had the salutary effect, for the slaveholder, of greatly incentivizing the enslaved to work hard toward this possible end, and also reduced any chance of class solidarity among them. The great majority, however, never made it out of slavery, and for them this "selective process would have been profoundly demoralizing" (Mouritsen, 2011: 204).

What held for Rome was true of nearly all slave systems. Beyond the fact that many of the enslaved, however hard they tried, simply lacked the skills, ambition, or energy to win the manumission race, a number of other factors intervened to prevent this outcome. For one, some slaves choose to abort the process by running away or by direct resistance, which, apart from a lucky few who were not recaptured or ended up in maroon settlements (Patterson, 2022 [1967]: Ch. 9; see also Chapter 7 in this volume) usually led either to their execution or to the permanent revocation of any chance of manumission. A second factor truncating the process was when the enslaved died of natural causes before achieving the strived for goal of manumission. Scheidel (2001: 29) estimated the life expectancy of elite Romans during the early empire at twenty-five to thirty years, although he did not think the lives of the enslaved and the lower classes were much shorter. A third reason was suicide. Sandra Greene (2017) shows that, for children, among whom the experience of natal alienation weighed especially hard, suicide and suicidal thoughts became an unconscious form of resistance, a tragic way of defying social death. In my early work on slavery in Jamaica (1967: 98–101), I mentioned that the enslaved, after the horrors of the middle passage and the harshness and cruel uncertainties of being seasoned in a strange land, showed marked symptoms of psychological trauma; some of them, especially Ibos from Nigeria, were considered especially prone to suicide. Finally, there are those rare cases where the trajectory runs in the reverse direction, namely, self-enslavement, comparative cases of which I discussed in *Slavery and Social Death*. Whether this proves that slavery can be a condition with honor, as Junia Furtado (2017) argues, is seriously open to question. What her case study of Joana does strongly indicate is the extremely precarious, "hand-to-mouth" condition of freed and free-born Blacks in certain parts of northern Brazil during the late eighteenth century. As I have shown (Patterson, 2018 [1982]: 130–1; this volume, pp. 21–2), free persons sold themselves into slavery for a variety of reasons: to escape poverty, as in Russia; to escape social and political isolation, as in nineteenth-century Kongo; as the only means of procuring land, as in medieval, tribal Germany; to escape military service, as in China during war-prone eras; and in Korea, especially during the Yi dynasty. In none of these cases did the reduction to slavery escape the extreme dishonor of the reduced status.

However, the sociological reality of slavery being a permanent state for most Roman slaves does not really undercut Bodel's view (and my own, stated in *Slavery and Social Death*) that the *ideology* of slavery as a process leading to freedom was an extremely important element of the Roman system of slavery. (Think of the persistence of the "American Dream" ideology, in spite of the nation's extreme and growing inequality.) It was, as Mouritsen's own study demonstrates, a critical component of the system, a goal and ideal encouraged by the enslavers and believed in by nearly all the enslaved and, as such, essential for the system's functioning and stability. And like all powerful ideologies, especially those partially realized by a successful minority, it was expressed in highly symbolic terms.

Thus, although incorrect in claiming that slavery was a temporary condition for *most* Roman slaves, Bodel's argument, viewed as an exploration of the symbolic structure of Roman slave life, still carries force, and its questioning of my own symbolic analysis remains to be answered. Is the metaphor of social death inadequate for a complex metaphoric sequence that culminates in the rebirth of the enslaved into the social life of freedom? I don't think so, and here is why.

First – and this is critical – my use of the metaphor of social death was not, as some have claimed, entirely or even primarily an external analytic device imposed on the data of slavery to make sense of it. The phenomenon of social death that I propounded was not an external, objectivizing theoretical construct meant to explain slavery, but a phenomenological account of the intersubjective lifeworld, the jointly constructed, lived experience of the enslaved and their enslavers. Central to that jointly produced lifeworld, Edmund Husserl's *Lebenswelt* (see Schutz and Luckmann, 1980) was the phenomenon of social death. A metaphor, to be sure, but, contrary to the common literalist view, metaphors are what we think and live by (Lakoff and Johnson, 1980). As George Lakoff and Mark Johnson have further shown, "our most fundamental concepts – time, events, causation, the mind, the self, and morality – are multiply metaphorical"; they are "a tool for understanding things in a way that is tied to our embodied, lived experience" (1999: 128, 543).

The metaphor of social death was the central phase in a symbolic dulotic trajectory that directly references a sociological sequence of statuses that, in its entirety, in the Roman case, ran as follows: natal security or birthright, in some cases recognized as freedom in the provenance society → captivity/enslavement → slavery (powerlessness re slaveholder; natal alienation; parasitic dishonor; *in rem* legal status; the incentivizing, shared ideology of freedom) → manumission → conditional freedom (*obsequium*; *operae*) → full freedom – membership of the *Lares Augusti* cult, worship of the deified emperor's "spirit/force" by the richest freedmen (Mouritsen, 2011: 249–60; Zanker, 1990: 317–19; Hopkins, 2010 [1978]: 211–13). Directly referencing this dulotic trajectory was the following symbolic sequence: social life → social dying → social death → social rebirth → conditional social life → full social life (incorporation).

Bodel's argument is that the metaphor of social death is questionable because real death is final. My first response to this is to repeat what was pointed out above: that this was not *my* metaphor externally imposed on the observed sociological trajectory, but my interpretation of a symbolic trajectory constructed by the enslaved, freedmen, and the slaveholders themselves, as well as freemen, a phenomenological reality of Roman life. Social death as metaphor is real and significant only through the interacting parties' accounts and performances of it. How do I know that the metaphor transforms death into something reversible? Both from what we know of how semiotic reasoning works and from the Roman and comparative data. First, there is no requirement that the signifier of a metaphoric process be a literal correspondence to the referent it signifies, a point long ago established by Saussure's dyadic theory of signs and also the more sophisticated triangular theory of Charles Peirce (1931–58, vol. 2: 228, 303) that preceded it (and upon which I draw). The symbolic mind can easily represent the referent (in our case, slavery) with whatever representation (Saussure's *signifier*; Peirce's *representamen*) it wills. That's the beauty, and utility, of metaphoric thinking. In the case of the Roman freedmen, the *representamen* was a social death that was dynamic and capable of being negated. How does the Roman symbolic mind do this? This is where Peirce's semiotics proves itself more valuable than Saussure's. The third element of the symbolic process, he has taught us, is the *interpretant,* which is the sense made of the *representamen* or signifier. So, in Peircean terms, we have a referent or object, slavery, represented by the signifier, death, which is interpreted as a dynamic process capable of a double negation – that of the pre-enslavement life it negated and of being negated itself by the symbolic process of rebirth. Nor does the symbolic process end here. One of the most important features of Peircean semiotics is its recognition of symbolic recursivity – the fact that the *interpretant* is itself a sign in the mind of the interpreter – "the meaning of a representation can be nothing but a re presentation," Peirce wrote – and, as such, can itself become a referent for a new triangular process of signification, and so on ad infinitum (1931–58, vol. 1: 339).

The data to support such symbolic thinking in regard to slavery are quite abundant, beginning with Bodel's own chapter. His cases show convincingly that freedmen symbolically negated death and had a deeply held belief in symbolic rebirth as expressed in their monumental inscriptions. My reading of these inscriptions is that the freedmen sought not so much to defy death as to celebrate its hardships and trials, the better to emphasize their triumph over it – O death, where is thy sting? – and the more to gloat over the glory of their rebirth. The symbolic logic of undoing death, and of rebirth, clearly implies a pre-existing condition of social death that held the possibility of undying and rebirth.

We also know this to be the case from the comparative data on the rituals of dis-enslavement, many instances of which I presented in *Slavery and Social Death* (2018 [1982]: 216–19). My earlier study of the funerary practices, as well as the ancestral and spirit beliefs of Jamaican slaves demonstrated this at length (Patterson, 2022 [1967]: 195–206). A simple yet poignant illustration is reported in Jerome Handler and Frederick Lange's archeological study of plantation slavery in Barbados, where it was found that the enslaved always buried their dead in the extended, supine position commonly found in West Africa, and with the head facing east toward Africa (1978: 174–81).

However, one of the most explicit cases in point is the remarkable discovery reported by Anthony Barbieri-Low in his work on Han China. As he notes, when *Slavery and Social Death* was published in 1982, there were so few historical records on manumission methods in China that one major scholar cast doubt on whether Han slaveholders were able to manumit the enslaved they held privately. Then came the discovery in 1983 of legal texts on the subject from the Zhangjiashan archeological site in Hubei Province. The technical term for manumission, we learn, means literally "to release" or "to avoid," but the astonishing payoff is revealed in the etymology for the Chinese words relating to manumission. Barbieri-Low writes:

> The word *miǎn* 免 is cognate with the word *miǎn* 絻 "mourning clothes/ mourning hair-dress" and the word *miǎn* 娩 "to give birth," a graph whose most ancient form *pictographically shows two hands removing a crowning baby from a woman's birth canal* ... These connections clearly demonstrate, at a fundamental linguistic level, the association of manumission with death and birth. (2017: 124)

The discoveries concerning manumission are also very instructive. It appears that there was a special status between slave and commoner reserved for freed persons, indicating the usual complex bundle of rights relating to different categories of statuses. However, of even greater interest is the finding that in Han China slaves became fully manumitted only with the death of the slaveholder, and, further, that

SLAVERY IN ANCIENT ROME AND EARLY CHRISTIANITY

if he died without heirs, his most favored slave inherited his property after being freed. This was both sociologically and symbolically congruent with a culture that so vividly represented the passage to freedman status as one from the generative womb of social death to the social life of the freed.

Let me close by pointing to what is undoubtedly the most important, and best-known, case of the symbolic interpretation of death as a dynamic process generating rebirth and new life: the Christian symbolism of spiritual death and rebirth (see Patterson, 1991: Part 4; Horsley, 1998, 2004: esp. Introduction and Ch. 7; Martin, 1990; Harrill, 1995; Briggs, 1989). Jesus, the founder of Christianity, had little to say about death and rebirth. Indeed, his not infrequent references to slavery were quite conventional for his times. It was Paul, Christianity's "second founder," who did so in his transformation of the belief system of the primitive Palestinian church. Essentially, what Paul did was to drastically change the early religion from a cult based on Jesus's life and radical teachings, to a religion *about* Jesus in which the central fact of his existence was not his life but his death. Paul, unlike the colonial subject Jesus, lived and worked in major slave centers of Rome and its main slaveholding cities, most notably Corinth, re-established at Caesar's direction by freedmen and the enslaved. Drawing on the source metaphor of freedom-into-slavery held by the freedmen, who were among the most important and influential converts to the young religion, Paul's Christology was a complete and exact spiritual introjection of the metaphor that, as I and others have argued, ran as follows: mankind once lived in Edenic freedom, secure in the bosom of God; then came the Adamic fall and enslavement to sin; this led to spiritual death ("the wages of sin"); out of which the convert was redeemed (Latin *redemptionem, redemptio* = the purchase, or ransoming, of someone out of slavery), paid for by Jesus's salvific crucifixion (a death for a death); which led to the rebirth of the Christian into a new life of freedom ("For freedom Christ has set us free; stand fast therefore, and do not submit again to the yoke of slavery": Galatians 5:1). But Paul did not end the spiritual symbolic trajectory here. The freedom celebrated in Galatians was more akin to the limited, conditional freedom of the Roman freedman still obligated to his former enslaver. In his letter to the Romans (written after Galatians though placed before it in the New Testament), Paul advocated the perfect freedom to which the Christian ultimately strived. This was the freedom that came with a new, sublime form of enslavement to God. Spiritually enslaved sinners, "having been set free from sin, have become slaves of righteousness."

When you were slaves in sin, you were free in regard to righteousness. But then, what return did you get from the things of which you are now ashamed? The end of those things is death. But now that you have been set free from sin and have become slaves of God, the return you get is sanctification and its end, eternal life. For the wages of sin is death, but the free gift of God is eternal life in Christ Jesus our Lord. (Romans 6:20–23; cf. Corinthians 4:5)

Now, the notion of true freedom being enslavement to God was a common Hellenistic-cum-Roman idea in Paul's time. However, I have argued that it would in all likelihood have achieved added force by its striking congruence with the ultimate state of freedom achieved by only the most successful freedmen, that of membership in the *Lares Augusti* cult, in which the freedman attained the almighty protection of the emperor (to the point of being able to dress like a senator and sponsor popular games) through worshipful surrender to his genius.

Whether or not this final stage of the spiritual dulotic trajectory was suggested to Paul by the freedmen membership in the *Lares Augusti* cult, there can be no doubt that running through his entire Christology was the metaphor of death as a creative process culminating in enslavement to God. Paul goes so far as to argue that the believer is "always carrying in the body the death of Jesus" and that "death is at work in us."

Consider the following symbolically loaded passage, the most remarkable celebration of the symbolic force of slavery as death and the one path to liberation from it:

For if we have been united with him in a death like his, we shall certainly be united with him in a resurrection like his. We know that our old self was crucified with him so that the sinful body [literally, "body of sin"] might be destroyed, and we might no longer be enslaved to sin. For he who has died is freed from sin. But if we have died in Christ, we believe that we shall also live with him. For we know that Christ, being raised from the dead, will never die again; death no longer has dominion over him. *The death he died he died to sin*, once and for all, but the life he lives he lives to God. So you must also consider yourself dead to sin and alive to God in Christ Jesus. (Romans 6:5–11)

Can the symbolic use of death as a dynamic force be made more explicit? This was, and remains, the foundational metaphor of the Christian creed, the religion that was to fashion European civilization, which for more than a thousand years was nothing other than Christendom, the civilization that would eventually come to dominate most of the peoples and cultures of the world. It was a preternaturally powerful, two-sided metaphor, as applicable to the inner, spiritual world, as to the outer, secular life, which could as readily serve the controlling interests of the powerful, as the radical yearnings of the oppressed. And for better, and for worse, or both, its primary symbolic source, let it not be forgotten, was the metaphor of slavery as social death.

What that protean metaphor left open was the question posed by John Swanson Jacobs to the "United States governed by six hundred thousand despots" that had condoned his enslavement, prompted by his reading of the Pauline text: "Who is the God that you worship? Is he a God of slavery, or a God of liberty?" (2024 [1855]: 61).

Coda

To Christian rulers, their scribes and philosophers, it was foundational that the metaphor be interpreted in purely spiritual terms. To the oppressed and their leaders, especially the radical rebels of the Middle Ages and early modern Europe, and the slave rebels of the Americas, its exterior meaning and its source in the brute realities of serfdom and enslavement were as obvious as they were inspiring. In her splendid study of the thought and language of the Anglo-Saxon slaveholding groups, Katherine Miller (2014) found that it was patently clear that the literal slave among them was "the 'pattern' for the human soul as the slave to God. Through this metaphor, Anglo-Saxons and their Biblical and Classical antecedents sought to understand and define their relationship with the divine in terms which were rooted in their own societies." Miller dismisses the "false distinction between slave words which can be used metaphorically and those which cannot," finding that the Anglo-Saxon synonyms for slave – *wealh, esne, þræl* – were commonly used with exactly the same meaning in all contexts, and that emphasis on the distinction "ignores the fact that the spiritual sense is rooted in everyday encounters with literal slaves, and that both metaphorical and literal slaves have many features in common" (2014: 271–2). Miller's finding is one that the revolutionary preachers John Ball of later medieval England, Thomas Muntzer of early modern Germany, Nat Turner of Virginia, the radical self-liberated John Swanson Jacobs, and the slave Baptist deacon, Samuel Sharpe, who led the great 1832 slave revolt of Jamaica that helped usher in the passage of the British abolition of slavery, would all have greeted with a loud amen.

III

Slavery in the Modern World

— 7 —

SLAVERY AND SLAVE REVOLTS: THE MAROON SLAVE WARS OF JAMAICA, 1655–1739

Introduction

This chapter has three objectives. First, to undertake a detailed study of Jamaican slave revolts and marronage during the first eighty-four years of the British conquest and rule of the island. These revolts, culminating in the defeat of the British slaveholder class, constitute one of the rare, and earliest, cases in world history of a slave population successfully revolting against their oppression, resulting in the legal recognition of their independence and right to self-determination by the defeated slaveholder class. Second, an attempt will be made to explain these revolts in structural and historical terms. That is, I will isolate the specific features of the Jamaican slave system that were necessary to, and, to the extent possible, sufficient for, an explanation of these revolts. And third, on the basis of this analysis, I will propose a general hypothesis regarding the causes of all slave revolts that may provide a theoretical guide for future research on the subject.

There are six parts to the study. Part 1 examines the British conquest of the island from the Spanish in 1655 and their subsequent failure to establish a colony of settlement along lines similar to parallel developments in early colonial North America between 1655 and 1700. Part 2 examines Black marronage by the enslaved left behind by the Spanish and revolts by the newly arrived enslaved African workers. Part 3 explores growing solidarity between the maroons and rebelling slaves in their resistance against the Whites between 1700 and 1720. Part 4 delineates the perfection of guerrilla warfare by the Blacks after 1720 and their eventual victory over the British who sued for peace in 1739. Part 5, "Snatching betrayal from the jaws of victory," examines

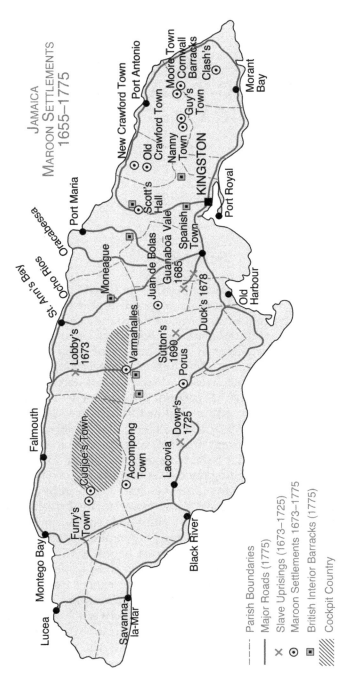

Figure 7.1 Map of Jamaica Maroon Settlements 1655–1755

the complex and still contested factors that went into the signing of the treaty of peace between the British and rebel leaders, especially Cudjoe, and the response of the disappointed slave population. Part 6, "Explaining slave revolts," is in three sections. The first section briefly probes the existential irrelevance of psychological factors in the explanation of the revolts; the second examines the question of whether these revolts are to be viewed as cases of marronage rather than genuine slave rebellions; and the third discusses the causes of slave revolts suggested by this record of resistance. We conclude with a set of hypotheses for a theory of slave revolts.

7.1: The British conquest and the failure of White settlement, 1655–1700

Few slave societies present a more impressive record of slave revolts than Jamaica. During the more than 180 years of its existence as a slave society, hardly a decade went by without a serious, large-scale revolt threatening the entire system. Between these larger efforts were numerous minor skirmishes, endless plots, individual acts of violence against the slaveholders, and other forms of resistance, all of which constantly pressed upon the White ruling class the fact that the system was a very precarious one, held together entirely by the exercise, or threat, of brute force amounting to outright genocide.

The first eighty-four years of the English occupation of the island (1655–1739) were marked by one long series of revolts, which reached a dramatic climax during the last fifteen years of this period, at the end of which the Whites, after coming close to disaster on several occasions, were forced to sue for peace and grant the rebels their freedom. It is customary to regard only these last fifteen climactic years as the so-called "First Maroon Wars." I hope to show, however, that almost all the revolts prior to 1740 were closely related and cannot meaningfully be separated from each other or from the events of the last decade and a half of the period.

Jamaica, the largest British-colonized island in the Caribbean, was captured from Spain in 1655 (as an afterthought following the failure to take San Domingue) as part of Oliver Cromwell's Grand Design on the Spanish possessions in the New World. During the more than 150 years of their occupation, the Spanish had done little to develop the island. When the British arrived, the population was estimated at no more than three thousand, of whom at least half were enslaved (Sedgwick to Whitehall, "Situation of the Island of Jamaica," CO,

1/14). (A key to the archival references can be found at the end of this chapter.)

For the first five years of the British occupation the colony remained under military rule, as the Spanish and some of their ex-slaves put up a strong guerrilla resistance (cf. Taylor, 1965 for a comprehensive, if somewhat biased, account). In 1660, when the last of the Spaniards had finally left, civil government was established and an early attempt was made at developing a colony of settlement. Attempts at populating the colony with White immigrants persisted formally until well into the eighteenth century, but a combination of factors ensured the failure of such attempts less than thirty years after the occupation. For most Europeans the climate was not the most hospitable. Worse, malaria and other fevers, endemic to the island, took a heavy toll on newcomers. Further, the disruptive presence of the buccaneers, internal political strife, and constitutional conflicts with the mother country resulted in great insecurity, which was intensified by the frequent revolts of the the enslaved and, toward the end of the seventeenth century, several destructive raids by the French fleet under Admiral Du Casse. Acts of God also played their part. The culmination of these was the famous earthquake of 1692, one of the worst in recorded history, in which two-thirds of the island's major commercial center sank beneath the sea, carrying nearly all its inhabitants with it (Anon, 1693; see also Marx, 1967).

But by far the most important set of factors leading to the failure of attempts at creating a colony of White settlers were economic. The major portion of the cultivable land of the island was rapidly monopolized by a group of land-grabbing planters who sought to establish an economic system that was quite incompatible with pioneering, small-scale settlements. By the turn of the eighteenth century, Jamaica was well on the way not only to recovery from the economic failures of the early, unsettled, small-farming period, but to a recovery based on the large-scale monocrop plantation model. African slavery was the cornerstone of this system. Against it, the small, even middle-sized, planters, depending on their own labor or those of a few slaves, could not compete. Those who were unable or unwilling to seek employment as overseers, bookkeepers, or tradesmen on the emerging large plantations had little choice but to migrate again (Patterson, 1967: 16–27, 33–51).

Between 1655 and 1661, more than 12,000 persons arrived on the island, yet, by 1662, hardly 3,600 remained. In 1696, the White population was down to fewer than 2,000, and, although this figure slowly increased in absolute terms during the eighteenth century, the ratio of Whites to Black slaves was to decline constantly, rarely exceeding 10 percent of the total population (Pitman 1917: Ch. 5; Gardner, 1873: 159).

By the second decade of the eighteenth century, the first group of successful planters had consolidated their fortunes and began to send their children to be educated in Britain; later, they themselves departed for the mother country, rarely to return to the place that was the source of their wealth (Ragatz, 1931; Patterson, 1967: 33–7). As the island approached its period of greatest prosperity, toward the end of the fourth decade of the eighteenth century, the wealthiest landowners, possessing well over three-quarters of the island's property (including the enslaved), were all absentees, living in great style in Britain, where they married into the petty aristocracy and made up the greater part of the West India lobby, the most powerful interest group in British politics at that time (Williams, 2021 [1944]: 91–7). In Jamaica, their affairs were managed, often with remarkable ineptitude – sometimes quite deliberately – by attorneys and agents who, with the few resident large-scale owners and the top echelons of the appointed officers, headed by the governor, made up the core of the local ruling class (Ragatz, 1928: Ch. 1; Patterson, 2022 [1967]: Ch. 1, sec. 3).

Politically, during the period of slavery, the island enjoyed a considerable degree of internal autonomy, having an elected House of Assembly, a governor – who was the Crown's representative in the island, and whose authority, after a long constitutional struggle, which culminated in 1728, depended largely on his strength of character and diplomatic skill – and a Council nominated by him (Whitsun, 1929; Spurdle, 1962). Whitehall, during the eighteenth century, remained a *deus ex machina*, which exercised its ultimate authority with considerable restraint so long as the colony remained His Majesty's "prizest possession."

The British legal system was imported with a few modifications to meet local needs. For the Whites, despite the gross lack of qualified legal personnel, the system worked well enough, guided as it was by the rugged individualism and democratic fervor that always, ironically, seem to characterize the elite castes of all oppressive colonial plantation systems.

For the non-White, and particularly the non-free, the legal system was a grim travesty. Traditional British law either completely neglected or, in the few cases where it obliquely touched on the topic, very clumsily handled the problem of slavery or other states of unfreedom. The local slaveholders preferred it this way. They made little attempt at formulating a slave code until the last quarter of the eighteenth century, and when they did, it was largely as an anti-abolitionist propaganda tactic and was rarely heeded in practice. For the nine-tenths of Jamaicans who made up the slave population, the slaveholder was the law. In him rested the power of life and death. Occasionally, a White person might have had to pay a fine for murdering his slave, but in the majority of such cases no legal action could be taken even to inflict the mildest penalty, since a Black person could not give evidence against any White person (Patterson, 2022 [1967]: Ch. 3; Smith, 1945).

Perhaps the most striking feature of the island during the first ninety years of British rule is the fact that it can only with difficulty be described as a society, if we take the latter term to denote, in the most general sense, a territorially based collectivity possessing some reasonably coherent and consistent system of values, norms, and beliefs. At the most, we can describe it as a society in an acute state of Durkheimian anomie. This was essentially a society of immigrants and transients – transients either longing for the day when they would have made their fortunes and returned to the mother country, or transients and forced immigrants whose sole ambition was escape from the horror of their enslavement, either through revolt or death. Unlike the slave systems of the American South or the majority of the Iberian colonies, Jamaica had no ruling class that, infused with the pioneer spirit, was committed to the social wellbeing and cultural development of their community (Pitman, 1917: 1–2; Genovese, 1961). For the resident White ruling class, the move to Jamaica was not an exodus involving a clean break with the past and visions of a glorious future and a new age of peace and prosperity, but a hasty migration motivated by greed and endured with much impatience. The sociological consequence was a shambled patchwork of social relationships which, in its excessive commitment to the sole goal of quick profits, discarded all aspects of the social institutions that are generally considered to be the basic prerequisites of normal social life: marriage, the family, education, religion (Jelly, 1826; Cundall, 1939; Long, 1774, II: 246; Mahon, 1839).

The White ruling class at least chose things this way. For the enslaved, it was a social catastrophe. They were brought in great numbers from all over the coastal belt of West Africa. In 1703, there were about 45,000 of them on the island. Fifty years later the slave population had almost tripled, to an estimated 130,000 souls. In 1800 the number had increased to 300,939, and in 1834, when the Emancipation Act was ratified, the population stood at an estimated 311,070. This high rate of increase was achieved almost entirely by the importation of fresh Africans; the estimated average annual rate of natural decrease was approximately 1.6 percent – so heavy was the mortality rate, especially during the first years of seasoning (Roberts, 1957: 36; Patterson, 2022 [1967]: Ch. 4).

The area of West Africa from which these Africans came is characterized by a considerable degree of tribal and cultural diversity. While the range of tribal provenance was wide (and even included a few odd importees from as far east as Madagascar), we have elsewhere indicated that well over two-thirds of the Africans who came to Jamaica derived from the areas now known as Ghana and Nigeria. During our period, however, the enslaved from Ghana constituted the single largest ethnic group and, for a short but not insignificant period (1700–25), the enslaved from Dahomey (then the Slave Coast) also made up a significant minority (Le Page and De Camp, 1960: Ch. 4; Patterson, 2022 [1967]: 142–4). We have elsewhere argued that the ethnohistorical data strongly suggest that, while elements of West African cultures did survive the process of enslavement (and would certainly have been most marked during our period), there was a general disintegration of the cultures of the imported Africans. Like their slaveholders' culture, but for somewhat different reasons, the Africans' beliefs, values, and ideas, not to mention the intricate structural contexts (which were of degrees of complexity varying from the loose segmentary organization of the Ibos to the formidable state of the Ashantis) within which they functioned, rapidly collapsed under the vicious impact of slavery (Patterson, 1966b).

During the first eighty-four years of the British colonization of Jamaica, then, we find this sorry sociological spectacle: a collectivity in which there were two quite distinct groups of people, both strangers to the land on which they met, both strangers to each other. Both groups were experiencing, in different ways, the dissolution of their traditional cultures. Both groups despised, distrusted, and loathed each other. Only the impulse of greed, the chains of slavery, and the crack of the cart whip kept them together. But such ingredients proved a poor social mortar. Early Jamaica was a brittle, fragile travesty of a society, which lingered during these years constantly on the brink of upheaval and revolt.

7.2: Early Black marronage and slave revolts, 1655–1700

In 1655, as their slaveholders fled under the onslaught of the invading English soldiers, fifteen hundred slaves formerly belonging to the

SLAVERY IN THE MODERN WORLD

Spaniards suddenly found themselves with a precarious though avidly grasped freedom. During the next five years, as the remnants of the Spanish settlers continued to put up their last-ditch guerrilla resistance, the British conquerors repeatedly tried to woo them to their side by offering clemency and good treatment. While a few mulattoes took up the offer, the entire population of Blacks maintained a careful distance between themselves and the strangers on the coast (Taylor, 1965: 101–2).

At first, the Blacks wandered uncertainly about the foothills of the parishes of St. Catherine and Clarendon, no doubt trying to make some sense of the situation, and at the same time devising a strategy for maintaining their freedom. Eventually, they formed themselves into three groups under elected leaders. One of these groups settled in the mountains overlooking Guanaboa Vale under a bold, astute leader called Juan Lubola (often referred to in the English records as Juan de Bolas) (Taylor, 1965: 98–9; CSP, 1661–8, no. 411). A second group established a village at Los Vermejales[1] under their leader Juan de Serras (Taylor, 1965: 99). This group eventually came to be called the Vermahalis or Vennehaly band by the British. The third group remains obscure. One writer has suggested that they took root somewhere in the valley running between the Clarendon plains and Porras (Porus).

Taking the view that, as far as Whites were concerned, the known evil was always to be preferred to the unknown, the ex-slaves continued to associate with the Spanish guerrillas scattered about the mountains. It was, however, a relationship of equals. They were not, as a conservative Jamaican historian has suggested, merely auxiliaries of the Spaniards, but independent guerrillas who associated with their former Spanish slaveholders when it suited their interests (Taylor, 1965: 100). Indeed, the Spanish guerrillas were far more dependent on the ex-slaves than the latter were on the Spanish, who relied entirely on their former slaves for their food supplies. Occasionally the guerrillas offered their vastly superior skills as mercenaries to their ex-slaveholders, but at the same time they plundered and harassed the British to their own ends quite independently, and certainly far more effectively than the Spaniards did, as the British unequivocally admitted in their dispatches.

---

[1] Los Vermejales was situated on a plateau in the mid-interior of Jamaica. Juan de Serras's band was referred to variously as the Vermejales, Vermehali, or Varmehaly Negroes. When the Blacks moved some miles to the west of the original site, they carried the name with them, and the new site later became known by the corrupted form of Vera Ma Hollis.

164

SLAVERY AND SLAVE REVOLTS

In June 1658 the Spanish guerrilla band, under their stubborn and devoted leader Ysassi, suffered a disastrous defeat at Rio Nuevo and were forced to retreat from the fort they had erected there. Not long after this, the head of the English regiment stationed at Guanaboa discovered the richly cultivated village of Lluidas Vale, and, instead of attempting to take it, sought an alliance with Lubola. The terms offered by the British were not disagreeable. In exchange for ceasing to support the Spanish, the freedom of Lubola and all his men would be recognized, as well as his right to govern his people. Realizing that the Spanish were then on their last legs, and being unprepared to risk the destruction of his two hundred acres of carefully cultivated crops (at that time the largest single source of locally grown food), Lubola agreed to the terms offered (see *JHA*, vol. 1; also CSP, 1661–8, no. 411). This, of course, spelled disaster for the Spanish guerrillas, who were now not only without their major supplier of food, but were also faced with the prospect of a British ally who knew all their secret hideouts and was more skilled in the techniques of guerrilla warfare. After this it was simply a mopping-up operation for the British soldiers. By 1660 the last of the Spanish had left.

Among the instructions given to the British commander in 1662, prior to the setting up of civil government, was an order to "give encouragements as securely you may to such Negroes, natives, and others, as shall submit to live peaceable under His Majesty's obedience and in due submission to the government of the island" (Instructions [no. 11] to Col. Doyley, 1662, *JHA*, vol. 1, Appendix). The following year, Lubola and his "Pelinco of negroes, about 150" were granted full civil rights, each man receiving thirty acres of land. Lubola was made a magistrate and his men formed into a "Black Militia" of "Lancers and archers." A few of the more adventurous even became private men of war (*JHA*, vol. 1, Appendix).

The remaining Black guerrilla bands had always viewed Lubola's alliance with the British with some suspicion. This was not allayed by his formal recognition and the remolding of his men into a Black militia. When, however, Lubola's enthusiasm for the conquerors led him to assist them in searching for, and destroying, the Blacks who continued to reject the British overtures, the latter realized that what may have begun as a slightly suspect, if understandable, act of realpolitik, had now degenerated into downright treachery. Sometime toward the end of 1663, Lubola was killed as he attempted to lead a party on the Vermejales Blacks (CSP, 1661–8, no. 1038).

Juan de Serras continued to harass the British, who made several unsuccessful attempts to dislodge him. When further attempts to negotiate with him failed, the British lost patience and, in 1670, he and all his men were declared outlaws, with a price of £30 on de Serras's head and £20 on that of all his followers. It was about this time that the term "Maroon" came to be applied to these Black guerrillas.[2]

Under pressure from the British, the group retreated to the uninhabited northeastern section of the island. The Whites were greatly relieved at their withdrawal and, since they were no longer molested by them, decided to leave them in peace. "In the course of years afterwards," a contemporary narrator informs us, "their companions were either dead or too old to guide parties to their haunts, the ways of them became utterly unknown to the white people and so they continued for many years" (Anon, n.d.). In the meantime, the newly arrived British settlers had begun to import their own slaves into the island. At first, most of these slaves came with the White migrants from Barbados and the other eastern Caribbean colonies (Patterson, 2022 [1967]: 135). Soon, however, the enslaved were coming directly from Africa. In 1662 there were about 550 Blacks on the island. Two years later, there were 8,000. During the brief period in which anything like a serious attempt at a White colony of settlement was under way, the slave population, as one would expect, grew relatively slowly, there being only 9,500 slaves in 1673. Twenty years later, however, that population had quadrupled and, as we have noted above, there were an estimated 45,000 slaves on the island in 1703.

For this sudden influx of Africans, the still-unsettled Whites were quite ill-prepared. The "pioneer" colonial system they sought to erect would soon collapse under the combined strain of land monopoly and African slave labor. There was the more immediate problem, however, of how to control the newly imported slaves.

In 1673, the first blow was struck by the enslaved. In the thinly peopled parish of St. Ann, two hundred slaves belonging to Major Sebly's plantation, nearly all of whom were Coromantee,[3] killed their enslaver and about thirteen other Whites; they then went on to plunder several smaller estates in the neighborhood, procuring all the arms and ammunition they could lay their hands on (Anon, n.d.). By the time the Whites had mustered a party, the rebels had all retreated to secure positions in the mountains around the borders of Clarendon,

---

[2] See Anon, n.d. The term "Maroon" is derived from the Spanish *cimarron*, meaning fugitive, wild, or "unruly," later "runaway slave." See Cassidy, 1961.

[3] The term "Coromantee" or "Coromantyn" was used by the Jamaican planters to describe the enslaved from the Gold Coast, more particularly, the enslaved of Akan-speaking origin.

St. Elizabeth, and St. Ann. The first party of Whites that went after them was "nearly destroyed," and this "not only discouraged other parties from going against them but also encouraged many other Negroes to rise, throw off their chains and join up with them" (Anon, n.d.). These groups of rebels formed the nucleus of what later became known as the Leeward band of Maroons.[4]

Five years after this uprising, in 1678, another serious rebellion took place. One Sunday afternoon, the enslaved on Captain Ducke's plantation, situated only four miles from the capital, St. Jago, noticing that the river that ran between the plantation and the town had risen so high that it appeared impassable, decided to seize the opportunity for freedom. The Whites on the estate were attacked, Major Ducke seriously wounded, and his wife killed. A Black traitor swam the river and gave the alarm in St. Jago, whereupon a troop of horse, after crossing the river with some difficulty, counterattacked. Some of the rebels were killed, and those who were taken prisoner were "put to exemplary violent deaths" (Barham, 1722).[5]

In 1685–6, there were several revolts, the participants of which joined with the growing bands of rebels encamped in the leeward part of the island. In early August 1685, all the enslaved belonging to a widow, Mrs. Grey, at Guanaboa rose in rebellion, along with those from four neighboring plantations, altogether making a party of about 150. They seized all the arms on Grey's estate, then attacked another plantation, where they killed one White and wounded another. A detachment of seventy soldiers was beaten off by the rebels, who then sought the refuge of the hills. Once out of the range of the Whites, they divided themselves into "2 or 3 parties." One party consisted of the "stoutest and best armed," who marched northward across the mountainous backbone of the island until they reached St. Ann. Pursued by the Whites, they suddenly changed course and headed east toward the parish of St. Mary, killing several Whites and destroying their settlements on the way. In the end, of the 150 slaves who rebelled, seven were killed in battle, thirty were captured, and fifty surrendered. The rest remained at large and were unsuccessfully hunted by Captain Davis and his party of imported Indian trackers. By September 1685, however, all the parties out against the rebels were recalled and paid off (Molesworth, 1685–8; CSP, 1685–8, nos.

---

[4] Not the revolt of 1690, as suggested by Dallas (1803, I: 26) or Hart (1950).
[5] Ducke was Attorney General of Jamaica in 1671 and a Member of Assembly for St. Catherine in 1679. When the estate was probated upon his death in 1683, there were ninety slaves, valued at £1,367. The total value of the estate was £2,020.52 (see Feurtado, 1896).

SLAVERY IN THE MODERN WORLD

339–72). This may have been the same rebellion led by the slave called Cuffee (Cofi: an Akan or "Coromantee" name). If so, they continued to harass the Whites until April 1686, growing each day "more formidable than ever." In November 1685, a £10 reward was offered for Cuffee and £5 for each of the "chiefest five others." When Cuffee was killed in April 1686, the number of parties out against them "were reduced to three" (CSP, 1685–8, nos. 445, 560, 623).

By this time, the different rebel bands had moved farther to the east, eventually taking up residence in the parish of St. George. Here they settled in three villages formed on the basis of tribal differences (Molesworth, 1685–8; CSP, 1685–8, nos. 869, 883). While roaming the woods about the border of St. George and St. Mary, the rebel bands came upon another strange group of fugitives of whom no one had yet heard. Sometime between 1669 and 1670 a slave ship with an unusual cargo of enslaved from Madagascar was wrecked near Morant Point at the eastern tip of the island. Those slaves who somehow managed to reach shore fled to the hills and, later, in association with several runaways, set up a cluster of villages in the more remote areas of the eastern hinterlands (CSP, 1685–8, no. 883). Joined now by the rebels formerly under Cuffee and possibly the parties from Guanaboa, they made up a formidable band, which often daringly descended in raiding parties on the plantations on the coastal plains. Three parties of Whites were constantly out against them, scouring the parishes of St. George, St. Thomas, and St. Mary, but their failure to check the onslaught of the rebels proved "so discouraging to the poorer sort of people, that those of St. George," according to the governor, "unless relieved, are prepared to desert their settlements" (CSP, 1685–8, no. 883). The governor considered the situation sufficiently grave to necessitate the enforcement of martial law, and stepped up the number and size of the parties. But they continued to have little success (CSP, 1685–8, nos. 965, 1021, 543, 1286).

Four years later a new uprising broke out. In July 1690, four hundred slaves, again mainly from the Gold Coast, belonging to Sutton's plantation in the parish of Clarendon, disposed of the person in charge of stores and, after seizing all the arms they could carry, proceeded to the next estate, where they killed the White overseer and set the house afire. The troops were called out, and twelve of the rebels were killed in the ensuing engagement. In the course of the following month, sixty women and children and ten men surrendered. With 318 of them still at large, however, the Governor (Inchiquin) feared "that [it] will be very dangerous to the mountain plantations." This group of rebels eventually joined ranks with the Leeward gang

168

SLAVERY AND SLAVE REVOLTS

already established in the mountains "and greatly strengthened their party, having good arms and plenty of ammunition" (Inchiquin to Lords, CO 138/7). Yet another rebellion took place in 1696 on the estate of Captain Herring, who was away at the time.[6] His wife and some of his children died in the uprising, and all the enslaved, along with several more from neighboring estates, went off to join the Leeward group (Anon, n.d.).

7.3: Black solidarity between enslaved rebels and maroons, 1700–1720

It is now time to take up the progress of the original group of former Spanish Black rebels, now well established in their maroon settlements. During the last thirty years or so of the seventeenth century, little had been heard of them. Runaway slaves who had made the mistake of seeking refuge with them were often treated so badly that the unfortunate fugitives sometimes fled back to their slaveholders or, when they could, joined ranks with other, smaller bands of runaways. At the commencement of the eighteenth century, however, the former Spanish-enslaved group had a radical change of policy. This change was induced partly by the successes of the rebels during the past three decades, and partly by their shortage of women, arms, and certain other basic necessities, such as salt and meat. They therefore made contact with the rebel bands that had established themselves in their part of the island and, at the same time, started to treat runaways more hospitably, often using the latter as guides when they raided the plantation stores of the Whites. At this time, they were settled in the hills between the north and southeastern parts of the island. In addition to several scattered villages, there was a sizable town of about three hundred people with one hundred acres of land, "well planted in provisions" (Anon, n.d.).

Between August and September of 1702, four parties were out searching for the rebel bands. Eventually, one of these parties, consisting of more than twenty soldiers, came upon the main rebel town, and a battle was fought that lasted for nearly six hours. The defenders of the rebel town boldly resisted the soldiers and, in the words of the governor, "faced our men so long as they had ammunition." When their

---

[6] Julines Herring of St. Elizabeth, whose estate was probated in 1690. There were 46 slaves at his death, 25 males and 21 females. The estate was valued at £1,274.5, including the enslaved, valued at £716 (see Centre for the Study of the Legacies of British Slavery, UCL database).

SLAVERY IN THE MODERN WORLD

limited stock of ammunition ran out, they were obliged to retreat, leaving three of the Whites wounded. Several of the rebels were killed and a few taken prisoner. The settlement was burned. A party of Whites was posted there, while the remaining three parties continued to pursue the rebels. "I take 'this thing',," commented the governor in his report on the matter, "to be of as much consequence as any I can think of at present" (Beckford to Lords, CSP, 1702, nos. 912, 928).

"This thing" became of even greater consequence in the ensuing months. So serious, in fact, that by the following January rather desperate underhand measures were being resorted to: Captain Codler, a leader of one of the White posses, was known to have entertained the wife of Bulley, one of the rebel leaders (under what circumstances we do not know) in a vain attempt at enticing the woman to betray her husband (CSP, 1703, no. 203).

While the Windward rebels continued to harass the Whites, another group of Coromantee slaves rebelled. Thirty of them "attacked two or three places, burnt only one house and wounded one man." Twelve were taken or killed and the rest made their escape to the hills, leaving the Whites "more apprehensive of some bloody design from them than any other enemy," which was no mean tribute, in view of the fact that the War of the Spanish Succession was then being waged and the islands were open game for French warships (CSP, 1704–5, no. 484).

In the meantime, the Leeward group of rebels was involved in some internecine disputes. Sometime not long before 1720, a Madagascan slave had led an uprising on Downs's plantation. With the enslaved from the plantation of his former enslaver, the Madagascan established a rebel camp in the mountains behind Deans Valley, where he augmented the number of his group by actively encouraging the enslaved on nearby plantations to run away and join him. He was, however, unable to hit it off with the main band of Leeward rebels under Cudjoe, which was encamped a little higher up. A power struggle ensued between the two leaders, and after several "bloody battles," the Madagascan was slain and his party incorporated with Cudjoe's ("Cudjoe's Fidelity," 1739).

In 1722 the resistance movement entered a new, critical phase. Since all available lands on the fertile southern coastal plains were taken up, the planters began to open up the area around the northeastern coast. These new estates cut off the communications of the Windward rebels from the coast, making the procurement of vital necessities even more difficult. To prevent further White expansion, the new settlements were systematically plundered, "murders were daily committed, plantations burnt and deserted, every person settled

170

near the mountains in dread both of the Rebels and mutinies in their own Plantations" (Anon, n.d.).

Let us briefly take stock of the situation in the mid-1720s, the time that is traditionally regarded as the formal commencement of the "First Maroon War." There were two main bands of rebels: the Leeward band, found in the precipitous areas near the center of the island, and the Windward, or northeastern, band. Each band was divided into several settlements centered on a main town or village and both were well organized.

At about this time the Leeward band formally elected a chief called Cudjoe, "a bold, skillful and enterprising man," remarkably adept at the techniques of guerrilla warfare. He was a short, stocky, powerfully built man with a humped back. On the occasion of his celebrated confrontation with the Whites who had come to his camp to sue for peace, he was dressed in knee-length drawers, an old ragged coat, and a rimless hat, and carried, on his right side, a cow's horn of powder and a bag of shots, and, on his left, a broad, sheathed machete, which dangled from a strap slung around his shoulder. His black skin, like those of his followers, was tinted red by the bauxite-rich soil found in the part of the island that he controlled (Dallas, 1803, I: 54).

Not all aspects of Cudjoe's character were, however, without blemish. He could be ruthless, even brutal, to his own men and, at times, unnecessarily selfish in his dealings with fellow guerrilla fighters. He was extremely ambivalent toward White people. He boldly resisted them as long as they sought to subdue him by the use of brute force and was generally highly suspicious of them. He was, however, all too easily seduced by their call for peace and friendship, and, as we will see, the account of his extraordinary behavior when he finally confronted the Whites who had come to negotiate is extremely puzzling (Dallas, 1803, I: 55–6; Anon, n.d.). These accounts were, of course, coming from White observers and they may well have misunderstood his mannerisms, or the cultural context of his gestures.

Unfortunately, we do not know a great deal about the leaders immediately under Cudjoe's command, appointed by him to lead the outlying villages. Two of these were his brothers, Accompong and Johnny, and the other two captains were Cuffee and Quao. From their names, it is clear that whatever the tribal composition of the followers, the leadership of the Leeward band was formed almost entirely of Coromantee slaves of originally Akan-speaking stock.[7]

---

[7] The names of the leading rebels of the Leeward group were: Captains Cudjoe, Accompong, Johnny, Cuffee, and Quao; in the Windward group the leading figures were:

SLAVERY IN THE MODERN WORLD

At the head of the main settlement of the Windward band – Nanny Town – was Cuffee, who was as skillful and shrewd a leader as Cudjoe, but, unlike the latter, both he and his successors, especially Quao, seem to have been more psychologically liberated in their attitude toward the White planters. Cuffee ruled his band of three hundred or so men with iron discipline, distinguishing himself from the rest by wearing a silver-laid hat and a small sword. All defectors and other delinquents in the group were punished by the gun (Sana, alias Ned, 1733).

There were many other leaders who attained distinction during the revolts. One of the most important was Kishee, "a great commander" of one of the northeastern groups who repeatedly outmaneuvered the Whites in the region of the Cotterwoods. He was eventually killed by a Black traitor called Scipio (*JHA*, vol. 3: 121).

The most legendary character of the wars, however, was Nanny, on whom, unfortunately, little is known positively. We know that she was the chief sorcerer or obeah woman of the main group of Windward rebels, and in this role exercised considerable influence over them. The Whites dreaded her and when, in 1733, she was killed by a slave, Cuffee, they thankfully rewarded him for his deed. Nanny, who gave her name to the main rebel town, now exists more in legend than in fact, but there can be no doubt that she existed and that the role she played tactically and psychologically – not only in boosting morale but in maintaining loyalty by her highly sanctioned oaths of secrecy – was of tremendous value (*JHA*, vol. 3: 121).[8]

Behind Nanny Town was another relatively large village called Guy's Town, after the name of its leader. It was well planted, and contained about two hundred well-armed men, and even more women and children. The rebels of this village tended to play a passive role during the war, fighting mainly to defend their passes. Apart from their usual settlements, the rebels had patches of eddoes, plantains, and yams scattered in remote areas over the countryside, which they used only during periods of retreat and emergency. Some of the bands also had a sexually segregated pattern of settlement, which ensured the protection of their womenfolk and children from the savagery of the White raiding parties (*JHA*, vol. 3: 62).

The rebels relied not only on their guerrilla skills in compensating for the vastly superior weaponry of the Whites, but also on a sophisticated intelligence system in which many of the enslaved still on the

Captains Cuffee, Kishee, and Quao. All, except Johnny, are names frequently found on the Gold Coast (now Ghana), especially among the Akan-speaking peoples.

[8] Nanny is now a national hero of Jamaica. On the surviving legend of Nanny among twentieth-century maroons, see Williams, 1938.

plantations functioned, providing the rebels with information about the plans of the Whites. A committee of the House of Assembly commented despairingly in 1733 that the rebels "are as well acquainted with our designs as we ourselves" (*JHA.*, vol. 3: 210; cf. also Dallas, 1803, I: 34). Many other slaves, in addition, provided the rebels with ammunition and sometimes even harbored them on the estates. The rebels also took full advantage of the dependence of the Whites on their enslaved in their campaigns. In one case, a large party of "baggage Negroes" was encouraged to mutiny and desert with all their provisions by the two Coromantee interpreters who were accompanying the party (*JHA*, vol. 3: 155).

7.4: Toward victory:
The defeat of the British slaveholder class, 1720–1739

In the mid-1720s, the two main parties together "amounted to some thousands," the Windward group being "the most numerous," and not, as is commonly believed, the Leeward group (Anon, n.d.). Regarding the tribal origins of the rebels, we do not, of course, know where the original band of Spanish ex-slaves came from, although the fact that ex-slaves from the Gold Coast eventually absorbed them would suggest that they too were from this area. The great majority of the rebels during the British era were Coromantee or Akan-speaking slaves from the Gold Coast. Another important group were also the Papaws, or the enslaved from the Slave Coast (now Dahomey). Ashworth, one of the White commanders, in answering the charge against him that he maliciously refused to support Sambo, the Black commander of one of the White parties, admitted that his opinion of the latter was lowered by the fact that Sambo, a Creole, could speak neither Coromantee nor Papaw (*JHA*, vol. 3: 158). It is significant that the two major groups of rebels came from the areas of the Guinea Coast where the great West African states of Ashanti and Dahomey were, at that time, at the height of their imperial expansion (cf. Panikkar, 1963, esp. Ch. 8; Claridge, 1964: vol. 1).

The situation, from the White viewpoint, became most critical in 1730 after repeated attempts at subduing the rebels had failed, and the rebels had become daily more bold and numerous. In June of that year, Governor Robert Hunter told the House:

> The Slaves in rebellion, from the increase of their numbers by the late desertions from several settlements, or from the bad success of common

SLAVERY IN THE MODERN WORLD

parties, are grown to that height of insolence that your frontiers that are no longer in any sort of security, must be deserted, and then the danger must spread and come nearer if not prevented. (1730–4: 708)

In the same address the governor told of the humiliating defeat and running away of a "grand party, consisting of 95 shots and 22 baggage Negroes, chiefly volunteers and detached men from the militia," when they had tried to take the main rebel settlement.

Panic soon began to set in among the White population. It was widely rumored that the rebels had communicated with the governor of the Spanish colony, of "Carcas," or "Cracas," offering to hand over the island to Spain when they had taken it over, on condition that the Spaniards guaranteed their freedom, a rumor that was not entirely without foundation (Tello, 1730; Quarrell, 1730).[9] Fear of the rebels largely accounted for a marked decline in the White population during this period, although the brutal treatment of indentured servants by their enslavers, in addition to the "low and languishing" state of the economy (due partly to severe drought and two recent hurricanes), was also responsible (Hunter, 1730–4: 11–12). In response to the dismal picture of the colony painted by the governor, the British government sent two regiments of foot soldiers to the island from Gibraltar (CO, 137/19, f. 19). Another large party was sent out from Port Antonio against the Windward rebels, but even before they had set out on their mission, the governor expressed grave doubts about what they could achieve, in view of the incompetence of the commanding officers (CO, 137, f. 17). His fears were certainly not groundless, for the party was thoroughly routed by the rebels, and one of the commanding officers was later court-martialed (CO, 137, f. 30).

In November 1731, yet another large party set out against the rebels. At last the Whites achieved some success. One of the villages was taken and burned after the inhabitants had abandoned it (CO, 137, f. 108). But the success was short-lived. Captain Thomas Peters, in command of the country party, withdrew a few days after taking the village. Whether this withdrawal was due to a counterattack by the rebels or just plain stupidity on Peters's part is unclear, but he was ordered to retake the town and failed to do so (*JHA*, vol. 3: 43). On January 4, 1732, the governor informed an emergency meeting of the legislature of the "news of the bad success of the parties sent out against the slaves in rebellion on the north side of the island," and

---

[9] "Carcas," or "Cracas," seems to be, from supporting evidence, a mistaken reference to Cuba, although Venezuela cannot be ruled out. See "Letter to James Knight. An Account of the Origins and Progress of the Revolted Negroes," C. E. Long Papers, 12431, BM.

SLAVERY AND SLAVE REVOLTS

of his fears of a general uprising (CO, 137, ff. 46–7). Knowing well about the lack of discipline and foresight – even in matters so grave – of the local Whites, he did not mince his words in his assessment of the dangerous situation they were in:

> There never was a point of time which more required your attention to the safety of this island than at present; your slaves in rebellion, animated by their success, and others (as it is reported) ready to join them on the first favourable opportunity, your militia very insignificant, the daily decrease of the numbers of your white people and increase of the rebel slaves; these circumstances must convince you of the necessity of entering upon more solid measures than have been hitherto resolved upon for your security; all former attempts against these slaves having been either unsuccessful or to very little purpose. (CO, 137, f. 19)

The governor passed on to the Assembly a suggestion made by the British government that a negotiated settlement be arrived at with the rebels, "by which they are to agree to be transported to some of the Bahama islands," but no one took that seriously. So great was the fear of the rebels and the inability of the Whites to resist them that a proposal by the governor to disband and settle the soldiers on favorable terms in the northeastern section of the island was tepidly received by them (CO, 137, ff. 47, 57). Since the defeat of the party in the early part of January 1731, numerous slaves had been encouraged to desert their slaveholders and join the rebels, a matter that was of increasing concern to the Whites. In addition, many of the "baggage Negroes" and Black-shots deserted to the side of the rebels, taking arms and baggage with them (see Letter to Lords, CO 137/20, ff. 47, 54, 67). An attempt to halt this trend by offering freedom to every slave who killed or brought in a rebel met with little success (*JHA*, vol. 3: 51).

In March 1732, two large parties set out against both bands of rebels. One of them, consisting of ninety-three armed Blacks and five White overseers, in addition to four columns of soldiers and twenty-eight "baggage Negroes," marched on the south side of the island against the Leeward band. The other party, consisting of 86 Whites, 131 armed Blacks, and 61 "baggage Negroes," marched from Port Antonio against the Windward group of rebels (CO, 137/20, f. 63; *JHA*, vol. 3: 77). The parties seemed to have met initially with some success, as three of the main settlements of the rebels, including Nanny Town, were taken. However, the counterattacks of the rebels, combined with "the desertion and backwardness of the baggage slaves," the incompetence of the White commanding officers (one of whom, Leo, was killed; the other, Peters, was later recalled, "having manifestly misbehaved himself"), the extremely heavy rainfall during the engagement, and the exhausted state of the island's treasury, not to mention the general scarcity of currency – the last an endemic economic problem – meant that these successes could not be followed up (*JHA*, vol. 3: 77, 81). Four parties of Blacks were sent out against the rebels, one of them under the most competent of the commanding officers in the service of the Whites, the Black freedman called, appropriately, Sambo (*JHA*, vol. 3: 99). However, in spite of the offer of freedom and spoils to the enslaved in the party, they met with little success, taking only one of the plantain walks of the rebels. One source of failure was the high desertion rate of the Blacks, which at one time became so serious that special guards had to be set up to cut them off (*JHA*, vol. 3: 81–2).

After the fall of Nanny Town, the main group of Windward rebels retreated toward Carrion Crow Hill, where they sought refuge with the Guy's Town group. Others scattered in small parties in the region of the Cotterwoods (Sana, 1733). Meanwhile, the main group of Leeward rebels set up a new town west of the recently destroyed one, in the parish of St. James. In November 1732 they suffered another setback when Whiles Town, a village not far from the main town, was taken by the Whites, who started to make plans to set up a permanent base there (*JHA*, vol. 3: 104). Early in 1733, the dislodged Windward rebels reorganized themselves and, under Kissey's brilliant leadership, retook Nanny Town. Morrison and Ashworth, the White commanders holding the town, had intelligence of the intended counterattack, but were so outclassed by the rebels that the knowledge was of little use to them (CO, 137/20, f. 120; *JHA*, vol. 3: 122, 154).

Perhaps the most impressive display of guerrilla warfare by the rebels was the second battle of Nanny Town, when they trounced the party sent out to retake it. In local terms this party was a formidable force. There were one hundred trained soldiers, taken from the two regiments sent from Gibraltar, a hundred local Whites, and two hundred seamen from a warship then stationed at the island (Hunter to Lords, CO, 137/20, f. 165). The party first divided itself into two divisions. The local Whites made up one of these, and they were sent up to Carrion Crow hill, above Nanny Town, to cut the rebels off from the rear. They did not get very far. On the way, they were ambushed by the rebels, and the entire division scrambled frantically back to Port Antonio without firing a shot.

The other division, which was supposed to have led the attack, placed the sailors at the front and the independent soldiers in the

176

rear, an arrangement that in no way pleased the sailors. Two miles away from Nanny Town, they were attacked by the rebels; after several skirmishes in which they were utterly outclassed, the sailors fell into a panic and a large number of them fled to the soldiers in the rear with tall tales about the massacre of most of the commanding officers. When, therefore, reinforcements were urgently requested from the front, many of the soldiers refused to budge. In any event, those who sought to obey the order were unable to, since their Black guide suddenly refused to show them the way through the woods. A fracas ensued in which the hysterical sailors turned on their own provisions and plundered them, possibly to ensure that they would not be able to carry out a sustained engagement against the dreaded guerrillas. Eventually, the entire party had to retreat in confusion. The guide who refused to lead the soldiers was later made a scapegoat, court-martialed, and shot (Williams, 1733; Swanton, c. 1733).

Conditions on the island had now grown really desperate for the planter caste. In August 1733, the rebels took possession of Hobby's plantation and easily repelled the parties sent out to relieve it (*JHA*, vol. 3: 195–6, 207). A planter wrote home to England in December 1733: "We are in terrible circumstances in respect to the rebellious Negroes, they got the better of all our partys, our men are quite despirited and dare not look them in the face in the Open Ground or in Equal Numbers" ("A Planter," 1733). That same month Governor Hunter (1733–4) broke another "terrible" piece of news to the British government. Way over in Hanover parish, at the western end of the island, another group of Blacks had risen in rebellion where the Whites "had least expected it." The revolt of the Blacks was now being waged at both extremities of the island, as well as in the center (CO, 137/21, ff. 16–17).

The war dragged on during 1734, with the planters getting the worst of almost all engagements. By now, however, "the greatest danger" for them was the remarkable number of the enslaved who were abandoning the plantations in order to join ranks with the main rebel bands or to set up their own guerrilla groups. In February alone, twenty-two enslaved "pulled foot" from Port Antonio, while, in St. Thomas, forty "able Coromantines" did the same (CO, 137/21, f. 44). Encouraged by their successes and by the moral and active support of the enslaved population in their area, the Windward rebels now resumed the initiative in the struggle. The letters to Britain took on a new tone of even greater apprehension. One planter wrote in March:

The Rebellious Negroes openly appear in Arms and are daily Increasing. An observer wrote "... they have already taken possession of three Plantations within eight miles of Port Antonio by which means they Cutt off any Communications between that Harbour by Land ... They have also attacked a place called the Breast Work where Several Men Armed were lodged to cover the workmen. (Extract, 1734, CO, 137/21, f. 57)

John Ayscough became governor after Robert Hunter's death in March 1734, and continued to lead the Whites' defenses as best he could, although he had grave doubts concerning the efficacy of the present methods employed against the rebels. Nonetheless, the Whites persevered, and on the twentieth of April two large parties attacked the main town of the Windward rebels. After a battle lasting five days, in which eighty members of the White party were killed, Nanny Town was recaptured by the Whites (Ayscough to Lords, 1734, CO, 137/21, ff. 174–5). This victory, however, had been won at such great cost, and its implications were so slight, that the news was received with little enthusiasm by the White population. According to Ayscough, "the country had been at the Expense of one hundred thousand pounds within these five years and no Benefit received or relief had." He reported also that many of the "Black shots" recruited by the Whites were in communication with the rebels and were supplying them with arms. Later in the year, he finally discharged all the parties. In October martial law was once more declared.

The Windward rebels, after retreating from their main town for the second time, now split up into two parties. In 1735, one of these, consisting of about three hundred men, women, and children, made an epic march of more than one hundred miles across the densely wooded and precipitous mountain ranges of the island in order to join ranks with Cudjoe's Leeward band. The Whites received intelligence of the march and hastily sent out parties to "oppose, disperse or destroy them," but the marchers "fought and forced their way on" (CO, 137/22, f. 37; Anon, n.d.). The march, apart from being a superb tactical maneuver, also paid certain psychological dividends in that the planters were left completely mystified and outwitted by it. "It is Supposed and feared," wrote Henry Cunningham, the new governor; "they are Settling themselves in some Strong fastness and when that is done, will begin their ravages Again, in Such parts of the Island, as may be of more Mischievous Consequences than they have hitherto attempted" (CO, 137/ 22, f. 40).

There is some uncertainty concerning what exactly transpired when the main body of Windward rebels met Cudjoe and his band. From

SLAVERY AND SLAVE REVOLTS

all available sources, it would appear that Cudjoe received them anything but warmly. His response was a bitter blow for the Windward
refugees. Cudjoe's reasons for his coolness, while understandable,
were very revealing. First, he claimed that he did not have enough
provisions for both parties. Second:

> He blamed them for great indiscretion in their conduct before the
> parties were sent against them and told them it was a rule with him
> always not to provoke the white people unless forced to it and showed
> them several graves where he said people were buried whom he had
> executed for murdering white men contrary to his orders and said their
> barbarous and unreasonable cruelty and insolence to the white people
> was the cause of their fitting out parties who would in time destroy
> them all. (Anon, n.d.)

Even allowing for the patronizing esteem in which the chronicler, like
most of the Whites after the war, held Cudjoe, which may have over-
emphasized his wariness and respectful attitude toward the Whites,
this alleged response is basically not inconsistent with the general
pattern of the man's character or the way in which he conducted the
war, which, in contrast to the tactics of the Windward rebels, was
essentially defensive.

Cudjoe's third reason, according to the above source, for rejecting
an alliance with the Windward rebels was the fact that as absolute
master of his own party he was not prepared to incorporate within his
domain independent companies who held allegiance to other leaders.
However, he did offer them temporary accommodation – for several
months, it would appear – until they were in a position to return to
their former quarters (Dallas, 1803, I: 27; note, however, that Dallas
erred in the date of this march).

At the beginning of 1736 there were three main rebel towns (Gregory
to Lords, CO, 137/22, f. 54). One was in St. George's parish, which
in the early part of the year was the main abode of the remaining
Windward rebels; another in St. Elizabeth under Accompong; and
the third in St. James under Cudjoe. The largest of these towns was
"supposed to contain in the whole about one thousand men, women
and children" (Gregory to Lords, CO, 137/22, f. 54). "Upwards
of three hundred," who had not joined the main settlements, were
scattered in small groups in the vicinity of the three great camps.
Presumably, Cudjoe's settlement in St. James was the largest party,
since it attracted most attention during the first part of the year. The
fact, too, that it was now accommodating the Windward refugees
would have swelled the numbers to the size mentioned.

179

In the latter half of 1736 the rebels remained fairly quiet, especially during the last four months, but so much had the planters despaired of ever defeating them that they were content to let sleeping dogs lie. Governor John Gregory wrote that he was at a loss to explain the relative quiet among the rebels, for "the Success of our Partys has not been so considerable, nor their numbers so much lessened" (Gregory to Lords, CO, 137/22, f. 110). Clearly, the Windward rebels at Cudjoe's camp were respecting his wishes, while those remaining in the northeast were biding their time as they recouped their losses and waited for the right opportunity to retake their beloved Nanny Town. Cudjoe as usual was playing his defensive game. All this, combined with the general view of the Whites, that "it would be advisable not to disturb them unless we could do it with some visible prospect of Success," accounted for the relative calm of the last months of 1736.

Figure 7.2 "Old Cudjoe making peace." Illustration from *The History of the Maroons* (1803) by Robert Charles Dallas, showing the Maroon leader Cudjoe. Engravers E. and J. Smith, after E. Smith

But it may have been the proverbial calm before the storm. The band of Windward refugees who had sought refuge with Cudjoe decided that they had had enough of his grudging hospitality and, in May 1737, set out on the grueling march back home to recover their lands. Gregory "had some intelligence of their design" but was unable to exploit it, for although he "took all precaution ... to prevent it ... their march was so silent and expeditious, and [his] orders so ill executed that ... [they] did not succeed" (Gregory to Lords, CO, 137/22, f. 141). Having failed to stop them, Gregory decided that the Whites had better swallow their pride and sue for peace. He made this suggestion to the Assembly, but they would have none of it. Clearly, with their usual lack of foresight, the Whites had been lulled into a false sense of security by the relative inactivity of recent months. However, during the course of that year and the one that followed – 1738 – the Windward rebels began to reassert their claims to both freedom and land in the form of raids, ambushes, and strong defenses of their positions, the pattern and outcome of which were strikingly similar to those of previous years. The White population gradually came around to Gregory's view that nothing could be gained in the battle bush and that a treaty appeared to be the only way of settling the matter.

Figure 7.3 Photograph of the town of Accompong in the parish of St. Elizabeth, Jamaica, in the early 20th century

SLAVERY IN THE MODERN WORLD

7.5: Snatching betrayal from the jaws of victory: Cudjoe and the Treaty of 1739

In February 1739, Colonel Guthrie, an able, popular, planter commander who had long been pressing for negotiations, was finally given the go-ahead by the governor, Edward Trelawny. After surviving a few ambushes in which several men were lost, Guthrie and a party of the Independent Company under Captain Sadler finally contacted one of Cudjoe's commanders. The Whites did everything to allay the strong suspicion of the rebels. Not only did they offer gifts and hostages, but the governor himself made the long and arduous march to a place hardly twenty miles from the main Maroon town to make himself available for the immediate ratification of the proposed treaty (Anon, n.d.). At a well-chosen defile, selected by the Maroons, Cudjoe finally met Guthrie under the protective eyes of the former's armed, hidden sentries. Cudjoe approached Guthrie, shook hands and, it is claimed, "threw himself to the ground, embracing Guthrie's legs, kissing his feet, and asking his pardon. He seemed to have lost all his ferocity, and to have become humbly penitent and abject. The rest of the Maroons, following the example of their chief, prostrated themselves, and expressed the most unbounded joy at the sincerity shown on the side of the white people" (Dallas, 1803, I: 56; Anon, n.d.).

On March 1, 1739, a fifteen-point peace treaty was signed between the Leeward Maroons and the Whites (see Appendix A at the end of this chapter). The treaty ensured the liberty and freedom of Cudjoe and all his followers and their right of ownership of all lands in the vicinity of their towns to the amount of fifteen hundred acres. They were to remain in the area but could hunt wild hogs wherever they wished, except within three miles of any White settlement. Runaway slaves who had joined Cudjoe within the previous two years were offered the choice of returning to their slaveholders with full pardon and indemnity or of remaining with the Maroons. Further, the former rebels, now free Maroons, were at liberty to sell their cash provisions in the markets of neighboring towns as long as licenses were obtained. If their rights were infringed by any White person they could apply to any commanding officer or magistrate for justice; likewise, any Maroon who injured a White person had to be delivered to the White authorities for trial.

During their lifetime, Cudjoe and all his successors were given full powers to punish all offenders within their camp, except those guilty of murder. To facilitate communication and "friendly correspondence,"

182

the Maroons were required to cut roads between their towns and the coastal settlements of the planters, and two White men, appointed by the governor, were to reside among them constantly.

Apart from the recognition of their freedom and land rights, however, perhaps the most important parts of the treaty were those clauses that required the Leeward Maroons to assist the Whites in repelling not only external enemies, but "to take, kill, suppress, or destroy . . . all rebels wheresoever they be unless they submit to the same terms"; and further, that all future runaways who sought refuge among them or were captured by them were to be returned to the Whites, for which service the Maroons were to be compensated.

The implications of the treaty as a whole, but particularly of the last two clauses, were not lost on all of Cudjoe's followers, nor on the enslaved population. They were extremely embittered by what they could only interpret as a completely unnecessary sellout. In the act of ratifying his own freedom, Cudjoe had sealed the fate of future freedom-fighters, for with the Maroons on the side of the Whites, no slave could hope to escape the tyranny of his slaveholder, either by running away or by rebellion.

While the Whites rejoiced at the way they had succeeded in doing, in a single act of negotiation, what years of fighting had failed to accomplish, disgruntled and outraged elements from among both Cudjoe's camp and the enslaved population began to make plans for a last-ditch stand that would nullify the effects of the treaty. The first move was made by several of Cudjoe's "chief men," who got in touch with the enslaved on neighboring plantations and incited them to revolt ("Cudjoe's Fidelity," 1739). The plot was nipped in the bud by Cudjoe, who arrested the four ringleaders and sent them to the governor. They were tried, two of them were condemned to death, and the other two were ordered to be transported. The governor, however, as an act of goodwill, pardoned them and returned them to Cudjoe. But Cudjoe would have none of it. At least it could be said of him that he was a man of his word, however contemptible that word. He hanged the two who were condemned to death and sent the other two back to the governor, insisting that they be transported. The governor granted his request and, like the rest of the White population, was doubtless very impressed with his zealous new ally.

The enslaved population, however, was not prepared to take the treaty lying down. A mood of restlessness ran like a quake through it. They complained, with cutting irony, that freedom had been granted to those who had rebelled, while the mass of the loyal continued to suffer enslavement. More directly, they viewed with great alarm

SLAVERY IN THE MODERN WORLD

the elimination of the only real avenue of escape from the barbarity of their slaveholders. Dissatisfaction "grew to such a height among them" that throughout the island, but especially in Spanish Town (St. Jago), they gathered into groups, where they made preliminary plans for revolt. The restive and mutinous spirit increased in intensity with each day. Whites were everywhere openly being abused.

Taking action just in time, the governor ordered a troop of horse against one of the larger groups of plotters and, in order to strike terror in the rest of the slave population, punished and executed most of them brutally, and transported the rest. The technique had the desired effect, and gradually the island-wide mood of unrest lessened (Anon, n.d.).

In the meantime, attempts were being made to bring the Windward rebels to sign the treaty, although the latter showed little taste for the matter, stubbornly continuing with the resistance. Colonel Guthrie very reluctantly assumed the responsibility once more of negotiating a treaty, and, assisted by the Maroons of Cudjoe's party, set off for St. George's parish. On his way he was "seized with a most violent griping pains in the bowels" and died a little after reaching his destination. It was strongly suspected that he was poisoned by one of the many slaves who "were in the utmost despair" over the settlement with Cudjoe and the prospect of a further treaty with the Windward Maroons (Anon, n.d.).

With the Leeward Maroons pledged to fight against them, and with their own party reduced in size, harassed, and weary from bearing the brunt of the war against the Whites for the past ten years, the Windward rebels, under their leader Quao, the last of the leaders before the end of the war (possibly Kissey's successor), had little choice but to sign a treaty similar in all but three less favorable respects to the one agreed with Cudjoe (see Appendix B at the end of this chapter). For example, where there was disagreement between Maroon and White hunters over a shot wild hog, the Maroons were required to hand the entire catch over to the Whites, instead of dividing it equally, as had been agreed on in the treaty with Cudjoe.

The atmosphere at the signing of the treaty at or near Crawford's town in St. George's Parish (now part of Portland parish) was quite different from that at the agreement with the Leeward rebels. The Windward Maroons never ceased to be suspicious of the Whites and made it quite clear that the treaty was signed with great reluctance and out of sheer necessity. The White hostage who was left in their midst during negotiations complained later that the hatred the Maroons expressed toward him and all Whites was so great that even

184

SLAVERY AND SLAVE REVOLTS

the children who gathered curiously around him poked his breast, with their fingers pointed as if they were knives, as they mockingly shouted "buckra, buckra" ("White man, White man"). His nervousness was not abated by the sight of the women who crowded around him, adorned with necklaces strung with the teeth of White men (Dallas, 1803, I: 73).

7.6: Explaining slave revolts

The existential irrelevance of psychological factors

How do we account for this remarkable tradition of revolt among the enslaved of Jamaica? Certainly, as slave societies go, this is an unusual, perhaps unique, record. One might initially be tempted to explain this record in largely social-psychological terms.[10] Such an attempt, however, would be not merely erroneous but irrelevant. Even if it could be proved that the Jamaican enslaved population was more prone to revolt than the enslaved from other societies, say the American South, we would still be left with the problem of explaining why this might be the case. The view, however, that a slave population can be more or less psychologically prone to revolt or, conversely, to dependence and docility, is, I think, without foundation, and rests on a highly simplistic view of slave personality, indeed, of human personality in general.

Enslavement, especially the genocidal, plantation type practiced in Jamaica, is a denial of all freedom and dignity, and, as such, a denial of humanity, of the very essence of the human condition, for it is an attempt at extreme objectification, at making the person a socially dead 'vocal instrument' in the view of the ancient Romans. Hence, it is an absurd denial.[11] Faced with such an attempted denial,

---

[10] For the best-known statement of this view, see Elkins, 1959. See also Genovese 1967. I cannot agree with Genovese that Elkins does not equate childishness with docility. He does not simply "give such an impression"; it is clearly implied in the thesis. Nor do I find anything "subtle" or elusive in the idea that Sambo is employed to account for "most forms of day-to-day resistance." Of some interest is the exchange between Genovese and Herbert Aptheker in *Studies on the Left*, vol. 6, no. 6 (1966). While I am in sympathy with many of the points raised by Professor Genovese in this exchange, I agree with Professor Woodward's contention that they need further substantiation. See also A. Sio's comments on the Elkins thesis in *Social and Economic Studies*, vol. 16, no. 3 (1967).

[11] For philosophical arguments likely to support what may be called the existential evil of slavery, see Marcel (1963); see also Camus (1954). See also Hegel's highly suggestive discussion in *The Phenomenology of Spirit* (2016 [1807]: 229–40).

185

SLAVERY IN THE MODERN WORLD

the slave, under certain conditions, may have appeared to acquiesce. This impression fails largely because it does not recognize, as Genovese points out, the all-too-human quality of contradiction. Stanley Elkins's "Sambo," the apparently acquiescing, submissive slave, no doubt existed on one level, but along with it – we might even add, implied by it – was hatred of the slaveholder, and the urge to destroy him, as the women and children of the Windward Maroon town made clear in their gestures toward the White hostage during the treaty negotiations . For one thing, "Sambo," even on the shallow level interpreted by Elkins, was found in all slave systems and was certainly not a "peculiarly American" phenomenon. It was a commonplace in Jamaica, this most rebellious of slave systems, and in the island there was even a name for it: "Quashee" (Patterson, 2022 [1967]: 174–81; see also Genovese, 1967: 294–8). The fact that "Sambo" could be found in Jamaica not only disproves Elkins's claim that it was a peculiarly American phenomenon, but questions the very basis of his interpretations of the so-called syndrome.

This is no place to relitigate the vexed matter of the personality of the enslaved for, as Finley (1960: 66) observed, "nothing is more elusive than the psychology of the slave." Our point here is to stress the irrelevance of psychological factors in the analysis of slave revolts. There is no correlation whatever between the modal personality of a slave population (whatever this may be) and their propensity to revolt. This view is best supported by glancing briefly at one of the major personalities of the First Maroon War. Cudjoe, who grew up in slavery, fully exhibited the kind of contradiction that is often found among the oppressed, one necessitated by the existential absurdity and sociological depravity of their condition (see Fanon, 2008 [1952], 1963; Patterson, 1966a). The discipline, skill, shrewdness, courage, and spirit of independence shown by Cudjoe throughout the wars is a model of the heroic person, incapable of being crushed by tyrannical conditions or overwhelmed by uneven odds. Up to the moment of his confrontation with Guthrie, he seems to be the very antithesis of Elkins's "Sambo." Yet suddenly, faced with the White officer suing for peace, he undergoes what appears to be an amazing metamorphosis of character. The gallant, rebellious hero becomes a prostrating supplicant kissing the feet of his enemy. The poverty of any psychological explanation of rebellion becomes quite clear at this point, for there is no way in which it can explain this extraordinary behavior.

And yet, Cudjoe's volte-face is hardly surprising. In its contradictory way it was quite consistent. Furthermore, even as he groveled at the feet of the great White "massah," one suspects that there was more to this extravagant show of humility than meets the eye. Is it perhaps the perfect *coup de grâce* of the rebel slave? Could it be that the real meaning of Cudjoe's extraordinary act was an expression of contempt for the White "master" by the very slave-like psychological technique of diverting the contempt on himself? There is no way, really, of knowing. But there is much in one theory of the psychology of oppression to support this view.[12] The social psychology of the Jamaican slaves, then, while of considerable intrinsic interest, is of little explanatory value in the interpretation of the causes of the revolts narrated above, for, as Eugene Genovese so well expresses it in his critique of Elkins, "Sambo existed wherever slavery existed . . . he nonetheless could turn into a rebel, and . . . our main task is to discover the conditions under which the personality pattern could become inverted and a seemingly docile slave could suddenly turn fierce" (1967: 294). Or, we may add, under which a hostile slave suddenly seems to turn docile.

Marronage, slave revolts, or both?

Before seeking to discover these conditions, however, one nagging explanatory problem peculiar to the type of historical data surveyed above needs to be resolved. It is the extent to which we should distinguish between Maroon and slave revolts and the role of Maroon activity, per se, as an explanation of those revolts of the Blacks still on the plantation. In other words, it may be argued that, first, the Maroons were not strictly enslaved and, as such, the rebellions cannot be regarded as slave revolts, and, second, that the very presence of the Maroons contributed to the climate of revolts, in that their existence was living proof of the vulnerability of the Whites, and encouraged the enslaved to challenge the system. Hence, while the Maroons partly explain revolts on the plantations, a separate set of explanations is required for the presence and activity of the Maroons themselves.

Clearly, the important factor here is the extent to which the revolts delineated above are related to each other and have their roots in the

---

[12] See the brilliant analysis by British existential psychoanalyst R. D. Laing in his *The Divided Self*, where he explains the "eccentricity and oddity" of certain persons in terms of their tendency to express their hatred through identification and excessive compliance with the wishes of the hated person, then finally giving vent to this hatred through "compulsive caricature" of the hate-object. "The individual begins by slavish conformity and compliance and ends through the very medium of this conformity and compliance in expressing his own negative will and hatred" (1965: 109).

SLAVERY IN THE MODERN WORLD

slave situation. The matter can be settled by answering three questions. First, were the revolts cumulative? Second, what was the nature of recruitment to the Maroon camps – was it primarily through reproduction or immigration of plantation slaves? And third, how did the original band of Spanish ex-slaves, who were obviously not derived from rebel activity on the plantations but were the product of a unique historical experience (the English conquests of the island), figure in the revolts during the British period?

On the first question, if the different revolts were completely unrelated, or, more specifically, if the groups that earlier established themselves in the hills had been little influenced by later rebels, then one could reasonably hold that they were not a factor in explaining later rebellions. This, however, was not the case. As we have seen, the revolts form a meaningful series of events. There were no historical discontinuities – no period marked a break in the sequence of events during which a separate Maroon identity was formed. The rebels of each revolt joined one or another of the major bands or were closely related to them. Obviously, the presence of rebel gangs stimulated the enslaved on the plantations to revolt and join them, but this does not justify the view that the Maroons should be treated separately. All social processes at some time become self-reinforcing. The important thing is to recognize the beginning and the end of the process and its essential features. The data indicate that an essential feature of the Maroons was the fact that they were merely one aspect of the revolt of the enslaved still on the plantations. Indeed, one may go further and suggest that all sustained slave revolts must acquire a Maroon dimension, since the only way in which an enslaved population can compensate for the inevitably superior military might of their slave-holders is to resort to guerrilla warfare, with all its implications of flight, strategic retreat to secret hideouts, and ambush.

The second question is closely related to the first. It may be argued that a generation of Maroons born in the hills outside of slavery had a separate identity from the enslaved; on the plantations, to the extent that the Maroon population was composed of members born in the camps, there would have been the kind of discontinuity that, it could be argued, would justify the distinction between their struggles with the Whites and those of the plantation slaves. There are two responses to this argument. First, even if the Maroon population at any given time after, say, 1700 was composed mainly of those born in the camps, one would still be justified in regarding the resistance as slave revolts. In the first place, there is no reason why participants in a slave revolt need only be slaveholders and plantation slaves. In

SLAVERY AND SLAVE REVOLTS

the eyes of the slaveholders, the Maroons were runaway slaves who had to be brought to subjection. In the eyes of the enslaved on the plantation, the Maroons were simply successful rebel slaves (hence the ironical observation by many of them at the end of the wars that those who had challenged the system were given their freedom). And in the eyes of the Maroons (that is, those already in the hills), the enslaved were all potential allies on whom they depended for provisions, arms, intelligence and new recruits.

In the second place, while the data are slight, it would appear that at any given moment after a second generation of Maroons became possible (after about 1700), the great majority of Maroons were nonetheless ex-slaves. If one compares the total population of the four major Maroon towns given by Long in 1749 with that suggested by the data on the Second Maroon War nearly half a century later, one finds that the natural rate of increase during times of peace was very low. One would hardly expect the natural increase of the population to be any higher during times of war. Indeed, the rigors of guerrilla warfare would place a strong curb on childbearing, not to mention the artificially increased mortality rate of the adult population. The perennial scarcity of women among the older generation of Maroons – it was, indeed, one of the main reasons for the early plantation raids of the Maroons – would seem to reinforce our view that the Maroon population hardly reproduced itself. The Maroon population, then, was primarily an ex-slave population, for its rapid increase during the first quarter of the eighteenth century can only be explained in terms of recruits from runaway slaves.

Finally, there is the question of the original band of Spanish ex-slaves. As the data indicate, however, this group was of no influence whatever on the slave revolts of the seventeenth century, since they deliberately cut themselves off from the rest of the island. If anything, they were a disincentive, since they treated those runaways who wandered into their camps so badly that few ventured anywhere near to them. During the eighteenth century, however, they did become one of the more formidable groups. But this was only after they had changed their policy toward rebel slaves. And, as we have seen, this change was occasioned by the success of the rebels in the Leeward section of the island. It was the enslaved who swelled the ranks and the arms of this originally small group (whose numbers were declining because of a scarcity of women), allowing them to become the major threat to the Whites. What is more, Quao, the most important leader of the Windward band, who eventually negotiated one of the treaties of peace, was a Creole. It would seem reasonable to regard

189

the revolts described above as genuine slave revolts, among the most successful episodes of resistance to this crime against humanity in the history of the world.

The causes of slave revolts

The conditions favoring revolts in Jamaica were both social and cultural, and while, naturally, these two sets of conditions were closely related, for purposes of analysis they will be considered separately. There were five or six features of the social structure of the Jamaican slave system that accounted for the rebellions.

First, there was the slaveholder/slave ratio. We have seen how, over a very short period of time, the slave group came to outnumber the ruling class by nearly ten to one. Sheer numbers, then, made adequate security measures impossible. There were simply not enough Whites to ensure proper surveillance of the slave group. The comparative data on slavery in the New World, and in antiquity, clearly indicate a correlation between low slaveholder/slave ratio and high incidence of revolts. Isaac Mendelsohn, for instance, states that the great numerical superiority of the slaveholder class throughout the ancient Near East accounts for the complete absence of slave revolts in that area (1949: 121).[13] And the famous revolt of the Helots (assuming that they were enslaved, a controversial issue) has been partly explained by the fact that "they outnumbered the free population on a scale without parallel in other Greek communities" (Finley, 1960: 66).

The second feature favoring revolt was the ratio of local (or Creole) to foreign-born (in this case, African) slaves. It would appear reasonable, and the available comparative literature lends support to the hypothesis, that the higher the proportion of the enslaved recruited from outside the system, the greater was the probability of rebellions taking place. Clearly, people socialized within the slave system would have been more adapted to such a system, more aware of the risks involved in revolting, and less inclined to bring down the *known* wrath of the ruling caste upon themselves than would the enslaved recruited as adults to the system. In his classic work on slave revolts in antiquity, *Struktur der Antiken Sklavenkriege*, Joseph Vogt claims that Poseidonios and other writers of antiquity "quite rightly"

---

[13] The correlation is fully supported by the comparative data on slave revolts of classical antiquity. See Vogt, 1957; Westermann, 1955a: 8–10, also his 1955b, an impossibly written but still important work, esp. Ch. IX; also Mommsen, 1878–1905, vol. 3: 308–9, 380–1.

emphasized the role of the enslaved who were formerly freemen in the famous Sicilian slave revolts (1957: 12).

Furthermore, the hatred of the Creole slave for his slaveholder would have been less single-minded than that of his African counterpart. All kinds of personal ties with members of the slaveholder caste – as a sexual partner, as a childhood playmate, as a favorite, even as a kinsman – would have corrupted and blurred the passionate desire for vengeance and the sense of injustice, if not of freedom. Personal ties, too, with other slaves would have operated in this direction – the fear of retaliation against a lover, child, or friend, for example. It is the old revolutionary story of which group had more to lose. A locally bred slave population might think that it had more than its chains to lose. A foreign-born slave population literally had only its chains.

The fact, then, that the great majority of Jamaican slaves during this period were of African origin – certainly no fewer than four-fifths – would have added a further element in favor of revolt. It may be contended that we are here assuming that the great majority of Africans enslaved in Jamaica were freemen before being captured, although many eighteenth- and nineteenth-century proslavery writers have suggested quite the contrary.[14] We have no reason, however, to believe that the majority of the enslaved from Africa were not freemen, and besides, even if they were not originally free, the argument would hardly be affected, since it is well known that slavery in West Africa at that period, as in most traditional societies, was of the household type, entirely different in nature from the industrial slavery that existed in the plantation systems of the New World. Enslavement would have been as much of a shock, and the sense of outrage no less intense, for an African household slave as it would have been for the average African freeman (cf. Forde, 1941; Smith, 1954; Siegel, 1945).

A third feature of the society favoring revolt were the opportunities for leadership and political organization that the system permitted. It was common knowledge among the planters – as indeed among all slaveowning castes – that it was a dangerous practice to recruit too many slaves from any one region or ethnic group, for the simple

[14] See Mungo Park's famous work, *Travels in the Interior Districts of Africa in the Years 1795, 1796, and 1797* (2023 [1807]). It has been claimed, however – and the internal stylistic evidence in addition to the known alterations of the original text by Park strongly supports the claim – that the proslavery, Jamaican, planter historian Bryan Edwards (author of The *History, Civil and Commercial, of the British Colonies in the West Indies*, 3 vols., 1807 [1796]) had a considerable influence, which he unscrupulously exploited by persuading the young traveler to exaggerate the extent to which Africans exported from the Guinea Coast to the New World were already enslaved.

reason that this offered a basis for solidarity and communication among a section of the enslaved group. As early as the late fourth century BCE, "the peripatetic author of the Oeconomica made the sensible recommendation that neither an individual nor a city should have many slaves of the same nationality" (Finley, 1960: 66; cf. also Aptheker, 1969: 63–4).[15]

In other words, the observance of this rule was an essential precondition of the well-known policy of divide and rule. But this was a rule the Jamaican planters refused to follow once they came to believe in their own stereotype that certain groups of Africans (especially Coromantees) made much hardier slaves after being seasoned or broken into the system.[16] Facilities for detribalization and seasoning at this time, however, were very poorly developed (if they were ever really effective), and, in the mad rush for profits, the enslaved, among whom must have been warriors and leaders of considerable experience, were hastened into the fields long before they had been in any way subdued.

During these eighty-four years, Coromantee (Akan) and, to a lesser extent, Papaw slaves made up a significant sector, perhaps more than half, of the slave population. However, not only were they the two largest single groups of slaves, but they were precisely the groups that were likely to be most dangerous, for it was during this period that the expansions of the relatively advanced political systems of Ashanti and Dahomey, with their strong militaristic traditions, were taking place. Coming mainly from the forest belt of West Africa, their normal method of combat would have been jungle warfare (Claridge, 1964, esp. vol. 1, pts. 3 and 4; Dalzell, 1793; Davidson, 1966: Chs. 18–19).

Add to this a fourth significant feature of Jamaica – its wild, forested countryside, with tall, rugged mountains, narrow defiles, precipitous slopes, and countless hidden valleys, all ideally suited to guerrilla warfare – and one immediately realizes what a powder keg the planters were constantly sitting on (Dallas, 1803, I: 39–45).[17]

[15] Spartacus, who led the most famous of the slave revolts of the late Roman Republic, was of Thracian origin and was able to exploit ethnicity in mobilizing his enslaved countrymen for revolt. The Thracians were joined by the major ethnic group – the Gauls – in this revolt. The parallel between the role of these two groups and that of the Coromantees and the Papaws in Jamaica is striking. See Vogt, 1957: 17, 36–7.

[16] There is a curious parallel between the reputation of Gold Coast slaves among Jamaican planters and that of Syrian slaves among the Roman latifundia owners of Sicily and Italy during the period of the late Republic.

[17] See also the aerial photograph and description of the cockpits in Robinson (1969); this book includes many photographs of eighteenth-century artists' impressions of maroon leaders as well as eighteenth-century maps of Jamaica, which the interested reader may wish to consult. The text, however, was intended for the non-specialist. For a modern

SLAVERY AND SLAVE REVOLTS

Another important feature of the society conducive to revolt was the high rate of absenteeism among the slaveholder caste. Absenteeism constantly creamed off the most successful and, presumably, most efficient members of the ruling caste, leaving the island in the hands of a group of attorneys and overseers whose treatment of the enslaved was not even mitigated by proprietorial self-interest. A resident owner could, at least, have been expected to be constrained by the brute fact that a wasted slave was wasted capital. No such constraint was imposed on managers who, being paid largely on a commission basis, had a vested interest in increasing profits (and also in compensating for their notorious managerial incompetence) by depleting the major capital asset of the property in their charge, namely, the enslaved. There is even evidence from a later period of the society that many of the overseers and attorneys – "swallowers up of estates," one owner called them – deliberately reduced their estates to bankruptcy in order to purchase them cheaply from their absentee employers (Patterson, 1967: 43–4; cf. Address of Assembly to Crown, 1750, CO, 137/25; Williamson, 2006 [1828]: 23).

Related to this is the fact that large-scale plantation agriculture, regardless of the degree of absenteeism, was itself a direct spur to harsh treatment of the enslaved, since the marginal value of each individual slave was thereby lessened, making them more dispensable. It takes, however, only one angry and inflamed slave with the right qualities of leadership to incite a revolt, whatever the size of the plantation. The shift to absenteeism and large-scale monocrop plantations, then, coming at the turn of the eighteenth century, when the relationship between the castes was still unsettled, inevitably created a situation where extreme brutality and, more important, inconsistency of treatment, were prevalent.

Earlier, we mentioned the general state of cultural disintegration prevailing among both slaveholders and the enslaved at this time. Several features of this cultural situation were particularly conducive to revolt. One was the lack of social commitment, the nearly complete absence of a cohesive set of collective sentiments and willingness to participate in collective action among the slaveholders. Clearly, since they saw their stay on the island as a temporary one, they would hardly be inclined to take unnecessary risks in defending it. The enslaved obviously had, somehow, to be kept in submission, but hardly anyone was prepared to lay down his life

account of the site of Nanny Town and the difficulties involved in reaching it even today, see Teulon (n.d.).

doing so. Indeed, even simple routine security tasks such as militia duties were considered unduly irksome and, apart from periods of crisis, the militia remained a largely defunct body. In a petition to the Duke of Newcastle in 1734, the Council and Assembly of the island unfairly tried to place the entire blame on "the cowardice and treachery" of the parties and the militia, "which mostly consisted of tradesmen and indentured servants" (*JHA*, vol 3: 229). They failed to mention, however, the utter selfishness of what one war-weary White petitioner referred to as "persons of the best property," who refused to perform militia duties, and regarding whom he went on to suggest "that means be found for the compelling them to do so" (*JHA*, vol. 3: 223). Perhaps the best example of the near total lack of public spirit, of a sense of shared concern for the fate of the society they ruled, was the outright refusal of many of the planters in the parish of Portland, where the rebels were most active, to allow their slaves to help in the building and replacing of barracks for the soldiers. Others would only provide slaves if they were compensated by the government, which they knew was bankrupt, largely because they themselves had refused to pay their taxes (*JHA*, vol. 3: 31). It is striking that the greatest slave revolt of antiquity, the Third Servile War between 73 and 71 BCE led by Spartacus, took place during the period of the late Roman republic when, as Finley (1960: 66) notes, there was a "marked breakdown of moral and social values."

One structural factor contributing to this lack of cultural cohesiveness and collective action was the highly uneven sex ratio of the White population. White women constituted no more than 30 percent of the total White population (Long, 1774, I: 376; also Williamson, 2006 [1828]: 117, 210–11). Jamaican slave society was no place for free women, children, and families (Patterson 1967: 41–2).[18] In the absence of wives, mothers, daughters, and sisters, the Jamaican "greathouse" never became the sanctified fortress of Southern "gynocracy" (Cash, 1960: 85–9, 115–26). The inflammatory thought of White women being raped by rebelling Black slaves seeking racial vengeance rarely spurred men on to '"gallant" deeds.

---

[18] At the height of the revolts, the White community was shaken by the divorce proceedings of one of the leading planters, whose adulterous wife had several "criminal conversations" (illicit sex) not only with her husband's White friends, but, as it transpired, with not a few of her own slaves (*JHA*, vol. 3: 493). It is not without significance that the most famous legend surviving the period of slavery concerns the diabolical sex murders of a beautiful, nymphomaniac, white witch, who consumed not only six of her husbands but countless sable beaus to boot. See de Lisser's novel, *The White Witch of Rosehall* (1929); also see Black's entertaining folk history, *Tales of Old Jamaica* (1966).

The Jamaican planters were therefore faced with a socioeconomic vicious circle. Their large-scale monopolistic farming practices drove most of the ambitious White lower and artisan class from the island and the most successful planters into absenteeism. This created a situation in which there were not only fewer Whites to defend the slave regime but, more seriously, a lack of development of a colonial settlement community worth defending. As we saw in our account of the revolts, the Whites often had to turn to coopted members of the Black population not only to defend them as foot soldiers and baggage carriers, but even to lead them into battle against the rebels.

Conclusion

This study of slave revolts during the first half of the history of British colonization and mass enslavement in Jamaica suggests the following hypotheses in explaining the causes of slave rebellion. In systems of slavery where the following conditions prevail, there will be a high tendency, increasing with the conjunction of such conditions, toward slave revolts:

- where the slave population greatly outnumbers that of the slave-holder class;
- where the ratio of local to foreign-born slaves is low;
- where the imported slaves, or a significant proportion of them, are of common ethnic origin;
- where geographical conditions favor guerrilla warfare;
- where there is a high incidence of absentee ownership;
- where the economy is dominated by large-scale enterprises (with many slaves per holding or estate);
- where the slaveholder class has not established a colony or independent society of settlement;
- and hence, where there is weak cultural cohesiveness and collective commitment, reinforced by a high (male/female) sex ratio, among the ruling population.

SLAVERY IN THE MODERN WORLD

Appendix A

Articles of the treaty executed by Colonel John Guthrie, Lieutenant Francis Sadler, and Cudjoe, the commander of the rebels, confirmed in an act of the Jamaican House of Assembly, May 12, 1739.

At the camp near Trelawney Town, March the 1st, 1739.
In the name of God, Amen. Whereas captain Cudjoe, captain Accompong, captain Johnny, captain Cuffee, captain Quaco, and several other negroes, their dependants and adherents, have been in a state of war and hostility for several years past against our sovereign lord the king, and the inhabitants of this island; and whereas peace and friendship among mankind, and preventing the effusion of blood, is agreeable to God, consonant to reason, and desired by every good man; and whereas his majesty George the second, king of Great-Britain, France, and Ireland, and of Jamaica lord, defender of the faith, etc. has by his letters patent . . . granted full power and authority to John Guthrie and Francis Sadler, esquires, to negotiate and finally conclude a treaty of peace and friendship with the aforesaid captain Cudjoe, the rest of his captains, adherents, and others his men; they mutually, sincerely and amicably, have agreed to the following articles:

First, That all hostilities shall cease on both sides forever.
Secondly, That the said Captain Cudjoe, the rest of his captains, adherents and men, shall be forever hereafter in a perfect State of Freedom and Liberty, excepting those who have been taken by them, or fled to them within the two years last past, if such are willing to return to their said masters and owners, with full pardon and indemnity from their masters and owners for what is past. Provided always, that if they are not willing to return, they shall remain in subjection to captain Cudjoe, and in friendship with us, according to the form and tenor of this treaty.
Thirdly, That they shall enjoy and possess for themselves and posterity forever, all the lands situated and lying between Trelawney Town and the Cockpits, to the amount of fifteen hundred acres, bearing Northwest from the said Trelawney Town.
Fourthly, That they shall have liberty to plant the said lands with coffee, ginger, tobacco and cotton, and breed cattle, hogs, goats, or any other stock, and dispose of the produce or the said commodities to the inhabitants of this island. Provided always, that when

196

SLAVERY AND SLAVE REVOLTS

they bring the said commodities to market, they shall apply first to the Custos, or any other Magistrate of the respective Parishes where they expose their goods to sale, fora license to vend the same.

Fifthly, That Captain Cudjoe, and all the captain's adherents, and people now in subjection to him, shall all live together within the bounds of Trelawney Town; and that they have liberty to hunt where they think fit, except within three miles of any Settlement, Crawl or Pen; provided always, that in case the hunters of Captain Cudjoe, and those of other Settlements meet, then the hogs to be equally divided between both parties.

Sixthly, That said Captain Cudjoe and his successors, do use their best endeavours to take, kill, suppress or destroy, either by themselves or jointly, with any other number of men commanded on that service by his Excellency the Governor or Commander in Chief for the time being, all rebels wheresoever they be throughout this island, unless they submit to the same terms of accommodation granted to Captain Cudjoe, and his successors.

Seventhly, That in case this island be invaded by any foreign enemy, the said Captain Cudjoe, and his successors herein and after named, or to be appointed, shall then, upon notice given, immediately repair to any place the Governor for the Time being shall appoint, in order to repel the said invaders with his or their utmost force; and to submit to the orders of the Commander in Chief on that Occasion.

Eighthly, That if any white Man shall do any manner of injury to Captain Cudjoe, his successors, or any of his people, they shall apply to any commanding Officer or Magistrate in the neighbourhood for Justice; and in case Captain Cudjoe, or any of his people, shall do any injury to any white person, he shall submit himself or deliver up such offenders to justice.

Ninthly, That if any Negroes shall hereafter run away from their Master or Owners, and fall into Captain Cudjoe's Hands, they shall immediately be sent back to the Chief Magistrate of the next Parish where they are taken; and those that bring them are to be satisfied for their trouble, as Legislature shall appoint.

Tenthly, That all negroes taken since the raising of this Party by Captain Cudjoe's people, shall immediately be returned.

Eleventhly, Captain Cudjoe, and his successors, shall wait on his Excellency, or the Commander in Chief for the time being, every year, if thereunto required.

Twelfth, That Captain Cudjoe, during his life, and the captains succeeding him, shall have full power to inflict any punishment they

197

SLAVERY IN THE MODERN WORLD

think proper for crimes committed by their men among themselves (death only excepted); in which case, if the captain thinks they deserve death, he shall be obliged to bring them before any justice of the peace, who shall order proceedings on their trial equal to those of other free negroes.

Thirteenth, That Captain Cudjoe with his people shall cut, clear, and keep open, large, and convenient roads from Trelawney Town to Westmoreland and St. James, and if possible to St. Elizabeth's.

Fourteenth, That two White men to be nominated by his Excellency, or the Commander in Chief for the time being, shall constantly live and reside with Captain Cudjoe and his successors, in order to maintain a friendly correspondence with the inhabitants of this Island.

Fifteenth, That captain Cudjoe shall, during his life, be chief commander in Trelawney Town; after his decease, the command to devolve on his Brother Captain Accompong; and, in case of his decease, on his next Brother Captain Johnny; and, failing him, Captain Cuffee shall succeed; who is to be succeeded by Captain Quaco; and, after all their demises, the Governor, or commander in chief for the time being, shall appoint, from time to time, whom he thinks fit for that command.

In testimony of the above presents, we have hereunto set our hands and seals the day and date written above.

> *John Guthrie. (L.S)*
> *Francis Sadler. (L.S)*
> *The mark L of captain Cudjoe.*

Appendix B

Articles of the treaty executed by colonel Robert Bennett, and Quao, the commander of the rebels, confirmed in an act of the Jamaican House of Assembly, May 27th, 1740.

The 14 Articles of the treaty, signed by Colonel Robert Bennett and the Windward leader, Quao, June 23rd, 1739. At or near either Crawford or Moore Town.

First, That all hostilities shall cease on both sides for ever, Amen.

Second, That the said Captain Quao, and his people, shall have a

SLAVERY AND SLAVE REVOLTS

certain quantity of land given to them, in order to raise provisions, hogs, fowls, goats, or whatever stock they may think proper, sugar canes excepted, saving for their hogs, and to have liberty to sell the same.

Third, That four white men shall constantly live and reside with them in their town, in order to keep a good correspondence with the inhabitants of this island.

Fourth, That the said Captain Quao, and his people, shall be ready on all commands the governor, or the commander in chief for the time being, shall send him, to suppress and destroy all other party or parties of rebellious negroes, that now are, or from time to time gather together to settle in any part of this island, and shall bring in such other negroes as shall from time to time run away from their respective owners, from the date of these articles.

Fifth, That the said Captain Quao, and his people, shall also be ready to assist his Excellency the governor for the time being, in case of any invasion, and shall put himself, with all his people that are able to bear arms, under the command of the general or commander of such forces, appointed by his Excellency to defend the island from the said invasion.

Sixth, That the said Captain Quao, and all his people, shall be in subjection to his Excellency the governor for the time being; and the said Captain Quao shall, once every year or oftener, appear before the governor, if thereunto required.

Seventh, That in case any of the hunters belonging to the inhabitants of this island, and the hunters belonging to Captain Quao, should meet in order to hinder disputes, Captain Quao will order his people to let the inhabitants hunters have the hog.

Eighth, That in case Captain Quao, or his people, shall take up run away negroes that shall abscond from their respective owners, and shall be paid for so doing as the legislature shall appoint.

Ninth, That in case Captain Quao, and his people, should be disturbed by a greater number of rebels than he is able to fight, that then he shall be assisted by as many white people as the governor for the time being shall think proper.

Tenth, That in case any of the negroes belonging to Captain Quao shall be guilty of any crime or crimes that may deserve death, he shall deliver him up to the next magistrate, in order to be tried as other negroes are; but small crimes he may punish himself.

Eleventh, That in case any white man, or other the inhabitants of this island, shall disturb or annoy any of the people, hogs, flock, or whatever goods may belong to the said Captain Quao, or any

SLAVERY IN THE MODERN WORLD

of his people, when they come down to the settlements to vend the same, upon due complaint made to a magistrate, he or they shall have justice done them.

Twelfth, That neither Captain Quao, nor any of his people, shall bring any hogs, fowls, or any stock or provisions, to sell to the inhabitants, without a ticket from under the hand of one or more of the white men residing within their town.

Thirteenth, That Captain Quao, nor any of his people, shall hunt within three miles of any settlement.

Fourteenth, That in case Captain Quao should die, that then the command of his people shall descend to Captain Thomboy; and at his death to descend to Captain Apong; and at his death Captain Blackwall shall succeed; and at his death Clash shall succeed; and, when he dies, the governor or commander in chief for the time being shall appoint whom he thinks proper.

In witness of these articles, the above-named colonel Robert Bennett and captain Quao have set their hands and seals, the day and year above written.

Robert Bennett. (L.S.)
The mark of X captain Quao

Key to archival references

CO   Colonial Office Records, Public Records Office, London.
CSP   Calendar of State Papers (Colonial; America and West Indies).
JHA   Journals of the House of Assembly, Jamaica.
BM, Sl.   British Museum, Sloane Manuscripts
Sedgwick to Whitehall, "Situation of the Island of Jamaica," CO, 1/14.
Instructions (No. 11) to Col. Doyley, *JHA,* vol. 1, Appendix.

— 8 —

SLAVERY AND GENOCIDE: THE US SOUTH, JAMAICA, AND THE HISTORICAL SOCIOLOGY OF EVIL

Genocide and slavery are, without question, mankind's two most heinous and ancient crimes. Understandably, there is now intense and growing scholarly inquiry on both subjects. However, the historiography of slavery is considerably older and more extensive than that of genocide, not because it is more ancient, but because preoccupation with genocide scholarship – indeed, the very word "genocide" – only began with the Nazi atrocities of World War II, while that on slavery was engendered by the anti-abolition movements of the late eighteenth and nineteenth centuries. Scholarship follows the banners of politics and popular moral contention. A surprising feature of the contemporary study and popular debates on these two subjects, however, is the fact that, with a few notable exceptions, they have largely remained siloed from each other.

This chapter has three parts. The first part examines the nature of genocide and the closely related problem of cultural genocide, sometimes called "ethnocide." The second part briefly discusses the relation between genocide and slavery in history. The third part examines comparatively two cases of slavery in the Americas: the US South and Jamaica. I argue that the US South is the paradigmatic case of slavery resulting in ethnocide, as all slaveries do, while Jamaica is the paradigmatic case of a slave society that crosses over into a special kind of genocide, what I call "protracted genocide."

8.1: The nature of genocide and ethnocide

Before getting to a definition of these terms, there is one general issue that scholars of both genocide and slavery have not sufficiently addressed, or have failed to clarify. We are still in need of a generic term that encompasses the different kinds of extreme inhumanities such as slavery, genocide, war crimes, ethnic cleansing, and so on. Raphael Lemkin (2008 [1944]), in his classic study wherein he coined the term "genocide," intended the term to serve this broader end; the sociologist Martin Shaw (2015: 199), in his valuable more recent study, has proposed returning to a revised version of this usage as the "master concept." This doesn't quite work, especially if we are to embrace atrocities such as slavery. The term "crimes against humanity" would seem to fit the bill perfectly. Interestingly, it was first used in this generic sense in the late eighteenth and early nineteenth centuries in the context of the movements to abolish the slave trade and slavery, later to describe the atrocities of European colonialism, especially Leopold II's barbarities in the Congo Free State, and then to describe the Armenian genocide; it was still employed in this generic sense in the first Nuremberg Tribunal, endorsed by the UN General Assembly in 1946 (Bassiouni, 1999). Unfortunately, the term was made less generic, in legal terms, by the statutes of subsequent international tribunals. The ICTY, (International Criminal Tribunal for the former Yugoslavia, 1993) and the later Rome Statute of the International Criminal Court (1998) defined it as a set of twelve acts (including murder, enslavement, and extermination) when committed *as part of a widespread or systematic attack directed against any civilian population.* This conceptually downshifted the term to armed military assault, thereby excluding genocide, which may occur outside the context of war. As the UN Office on Genocide Prevention (n.d.) notes: "In contrast with genocide, crimes against humanity do not need to target a specific group." Furthermore, the inclusion of enslavement is confusing since most of the enslaved most of the time are not under armed attack; hence the term is confined to slave capture rather than the institution that it initiates. To complicate matters further, "crimes against humanity" have not yet been codified in any international treaty, so the term now lingers in a kind of legal and conceptual limbo.

It was possibly with this in mind that one of the most distinguished scholars of genocide, the late historical sociologist Helen Fein, a founder of the International Association of Genocide Scholars, in her last work (2007) proposed the term "life-integrity rights," defined as a class of six pre-political rights, the violations of which served the generic purpose. The first of these is the right to life, which she calls, correctly, "the most fundamental among human rights." Genocide she considers to be the most extreme violation of this fundamental right

202

to life, along with others such as mass killings, summary/extrajudicial executions, and "disappearances." The fourth of Fein's life-integrity rights she defined as the "freedom to own one's body and labor," and first among its violations is "slavery, forced labor, debt slavery and equivalent institutions." Here I part company with Fein, since she is implicitly conceiving slavery in civil law terms, derived from ancient Roman law, which, as I have shown, is true mainly of Western slaveries (Patterson, 2018 [1982]: 1–34, Ch. 3). Furthermore, freedom as a pre-political right does not precede slavery but is historically derivative of emancipation from it (Patterson, 1991). However, as much as I am drawn to the concept of "life integrity rights," it is too cumbersome a term to be used as a generic "master concept." Language matters.

More recently, Michael Mann (2005) has proposed seeing ethnic cleansing as a generic term, with genocide its most extreme form, a product of modernity, arising usually under conditions of immature democracy in which ethnic conflict trumps class before the full development of class-based conflict in modern democratic capitalism. There are so many exceptions to his generalizations that they are simply not tenable. Mann joins another sociologist, Zygmunt Bauman (1989) in claiming that the holocaust – and for Mann all ethnic cleansing – is a distinct product of modernity. As a historical sociologist deeply engaged with the non-Western and pre-modern worlds, I have little patience with this modernist obsession of sociology, which is simply a broader aspect of the discipline's chronic presentism and parochial Westernism (see Chapter 3). The fact that Mann is a historical sociologist whose earlier work digs deep into the pre-modern world makes his untenable claim even more puzzling (see the review of modernist approaches to genocide by Shaw, 2015: 172 –87). There were innumerable, unambiguous cases of genocide, by any definition, in the ancient and medieval worlds, several of which we cite in the next section. Of the premodern genocidal assaults on the Jews, Maya Irish (2023) pointedly notes, "medieval and modern anti-Jewish violence have far more in common than many scholars are willing to admit."

Genocide is now used in both a strictly legal and a broader sociological sense. As noted above, the term was coined by Raphael Lemkin, a Polish-born Jewish lawyer, in response to the holocaust or Shoah. He defined it as "the destruction of a nation or of an ethnic group" (2008 [1944]: 79). The United Nations codified it more precisely in a legally binding document in the 1948 Convention on the Prevention and Punishment of the Crime of Genocide, which (as of April 2022) has been ratified by 153 states. The International Court of Justice (ICJ) now considers it a peremptory norm of international law that admits of no derogation. Even for those who have not ratified it, the definition is considered by the ICJ to be part of general customary international law.

According to this definition, genocide involves "any of the following acts committed with the intent to destroy, in whole or in part, a national, ethnical, racial, or religious group, as such":

(a)   Killing members of the group;
(b)   Causing serious bodily or mental harm to members of the group;
(c)   Deliberately inflicting on the group conditions of life calculated to bring about its physical destruction in whole or in part;
(d)   Imposing measures intended to prevent births within the group; and
(e)   Forcibly transferring children of the group to another group.

The Convention specifies two basic elements: a "mental" element defined as "the intent to destroy, in whole or in part, a national, ethnical, racial or religious group, as such," and a physical element, which includes the five kinds of acts listed above.

However, almost every aspect of the definition has been contested by academics and genocide scholars. One key issue is intent: to what extent is it necessary for mass killings to be considered genocide (Shaw, 2015: Ch. 7)? The convention holds that "there must be a proven intent on the part of perpetrators to physically destroy" the kinds of groups specified, which is what gives the crime of genocide its uniqueness. Alex Hinton has pointed out that the emphasis on intent, and the exclusion of the mass killing of political groups from the definition of genocide, was the result of political pressure from America and other advanced nations with colonial histories. America, in particular, feared being charged with genocide for its history of slavery and Jim Crow (the lynching of Blacks was still common in 1948) and did not ratify the convention until 1988 (Hinton, 2022: 136). Controversy on this dates back to Jean-Paul Sartre (1968), who argued that the American bombing and killing of thousands of civilians in Vietnam constituted genocide, regardless of whether Americans intended to destroy Vietcong soldiers and villagers *as such*. The issue of intent became central to the defense of America: however horrible the bombings were, and however many Vietnamese lost their lives, defenders argued, it was never the intent of the American armed forces to deliberately exterminate the Vietnamese people because they were Vietnamese. They were, after all, fighting alongside the PAVN, or People's Army of Vietnam. Genocide emerges only with the targeted slaughter of a specific group. It could, as easily, be countered from the Vietcong side that the PAVN were traitors siding with an external enemy and that the extermination of large numbers of a group can still qualify as genocide, whoever the attackers' allies and whatever their explicitly stated intentions. A similar quandary exists in interpreting the frequent massacres of Indigenous people of North America during the seventeenth century, what Blackhawk (2023b) calls the "century of horrors as destructive waves radiated out from zones of European invasion," in which Indigenous peoples also frequently waged war upon each other "in ways that depopulated regions and shocked Europeans." These internecine conflicts, however, were largely in response to changes brought about by European contact. Proving intent, or lack thereof, is clearly a complex matter.

Another issue is the targeted killing of political groups, which the Convention excludes from the crime of genocide, while others strongly argued otherwise (Kuper, 1981; Shaw, 2015: 90–6). Stalin's nationalization of land and agricultural policy, which resulted in the mass starvation to death of millions of Russian and Ukrainian peasants (the Holodomor, leading to death by starvation of four million people, some 12 percent of the Ukrainian population) (Naimark, 2023: 162–85) and Mao's cultural revolution (Dikötter, 2023: 429–49), which resulted in famine and the death of an estimated thirty million Chinese, are considered by many to be cases of genocide. However, others argue that it was never Stalin's or Mao's *intention* to target and kill their people because they were Russians and Chinese; their intentions were misguided attempts to improve their lot through socialist revolution. It is hard to take this seriously.

Preventing a people from reproducing, especially on a mass scale, is considered genocide, as outlined in the UN 1948 Declaration. Fein (2007: 134–6) notes that "genocidaires might choose to prevent reproduction within the group or to appropriate the progeny in order to destroy the group in the long run." There is also the question of how many people must die for an atrocity to be considered genocide. Some consider the murder of a single member of a group because of their group identity to be a genocidal killing. Here, Shaw's (2015: 193) proposal and definition of the term "genocidal violence" is well taken. I believe this was at the heart of the horrified global reaction to the killing of George Floyd in Minneapolis in 2020. The inhumanly blank stare on the face of Floyd's uniformed White killer somehow mirrored everything one imagined of an SS guard turning on the gas at Auschwitz.

The editors of *The Cambridge World History of Genocide* (2023), as well as earlier genocide scholars such as Helen Fein, have argued for a broader, more sociological conception of genocide, while accepting the UN definition as an established fact of international law, since, as Fein noted, it is "useful to maintain a common universe of discourse among genocide scholars, international lawyers, and human rights monitors" (2007: 132). Fein's sociological definition has been extremely influential: "Genocide", she wrote, "is sustained purposeful action by a perpetrator to physically destroy a collectivity directly, or indirectly, through interdiction of the biological and social reproduction of group members, sustained regardless of the surrender or lack of threat offered by the victim" (2007: 132). Building on this and earlier volumes in the series, the editors of the third and final volume of *The Cambridge World History of Genocide* summed up as follows:

> Genocide is a form of violence that targets groups and where the purpose of violence is the destruction of groups. Genocide is the attempt to destroy groups, in whole or in part, as the Convention states. We can think of genocide then as a form of group-selective, or "categorical," violence in that the criterion that perpetrators use to target individuals is their ostensible individual membership in a group. They are selected for violence because they are "Muslims'," "Jewish," "Rohingya," "Tutsi" and so forth. In contrast, other kinds of violence, like most crimes against humanity (e.g. murder, enforced disappearances, enslavement, imprisonment, torture, forcible transfer of populations), are not group-selective. Such violence is targeted against civilians (not necessarily because of their group membership), and is large-scale or systematic. The concept of "extermination" can include but does not necessarily imply group selective violence, though it does imply attempted complete destruction. (Kiernan, Lower, et al., 2023: 11)

I find this somewhat useful, though I disagree with the statement that enslavement is not "group-selective," to which I return in the next section. For now, we can summarize the essential features of genocide, based on studies that draw on social science analyses while remaining faithful to the core elements of the 1948 and later UN genocide conventions.[1] Genocide is, first, organized violence against

---

[1] While, as a sociologist, I am sympathetic to Shaw's (2015: 5) view that we should not be "unduly deferential" to the legal definitions and discussions of the subject, and be more alert to issues of agency and structure, it seems that these legally influenced approaches have become too entrenched not to be taken seriously.

a targeted group of people; involving, second, mass killings on a large scale; with, third, the intention of eliminating them. In Scott Straus's view, "the attempt at group destruction remains the etymological root of the concept and its central meaning."[2] This takes us back to the issue of intent. Is group destruction the purpose or logic of the victimizers' action? The problem here is that there is often no explicitly stated plan or ideology of destruction in what are clear cases of the intended mass destruction of a group. Furthermore, the original UN Declaration states that showing or proving motive is not a requirement for genocide, which, incidentally, excludes the popular view of genocide that it is necessarily motivated by a racist ideology. Racism is only one of several motivating ideologies that might instigate genocide, with others such as the desire to appropriate the victims' land (true of several of the mass killings of Indigenous peoples), or hatred of the victims' political views (the Cambodian genocide), or their religious views (the massacres of Muslims during the Crusades), or even the belief that they are the perpetrators of witchcraft (resulting in the mass killing of women during the period of the Black Death).

More problematic are cases where genocide emerges as "collateral damage" from actions not explicitly aimed at the group's destruction, but known and seen to be an inevitable outcome of the action. If, for example, a group of colonial exploiters knew that their economic treatment of the exploited group had fatal outcomes leading irrevocably to the destruction of large parts, or the entirety, of the group (as, for example, the Spanish colonizers of Jamaica knew to be the case with the rapidly declining Indigenous Tainos from the first decade of the sixteenth century), at what point does one call such exploitation genocide, even if the colonial exploiters insist that they had no intention of destroying them, that, indeed, they wanted the Tainos to stay alive for their badly needed labor, and that they also truly desired to convert them to the Catholic Church and the holy bosom of Christ, as their Queen, Isabella, had solemnly directed?

Finally, there is the question of cultural genocide or ethnocide, which has been criticized for risking confounding the terms "culture" and "ethnicity." Many of those who work in genocide studies are concerned with the destruction of a people's culture. This was already indicated in the work of Raphael Lemkin (2008 [1944]: 91), who considered such destruction a form of genocide, although, after some consideration, the 1948 UN Convention decided not to include the term. A draft of the UN Declaration on the Rights of Indigenous

---

[2] Scott Straus, personal communication.

Peoples used both the terms ethnocide and cultural genocide, with clause (d) prohibiting "Any form of assimilation or integration by other cultures or ways of life imposed on them by legislative, administrative or other measures"; but both terms were dropped in the final document, although the prohibition against "forced assimilation or destruction of their culture," "the right to belong to an indigenous community or nation, in accordance with the traditions and customs of the community or nation concerned," as well as "the right to practice and revitalize their cultural traditions and customs" were all retained (UN, 2007: 10, 11).

Cultural destruction was pivotal in the work of an important philosopher of genocide, the late feminist philosopher Claudia Card, who used the concept of social death as a central component in her definition of genocide. For Card, social death is what distinguishes genocide from other forms of mass killings. This is how she sums up her argument:

> This essay develops the hypothesis that social death is utterly central to the evil of genocide, not just when a genocide is primarily cultural but even when it is homicidal on a massive scale. It is social death that enables us to distinguish the peculiar evil of genocide from the evils of other mass murders ... Social vitality exists through relationships, contemporary and intergenerational, that create an identity that gives meaning to a life. Major loss of social vitality is a loss of identity and consequently a serious loss of meaning for one's existence. Putting social death at the center takes the focus off individual choice, individual goals, individual careers, and body counts, and puts it on relationships that create community and set the context that gives meaning to choices and goals. If my hypothesis is correct, the term "cultural genocide" is probably both redundant and misleading – redundant, if the social death present in all genocide implies cultural death as well, and misleading, if "cultural genocide" suggests that some genocides do not include cultural death. (2003: 63)

The philosopher James Snow (2016) thinks this addresses a major problem in the too-great emphasis on the number of killings as a measure of genocide, because this way of framing genocide "marginalizes the voices and experiences of victims who may not succumb to biological death," but nevertheless suffer the loss of family members and other loved ones, and the destruction of those foundational institutions that generate and sustain such relationships.

While I find Card's position instructive, I must agree with the generality of genocide scholars, namely that targeted physical death is so entrenched in our conception of genocide that it cannot be displaced as the central component of the crime. Thus, while I agree with Card that ethnic cultural decimation is critical for the existence of genocide, and is a major element distinguishing it from other kinds of mass killings such as those in warfare, one can still meaningfully distinguish between cultural extermination, or ethnocide as it is sometimes called, and genocide. All genocides include some form of ethnocide (and social death) but not all ethnocides entail physical extermination or mass killings.

Cultural genocide has been made unlawful in several international treaties and is considered a crime against humanity. Article 2 of the Convention on the Prevention and Punishment of the Crime of Genocide (UN, 1951) considers "transferring children of the group to another group" an element of genocide, as does Article 27 of the International Covenant on Civil and Political Rights, which mandates "the rights of ethnic, religious and linguistic minorities . . . to enjoy their own culture, to profess and practice their own religion, and to use their own language" (UN, 1966). More recently, UNESCO (1981), in collaboration with representatives of the Indian Peoples of America, issued the *Declaration of San José*, which held that ethnocide occurs when "an ethnic group is denied the right to enjoy, develop and transmit its own culture and its own language, whether collectively or individually," and declared that "ethnocide, that is, cultural genocide, is a violation of international law equivalent to genocide." A useful work by Elisa Novic (2016), which attempted to formally define the concept in international law, concluded that its core idea is the intentional destruction of group cultures, and settled on the term "cultural genocide."

The question of whether cultural destruction amounts to genocide, even in the absence of mass killings, or should be distinguished from physical genocide, has become an important public issue prompted by revelations concerning the treatment of Native American children in Canada and the United States. Thousands of these children were forcibly removed from their families and re-educated into Western culture by the Catholic Church, as well as both the US and Canadian state authorities, during the nineteenth and early twentieth centuries. The Truth and Reconciliation Commission of Canada (TRC) found that, up to the 1990s, more than 150,000 aboriginal children were separated from their families and communities; in the United States between 1890 and 1960, officials enrolled between 6.6 and 14.2 percent of all Native Americans in boarding, day, and mission schools (McBride, 2023). There is general agreement that this amounted to ethnocide or cultural genocide, but was it actually genocide? The evidence accumulated by the TRC – and I agree – would suggest that it was. Quite apart from the trauma of forced separation from their families and natal cultures, thousands died from neglect and punishment; in addition, such actions prevented these groups from eventually reproducing. Pope Francis (2022) has placed the Catholic Church's seal of genocide on these atrocities in his public apology for these acts, which he called genocide without qualification.

Quite apart from the issue of ethnocide, a growing literature now clearly demonstrates numerous cases of genuine physical genocide among the Indigenous populations of America, beginning from soon after the arrival of Europeans in the early seventeenth century. The massacre of the Pequot of New England between 1636 and 1640, which facilitated the English settlement of the region; of the Kikotan of Virginia in 1610; and the state-sponsored killing of some 80 percent of California Indians between 1846 and 1873: these are only a few of the more extreme cases (Madley 2023a, 2023b). As Ned Blackhawk (2023a) observes, there is now "near consensus" among scholars that "genocide against at least some indigenous peoples had occurred in North America following colonization" and, citing Madley, that "the near-annihilation of North America's indigenous peoples remains a formative event in U.S. history." David Stannard (1993: ix–x, 146) states the matter even more forcefully in his view that the European invasion and settlement and resulting demographic collapse of the Indigenous population amounted to "the worst human holocaust the world had ever witnessed."[3]

Cultural and physical actions that prevent reproduction also amount to a form of genocide, a position of importance to my argument in the third section. Indeed, this may be the worst form of genocide today. I refer here to one side of the crime of "gendercide," which, oddly, is only mildly punished in some societies and is not illegal in most Western societies, including the United States. What is gendercide? It is remarkable that I have to define what it is, since many have not heard of it, even though it involves millions of deaths. It is striking, also, that the recently published *Cambridge World History of Genocide*, now one of the most authoritative current works in this area, has no separate chapter on the subject, and it is only occasionally mentioned in all its forty chapters. Gendercide, a

---

[3] Stannard's estimate of the pre-Columbian Indigenous population in the hemisphere of 100 million is considered rather high. Russell Thornton's (1990: 29–32) estimate of 75 million is considered more likely, with 5 million estimated in the present coterminous United States and about 2 million in what is now Canada.

term coined by Mary Warren (1985), refers to the deliberate killing of individuals based on their gender, or the selective prevention of the birth of fetuses of a particular gender. In most cases, females are targeted, but males have been victims from ancient times, with the term "androcide" used by some to refer to the targeted killing of males (Jones, 2000). While agreeing with Shaw (2015: 90) that such killings are to be seen as the gender dimension of genocide, I wholly disagree with his view that the term is redundant. Gender-specific acts are properly considered separately in the social sciences, as the subdiscipline of gender studies have long made clear. To dismiss gendercide as redundant is equivalent to dismissing misogyny as a concept on the grounds that it is merely a dimension of misanthropy. It is shocking that very few countries, and no Western state, have made the selective destruction of female fetuses illegal.

In his important comparative study, Jones demonstrates that "gendercide – inclusively defined as *gender-selective mass killing* – is a frequent and often defining feature of human conflict and perhaps of human social organization extending back to antiquity" (2000: 166), and that the practice is ubiquitous in recent politico-military conflicts worldwide, even though largely neglected, including by genocide scholars. The selective murder of thousands of young men of "battle age" was a war policy of the Serbs in their detention and killing of ethnic Albanian men. Similar male gendercides occurred in Jammu and Kashmir, 1999; Colombia, 1998; Rwanda, 1997; Bosnia-Herzegovina, 1992; Sri Lanka, 1991; Peru, 1990; Delhi, India, 1984; and Iraqi Kurdistan in 1983 – to name only the most extreme cases. As we saw in Chapter 5, the practice of massacring men and enslaving women and children was typical of ancient and tribal warfare. It is interesting to note that the Nazi holocaust began with the targeted killing of males, using poison gas, with the selective killing of Russian men, and that the first death camp at Dachau, created in 1933, initially focused exclusively on the killing of homosexual and other males. It is significant too, that among the more banal of the racist edicts leading into the mass-killing phase of the holocaust was the prohibition on selling soap or shaving cream to Jews, thereby marking out Jewish men by their beards (Dwork, 2023).

Regarding the targeted killing of females, the United Nations (2020) estimates that, at a minimum, there were in 2020 more than 140 million missing women globally, primarily as a result of gender-targeted abortions that became more widespread with the advent of inexpensive ways of identifying fetal gender in the 1980s, particularly in Asia. The sex ratio of a population is a biological constant, with a natural sex ratio at birth of 105 boys to 100 girls. However, boys are more susceptible than girls to early infant maladies, and the natural ratio evens out within a few months of birth. A population with a heavily skewed sex ratio toward males who survive suggests that females have been eliminated, either through abortion or female infanticide, as is prevalent in some regions of India. While South Korea, China, and India have implemented sex-selective abortion bans, these have not been entirely successful, except in Korea. The European Parliament called for the criminalization of gendercide in 2013, but member nations have not acted on it. The US Congress also passed a "Stop Gendercide Act" as part of the Trafficking Victims Protection Act of 2018, but it has had little impact on law or practice.

8.2: Slavery and genocide in history

Let me turn now to the question of the relation between slavery and genocide. There have been surprisingly few works that have examined this subject. Among those who have addressed the subject, the most controversial was Stanley Elkins (1959), who claimed to have found striking parallels between the "Sambo" personality of the African American slave in response to the "total institution" of the plantation, depicted mainly in the stereotypes of their White slaveholders, and the psychological reaction of some Jewish inmates to the similar "total" institution of the concentration camp and their relations with their German concentration camp officers. Elkins pointed to similarities between the "utter dependence and childlike attachment" of the enslaved with the White slaveholder, and the identification with the Nazi concentration camp guards reported in some accounts of concentration camp survivors. Both, he claimed, were infantilized by their oppression and became docile and psychologically dependent on their slaveholder and Nazi oppressors, respectively. The furor in response to this work was intense, although Elkins boldly defended his ground to the end (Lane, 1971; Elkins, 1975). Most genocide scholars avoided the comparison after that or, like Jeffrey Herf (2007) and Seymour Drescher (1996), emphasized the differences.

However, several notable genocide scholars have compared the two forms of oppression, some drawing on my work, *Slavery and Social Death* (1982). The now classic work on the Jews in Nazi Germany by Marion Kaplan (1998: 34–6, 150–60, 173–9, 184–200) argued that, "in the 1930s Nazi Germany succeeded in enforcing social death on its Jews – excommunicating them, subjecting them to inferior status, and relegating them to a perpetual state of dishonor," while genocide, in the strict sense of mass killings, began with the death camps in 1940. Daniel Goldhagen's controversial work, *Hitler's Willing Executioners*, argued in a similar vein (1997: 168–9), as did the work by the philosopher of evil Laurence Thomas (1993), who focused on the notion of natal alienation at the heart of the concept of social death.

The main argument of these works is that, while comparable in their approach to evil, there was a fundamental difference between New World slavery, as well as slavery in general, and the Jewish holocaust, as well as all genocides: the slaveholder wanted to maintain the life of the enslaved in order to use their bodies, whereas the whole point of the holocaust after 1940 was the targeted killing and elimination of the Jewish people. But what if, in the course of exploiting them economically, the enslaved were worked to death? On this, an observation by Helen Fein is instructive. "Planners of genocide who seek total annihilation," she wrote, "are not concerned with exploitation in any rational economic sense. The way in which genocide 'trumps' exploitation was shown in how Jewish slaves were worked to death during the Holocaust in slave-labor camps . . . Slave owners, by contrast, have an economic interest in preserving their slaves as capital" (2007: 21).

One scholar of genocide who sharply departs from this view is Alex Hinton (2022), who vigorously argues that the Black American experience in America amounts to genocide, especially when considered in its entirety. Borrowing the term "structural genocide" from Patrick Wolfe (2006), Hinton argues that genocide is best seen as a process unfolding over time, a view also held by both Lemkin and Fein, and one that entails the destruction of a people's heritage and social being. This had been the argument made by William Patterson and Paul Robeson in the petition *We Charge Genocide*, on behalf of the Civil Rights Congress, a radical Black group, which was presented to the UN in 1951 (and again in 1970 by an Emergency Conference Committee chaired by Ossie Davis); it was summarily dismissed on both occasions (Patterson, 1970). Lemkin himself was among those rubbishing the petition after its first submission, on the familiar grounds that slavery was not genocide because the slaveholder sought to preserve the life of their slaves the better to exploit them and, further, that Blacks were doing relatively well after slavery. It was not one of Lemkin's finer moments, since it contradicted his own arguments on culture and genocide (on which, see Moses, 2010), arguments that Hinton cites in his defense of the petition:

In his unpublished notes, Lemkin includes "slavery – exposure to death" as a physical technique of genocide along with "separation of families," which was also common with enslaved peoples. For Lemkin, influenced in part by German philosophy, the key element was the destruction of the "spirit" of a people. Forcibly removing people from Africa and placing them in a situation in which they were racially codified, regulated, and dehumanized as "Blacks" (and other slurs) would seem to meet Lemkin's criteria for genocide. From this perspective, the plight of Blacks in the United States at the time of the *We Charge Genocide* petition, particularly in the Jim Crow South, could arguably be viewed as part of a long-term genocidal process – one that also involved crimes against humanity. While Lemkin did consider the destruction of Indigenous people as genocide, he also failed to mention Native Americans in the context of the *We Charge Genocide* debate. Instead, and continuing a pattern that has persisted into the present, Lemkin helped sweep consideration of the legacy of genocide and atrocity crimes in the United States under the rug. (2022: 142)

I might add that many other slave systems in antiquity and the New World amounted to genocides rather than simply crimes against humanity. In antiquity, there were several unambiguous cases of genocide. Among the ancient Greeks, slavery in the Laurion silver mines of fifth- and fourth-century BCE Attica, where up to 35,000 toiled naked under hot, brutal conditions, stands out (Lauffer, 1979: 57–61); so too did the various "urbicides," or total destruction, mass killings, and enslavement by the ancient Greeks against other Greek city-states as well as non-Greek urban centers. According to Herodotus, Arisba on Lesbos was "andrapodized," meaning that, after the men had been slaughtered, the women and children were sold into slavery like mere *tetrapoda*, or four-footed animals. And in what was possibly the most extreme case of genocide among the Greeks, in 424 BCE, Aegina was destroyed and those not massacred in the siege were taken back to Athens and slaughtered in cold blood (Cartledge, 2023). Clear cases of genocide by the Romans include the destruction of Carthage, Numantia, and Corinth (Taylor, 2023a) and possibly Caesar's conquest of Gaul (Taylor, 2023b). Late medieval and early modern Europe presents what is one of the most extreme cases in all history of genocide as complete annihilation, that of the Spanish destruction of the peoples and cultures of the seven Canary Islands between 1402 and 1496, entailing "the erasure of their names, language, custom, economy, land ownership, ecological environment, beliefs, culture, social structure, and political organization" by means of "enslavement, deportation, disease, and the strategic use of terror"

(Tostado, 2023). In the New World, slavery in the coffee county of nineteenth-century Vassouras, Brazil (Stein, 1986), in eighteenth-century St. Domingue, later Haiti (Burnard and Garrigus, 2016),[4] and in nineteenth-century Cuba (Fraginals, 1976) all went well beyond mere crimes against humanity into the category of genuine genocides, along lines similar to what I document below.

8.3: Slavery and protracted genocide in Jamaica, 1655–1838: A counterfactual comparison with US slavery

My problem with works discussing slavery and genocide is that they take too monolithic a view of New World slavery. There was significant variation among the New World slave systems, which complicates comparing slavery with genocide. There were differences due to the imperial framework under which they operated; differences due to the cultural origins of the slaveholder classes; differences in kinds of economies, from those with small-scale family farm systems as the norm to the dominance of large plantation systems; differences in patterns of residence of the slaveholder class, from those that were predominantly local in residence to those in which the wealthiest slaveholders were absentee; and so on.

In exploring the problem of genocide, ethnocide, and slavery, I find that the US South and Jamaica constituted two paradigmatic cases. For Blacks in the US slave system, the experience was one of classic ethnocide – deracination from their African cultural background and reduction to a state of social death in which they did not belong to the society in which they found themselves, even though, by the early eighteenth century, the great majority were born there. This, like all slaveries, was a crime against humanity, as is now clearly mandated in the Rome statute (1998) on genocide and related crimes. Their experience, however, was not that of genocide, as their demographic history makes clear.[5] For Jamaican Blacks, on the other hand, I

---

[4] At one point during the late eighteenth century, Haiti accounted for a third of the entire slave trade to the Americas.

[5] I think a better case for the charge of genocide in the experience of Black Americans can be made for the Jim Crow, neo-slavery era, when thousands of Blacks were brutally murdered in extra-judicial killings that were attended by large numbers of Whites from all levels of the society, including ordained ministers of religion. There is no doubt about the intent of the *génocidaires*, the racial targeting of the Black population and the collective desire to exterminate them, especially by lower-class whites not dependent on their labor, who, indeed, saw them as competitors. I have shown (Patterson, 1998a) that the ritualized savagery of the killings in many cases had an almost cannibalistic aspect.

SLAVERY IN THE MODERN WORLD

will show that the system was one of protracted genocide, with a cumulative physical destruction of what amounted to nearly 6 million persons. The remainder of this chapter will offer evidence for this claim.

Both the US South and Jamaica were plantation systems that originated in British imperialism, with slaveholder classes from Britain. Until 1776 they were both also part of the British empire. Although both were plantation systems, the scale of slave-ownership differed: the average ownership was only about ten slaves in the United States, while, on a typical large Jamaican plantation, the average ownership was more than one hundred slaves. In the US South, the majority of people were free and White. In Jamaica, from the early eighteenth century, the vast majority were Black and enslaved, the enslaved population outnumbering Whites and the relatively few free non-Whites, by more than ten to one. For the Whites who survived the tropical diseases, Jamaica became a source of great riches, far beyond that of US Whites.[6]

One fundamental difference between the two systems was the survival rate of the Black populations. In America, the planter class from early on calculated that it made economic sense to encourage the reproduction of their slave population, a decision encouraged by the cheaper cost of food in the United States, where there was a large, free farming population and abundant land. As we will see, the kind of crops they grew – tobacco and, later, cotton – also made a reproductive slave strategy more profitable. This was in sharp contrast with Jamaica, where the sugar crop and slave trade led the slaveholding class to an economic calculation in which reproduction was seen as too costly and was replaced by one in which young Africans were bought and worked mercilessly with little concern for their welfare.

Death was everywhere in Jamaican slave society, as I showed in *The Sociology of Slavery* (1967) and its literary sequel, *Die the Long Day* (1972) – the physical death they tried to shun, the social death that they could not. I use the term "protracted" or "slow-moving" genocide to explain the demographic and social situation of the Black population of Jamaica during the period of British slavery, from 1655 to 1838, somewhat similar to the protracted destruction of the Canary Islanders between 1402 and 1496.[7] This is not a metaphor.

Yale Historian James Whitman (2018), has shown that the Nazi movement was strongly influenced by American race law and practice during this period (see also Cooper, 2012).
[6] There is now a large bibliography on slavery in Jamaica, on which see Patterson, 2022.
[7] The island was discovered by Columbus in 1494 and settled by the Spanish in 1509, who held it until 1655, when it was conquered by the British.

With the data from the Atlantic slave trade database now available, it is possible to calculate more precisely the real death toll of Jamaican slavery by using a simple counterfactual strategy. What is needed is another slave society that shows what might have been possible – a counterfactual – had the British proto-Leviathan in Jamaica not pursued the demographic strategy of buying, ruthlessly overexploiting, and replacing their enslaved from the African slave trade. The demographic experience of the ethnocidally enslaved in North America provides just such a counterfactual case.[8]

The distinguished American historian Richard Dunn has given us an indelible meso-level demographic analysis of these "two radically different slave systems in action," wherein the Jamaican planters treated the enslaved "as disposable cogs in a machine: importing slaves from Africa, working them too hard, feeding them too little, exposing them to debilitating disease, and routinely importing new Africans to replace those who died," in contrast to the demographic growth of the enslaved in Virginia (2014: 73). To be sure, the American slaveholders were no angels, for, as Michael Tadman (2000) has shown, the reproductive choice was made easier for them by virtue of the fact that the crop from which they made their wealth was not sugar; that, indeed, where they were sugar planters, as in Louisiana, they were just as inhumanly destructive as their Jamaican counterparts, with similarly lethal demographic consequences.

Two arguments against this counterfactual strategy must be considered. The first, that environmental and epidemiological factors prevented such a reproductive approach by the Jamaican planters, can be dismissed with one word: Barbados – a very similar West Indian slave society that was so successful at reproduction that it was capable of providing other eastern Caribbean islands with enslaved and ex-enslaved before and after abolition. Furthermore, it appears that the disease environment of the US South was not that much better for the enslaved than that which prevailed in Jamaica, reflected in the fact that mortality rates were not very different, although there is some question about this (Fogel and Engerman, 1979; but cf. Tadman, 2000: 1558).

The second argument, that the American slaveholders were both more willing and better able to feed their enslaved because of their

---

[8] The striking differences in the demographic patterns of North America and the West Indies were remarked on from the late eighteenth century and used in abolitionist advocacy (see Higman, 1984: 305–6). They were also noted by DuBois (1935: 4); Philip Curtin (1969: 88–9) drew closer attention to them, as did Fogel and Engerman (1974: 25).

large farming communities, while generally true, should be carefully qualified. Tadman has shown that there were huge mortality differences between Blacks and Whites in America, and that the more favorable reproduction rate of American Blacks than those in the Caribbean came at great cost to the former. In other words, it was not all that costly to American planters to ensure the much greater reproduction of the enslaved. The difference is explained in terms of the extremely exploitative demands of the sugar plantation system, where more profits could be made by relying on the slave trade to both replenish and increase the population and provide more males than females. Furthermore, as many studies have now shown, Jamaica was an integral part of the Atlantic economic system for the entire period of slavery and bought much of its staples and food from America. Additionally, profit margins in Jamaica far exceeded those of the American slave South. From Trevor Burnard's calculations, in the late eighteenth century the wealth of Southern planters "paled beside that of Jamaica," and "the average White in Jamaica was 36.6 times wealthier than the average White in the Thirteen Colonies" (Burnard, 2001: 519–20). Therefore, had they so desired, the Jamaican planters could easily have bought more food and other necessities to pursue a successful reproductive strategy, as Barbadian slaveholders successfully did, instead of overworking and underfeeding them (Sheridan, 1965: 292, 311). On the evidence of the planters themselves, the cost of rearing an enslaved person to the age of fourteen in 1831–32, was not much higher in Jamaica than Barbados: 112 pounds sterling, compared to 109 sterling in Barbados, much lower than in other slave colonies such as Trinidad where it was 162 sterling (Hall, 1962: 307). Given that Jamaica is over 25 times the size of Barbados, with far more resources complementing the plantation system than in mono-crop Barbados (cattle pens, numerous rivers for irrigation and mill-power, protected harbors, relatively abundant forests, several commercial centers, and its large export-oriented coffee sector which very likely exercised a positive joint demand for the dominant sugar crop, given that consumption of the former strongly activated the need to consume the latter in the British and American markets), with a more rational, less blindly exploitative strategy, it could easily have far exceeded Barbados, and replicated America's reproductive performance. Instead, planter economic calculations resulted in a slave system where "the lives of the enslaved population in Jamaica were the most miserable in the Atlantic World, especially in the first half of the eighteenth century, when ... the great majority of slaves were traumatized, brutalized, and alienated migrants from Africa" (Burnard and Garrigus, 2016: 38).

It must be concluded, then, that the demographic strategy of the Jamaican slaveholder was one of clear choice. As demographic historian Kenneth Kiple (1985: 104–19) notes, "as long as a master had control over a slave's life, he controlled to a large extent what he consumed," and obviously his physical survival. As I was among the first to point out (Patterson, 1967: Chs. 6–8), and Kiple later specified at length, Jamaican slaves spent their lives hungry and malnourished, on the verge of starvation with numerous nutritional diseases resulting in endemic bone and dental problems, debilitating mood swings, pellagra, beriberi due to widespread thiamine deficiency, dropsy, and dirt-eating, which was a desperate response to calcium and other mineral deficiencies as well as pure hunger. All of this weighed especially hard on children, whom "malnutrition tormented twice, working much of its debilitating and often deadly effects through poor maternal nutrition before even touching the child via his own nutritional intake" (Kiple, 1985: 103). This is reminiscent of the early concentration camps of Germany such as Dachau and the numerous ad hoc detention centers where malnourished inmates were worked near to death before the final phase of direct killings (Pohl, 1923).

This being so, consider Figures 8.1 and 8.2. Figure 8.1 shows the relative percentages of slaves taken to Jamaica and the North American mainland by decade between 1651 and 1830. Between 1651 and 1660, North America received far more slaves than Jamaica. In 1655 Jamaica was captured by the British from the Spanish and, instantly, everything changed. Between five and ten times more slaves were delivered to Jamaica than to *all* of North America during the six decades after 1660 and the last three decades of the eighteenth century, and more than twice as many in the decades in between. Figure 8.2 shows the cumulative effect in absolute numbers: between 1650 and 1830, a total of 1,017,109 Africans were disembarked in Jamaica, while only 388,233 were taken to North America. However, in 1830 there were 2,009,048 enslaved in America and, including free Blacks, some 2,328,442 Black souls. At that time, there were only 319,070 enslaved in Jamaica and, all told, 357,147, including people of some Black ancestry.

What this astonishing difference amounts to is this: had Africans and their descendants experienced the same rate of increase in Jamaica as had occurred in North America (a quite modest reproductive bar), the theoretically possible 1830 enslaved population in the

219

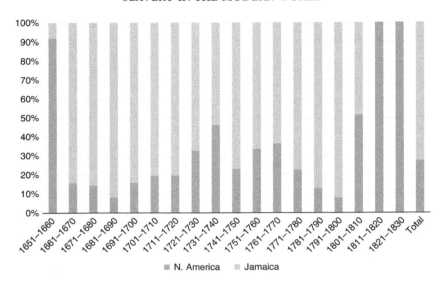

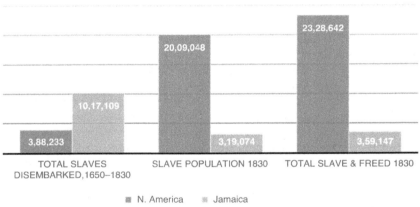

Figures 8.1 and 8.2 Graphs composed by author from Trans-Atlantic Slave Trade Database. https://www.slavevoyages.org/assessment/estimates

island would have been 5,262,522 and its total Black population (including free colored or people of mixed ancestry) would have been 6,090,499. Taking account of the 359,147 survivors in 1830, and using North American slavery as a counterfactual yardstick, we must conclude that there were 5,731,302 missing Black Jamaicans in 1830, which is a measure of British protracted genocide of Black people in the island between 1655 and 1830. To express this in the stronger causal terms of a counterfactual conditional: *had it not been for the distinctive features of Jamaican slavery, 5,731,302 Jamaican lives would not have been lost.* (My estimate, I hasten to add, is confined to the Jamaican enslaved population, both the Africans brought there and their descendants, with no implications for African lives lost in Africa.[9]) This figure, we might note, is not much smaller than the 6 million Jews eliminated in the Nazi holocaust. Jamaican slavery, we conclude, was a clear case of genocide.

To be sure, there are varieties of genocide (on which, see Rosenbaum, 1996; Bloxham and Moses, 2010: Parts 3 and 4; Kiernan, 2023). The British genocide of Blacks in Jamaica took place over 183 years rather than the twelve years of the Nazi holocaust and the two to four years of the Ottoman genocide of at least 1.1 million Armenians between 1914 and 1918. Furthermore, the fact that Jamaican Blacks were not totally exterminated does not make their experience any less genocidal. As Lemkin pointed out in his classic statement, "total extermination was not necessary for genocide to occur" (cited in Moses, 2010: 21). Some Jews survived. Some Jamaicans survived. Lemkin also observed that genocide was best viewed as a process over time rather than as an event.

From all this, it is clear that what happened in Jamaica between 1655 and 1838 was genocide in every sense of the term, for what we find is both ethnocultural destruction (ethnocide), physical killing, and brutalization on a large scale, and the denial of existence to 5,731,302 souls. While both were genocide, there are three differences between the Nazi and the Jamaican genocides. The first is temporal, the fact that the Jewish social death – the ethnocide accompanying genocide – lasted for 12 years (1933 to 1945), while that of Jamaicans lasted for 183 years of deracination: the loss of connection with their past, of any recognized sense of any rights in, or belonging to, the land of their birth, to their own children and parents, to their very selves and bodies. The second, already mentioned, that the Jewish *physical* elimination was concentrated over a short period of approximately 5 years, while that of Jamaicans lasted for 183 years in the drip, drip, drip of shortened lives and curtailed fertility, lives that led one mid-eighteenth-century enslaved man, speaking no doubt for countless others, to say to his tormenting enslaver: "If this be living, he did not care whether he lived or died" (Hall, 1989: 204).

---

[9] The question of the demographic impact of the Atlantic slave trade on West Africa is a complex one, which this argument avoids (see Manning, 1992).

The third concerns the nature of the elimination, and is likely the most contentious: in the case of the Jews, actual living bodies were destroyed; in the case of the Jamaicans, in addition to the abbreviated lives and outright individual murders, mass executions, and suicides, potential living bodies were preventively destroyed – lives that would almost certainly have happened, should by any and all human standards have eventuated, under the quite reasonable counterfactual condition. As we noted several times previously, both the 1948 Genocide Convention and subsequent reaffirmations make the prevention of births a central element of genocide. The absence of these 5,731,302 Jamaican lives is not a hypothetical. It was a deliberate curtailment. Like female gendercide, the deliberate preventive obliteration of up to 150 million females mainly through sex-selective termination of pregnancies was not just a crime against humanity, but genocide. The comparison with gendercide is clarifying in that it emphasizes the fact that genocide need not involve deliberate killings, actual bodies, or concerted mass murder (although these frequently happened in Jamaica, especially after real and attempted plots of rebellion, as well as in gendercide with infanticide). As Mary Warren pointed out: "not all instances of genocide involve direct or deliberate killing. Deaths or cultural disintegration deliberately or negligently brought about through starvation, disease or neglect may also be genocidal. Indeed, some acts of genocide *do not involve any deaths at all, but rather consist in the wrongful denial of the right to reproduce*" (1985: 22–3; emphasis added).

Let us, finally, consider the issue of intent to exterminate, which, as noted earlier, has become a contentious matter in the definition and study of genocide. There is an important preliminary matter that is rarely discussed in considerations of whether New World slaveries constituted genocide. This is the fact that the issue is usually conceived in terms of the descendants of the Africans who were transported from Africa, rather than from the perspective of the 12.5 million Africans who were forcibly brought to the Americas in what still remains the largest forced migration in human history. It is important to point out that this experience of being hunted down, captured, and transported under horrendous conditions during the middle passage is itself an unambiguous act of genocide, greater than any other in the modern world. The classicist, Tristan Taylor, in his excellent study of genocidal episodes in ancient Roman history (2023a), makes the point well and the relevant passage deserves to be quoted in its entirety since it is equally applicable to the experience of Africans at the hands of modern Europeans:

SLAVERY AND GENOCIDE

The fact that the Romans enslaved the population of these cities that survived the siege and sack, rather than killed them, raises the question of whether the intention was to "destroy" the group "as such." Although enslavement itself was not necessarily a path to swift death in the Greco-Roman world (not all were sent to live short lives in the mines), the impact of mass enslavement and dispersal of the population *was as consequential as massacre for a group's elimination*. Most would be dispersed to separate unknown fates in unknown destinations, unable to continue the group of which they were a part through both the prevention of endogamous biological reproduction and their inability to perform the various cultural acts constitutive of the group's collective identity. In considering the Convention definition of genocide, mass enslavement could thus be considered as an act that imposed conditions of life calculated to bring an end to the group. In relation to children, enslavement also involves their forcible transfer between groups, and indeed as the entire surviving group was dispersed, endogamous biological reproduction was prevented, acts also listed in the Convention definition. It cannot be doubted that the Romans were aware that mass enslavement would have such consequences.

Nor can it be doubted that the British, French, Dutch, Portuguese, Spanish, Danish, and Swedish slave-traders who transported those 12.5 million Africans, and the Europeans who bought and enslaved them, were aware of the consequences of their action. The enslavement and transportation of 12.5 million Africans to the Americas was not just a "crime against humanity," as the Rome Statute would have it; it was the modern world's greatest act of outright genocide. Whether it is called "pragmatic" or "ideological" genocide is a distinction that descendants of this Black holocaust are justified in considering spurious.

Let us return, however, to the matter at hand: whether the Jamaican experience of the 1,017,109 Africans who ended up in that island, and their descendants, amounted to another outright crime of genocide. All the genocide conventions, starting with the UN 1948 Declaration, include the deliberate denial of reproduction to a group as one fundamental element of genocide. As we have seen, the evidence is abundant that the Jamaican planters *intended* to prevent their slaves from reproducing for 153 of the 183 years of British slavery. Only during the last thirty years of the system, after their external source of slaves was cut off by the abolition of the slave trade in 1807, did they begin to make desultory and largely unsuccessful attempts to encourage and provide the conditions for slave women to reproduce. Before that, they intentionally did everything to prevent reproduction. They did so, first, through the mass assault on enslaved women, nearly all

223

of whom were repeatedly raped from the age of puberty and even earlier. This was a deliberate and systematic form of terror, meant not simply to satisfy the sexual needs of the slaveholder but, as Burnard (2004: 156–62) has pointed out, an exercise in total power: "White men molested slave women in part because they could do so without fear of social consequence and in part because they constantly needed to show the enslaved the extent of their dominance. The institutional dominance of White men had to be translated into personal dominance." The rape of the enslaved woman was an expression of dominance not only over her but also over the men of her group, a pattern of exploitation found in all slave societies, as Ruth Karras, a scholar of medieval England and Scandinavia, has cogently pointed out:

> There is a significant overlap between the factors of desire and domination. For men of the enslaving class to assert that privilege is an act of domination over people of other groups, notably people of whatever ethnic or racial group or social class was being enslaved in that particular culture . . . sex with one's enslaved women or men could carry with it a message of dominance over other men: men who are raped; enslaved men who are less masculine because they are unable to protect the victims; men whose wives, daughters, sons, sisters, brothers have been captured and raped (even if the men in question are dead, their posthumous reputation may still be dominated). (2023: 216)

The systematic mass rape of enslaved women also had a health component detrimental to reproduction. There is evidence that the great majority of enslaved women suffered from the European strain of gonorrhea, especially the more vulnerable African women, among whom, on one estate for which we have accurate data, every woman was infected within three months of her arrival (Hall, 1989: 135). There was no cure for gonorrhea until the twentieth century. Untreated, it causes pelvic inflammatory disease that permanently damages the reproductive system, leading to infertility, miscarriage, and stillbirth. There was also a psychological dimension to the mass rape of enslaved women, which directly affected their reproductive capacity. Helen Fein has pointed out that:

> Genocidaires might choose to prevent reproduction within the group or to appropriate the progeny in order to destroy the group in the long run. Rape, forced marriage and sexual slavery, enforced pregnancy, forced adoption and conversion of children, and forced abortions are means to this end. Rape is not just a means of torture, causing serious bodily and mental harm to women. Rape also threatens the future of the group by often impeding the future marriage of unmarried women,

SLAVERY AND GENOCIDE

who are shamed by the stigma, and threatens the classification of the child as a member of the mother's group rather than that of the rapist. (2007: 134–6)

Quite apart from the fact that marriage was forbidden among the enslaved, there is ample evidence that the chronic rape of enslaved women by their White enslavers not only created lasting trauma among the enslaved women but ravaged their relationship with enslaved men, leading to enduring relational problems that affected slave women's desire and capacity to reproduce (Patterson, 1967: 159–74). Furthermore, consistent with Fein's observation, the mulatto progeny of the rape of enslaved women notoriously sought to define themselves out of the Black group and racial identity of their mothers (the source of the island's, and broader Caribbean's, vicious colorism), an identity rejection strongly encouraged by the enslavers who, given their extreme numeric minority of less than one in ten of the total population, needed their alliance.

Beyond problems of conception and reproduction caused by rape, other factors prevented reproduction. One was the shortage of women among the enslaved. Because of the reliance on forced migration through the slave trade for population replacement and growth, and the slaveholders' bias toward purchasing males for the plantations, there was a severe gender imbalance in the slave population throughout the period of slavery. The effects on reproduction and the stability of male–female relationships can easily be imagined. Still other factors prevented reproduction. When women, against all the odds, became pregnant, they found conditions created by the enslavers threatening their pregnancy at every turn. Thus pregnant women were forced to work – on most plantations in greater numbers than men, who were disproportionately employed in skilled tasks – in the grueling cane fields nearly up to the day of delivery, greatly increasing the risk of miscarriages. Furthermore, they were refused any extra support for those infants who were delivered; mothers who managed to give birth were forced to return to the canefield within days of their delivery, leaving their infants in the care of aged, often unhealthy, weak and malnourished women who were given little or no means to care for them, resulting in extremely high rates of infant mortality. Finally, those few children who survived infancy were put to work in children's gangs at an early age, making it unlikely that many would survive to adulthood. Slaveholders outwardly wished for their death, since they calculated that the cost of feeding them was not worth the risk of their dying before reaching the age at which they would begin to pay for their keep. It was far more efficient to simply buy a young male off the slave ship (Patterson 2022 [1967]: 254–74).

This all amounted to protracted genocide. Fein is emphatic on this cause of genocide, which is an element of the crime, and on the fact that, by its nature, it tends to occur over time. Citing the UN 1948 Genocide Convention, Fein wrote:

> "Causing serious bodily or mental harm to members of the group" and "deliberately inflicting on the group conditions of life calculating to bring about its physical destruction in whole or in part" can include imposing disease-producing conditions and starvation in communities, camps, and ghettos; slave labor; torture; and poisoning air and weather. This is *"genocide by attrition"* which I have documented in Sudan, in the Warsaw Ghetto (1941–1943), and in Democratic Kampuchea (1975–1979). (2007: 133; emphasis added)

To conclude, for 183 years Jamaicans had their ancestral memories and traditional cultures destroyed; their actual lives devastated, ruthlessly exploited, and severely shortened; their bodies frequently lashed to the point of passing out and death; their attempts at self-defense met with gibbeting, beheadings, quarterings, and slow death from starvation while hung from public posts, to be eaten by vultures and wild dogs; their familial bonds shattered; their female bodies obsessively raped with impunity and infected with life-shortening variants of venereal diseases not present in Africa; their reproductive rights denied; their infants neglected; their children malnourished, naked, and neglected, leading to the accumulation of 5,731,302 missing persons. One can think of few more heinous cases of outright genocide.

Coda

When British slavery was finally abolished in 1838, Jamaicans, as we have noted, had experienced it for 183 years. The island has never fully recovered from the uniquely violent decimation of that first half of its history. "One of the characteristics of traumatic memory," Dan Stone has written, "is that it cannot be suppressed at will," and societies remain scarred long after its experience (2010: 102, 114). The Prime Minister of Jamaica, the Honorable Andrew Holness, in his 2021 Emancipation Day speech commemorating the abolition of slavery in the island, noted that it had been 183 years since abolition, and he talked of the role that the last great rebellion of the enslaved, led by National Hero Samuel Sharpe, had played in bringing it about.

He then added something with which his entire nation would have somberly agreed: *"The use of violence has followed us from our history."* Today, Jamaica remains one of the most violent nations in the world, as it was in the eighteenth century, with a homicide rate that places it in the top five of all nations, and a rate of femicide, the murder of women, consistently at the very top of the world's nations, a self-destructive pattern of gendercide directly inherited from the violent interpersonal traumas of the slave plantation (UN, 2019). The "dead yards" of the nation's slums (Thomson, 2011) bear ghoulish witness to the plantation dead yards in that first half of its existence.[10] For Jamaica today, as for all other peoples who descend from the remnants of genocide who physically survived, "the politics of post-genocidal memories are matters of life and death" (Stone 2010: 115).

That first half of Jamaica's history has never been fully told. If the truth be told, it can never be fully known. Genocide, fast or slow moving, is existentially unknowable. Unimaginable. As Ken Kiernan (2023) observed, "Genocide has a way of imposing silence." We try as historians and sociologists to fathom and feel its horror, its sorrow, its unrelenting grief, its preternatural evil. But in its hollow-ing banality,[11] it defies all understanding. Having reached the limits of historical and sociological understanding, I tried to imagine that first half of our past in the literary sequel to the *Sociology of Slavery*, my novel, *Die the Long Day*, which drew on the materials I had col-lected for the earlier sociohistorical work to recreate a day of death and celebratory mourning on an eighteenth-century slave plantation. During the mourning for the murdered heroine, an old Fanti woman, slightly crazed, wanders amidst the mourners, repeatedly wailing in a voice as dark as death, a dirge that was all she had remembered from her deracinated African past. It went like this:

Do not say anything,
O Mother, Sister,
Do not say anything.
For anything you say will be too much,
And nothing you say will be enough.

---

[10] For a more historically grounded reflection on the historical roots of contemporary violence in Jamaica, see Lemonius, 2017.
[11] I echo here Hannah Arendt's 1963 *New Yorker* essay, "Eichmann in Jerusalem: A Report on the Banality of Evil," by which she meant the normalization of wickedness, which is about as apt a description of Jamaican slave society as I can think of.

IV

Slavery Today

— 9 —

HUMAN TRAFFICKING, MODERN-DAY SLAVERY, AND OTHER FORMS OF SERVITUDE

A striking development since the 1980s has been activism around claims of modern-day slavery and the trafficking of persons into servitude. This trend has been fueled by an unusual degree of celebrity engagement, press coverage, and popular interest (Gulati, 2012; Haynes, 2014). A search of the English text corpus in Google Books Ngram Viewer, a tool used to chart the frequency of a term's usage in published literature over time, shows that the use of the term "slave labor," since its sharp surge during the American Civil War era of the 1860s, rose to another peak during the civil rights era and began to rise again in the mid-1980s. Interest in the term "forced labor" quickly picked up after the 1920s and since then has followed a similar trend to that of "slave labor" (see Figure 9.1). Figure 9.2 indicates that references to various terms related to servitude started to take off in about the early 1990s, the most significant being "human trafficking." One study (Limoncelli, 2017) also finds that the number of NGOs addressing the problem of trafficking globally began to grow in the mid-1980s. By one count, as of July 2023, there are some 2,569 antislavery organizations operating both within countries and internationally (Polaris, 2023).

We are led to inquire into the nature and extent of the phenomena that prompted this surge of interest and activism. The common conflation of all forms of forced labor with slavery and the often exaggerated claims about the number of modern slaves, such as the fallacious assertion that there are more slaves today than at the height of the Atlantic slave systems in the eighteenth and nineteenth centuries (Bales, 2007, 2012; van den Anker, 2004),[1] have led to

---

[1] Estimates of global slavery today include bonded laborers, who make up more than half the totals. Bonded laborers existed in even greater numbers in the eighteenth and

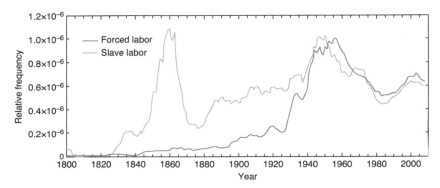

Figure 9.1 Ngrams on use of terms "slave labor" and "forced labor," 1800–2010

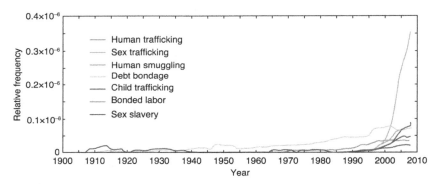

Figure 9.2 Ngrams on use of seven related terms re trafficking and slavery, 1900–2010

justifiable skepticism among many scholars (Bunting and Quirk, 2017). Nonetheless, servitude – including, at its extreme, modern-day forms of slavery – is experienced by a non-negligible proportion of the global population, nearly one of every 150 living persons, by one authoritative estimate. The issue poses urgent challenges for leaders, policymakers, legislators, and scholars.

There is currently a substantial and growing interdisciplinary literature on the nature, types, and extent of modern servitude (Goździak and Bump, 2008). We will not attempt to cover this entire literature here. Instead, we seek to clarify the main terms in the field and identify some of the more important substantive and methodological issues

nineteenth centuries, but are excluded from global estimates of slavery in these earlier periods.

in its study. The first section examines the most basic terms in the field and several serious terminological and definitional questions they raise; the second section discusses types of servitude and the continuum of experiences associated with each type; the third section assesses approaches and problems in estimating the size of the populations of interest; and the fourth section briefly discusses the multilevel factors that contribute to the rise of modern slavery and other forms of servitude. A concluding section briefly assesses the effectiveness of the antitrafficking movement, indicates some of the important gaps in the field, and urges greater engagement of sociologists with the subject.

9.1: Servitude, slavery, trafficking, and smuggling

There is general agreement that the study of trafficking and modern slavery is beset by serious definitional problems. In a critique of what she calls "exploitation creep," J. A. Chuang (2014) has noted a growing tendency to categorize all forms of exploited labor as forced labor and also to equate them with trafficking and even slavery. Muddled definitions and operationalization challenge the validity and comparability of empirical findings. This problem has been compounded by the otherwise valuable joint International Labour Office reports on modern "slavery" (2017b; ILO et al., 2022). Thus we begin by making clear what we mean by the most basic terms in the field: servitude, forced labor, slavery, trafficking, and smuggling, along with what we term "abusive migration."

Servitude: Reviving a serviceable old term

Definitional problems begin with how to designate the most generic term in the field. Until 2017, the ILO, the most authoritative body on the subject, had settled on the term "forced labor," occasionally using "servitude" as a synonym. The term "forced labor," whatever its limitations, had the advantage of avoiding the tendency of antitrafficking and abolitionist activists to identify all forms of exploitation as slavery. Unfortunately, in its much anticipated 2017 report on the subject, and continuing in its more recent 2022 report, the ILO changed its position to that of one of its new collaborators, the Walk Free Foundation, which advocates "modern slavery" as the umbrella term for all forms of modern exploited labor. The need for a new generic term, I suspect, was also driven by the decision, which I applaud, to include for the first time forced marriage as a form of

SLAVERY TODAY

servitude. This made "forced labor" as the generic term somewhat problematic since forced marriages do not necessarily entail forced labor. I agree that another inclusive term would be more appropriate, but strongly disagree with the change to "modern slavery," not only because it misapplies and dilutes the term "slavery" (Kurasawa, 2017), but because it introduces a classificatory confusion in the analysis of a subtype of so-called slavery. The ILO divides modern slavery into forced labor and forced marriage, but one kind of forced labor is then identified as "work imposed in the context of slavery or vestiges of slavery," making the concept of slavery a subcategory of itself (ILO, 2017b: 17)

The umbrella term I propose is one that has long been used for this purpose, including by the ILO, namely, "servitude" (Bush, 2000: 3–5). Adapting and extending the earlier standard definition of forced labor, servitude can be defined as *that condition in which the work, service, or relationships of another person are not freely offered or, if voluntarily initiated, cannot be left or refused, and are maintained under the threat of physical or psychological coercion, violence, or some other penalty.* So defined, servitude embraces all known forms of exploitation or coercion, including forced labor, political imprisonment, forced marriage, sexual exploitation, enslavement and other degrading forms of domination not centered around labor exploitation. This definition of servitude also acknowledges an aspect of modern forms of exploitation too often neglected, that relations of domination are often fluid (Hoang and Parreñas, 2014); they are, not uncommonly, initiated by the victim or agreed to by them, then later become coercive (Andrijasevic, 2010; Cheng, 2014). *Forced labor* is all those forms of servitude in which the exploitation of labor, sexual and nonsexual, for profit is the primary motivation of the exploiter. Forced marriage, the other major category of modern servitude, refers to situations where persons, regardless of their age, have been forced to marry without their consent and, even with initial consent from adults, are forced to remain in the relationship against their will.

The ILO group estimates that, on any given day in 2021, there were 49.6 million persons in servitude,[2] of whom 27.6 million were in forced labor and 22 million in forced marriage (ILO et al., 2022: 2). Of this total, 54 percent were females and 46 percent males. Forced labor, following the 1930 Forced Labor Convention, was defined

---

[2] In this chapter I substitute the term "servitude" for what the ILO (2017b) called "slavery," except in those extreme cases on the continuum of servitude where I deem the term slavery to be appropriate.

as "all work or service which is exacted from any person under the menace of any penalty and for which the said person has not offered himself voluntarily" (2022: 2). Of the 27.6 million persons in forced labor 57 percent were males and 43 percent females. At the same time, of the 21.99 million persons in forced marriages, 68 percent were females and 32 percent males. A quarter of all persons in servitude were children. Forced labor grew by 2.7 million persons between 2016 (the pinpointed date of the previous estimate) and 2021, the increase attributed, in part, to the global rise in poverty caused by the COVID-19 pandemic.

Servitude may last from a few days or weeks to years in the case of bonded labor, or a lifetime for women in forced marriages, with an average of nearly two years for adult victims and 2.2 years for children. The average age for International Organization for Migration-registered victims of trafficking is 27, with half of all victims aged between 19 and 33 (CTDC, 2022). The great majority (59 percent) of people in servitude reside in the Asia Pacific region, followed by Africa (14 percent), Europe and Central Asia (13 percent), and the Americas (10 percent). However, in terms of prevalence per thousand persons, the Arab states have the highest proportions, with 10.1 of every 1,000 persons in servitude, followed by Europe and Central Asia (6.9 per 1000), Asia and the Pacific (6.8), Africa (5.2), and the Americas (5.2). As one would expect, the poorest countries have the highest prevalence of servitude per thousand persons.

The ILO and its collaborators are highly reputable organizations on the topic of servitude and exploitation. Aside from our misgivings about their terminology, we conditionally accept these figures as the best available working estimates, subject to critical examination and continuing revision.[3] In the section below, "Measuring servitude," we discuss the available approaches and their limitations in estimating the often hidden victims of servitude.

Slavery

In *Slavery and Social Death* (1982) I argued that the widely accepted definition of slavery by the League of Nations Slavery Convention of 1926 as "the condition of a person over whom any or all the powers attaching to the right of ownership are exercised" (UN OHCHR,

---

[3] The ILO (2017b) global estimates of modern slavery were derived from national household surveys and the IOM database, which is a complete shift from the capture-recapture method used in previous rounds. We discuss the methodologies used in making estimates of the different types of servitude below.

1926: 1), while not inaccurate in regard to ancient Roman and modern capitalistic slave systems, is insufficient for any global consideration of slavery. Slavery was found to be a heritable condition of social death (legal, civic, and symbolic) and degradation, a permanent outsider status sanctioned by the state, and institutionally reinforced by the broader culture and society (see also in this volume pp. 15–20 and Chapter 2). With a few notable exceptions, discussed below, slavery in this classic traditional form is largely extinct in the modern world and is formally illegal, or constitutionally prohibited, in nearly all states. However, certain extreme forms of modern servitude may be sufficiently slave-like to justify being called "modern-day slavery."

To clarify the exact legal meaning of the term modern-day slavery, an international research network of legal and social science scholars (in which I was included) met over a period of two years and produced the Bellagio-Harvard Guidelines on the Legal Parameters of Slavery (see Allain, 2012: esp. 375–80). Using the 1926 Slavery Convention's definition as a starting point, the group determined that its critical phrase "powers attaching to the right of ownership" should be understood, in contemporary terms, to mean power and "control over a person in such a way as to significantly deprive that person of his or her individual liberty, with the intent of exploitation through the use, management, profit, transfer or disposal of that person" (Allain, 2012: 376). Violence, deception, and other kinds of coercion are typical measures of control. Furthermore, the group concluded that "possession is foundational to an understanding of slavery, even when the State does not support a property right in respect of persons" (2012: 376). Effective possession may take the form of physical constraints or more abstract means such as enforcing a new identity through religion or marriage.

Building on the Bellagio-Harvard Guidelines, modern-day slavery can be defined as that condition in which one or more individuals or organizations exercise complete control and possession of another person's body, labor, capabilities, and movement through the overt or threatened use of violence or other forms of coercion. This is one extreme end on the continuum of modern servitude, and I advocate the use of the term "modern slavery" only in such instances. Moreover, modern-day slavery is not to be confused with situations where individuals are forced by extreme poverty and chronic inequality to voluntarily offer their labor in exchange for advances in income that result in exploitation such as debt bondage, if the conditions of complete control, possession, and inability to leave are unmet. This is what the World Bank calls "consensual exploitation," which, it

HUMAN TRAFFICKING, MODERN-DAY SLAVERY, AND SERVITUDE

argues, is best addressed through social and labor law rather than the criminal justice system (Koettl, 2009; for a different view, see Kara, 2014: 27–37).

Although I abide by this definition in this chapter and in my analysis and teaching of modern-day slavery, I should emphasize that it overlaps with, but is not the same as, historical slavery, the condition analyzed in the other chapters of this volume. In the first place, slavery is today illegal in all the nations of the world. Of course, the degree to which laws against slavery are taken seriously and prosecuted varies considerably across nations. This means that if the modern-day slave escapes from the control of their slaveholder, they cannot be returned and, indeed, can expect the protection of the authorities who, in the great majority of modern societies, will proceed to prosecute the slaveholder. Second, descent-based slavery is outlawed in theory and practice in all but five countries of the world. Descent-based slavery is the condition in which persons are born into slavery and their status is inherited by their children. As indicated earlier, the average length of time for the typical modern-day slave is measured in months, not a lifetime, with the exception of women trapped in marital slavery from which they desire to be liberated, and a few cases of extreme bonded labor. Third, while some modern-day slaves might be murdered by their slaveholders, this is rare, and in nearly all societies the offense carries the same penalty as that for free persons. In all traditional descent-based systems of slavery, the slaveholder had the power of life and death, without penalty, over their slaves, with laws forbidding the practice almost always being dead letters (discussed in Chapter 1). Finally, while the modern-day slave, when under the total violent control of the slaveholder, may experience something akin to social death, as has been reported of some enslaved prostitutes under the total control of their pimp-masters (Farley et al., 2004: 58), this is always a temporary condition in the modern setting and it lacks one of the fundamental elements of traditional social death – the fact that the condition was sanctioned and protected by the government, attitudes, culture, norms, and behavior of all free, non-slave members of the society in which the enslaved were held, and the enslaved usually had no home to return to. The five societies in which traditional, descent-based slavery is still practiced are briefly discussed below.

Definitions, however, are not etched in phenomenological granite. From a Wittgensteinian perspective, it may be argued that, if the occurrence and understanding of the characteristic elements of a practice in one period, say, the present, bear sufficient "family resemblance" to, and continuity with, its practice in another previous period, we may be justified in approximating the one to the other, as long as the differences are recognized and understood. Wittgenstein and his followers have gone so far as to argue that a category continues to exist even if nearly all the set of characteristic elements of a previous period have been gradually replaced, in an overlapping sequential process, by other characteristic elements. The basic idea is that categories are graded structures with central tendencies. I don't know if I go that far, but this is not the place to argue the matter (see Barsalou, 1985; for my own related, though by no means similar, view on the problem of continuity, see Patterson, 2004). We take the conception of modern-day slavery, clarified in the Bellagio-Harvard guidelines, as given, and carry on with the task at hand.

Trafficking

Trafficking has been formally defined and the definition adopted by nearly all nations in the so-called Palermo Protocol of 2000:

> "Trafficking in persons" shall mean the recruitment, transportation, transfer, harbouring or receipt of persons, by means of the threat or use of force or other forms of coercion, of abduction, of fraud, of deception, of the abuse of power or of a position of vulnerability or of the giving or receiving of payments or benefits to achieve the consent of a person having control over another person, for the purpose of exploitation. (UN OHCHR 2000: 42)

The protocol views the consent of the victim as irrelevant in defining trafficking where any of the specified means are used. The transportation of a child under the age of eighteen unexceptionally qualifies as trafficking, regardless of the means or the agreement of the child. This definition is not without issues, such as what constitutes deception and exploitation in light of varying labor standards, and what the role of agency is in defining trafficking, particularly in the case of persons under the age of eighteen who move in the face of brutal survival options (Davidson and Anderson, 2006; Gallagher, 2017; Huijsmans and Baker, 2012). Forced movement, internationally or domestically, is central to what constitutes trafficking. In other words, people in forced labor without going through forced movement do not count as victims of trafficking. We consider trafficking to be a process that may lead to different outcomes, rather than an end state (Allain, 2017). We do not agree with the growing tendency to apply the term trafficking to all forms of forced exploitation, although, here again, a sort of Wittgensteinian creep may be taking place.

HUMAN TRAFFICKING, MODERN-DAY SLAVERY, AND SERVITUDE

While trafficking usually results in some form of exploitation tantamount to forced labor, slavery being the most extreme, it is possible for a trafficked person to end up in a situation that, although exploitative, does not amount to forced labor. For example, many of the villagers recruited by labor brokers in the Chinese construction industry end up with living conditions and wages lower than they had bargained for, but as J. Chuang (2014: 59) shows, "the complex relation of debt and consent" between them and their brokers, while exploitative, falls short of the definition of forced labor. The same holds for thousands of Filipina women in the Tokyo hostess industry who were declared to have been trafficked and summarily deported back home against their will to conditions that they considered much worse than their situation in Tokyo (see Parreñas, 2011). "Soft trafficking," according to Frederick (1998), describes a survival strategy in which rural South Asian young women trafficked by family members into urban sex work end up supporting themselves and family back in their home villages (Skrivankova, 2017). Genuine trafficking may also result in servitude but not forced labor, as was true of Japanese Americans arrested, trafficked, and incarcerated in concentration camps by the US government during World War II (Herzig-Yoshinaga, 2009).

Trafficking is now a global phenomenon. The UN Office on Drugs and Crime recorded more than five hundred detected flows of trafficking between 2012 and 2014, many of which overlap with key migration routes; 60 percent of detected victims were moved across borders (UNODC, 2016). However, the most recent report of the UNODC (2022) on trafficking found, for the first time, an unexpected 11 percent drop in the number of persons trafficked between 2019 and 2020, especially in low- and mid-income countries. The most significant declines were for sexual exploitation (down 24 percent) and cross-border trafficking (down 21 percent). Furthermore, for the first time since it started to collect data on the problem, the percentage of persons detected for forced labor was equal to those detected for sexual exploitation (40 percent each). The reasons for this change, and what to make of it, are not clear. The Covid-19 pandemic was obviously involved. Some organizations, most notably the US State Department's *Trafficking in Persons* report, have claimed that the risks of trafficking for vulnerable and marginalized populations were greatly exacerbated by the pandemic, which also diverted the resources of official agencies from antitrafficking work to other problems created by the pandemic (US State Department, 2021: 2–23; see also ILO et al., 2022). While the restrictions on travel and gatherings in public spaces may have reduced the opportunities for trafficking, it is more likely that venues were changed and that activities became more secretive. The most likely explanation, as the 2022 UNODC report itself suggests, is that law enforcement in regard to trafficking was curtailed by the pandemic (ILO et al., 2022: 27).

Smuggling

Smuggling of persons entails their illegal entry into a country, often facilitated by third parties (UNODC, 2004). Like trafficking, it is a process rather than an end state, and the line between the two can sometimes be blurred. Smuggled persons voluntarily engage in the process, usually paying the smuggler and ending the transaction or relationship once the destination is reached. Smuggling always entails the illegal crossing of international borders, whereas trafficking may be domestic or involve legal crossing of borders. Human smuggling is a crime against the state, whereas trafficking is considered a crime against the person. Most advanced states now view the trafficked person as a victim, while the smuggled person is considered a law-breaker, although the UN protocol on the practice allows for the prosecution of smugglers, but explicitly excludes the prosecution of the smuggled (UNODC, 2004: 55, Article 5).

The number of smuggled persons surged in the 1980s and 1990s following tighter border control by destination states (Gallagher and David, 2014; Kyle and Koslowski, 2001). Audrey Singer and Douglas Massey (1998) found that 75 percent of unauthorized Mexicans entering the United States used coyotes or smugglers. The IOM reported some 2.5–3 million irregular migrants in Thailand, 80 percent of whom were smuggled (McAuliffe and Laczko, 2016). In 2010, the IOM estimated that 10–15 percent of the world's then 214 million migrants were irregular, equivalent to between 20 and 30 million persons (2010: 29). The numbers have increased, especially considering the European refugee crisis beginning in 2015, although no reliable estimate is currently available. There are different kinds of smugglers, "along a spectrum, from unconnected or loosely connected individuals making a modest profit from a limited smuggling market . . . to large, sophisticated organizations making significant profits from migrant smuggling offences" (UNODC, 2023: 3). Not all unauthorized migration is criminal or profit-driven; examples include altruistic smuggling, smuggling for humanitarian reasons, and self-smuggling (McAuliffe and Laczko, 2016). The UN Protocol on Smuggling explicitly excludes the prosecution of persons or organizations that aid illegal entry of migrants for humanitarian purposes. Experiences

HUMAN TRAFFICKING, MODERN-DAY SLAVERY, AND SERVITUDE

during or after the smuggling process also diverge. Sociologist Danilo Mandic and others (Mandic, 2017; Ahmet and Toktas, 2002) found that refugees into Europe often fear corrupt government officials and their anti-smuggling policies more than their smugglers, whom they view in pragmatic terms as more in line with their interests. In this case, smuggling is more accurately viewed as a transnational service industry linking smugglers as service providers with their smuggled clients (Bilger et al., 2006). At the other extreme, a smuggled person may become trafficked (Aronowitz, 2009; Human Rights Watch, 2014). In Yemen, for example, some smugglers abduct their clients after arrival, releasing them only after their families pay a hefty ransom. Sometimes, debt to the smugglers, either pre-agreed or later unfairly enforced, results in labor exploitation during the journey or at the destination (McAuliffe and Laczko, 2016). The current vast number of refugees and displaced persons due to conflicts or persecution suggests a potentially substantial overlap between trafficked persons, refugees, and smuggled migrants (UNODC, 2016).

Not all states have adopted the UN Protocol on Smuggling, and there is as yet no general agreement, even in the jurisprudence of advanced states, on the articles of the Protocol regarding the nonliability of smuggled migrants. While the Protocol supports the criminal prosecution of organized smuggling enterprises, and all forms involving payments by migrants to the smugglers, it limits the criminal justice response to the migrants and emphasizes their rights in international law. Thus, Article 5 states that "Migrants shall not become liable to criminal prosecution under this Protocol for the fact of having been the object of conduct" by the smuggler; and a "Saving clause" (Article 19) protects the rights of migrants under international humanitarian, human rights, and refugee status laws, especially the principle of non-refoulement (UNODC, 2004). However, legal and ethical complexities arise when migrants themselves partly engage with or help their smugglers, such as by navigating the boats or land vehicles that are provided by their for-profit smugglers (UNODC, 2023).

Abusive migration

Closely related to the smuggling process is what may be called "abusive migration" (see Haynes, 2009). It refers to the situation where a person legally enters a country with permission to work, usually under contract to a local employer, but the legitimate and mutually beneficial migrant employment subsequently transforms into one of forced labor. In some cases, deception or coercion started from the recruitment stage in the sending country (Harroff-Tavel and Nasri, 2013: 31–5). The *kafala* or sponsorship system of the Middle East offers a typical example. The prevalence of abusive migration, especially in Asia and the Middle East, results from both the pull of economic opportunities in the destination countries and the push of economic insecurity and transactional migration brokers in sending states (Peng, 2017). Although the sample of 354 migrant workers in the Middle East interviewed by Hélène Harroff-Tavel and Alix Nasri (2013) was not selected at random, it is remarkable that over 75 percent of the interviewed were assessed to be in forced labor. Several of the Gulf states have now formally abolished the *kafala* system, but observers indicate that migrants do continue to be exploited (Migrant-Rights.Org, 2018).

The 2017 ILO *Global Estimates of Modern Slavery* report gave no explicit estimates on trafficking and smuggling. However, it reported that a little under a quarter (23 percent) of all persons in servitude are exploited outside their country of residence, and that cross-border movement is more common in exploitation for sexual purposes (74 percent) than in other forms of forced labor (14 percent) (2017b: 29–30). The more recent report (ILO et al., 2022: 36) notes that 15 percent of all adults in forced labor in 2021 were migrants. The fact that, in 2019, only 5 percent of the total global labor force were migrants means that migrants are disproportionately represented among workers who are in forced labor. Nonetheless these figures also make clear that the great majority of persons in servitude are exploited in their own country and are not necessarily trafficked. Some, to be sure, are internally trafficked, but the common practice of attaching the term "trafficked" to all persons in forced labor is misleading.

9.2: Forms of servitude

Authorities disagree on how to classify, and what to include, in the typology of servitude. For instance, the UN includes illegal adoptions and organ trafficking, whereas the US State Department in its annual TIP report on trafficking does not. We use the following typology: traditional and modern slavery, bonded labor, international migrant forced laborers (or simply IMFL), domestic servitude, sexual servitude, child servitude, marital servitude, and state servitude.

Traditional, descent-based slavery

Different from modern-day slavery, as defined previously, traditional, descent-based slavery refers to those intergenerational systems that have persisted from the nineteenth century and earlier, not having been abolished, in spite of laws enacted to the contrary. They are found mainly in Mauritania, Niger, Sudan, Mali, and Côte d'Ivoire. Some research suggests that, far from declining, the number of people in these systems is increasing, especially in Sudan, long in the throes of a brutal war of secession followed by civil war. In Niger, an observation- and interview-based study in 2004 identified 810,363 persons in traditional hereditary slavery in a total population of 15.2 million (Abdelkader, 2004). Most experts agree that a substantial number of traditional slaves exist in Mauritania, but only one survey has been attempted, that of the Global Slavery Index (2017), which estimated that 43,000 persons were living in slavery in 2016, or 1.06 percent of a total population of 4 million. One estimate of the slave population of Sudan placed it at between 10,000 and 15,000 in 2000 (Jok, 2001); more recently, traditional slavery has been supplemented by modern slave trafficking, the country becoming a "transit source and destination country" for modern-day slaves (US State Department, 2017, pp. 371–3). Traditional slavery is also reliably reported to exist in Mali, especially in the north, where Tuareg slaveholders continue to lay claim on thousands of ex-slaves in spite of the legal abolition of the institution in the 1960s (Tran, 2012; US State Department, 2017). Several human rights organizations in Mali estimate the present size of the slave population there to be 800,000 who were born in slavery and approximately 200,000 who continue to live under the direct control of their slaveholders (UN Human Rights, 2023). It is a sad irony of the modern world that Africa, the continent that suffered so monstrously – demographically, politically, economically, and psychologically – from the long centuries of the Atlantic slave trade should remain the last region with traditional, descent-based slavery of exactly the kind to which millions of its people were subjected by Europeans in the Americas.

Bonded labor

Bonded labor has been defined in international law as follows:

> The status or condition arising from a pledge by a debtor of his personal services or of those of a person under his control as security for a

debt, if the value of those services as reasonably assessed is not applied towards the liquidation of the debt or the length and nature of those services are not respectively limited and defined. (ILO, 2001: 124; see also Ruwanpura and Rai, 2004: 5)

In practice, as Srivastava (2005) notes, it denies employees the right to choose their employer or to negotiate the terms and conditions of their contract.

The ILO estimates more recently that 20 per cent of forced labor victims are in debt bondage, resulting from the traditional form of a loan or more modern means such as recruitment and agency charges (ILO et al., 2022). Traditional bonded labor exists mainly in India, Nepal, Bangladesh, and Pakistan, and occurs in agriculture and a wide range of industries, especially the brick, carpet, stone-breaking, tea, and shrimp industries (Kara, 2014; Srivastava, 2005). Its persistence is attributable to landlessness, poverty, lack of alternate economic opportunities, caste and ethnic discrimination, illiteracy, consumption spikes at rites of passage (especially weddings and religious events), corruption of officials, and failure to enforce anti-bond labor laws (Kara, 2014; Srivastava, 2005). Apart from the more traditional kinds of bonded labor, which are vestiges of caste and somewhat feudal in nature and which have declined sharply in modern times, most bonded labor in South Asia, especially India, seems to rely on seasonal internal migrant labor, organized by labor recruiters. Sometimes, deception regarding wages and threats of violence is used to exploit migrants; in such cases they are trafficked. And yet, mostly, the migrants, especially returnees, know exactly what to expect; it is the threat of destitution that drives them into the renewal of harsh labor contracts (Srivastava, 2005). Persons in debt bondage are found in a range of industries: 31 percent are in agriculture; 27 percent are in construction; 20 percent are in domestic service; and 14 percent are in manufacturing (ILO et al., 2022: 43)

There is a pronounced ethnoracial component to debt bondage. A disproportionate number of them belong to marginalized ethnoracial groups, such as the darker-complexioned scheduled castes of India and Indigenous peoples of the Americas. Peonage in the United States, which ensnared Blacks until the 1950s and still persists among some migrant groups in the US (Blackmon, 2008; Daniel, 1972) and in Central America, such as the Diriomenos of Nicaragua (Dore, 2006), bears close resemblance to its Asian counterpart. However, a more modern version of bonded servitude, what the ILO (2001:

HUMAN TRAFFICKING, MODERN-DAY SLAVERY, AND SERVITUDE

2) previously labeled "forced labor in agriculture and remote rural areas," reduces individuals to servitude through isolation and entrapment (*enganche*, "hooking") in indebtedness for transportation to, and living costs in, remote areas. This kind of debt bondage is present in both agriculture and charcoal production in South American countries such as Bolivia – especially among nut harvesters – the Chaco region of Paraguay, Peru – especially for illegal logging in the Amazon – and Brazil (Bedoya et al., 2009; ILO, 2001).

Siddharth Kara's work (2014) has certainly demonstrated the resemblance of debt bondage in South Asia to modern slavery in terms of the economic harshness, subjection to their bondholders, degradation, isolation, and restriction on movement during the contracted period. Kara distinguishes between demand and supply side factors in accounting for the prevalence and persistence of debt bondage. On the demand side, he cites legal deficiencies such as the absence of minimum wage laws, insufficient scope of vicarious liability laws, land laws that promote landlessness of peasants and insufficient penalties for the crime of bonded labor. Systemic factors include the failure to enforce labor laws, government corruption, corrupt reporting mechanisms, and the Jamadar labor contracting system. On the supply side, he emphasized widespread poverty, lack of credit resources and alternate income opportunities, inadequate infrastructure such as proper roads to market, illiteracy, poor health, the absence of rehabilitation for freed bondsmen leading to their re-indebtedness, environmental disasters, being made worse by climate change, and chronic bias against subordinated castes.

International migrant forced laborers

IMFL are those who end up in servitude outside their native countries. The term "labor trafficking" is increasingly used to refer to this category, but it is misleading (Owens et al., 2014; Zhang, 2012). Only a small proportion of this group have been trafficked; most, in fact, end up in exploitative conditions following smuggling, including self-smuggling, or abusive migration (Doomernik, 2006). As stated above, the ILO (2017b) estimates that nearly a quarter (23 percent) of all persons in servitude were exploited outside their country of residence. Belanger's (2014) study of Vietnamese migrants in East Asian countries found that two-thirds experienced no form of forced labor, while the remaining one-third that did ranged on a continuum from abuse to extreme forced labor. In the United States, most persons who experience forced labor in agriculture are unauthorized migrants, but a substantial minority are authorized migrants who entered under the H-2B visa program (Bales and Soodalter, 2009; Owens et al., 2014). A study of North Carolina farmworkers found that a quarter of them were trafficked, while 39 percent experienced other forms of abuse (Barrick et al., 2014). In San Diego, Zhang et al. (2014) identified 30 percent of the farmworkers as labor trafficked, and 55 percent suffered forms of labor abuse. In the restaurant industry, the second largest employer of immigrants, where there is widespread labor exploitation, most victims entered with lawful visas. Their exploitation results in part from harsh working conditions and in part from voluntary agreement to bonded debt with recruiters in their home country (Owens et al., 2014). In Britain, the immigration system – a complex bureaucratic arrangement that creates a hierarchy of vulnerability – can be used by employers to impose on legal migrants varying degrees of exploitation (Scullion et al., 2014). A major factor contributing to abuse and possibly forced labor throughout the world is the use of labor contractors, especially in the agricultural sector (Barrientos, 2011). In the United States, these recruiters handle the recruiting, transportation, housing, and payment of farm workers, creating such great distance between grower and worker that many do not even know the name of the farm-owner or farm where they work, relieving the farm-owners of any responsibility for worker abuse (Barrick, 2016).

Possibly the worst cases of IMFL today occur in the Thai fishing industry, where trafficked, smuggled, and legal workers are subjected to work conditions and personal abuse amounting to outright slavery that includes murder with impunity (Chantavanich et al., 2016; EJF, 2015; Urbina, 2015). One UN report found that 59 percent of trafficked sailors witnessed a fellow worker murdered (EJF, 2015). Official corruption and widespread pirate fishing facilitate this regime of brutal labor exploitation. The Thai fishing industry, which employs more than 150,000 laborers, nearly all immigrants, well illustrates the degree to which globalization links the enslavement of workers in one side of the world with household demand in America on the other side, along with other advanced countries. The industry thrives on the demand for fish meal for pet food in the United States and generates an export value of US$150 million per year for Thailand. Although Thailand has been singled out for the extremity and degree of forced labor found there, the abuse of workers, amounting to forced labor, is found worldwide in the offshore fisheries sector (Surtees, 2012; Marschke and Vandergeest, 2016; see also ILO et al., 2022: 33).

Domestic or household servitude

Domestic or household servitude, in its international form, is often associated with smuggling and abusive migration, although most forms of forced household labor take place within national borders. Currently, migrants make up only 17 percent of the world's 67 million domestic workers. There were an estimated 1.4 million persons in forced domestic labor in 2021, amounting to 8 percent of the total. This form of forced labor is highly gendered: 1 million of the total were women; a little under 0.4 million were men (ILO et al., 2022). The IOM (2012: 7) singled out gender as "the most important factor shaping migrants' experiences – more important than their country of origin or destination, their age, class, race or culture." Domestic labor is distinctive in that it is not normally considered part of the formal economy, except for the minority who work for cleaning firms. Hence, women in domestic servitude find themselves highly dependent on their employers, often other women, who do not see their homes as workplaces or their relationship with their maids as an employer/employee relationship governed by labor laws (Hondagneu-Sotelo, 2007). In addition, domestic work can demand very intimate, bodily kinds of labor such as caring for the children of the household and substituting for the mother's roles in a variety of other ways, which induces a tendency toward extreme control of the person doing such work (Anderson, 2000; Parreñas, 2015; Tizon, 2017). It is hardly surprising, then, that this form of labor often becomes not just exploitative but forced and, especially where labor laws are lax, resembles enslavement (Bales and Soodalter, 2009; Fernando, 2013; Kara, 2014; Sunderland, 2006). Migrant domestic workers are often tied to a single employer because of visa restrictions, which makes them more vulnerable to abuse.

Sexual trafficking and servitude

Sexual trafficking and servitude have received the greatest attention from researchers on forced labor, both academic and nonacademic. By sexual servitude we refer to trafficked and nontrafficked cases of forced prostitution, rather than to all forms of sex work. It must be emphasized that not all sexual servitude results from trafficking (Agustin, 2007; Belanger, 2014; Cheng, 2014; Davidson and Anderson, 2006). Women who are forced or coerced by circumstances, emotional deception, or addiction into prostitution in their own communities are not trafficked (Dewey, 2014; Kennedy et al.,

2007; Levitt and Venkatesh, 2007). Underage California prostitutes, some as young as ten years of age, still living at home and attending school, are not strictly trafficked, although the term is increasingly being used as a synonym for being pimped. Nonetheless, they are often in complete economic, emotional, and sexual servitude to their pimps, whom they consider their boyfriends and who have psychologically entrapped them to the point where they will act only "if he lets me" (Morris, 2016: 96–101). It is also not necessarily the case that all women transported within or between national borders for sexual work are trafficked (Brennan, 2004; Chin and Finckenauer, 2012). Many do so voluntarily in attempting to improve their economic situation or to lead less oppressive or more interesting lives (Andrijasevic, 2010).

The *Global Estimates* report indicates that there were 6.3 million persons in forced commercial sexual exploitation on any given day in 2021 (ILO et al., 2022: 45), of whom 1.7 million were children; 80 percent of this total were women and girls. The ILO and its collaborators follow UNODC in claiming that at least a half of all cases of commercial sexual exploitation were the result of trafficking. However, the group concedes that the "trafficking mechanisms can be complex." The Covid-19 pandemic, followed a couple of years later by the Russian invasion of Ukraine, greatly increased the risk of sexual trafficking, especially in Ukraine, which was already a major source of sexually trafficked women in Western Europe. Other conflict areas that have increased vulnerability to sexual trafficking include Venezuela, Colombia, the Democratic Republic of the Congo, Somalia, Sudan, South Sudan, Myanmar, and Syria (UNODC, 2018: 9, 23–7).

There can be no doubt that the term "sexual slavery" applies particularly to one subgroup of prostituted persons: namely, girls and women (and some boys) who have been trafficked or reduced to a condition of total dependence on their pimps or madams. As I have argued elsewhere (Patterson, 2012), their experiences draw stark parallels to traditional slaves in terms of their emotional, social, and legal isolation; their brutal seasoning into sexual work through beatings, rape, and forced addiction to drugs; their constant psychological torture, such as threats of violence to their family and the disclosure of their degradation; and, if unauthorized migrants, disclosure to deportation authorities. Additional slave-like qualities come from the complete dependence on their pimps, who often hold the power not only to sell their sexual services but to transfer possession of their bodies to other slaveholders, bodies that are often branded with the name of their pimps. Such sexual enslavement has been well documented not only by researchers, but also in the narratives of former sexual slaves (Dank et al., 2014; Dinan, 2002; Farley et al., 2004; Farr, 2005; Giobbe, 1993; Hossain et al., 2010; Miller, 2002; WHO, 2005; Williamson and Cluse-Tolar, 2002). Perhaps the most egregious cases of outright sexual slavery in contemporary times are girls and women captured and exploited by ISIS (the Islamic State of Iraq and Syria), Boko Haram, and other militant Islamist groups (Malik, 2017), as well as those forced into sexual slavery during civil wars in non-Islamic Africa and other areas (Bunting, 2017).

The literature on sexual servitude has attracted a range of criticisms: the disproportionate focus on sexual labor over nonsexual forced labor; an overemphasis on the social, political, cultural, and moral biases of Western, especially American, societies; categorical conflation of all sex work with trafficking; the downplaying of the socioeconomic contexts within which sex work is embedded; exaggerated claims about the number of persons sexually trafficked; and shortage of evidence-based work (Andrijasevic, 2010; J. A. Chuang, 2010, 2014; Hoang and Parreñas, 2014; Sanghera, 2016; Weitzer, 2007, 2011; Zhang, 2009). While these criticisms are legitimate, it is also important not to go to the other extreme of underestimating the extent of sexual servitude. The average, global annual duration in sexual servitude between 2014 and 2016, according to the IOM (2017: 3) was 1.7 years. An analysis of sex trafficking of minors in the US between 2010 and 2015 found an average duration of 1.8 years for females and 2.3 years for males (McCain Institute, 2021: 3). Sexual servitude on average lasted 23.4 months. We should note further that the level of sexual exploitation does not end with the category of sexual servitude. The ILO (2017) points out that most victims of servitude suffer multiple forms of coercion. For women, this often means sexual violence. Women and girls' majority share (54 percent) of the total population in modern day slavery – 11.8 million of the 27.6 in forced labor and 14.9 million of the 22 million in forced marriage (ILO et al. 2022) – thus leads us to reconsider whether the emphasis on sexual exploitation is really all that off the mark.

The contested nature of this literature is further fueled by a fraught debate in the field over the socioeconomic effects and ethics of commercial sex work (Dickenson, 2006; Kesler, 2002). On the one hand are scholars and activists who hold that all commercial sexual transactions are socioeconomically exploitative and amount to a degradation of women's bodies, in which issues of agency and a woman's right to do with her body as she pleases are irrelevant morally, legally, and socioeconomically (Bales and Soodalter, 2009; Barry, 1996; Farley, 2004; Kara, 2017; Kristof and WuDunn, 2010; MacKinnon, 1993). Hence, prostitution should be prohibited and criminalized. On the other hand are those who emphasize the socioeconomic circumstances that propel women into sex work, as well as their right to exercise agency in the choice of how to use their bodies, especially when few alternatives for survival exist (Bernstein, 2007; Chuang, 2010; Hoang, 2015; Weitzer, 2007; Wijers, 2017). Both sides actually often agree that women are forced into prostitution, but they differ on the agent of their coercion: prohibitionists emphasize the role of traffickers and pimps, whereas anti-prohibitionists emphasize socioeconomic constraints. The issue of agency further complicates this neat dichotomy given the disputable degree to which women under dire circumstances can be said to exercise agency, or the fluidity between the voluntary and involuntary under such circumstances (Andrijasevic, 2010; Cheng, 2014; Dewey, 2014; Dickenson, 2006; Kropiwnicki, 2011; Peters, 2014; van Liempt, 2006). There is growing consensus that the prohibitionists' hardline antitrafficking emphasis on prosecution and rescue-and-release strategies has often done more harm than good, sometimes worsening the condition of trafficked victims and voluntary sex workers alike (Dewey, 2014; Farrag et al., 2014; Hoang, 2015; Kempadoo et al., 2012; Parreñas, 2011; Zheng, 2014). The anti-prostitution pledge of the US government, which requires nongovernmental organizations (NGOs) receiving federal anti-HIV/AIDS or antitrafficking funds to oppose all prostitution (declared unconstitutional by the US Supreme Court in 2013 for US NGOs, although still applicable to foreign NGOs receiving funds from the US government), has inadvertently hampered public health campaigns in several countries (Hudson, 2010; Weitzer, 2007).

Of special interest is the unusual situation in the United States with regard to sex trafficking and sexual servitude. Unlike other advanced countries, which are primarily destinations for women sex-trafficked from poorer nations, the United States is both the destination and the source of a large proportion of its sex workers, trafficked and nontrafficked. It is extraordinary that a large number of the migrant children trafficked into prostitution in the United States were brought into the country by their parents or by smugglers paid by relatives (Goździak, 2016). While none of the 140 migrant children studied by Elżbieta Goździak was physically forced to America, they were nonetheless trafficked and, in our view, in childhood servitude.

Many of those domestically trafficked and sexually exploited are runaway minors (Dank et al., 2014). A major factor of Americans' vulnerability to sex servitude is the US's relatively weak welfare state and high level of inequality. Women in Western Europe and other advanced economies do not face the desperate economic plight of many American working- and lower-class women, especially single mothers (Dank et al., 2014). Black and Native American women, and, more recently, Hispanic women, in particular, are pressured to turn to sex work for survival by ethnoracial sexual stereotypes and economic hardship (Morris, 2016). America's chronic drug problem, fueled in good part by the punitive practices of the state's counterproductive war on drugs, worsens the situation (Dank et al., 2014; Hoffman, 2017). The long existence of a pimp or "mack-man" and "playa" configuration within the street culture of Black lower-class men cannot be discounted as a contributing factor (Dank et al., 2014: 130–2; Giobbe, 1993; Miller, 2008), although recent work has documented mutual financial benefits in their relationship with mature, usually part-time, sex workers (Dank et al., 2014; Levitt and Venkatesh, 2007).

Child servitude

Child servitude, considered by some as "one of the most heinous crimes of modern times," presents several conceptual issues (Craig, 2010: 5). The line between legitimate, if hard, work and abuse can be fuzzy, especially when the children are working with their family. Variations in cultural conceptions of the nature of childhood and the starting age of adulthood complicate the discussion of agency, vulnerability, and fluidity of labor conditions (Blagbrough, 2017; Huijsmans and Baker, 2012; Seeberg and Goździak, 2016). Nonetheless we need some precision, even though arbitrary, if progress is to be made in the study and eradication of this problem. The international treaty definition of a child as any person under the age of eighteen, unless legally defined below this age, is now largely accepted (UN General Assembly Resolution 44/25, 1989). The ILO recognizes four broad categories of children who work: children in employment, who are those engaged in any form of work, including permitted, unpaid light work; children in child labor, who are all those employed in productive labor; children in forced labor, who are those in any form of servitude; and children in hazardous work, who are those involved in activities that are harmful to their health, safety, or morals. Child servitude need not be hazardous (for example, some kinds of domestic servitude) and hazardous work is not necessarily servitude (for example, children working with their parents in hazardous occupations such as goldmining, brick-making, and some kinds of farming; ILO, 2011).

The ILO's (2017a) special volume on child labor shows that 152 million children, or 10 percent of the world's total child population, counted as child laborers. A majority of children worked with their families (69 percent), whereas 27 percent sought paid employment and 4 percent were self-employed. Child labor was overwhelmingly concentrated in agriculture (71 percent). Industry and services, respectively, absorbed the remaining 12 and 17 percent of child labor. Some 73 million children work under hazardous conditions.

The 2022 ILO report on modern servitude, however, estimated the number of forced child laborers at 3.3 million on any given day in 2021, down from 4.3 million in 2016 (ILO et al., 2022). This number is likely an underestimate, given the hidden and illicit nature of the phenomenon. Nonetheless, half of all children in forced labor are commercially sexually exploited (1.69 million). They are abducted, drugged, and used especially in the tourist and pornography industries; the internet, especially social media, has greatly facilitated this form of child sexual exploitation. The Counter Trafficking Data Collaborative (2022) found that a third of all identified children are trafficked between the ages of fifteen and seventeen. More than half of female victims are between fifteen and seventeen, while about 40 percent of males are under the age of twelve. The CTDC reports, further, that 21 percent of children are forced into domestic work, 10 percent into begging, 7 percent in the hospitality sector, 6 percent in street and small-scale informal retail, 6 percent in illicit activities and 5 percent in agriculture (see also ILO et al., 2022: 49). The study found that the rate of family involvement in the trafficking of children is four times higher than is the case for adult trafficking.

In addition, 9 million of the 22 million conservatively estimated to be in forced marriages were children (44 percent), up from 5.7 million children in 2016 (ILO, 2017a; ILO et al., 2022). The US Department of Labor (2015) identified poverty, cultural traditions, political and military instability, and legal ineffectiveness as drivers of child labor. The 2017 ILO report supports this assessment. For instance, in the five to fourteen age group of child laborers, 36 million children (32 percent) were out of school, and academic performance of those in school was compromised due to their work (ILO, 2017a). One somewhat bright side to these grim figures is that they have consistently declined worldwide, with a net reduction of 94 million children in child labor between 2000 and 2016. The rate of improvement, however, slowed down over the 2012–16 four-year period, and, in

Africa, the trend of child labor actually began to climb again (ILO, 2017a).

Beyond the sexual exploitation of children and their use in hazardous work, we highlight two of the worst forms of child servitude, which, in our view, amount to genuine slavery, and a third that, while frequently called slavery, challenges the unrestrained use of this term. First are children recruited as soldiers, many of whom are brainwashed into becoming especially violent killers. This represents one of the most extreme violations of international human rights (Waschefort, 2017). Consistent with the provisions of the Optional Protocol to the Convention of the Rights of the Child, the US State Department defines child soldiers as persons under eighteen directly taking part in hostilities, or compulsorily recruited into governmental armed forces, police, or other security forces; and any person under fifteen, even if voluntarily recruited to such forces. It also includes any child under eighteen engaged in nonstate armed forces (US State Department, 2023: 67)

Child soldiers are found all over the world, including Europe (Singer, 2006). The UN estimates that about 10,000 are abducted each year into armed conflict. The worst cases appear each year on a UN Secretary General's List of Shame, which currently includes seven countries: Afghanistan, Democratic Republic of Congo, Myanmar, Somalia, South Sudan, Sudan, and Yemen. The US 2023 TIP Report added the following countries: Egypt, Eritrea, Iran, Libya, Mali, Russia, Rwanda, Syria, Turkey, and Venezuela. The Taliban in Afghanistan and ISIS in Iraq and Syria, for example, deployed children on a large scale, in some cases as suicide bombers (Child Soldiers International, 2017–18; UN Security Council, 2016). They are also used to clear mines, plant explosives, and commit especially gruesome acts of terror. Some children are recruited by abduction, some due to poverty and loss of family, and others to escape domestic slavery and abuse. Those who survive bear permanent psychological and physical scars (Machel, 2001).

The increase in the number of child soldiers is due in large part to increased disasters and military conflicts around the world. A quarter of all children (535 million) now live in countries racked by such disasters and conflicts, and children make up over half of the 65 million persons displaced by war (ILO, 2017a). Two other factors often cited are the invention of lightweight small arms suitable for child use and a change in the traditional rules of war that forbade the targeting and recruiting of children (Singer, 2006). These explanations have, however, been contested by Rosen (2005, 2012), who points out the extensive use of child combatants in wars of the past, most notably in the American Civil War, in which between 250,000 and 420,000 boy soldiers fought and killed, some as young as eight years of age.

The second issue to which we draw special attention are child slaves in the cocoa farms of West Africa, especially Côte d'Ivoire, but also northern Ghana, Nigeria, and Cameroon (Bertrand et al., 2015; US Department of Labor, 2015). Of the world's cocoa, 70 percent comes from West Africa, and, like the fishing industry in Thailand, cocoa production is driven by a highly desired product in the advanced world: chocolate. The processing and lucrative value chains of the global chocolate industry are now dominated by eight vertically and horizontally concentrated companies. The industry is valued at more than US$101 billion, but little of the wealth goes to the world's 5–6 million cocoa farmers, who receive only 6.6 percent of the total value added to a ton of cocoa beans sold, and who earn, on average, about $2.07 a day in Côte d'Ivoire, just above the global daily poverty rate of $1.90 (Gayi and Tsowou, 2016: 13–19), but well below it in per capita terms when their dependents are taken into account. Accordingly, in spite of high adult unemployment, cocoa farmers turn to child labor on a massive scale. In Côte d'Ivoire 31.5 percent of children in rural areas aged between five and fourteen work full time and another 21.5 percent work part time (US Department of Labor, 2015). In many cocoa farms, the labor conditions of child workers amount to outright slavery, with many deceptively taken from their parents in neighboring countries (Bertrand et al., 2015).

The third case of exploited child labor highlighted here illustrates the common problem of conflating exploitation with slavery: the so-called restaveks of Haiti. These are extremely poor children sent to work as domestics in the homes of others who are often only slightly better off. More than 225,000 children are estimated to work as restaveks, two-thirds of whom are girls. They are present in 22 percent of all households in Haiti. The severe exploitation and educational deprivation of restaveks have been well documented (Beyond Borders et al., 2014; Smucker et al., 2009). However, the Haitian case poses particular challenges in estimating the extent and nature of servitude in a local socioeconomic context. A quite balanced study (Sommerfelt, 2015) confirms that many children between the ages of five and fourteen are indeed in domestic labor (between 233,000 and 350,000), with limited educational opportunities and heavy workloads; the study also observes that hard work is commonplace among all poor Haitian children and that, for many of them, the system of fosterage might be a lesser evil than malnourishment and extreme deprivation with their impoverished parents. Thus, while the condition of these children can reasonably be described as servitude, only a minority at the bad end of the continuum of treatment can truly be called enslaved in the Haitian socioeconomic context, activist rhetoric notwithstanding. Child domestic servitude also aptly describes the Nepalese *kamaliri* system, in which lower-caste *tharu* girls are sent to work in the homes of upper-caste urban Nepali (Giri, 2010; Kara, 2014). As in Haiti, the harsh end of this system is certainly slave-like, but before we can draw conclusions about the slave-like nature of the system, the entire local economic and cultural context should be considered.

Marital servitude

Marital servitude, including child marriage, is an ancient institution, but only in 1979 was it formally recognized as a form of servitude, following the UN Convention on the Elimination of All Forms of Discrimination against Women (a treaty signed, but not ratified, by the United States). The 2017 ILO report included, for the first time, forced marriage as a form of modern servitude. The 2022 report estimates, conservatively, that at any time in 2021, some 22 million persons were living in forced marriages, up from 15.4 million in 2016 (ILO et al., 2022: 59–74). This amounts to three in every one thousand persons alive in 2021. The great majority of persons in forced marriage were females (68 percent), and 37 percent were children under the age of eighteen; 41 percent were younger than sixteen. Girls were far more likely than boys to be married while still in their childhood: 87 percent versus 13 percent (ILO et al., 2022: 66). Although the great majority of forced marriages are in Asia and the Pacific region (14.2 million, amounting to 65 percent of the total), followed by Africa (13 percent), Europe and Central Asia (10 percent), the Americas (7 percent), and Arab states (4 percent), the actual prevalence is different. Women and girls experience the highest prevalence (per thousand of population) in the Arab States (4.8 per thousand), followed by Asia and the Pacific (3.3), Europe and Central Asia (2.5), Africa (2.4), and the Americas (1.5). However, the ILO and its collaborators admit that these figures are very likely underestimates, especially those on child marriages.

For alternate data on child marriages, we turn to UNICEF (2023), whose estimates are based on national surveys. For the period 2015–22, UNICEF reports that 4 percent of girls were married by the age of fifteen and 19 percent by the age of eighteen; during this same period 3 percent of boys were married by the age of eighteen. The highest percentage of such marriages were in sub-Saharan Africa, especially West and Central Africa, where 11 percent of girls were married by the age of fifteen and 33 percent by the age of eighteen; comparable figures in Eastern and Southern Africa were 9 percent and 32 percent. Next to Africa was South Asia (6 percent and 26 percent), followed by Latin America and the Caribbean (2 percent and 16 percent) and the Middle East and North Africa (2 percent and 21 percent). Among boys, the figures were only between 3 percent and 4 percent. These results are surprising, compared with those reported by the ILO and its collaborators.

UNICEF considers marriage before the age of eighteen to be "a fundamental violation of human rights" (UNICEF, 2023) and, like the ILO, I consider it to be a form of servitude. Although many countries are in violation, the right to "free and full" consent to marriage is recognized as fundamental in the UN Declaration of Human Rights and I agree with UNICEF that children are not sufficiently mature to give such consent. Child marriages result from the interaction of several factors: "poverty, the perception that marriage will provide 'protection', family honor, social norms, customary or religious laws that condone the practice, an inadequate legislative framework and the state of a country's civil registration system" (UNICEF, 2023). These marriages have adverse effects, such as curtailed – if any – education for girls, and heightened risks of illness and death from pregnancy and childbirth. Child wives are also far more likely to experience abuse, overwork, and psychological trauma (Turner, 2013; UNICEF, 2014)

Two developments unique to the last third of the twentieth century further intensified the growth of modern marital servitude. In many Asian countries, particularly China, India, and South Korea, the traditional preference for boys and the availability of modern technology to determine the sex of the fetus resulted in girl fetuses being aborted on a vast scale, also known as "gendercide" (Hvistendahl, 2012). In China, the government's one-child policy further exacerbated the gender imbalance. As a result, many areas in Asia now experience a significant shortage of women of marriageable age, with a gender ratio of 130 males to every 100 women in some parts of northern India and China (*The Economist*, 2010; Guilmoto, 2007; Hvistendahl, 2012; Tiefenbrun and Edwards, 2008). This unmet demand for women as brides, or simply as sexual partners, has led, in turn, to a new wave of female migration and, in some cases, bridal trafficking or enslavement. A brisk smuggling of single women from Vietnam operates in parts of rural China bordering on Vietnam. Most women move voluntarily in search of Chinese husbands; others are recruited. Some find successful unions; many, however, are falsely promised traditional arranged marriages only to discover themselves trapped in abusive relationships (Son et al., 2011). In northwest India, where the problem is acute, bride-buying is a huge and brutal business in which many women end up as sex slaves jointly owned by several men in the same village (Raza, 2014).

Child marriages or forced marriages constitute problems not only for developing countries. The US Census identified 57,800 Americans aged between fifteen and seventeen reportedly being married in 2014. A search of available marriage license data in thirty-eight US states revealed more than 167,000 instances of child marriages between 2000 and 2010 (McClendon and Sandstrom, 2016). One activist group estimates that some 300,000 children were married in the United States between 2000 and 2018 (Unchained at Last, 2023). It was unclear what share of child marriages were coerced. A survey of US governmental and nongovernmental agencies concluded that the agencies together encountered 3,000 known or suspected cases of forced marriage between 2009 and 2011 (Tahirih Justice Center, 2011). It is remarkable that, as of 2023, five US states have no statutory minimum age of marriage allowing for no exceptions. Only ten states have banned marriages under the age of eighteen without exception.

The Forced Marriage Unit (2017) in the United Kingdom handled 1,428 likely forced marriage cases in 2016, of which 26 percent involved victims under the age of eighteen. Existing evidence suggests that forced marriages in advanced countries tend to occur mainly within immigrant communities and are due to a strong compliance to custom, but some involve nonimmigrants. Benjamin Lawrence (2017) has drawn attention to what he calls the "forced marriage paradox," in which refugees and asylum seekers from this form of enslavement are legally obliged to use the terminology of legitimate marriage to describe the individuals and circumstances from which they are seeking protection in the petition process, thereby perpetuating the violence against the survivors.

State-imposed forced labor or compulsory public works

Finally, there is state-imposed forced labor or compulsory public works, in which the state exploits individuals under its control for its own gain or that of companies in the private sector. In 2012, the

ILO estimated this form of forced labor at 2.2 million persons, or 10 percent of the global total forced labor population. By 2016 it had reached 4.1 million, or 16.3 percent of total forced labor (ILO, 2017b). The most recent estimate suggests a decline to 3.9 million persons in 2021, of whom 78 percent were males and 8 percent were children (ILO et al., 2022).

States place their citizens into servitude for a variety of reasons. In 2016, 64 percent of state-imposed labor was for economic development, while nearly 15 percent involved conscripted persons forced to do nonmilitary work, 14 percent compulsory prison labor, and 8 percent communal services beyond normal civic obligations (ILO, 2017b). In 2021, a different classification was adopted. The ILO found that 2.2 million or 55.8 percent of persons in state servitude were the result of the abuse of compulsory prison labor, while 1.1 million (26.9 percent) were the result of the abuse of conscription and 17.3 percent were due to forced labor for economic development as well as the performance of "work beyond normal civil obligations or minor communal services" (ILO et al., 2022: 51). Although the 1957 Forced Labor Convention prohibits these kinds of exploitation by states, this form of servitude is difficult to eliminate given the exceptions allowed by international norms. The imposition of compulsory work for nonviolent political offenses has increased in recent years. Countries that have been formally identified by the UN's Committee of Experts on the Application of Conventions and Recommendations (CEAR) include Burundi, Algeria, Benin, Kazakhstan, the Russian Federation, the United Arab Emirates, and the United Republic of Tanzania. Also under more recent observation are Azerbaijan, Fiji, Zimbabwe, and, especially, North Korea (ILO et al., 2022: 52).

Absent from this list are Myanmar and Eritrea. Myanmar has long forced large numbers of its citizens to perform compulsory labor for the military, not to mention its recruitment of children in the armed forces and the genocidal killing and displacement of the majority of its Rohingya minority. In October 2023, the Myanmar Commission of Inquiry concluded that "the military continues to exact different types of forced labour in the context of armed conflict" in addition to flagrant violation of "basic civil liberties and trade union rights" (ILO, 2023).

Eritrea has been identified as the country with the second highest prevalence of modern-day slavery, with 9 percent of its population, some 320,000 people, victims of servitude. Its compulsory national conscription system ensnares citizens between the ages of eighteen and forty, who are forced to do nonmilitary work. For many, the length of conscription can be indefinite, and there are credible reports of people spending decades in what amounts to compulsory service to the government (Walk Free, 2023a). Human Rights Watch (2019) has found that indefinite conscription violates the human rights of young Eritreans, and severely restricts their access to education; many are conscripted before completing secondary school. This has driven some 507,300 young Eritreans into exile. Several Western corporations have been accused of benefiting from this state-compelled labor, notably the Canadian mining company Nevsun Resources, which entered an out-of-court settlement before the Supreme Court of British Columbia with former Eritrean mineworkers who claim to have been victims of "gross human rights violations such as slavery, forced labour, torture and crimes against humanity during the construction of copper and gold mines in Eritrea," committed by one of Nevsun's subsidiaries in complicity with the Eritrean government (Carolino, 2020).

Examples of state-imposed servitude in the not-too-distant past include the Nazi slave concentration camps, the Soviet Gulags, the Chinese laogai (reform through labor) and laojiao (re-education through labor) prison labor systems (Funakoshi, 2013), and the American incarceration and "re-enslavement" of African American men in the Jim Crow South under spurious vagrancy charges, followed by forcing them to work in chain gangs or renting them out to companies such as U.S. Steel (Blackmon, 2008). Current US laws prevent the exploitation of prisoners who work, but with the largest prison population in the world, many located in the states of the former Confederacy, the risk of abuse is real, and several reports have emerged of supposedly rehabilitative work crossing the line into forced labor for profit (Sloan, 2010). In 2016 some 24,000 prisoners in twenty-nine prisons across the United States went on strike to protest inhumane conditions and unfair pay for work (Goad, 2017).

Elsewhere, one of the largest forms of modern public forced labor is the state-run harvesting of cotton in Uzbekistan (Human Rights Watch, 2013; US State Department, 2017). Cotton is the country's main crop, accounting for 17 percent of its exports. The state forced more than 2 million persons to work in the harvesting of the crop, mandating cotton production quotas on regional and local officials. Government workers and children were among those forced to work during the harvest. Persons who refused were penalized and sometimes beaten. Pressure from activists led to the banning of children from the fields after 2012, although many violations continue. The practice subsided when some three hundred Western firms signed the Uzbekistan Cotton Pledge, committing them to not knowingly sourcing cotton from the country until the government stopped using forced labor in the sector. Progress has been monitored by the ILO. Recent reports indicate that while the practice has declined, it persists, with forced work by civil servants under the guise of "volunteer work" at the rate of 10 cents per kilogram of cotton, which amounts to $3 per day for the fastest pickers.

China has been accused of arbitrarily detaining more than 1.8 million Uyghurs, Kazakhs, Kyrgyz, and other Muslim minority groups in the Xinjing Uyghur Autonomous Region of the country, in a system of extrajudicial mass internment camps for "political re-education" as part of its "counterterrorism" and "counterextremism" campaigns. Human rights groups have accused the Chinese government of using forced labor, especially in the production of cotton and tomatoes, mass surveillance, and even torture of the leaders of these ethnic groups. Mass sterilization of women has also been claimed. There is credible report of inmates being forced to work in subsidized factories at a fraction of the minimum wage in what are deemed "poverty alleviation" programs. The Chinese government acknowledges that it had established "vocational education and training centers, in accordance with the law, to eradicate the breeding ground and conditions for the spread of terrorism and religious extremism" in the region (OHCHR, 2022: 14). Persons sent to these training centers indicated in interviews that they were detained under compulsion and were not allowed to leave. A long-delayed report by the UN OHCHR, published in August 2022, confirmed many of these allegations. The report stated that "allegations of patterns of torture, or ill-treatment, including forced medical treatment and adverse conditions of detention, are credible, as are allegations of individual incidents of sexual and gender-based violence." The report concluded that "restrictions and deprivation more generally of fundamental rights, enjoyed individually and collectively, may constitute international crimes, in particular crimes against humanity" (OHCHR, 2022: 46).

North Korea is ranked by the Global Slavery Index (2017) as the country with the highest number of slaves in the world, nearly all slaves of the state. The US Trafficking in Persons Report found that the "government sponsored human trafficking through its use of forced labor in prison camps and labor training centers, facilitation of forced labor of students, and its provision of forced labor to foreign companies through bilateral contracts" (US State Department, 2017: 234). There are an estimated 80–120,000 persons in political

HUMAN TRAFFICKING, MODERN-DAY SLAVERY, AND SERVITUDE

prison camps and labor training centers. Defectors report that trafficking victims forcibly repatriated from China are sent to prison camps, tortured, and sometimes executed. School children over the age of fourteen are forced to work without pay for up to a month twice yearly and are also exploited by school principals and teachers (Human Rights Watch, 2017; US State Department, 2017). People are enslaved for crimes committed in their effort to ward off starvation, including privately producing food, stealing food, and acts of desperation such as cannibalism, and for political crimes as well as common criminal acts (Howard-Hassmann, 2017).

9.3: Measuring servitude

Measuring the extent of modern-day slavery and other forms of servitude is an important first step in understanding the phenomena and designing effective policy. However, the illicit nature of trafficking activity, social isolation of victims, and inconsistent definitions have made it a challenging task. There are also special ethical and methodological issues posed by the illicit and often migratory nature of these activities (Vargas-Silva, 2012). Few empirical studies in trafficking included original systematic data collections. Most publications restate commonly cited figures from a few established reports, which are themselves questionable (Zhang, 2009). The paucity of reliable data has prompted some scholars to forgo systematic estimation on the macro level in favor of micro-level field studies (Weitzer, 2014, 2015; Zhang, 2009).

We acknowledge the limitations in existing macro-level estimates, but we also recognize their value in guiding future research and policy, and the research community is making constant efforts to improve estimates of the population under servitude. It is, van Dijk and Campistol (2017) note, a work in progress. In this section we examine current estimation methods and their applications (see summary in Table 9.1). Like most estimates in this literature, the numbers presented here are prone to biases. They nonetheless provide a useful overview of the severity of servitude and exploitation worldwide.

One common data source for servitude and trafficking comes from the official administrative records of national authorities, such as the criminal justice system and immigration services, as well as international organizations and NGOs. Counting officially detected victims and offenders has revealed useful patterns of servitude and related

SLAVERY TODAY

Table 9.1. Estimation methods and applications

Method	Examples of applications	
	Global level	Local/national level
Administrative records	US Department of State Trafficking in Persons Report (US State Dep. 2017), UNODC Global Report on Trafficking in Persons (UNODC 2016)	Eurostat Report on Trafficking in Human Beings (Eurostat 2015), unauthorized immigrants in the United States (Baker & Rytina 2012)
Direct counting		Sex workers in Cambodia (Steinfatt 2011, 2015)
Multiplier method	ILO global estimates of forced labor (ILO 2012, ILO et al. 2017)	Sex trafficking victims in Texas (Busch-Armendariz et al. 2016), slaves in Europe (Datta & Bales 2013)
Surveys		Child domestic servants in Latin America (Levison & Langer 2010), Haitian child domestic labor (Sommerfelt 2015), national data used in global estimates of child labor (ILO 2017a), child marriage (UNICEF 2014), migrant workers (ILO 2015), modern slavery (ILO et al. 2017b)
Capture-recapture		ILO (2012) global estimates of forced labor
Multiple systems estimation (variant of capture-recapture)		Modern slavery in the United Kingdom (Bales et al. 2015), trafficking in the Netherlands (van Dijk & van der Heijden 2016)
Respondent-driven sampling (network-based method)		Migrant farm workers in San Diego (Zhang 2012), commercially sexually exploited children in New York City (Curtis et al. 2008)
Geomapping		Migrant farm workers in North Carolina (Barrick et al. 2015)

HUMAN TRAFFICKING, MODERN-DAY SLAVERY, AND SERVITUDE

Table 9.1. *continued*

	Examples of applications	
Method	Global level	Local/national level
Internet advertisement data		Sex trafficking in Hawaii (Ibanez & Suthers 2014), sex workers in Oslo, Norway (Brunovskis & Tyldum 2004
Underground economy size		Underground commercial sex economy in eight US cities (Dank et al. 2014)
Mixed methods	ILO (2017a) global estimates of child labor, ILO (2015) global estimates of migrant workers, Global Slavery Index (Walk Free 2016), ILO (2012) and ILO et al. (2017b) global estimates of forced labor and modern slavery	Sex workers in Oslo, Norway (Brunovskis & Tyldum 2004), commercially sexually exploited children in New York City (Curtis et al. 2008), Haitian child domestic labor (Sommerfelt 2015)

activities. However, the information is limited in that the conviction rate for trafficking remains low, and cross-national or temporal trends may be inaccurate, reflecting differences in definitions and prosecution rather than real changes in trafficking flows. Drawing from government law enforcement data, the US Department of State Trafficking in Persons Report (US State Department, 2017) identified 14,897 cases of prosecutions, a smaller number of convictions (9,071), and 66,520 officially detected trafficking victims in 2016, about a quarter of whom were subject to labor trafficking. The yearly counts display an overall rising trend in the number of victims from 2009 to 2016, but a breakdown by region reveals diverse trajectories. For instance, the number of victims of trafficking identified in Europe stabilized around 11,000 between 2011 and 2016, whereas the East Asia and Pacific region and the South and Central Asia region both observed an unusual surge in 2015, followed by a sharp drop in 2016. These fluctuations are likely in part due to changing law enforcement efforts and inconsistent reporting. The Covid-19 pandemic greatly complicated attempts to estimate the extent of servitude, as can be imagined. As the ILO noted, it makes comparisons both over time and between countries very difficult, since it affected "not only the situation of workers worldwide but also the modalities of data collection in the surveys" (ILO et al., 2022: 109). For this reason, one should view comparisons between the 2017 and 2022 reports with great caution. The UNODC *Global Report on Trafficking in Persons* (2016) provides further details about patterns of trafficking in terms of both victims and offenders. The differentiation between countries of origin and countries of destination, in particular, allows for the distinction between internal trafficking and trafficking across borders and the identification of flows of movement.

Local-level analysis of administrative records also exists. The 2015 Eurostat Report on Trafficking in Human Beings reported 8,805 prosecutions of human trafficking cases associated with 30,146 victims in the European Union (EU) member states in 2010–12. In the United States, an estimate of 11.4 million unauthorized immigrants in January 2012 was derived by subtracting the number of legal permanent residents recorded by the US Department of Homeland Security from the size of the foreign-born population provided by the American Community Survey from the US Census Bureau (Baker and Rytina, 2012). Also applying the counting method, Steinfatt (2011, 2015) relied on taxi drivers to map sex venues, directly counted active sex workers, and surmised trafficked victims in Cambodia. Calculation based on the empirical counts then yielded an estimate of 27,925 sex workers in Cambodia in 2008, among whom 1,058 were trafficked.[4]

The multiplier method relies on a known population size and the ratio between it and the size of the population of interest, with the ratio often derived from representative surveys or secondary sources. For example, a study in Texas multiplies the community size by the victimization rate to derive the number of sex-trafficking victims (Busch-Armendariz et al., 2016). Knowing the number of reported victims and the ratio of the reported cases relative to undetected cases can yield an estimate of the total population. This approach was used to estimate the number of modern-day slaves in Europe (Datta and Bales, 2013) and was also part of the ILO's methodology for the 2012 *Global Estimate of Forced Labour*. The accuracy of the population ratio, particularly in the case of hidden and illicit activities like trafficking and modern-day slavery, is critical for the validity of such estimates.

---

[4] See Steinfatt (2011) and Weitzer (2015) for detailed discussion of the Cambodian sex worker estimation methodology.

HUMAN TRAFFICKING, MODERN-DAY SLAVERY, AND SERVITUDE

In the absence of systematic data collection, the survey of a convenience sample of migrants and refugees en route in the Mediterranean offered a timely, if tentative, understanding of human trafficking and exploitation in the region (IOM, 2016).

Survey research has been increasingly adopted to make global or regional estimates of forced labor and migrants, although great caution should be exercised in the application of nationally representative surveys to the study of all types of servitude, given the rare, illicit, and stigmatized nature of these activities. Levison and Langer (2010) estimated the trends in child domestic servants in six Latin American countries between 1960 and 2002 from micro census data. The aforementioned study of Haitian child domestic labor (Sommerfelt, 2015), also utilizing nationwide household surveys, further demonstrates how estimates can vary considerably depending on the definition of the population under study.

Another common estimation method, originating in ecology, is capture–recapture, which originated in the estimation of animal populations (ILO, 2012; van der Heijden et al., 2015). Researchers first draw a sample from the population, then mark and release it. They then draw another independent sample from the same pool and count the number of marked individuals from the first sample that are recaptured. Since the proportion of marked individuals in the second sample should equal the proportion of marked individuals in the total population, dividing the size of the first marked sample by the proportion of marked individuals in the second sample returns an estimate of the total population size. More formally, if the first sample size is A, the second sample size B, and the overlapped or recaptured size C, the formula for estimating the total population is $A \times B/C$. In studies of human populations, recording individuals who have come in contact with certain institutions or services is viewed as the equivalent of marking captured individuals. Variations of this methodology utilize a single sample or more than two samples (van der Heijden et al., 2015). The widely cited 2012 ILO estimates of forced labor worldwide used the capture–recapture method. In this context, the unit being counted was a reported case of forced labor from secondary sources, ranging from media reports, official sources, and NGOs, to academic reports. The research team compiled a single list of reported cases, recorded the frequency of each case appearing in the list and estimated the total number of reported cases of forced labor. This quantity, divided by the proportion of reported cases in total forced labor obtained from surveys, then yielded the

SLAVERY TODAY

estimate of total forced labor, both reported and unreported (ILO, 2012).[5]

A variant of capture–recapture, the multiple systems estimation method, uses more than two samples and relaxes the assumption of independence among samples.[6] A UK study compiled multiple lists from authorities, nongovernment agencies, and the public, and estimated that the number of victims of modern slavery in the country was between 10,951 and 11,418, which included 2,744 known cases, or about a quarter of all cases (Bales et al., 2015). Applying the same methodology, van Dijk and van der Heijden (2016) estimated a total of 17,800 trafficked victims in the Netherlands, with only 10 percent of the victims detected. The multiple systems estimation method can be implemented in many other countries and provides valuable data sources for global and regional estimates in addition to nationally representative surveys, which may perform poorly in situations with low victimization rates. When using this method, consistency in the definition of the populations being studied is of special importance in choosing comparable lists.

Besides the conventional methods, researchers have devised novel methodologies to study servitude, although with a focus on micro-level contexts. For instance, network-based methods are suitable for trafficked populations with a certain degree of social connectivity, such as street sex workers and trafficked laborers. As in snowball sampling, with respondent-driven sampling (RDS), existing study subjects are each offered incentives to recruit a certain number of members from their personal contacts. The recruitment with RDS continues until the targeted population is saturated or the desired sample size achieved. A weighting scheme is also applied to correct biases and make inferences about the whole population beyond the snowball sample (Heckathorn, 1997). Zhang (2012) implemented RDS to estimate the prevalence of trafficking among unauthorized migrant workers in San Diego. Based on interviews with 826 participants, he concluded that 58 percent of authorized migrant laborers experienced

---

[5] See van der Heijden et al. (2015) for a detailed discussion of assumptions, variations, and applications of capture–recapture methodology and its application in the ILO (2012) global estimates of forced labor.

[6] The independent assumption between samples is often violated in studies of human populations. Suppose we apply the capture–recapture method to a list of trafficked victims identified by the police and a list identified by service providers to derive the total number of trafficked victims. The agencies are likely to refer the victims to one another, and the inclusion in one list is likely dependent on the inclusion in another. Therefore, the multiple systems estimation method, which relaxes the independence assumption, is valuable.

at least one form of trafficking violence or abusive treatment. The degree of trafficking violation varied significantly by occupation, from 35 percent found in construction to 16 percent in agriculture.

RDS has also been used to study sex exploitation. In addition to estimating the composition and characteristics of the population, as in Zhang's (2012) application, the New York City study of commercially sexually exploited children (CSEC) measured the population size (Curtis et al., 2008) using the capture–recapture method with the RDS sample and the official arrest statistics. It further validated the capture–recapture estimate with a network estimation approach based on personal network sizes and the number of recruitment coupons circulated. The two methods generated comparable estimates for the population size of the CSEC population in New York City – 3,946 and 3,796, respectively. Despite the advantages and potential of network-based methods, the researchers caution that this study is likely to miss subjects who lack physical mobility or network ties.

The internet and digital technology are now included in researchers' repertoire in studying servitude. One study of labor trafficking developed a sampling frame of potential victims by identifying geographical areas with labor-intensive farming practices and enumerating dwellings in the selected areas using digital images and Global Positioning System coordinates (Barrick et al., 2015). With regard to sexual servitude, while the internet and online advertisements have facilitated the sale of sex and related exploitation, they also offer digital footprints for law enforcement and researchers to uncover the activities. An analysis of online advertisements for adult services on Backpage Hawaii, for example, revealed common sex-trafficking indicators, as well as movement patterns of potential victims (Ibanez and Suthers, 2014). Recognizing the different ways in which women in prostitution contact clients, Brunovskis and Tyldum (2004) generated a roster for telephone surveys from print media and online advertisements to study female prostitutes who contact clients through advertisements in Oslo, Norway, complementing the capture–recapture method with repeated field visits used to derive the number of street sex workers.

Finally, diverging from the literature that focuses on population size, the Urban Institute estimated the size of the underground economy (Dank et al., 2014). It measured the total size of the underground economy in eight American cities by the amount of currency in circulation. It then used relative information about the underground commercial sex, drug, and weapons markets to obtain the size of each market in absolute terms. In 2007, the underground commercial

SLAVERY TODAY

sex economy in the cities under study was estimated to range in value from US$39.9 million in Denver to US$302 million in Miami.

Many empirical studies adopt mixed methods to improve estimates or develop a more comprehensive understanding of the phenomenon. Some employ both quantitative and qualitative methods (e.g. Sommerfelt, 2015). Other studies apply multiple estimation methods to derive or validate the same quantity. As national datasets are lacking in certain countries, mixed methods of data-gathering and extrapolation or imputation fill in the missing data and pave the way for global aggregate measures, as in the case of the ILO's 2017 *Global Estimates of Child Labour* and 2015 *Global Estimates of Migrant Workers*. The *Global Slavery Index 2016* developed by the Walk Free Foundation combines direct estimation from nationally representative surveys (25 countries), multiple systems estimation (2 countries), and extrapolation based on equivalent country risk profiles (139 countries).[7] As noted earlier, in its most recent global estimates of modern servitude, the ILO collaborated with the Walk Free Foundation and the IOM. It abandoned the capture–recapture method used in the previous rounds and instead estimated the population size for forced labor in the private economy, as well as forced marriage, using nationally representative household surveys – forty-eight countries for the 2016, and sixty-eight for the 2021 study – and aggregating national results to global or regional estimates with sampling weight adjustments. For the 2021 study, a total of 77,914 respondents aged fifteen and older were interviewed, during which information on immediate family members was gathered, resulting in a full network sample (respondents and their family network) of 628,598 persons (Walk Free, 2023b). National estimates were calculated by means of individual and country-level risk factors of modern-day slavery. Multilevel models were used to extrapolate the results of the country-level findings beyond the 2021 sample of sixty-eight countries. The low report rate of forced sexual exploitation and child labor in the surveys led to the use of the multiplier method, drawing on the number of people in forced labor from survey data, and the odds ratio of sexual exploitation or child labor relative to forced adult labor from the IOM database. However, forced labor imposed by the state was estimated based on secondary data sources.

As can be imagined, this complex methodology, and limitations in the data used, require some caution in interpreting the findings, as the

---

[7] See Gallagher (2014), Guth et al. (2014), and Weitzer (2015) for critical discussion of the methodology of the *Global Slavery Index*.

HUMAN TRAFFICKING, MODERN-DAY SLAVERY, AND SERVITUDE

authors of the reports made clear. Several of the most populous countries were not surveyed for the 2022 report, notably China, India, and Pakistan. The imputation method introduced errors. Covid-19 created special problems, especially the reliance on telephone rather than face-to-face interviews, as had been done in previous global estimates. Changes in methodology and data coverage also make the 2021 estimates of forced labor not comparable with previous estimates (Walk Free, 2023b). In addition to these limitations, it is regrettable that the capture–recapture technique, last used for the 2012 estimate, was abandoned for the 2016 and 2021 studies. The implication of these methodological discontinuities for the estimates deserves further examination. Moreover, as multiple estimates over the same geographical areas become available, it is important to compare across estimates and assess the impact of different definitions, operationalization procedures, and estimation methodologies on the estimates.

In spite of these clearly acknowledged methodological problems, we still strongly support the heroic statistical effort that went into the production of these most recent global estimates. They are far superior to the groundless statistical claims that had previously been made by activists and even academic and government professionals in the field who simply repeated wild guesses that gained false credibility with each repetition.

9.4: Explaining the rise of modern servitude

What accounts for this extraordinary increase in the number of persons held in servitude over recent decades? A full explanation would require another chapter. Here we tentatively suggest the conjunction of six broad sets of macro-, meso- and micro-socioeconomic and cultural factors (see Aronowitz, 2009; Bales, 2012; Cameron and Newman, 2008; ILO, 2005; Shelley, 2010; Tiefenbrun and Edwards, 2008; van den Anker, 2004): global economic and political changes, domestic economic changes, sociological developments, politico-legal changes, the growth of gender imbalance due to a combination of medical and political changes, and personal factors.

The ILO (2005: 63) has called forced labor "the underside of globalization." The intensification of globalization in the latter half of the twentieth century set in motion several factors that facilitated both the demand for, and the supply of, forced labor. The postwar economic boom in the West and later in parts of Asia, and, more broadly, the growing integration of the world's economies, in its first phase greatly increased the demand for cheap labor. This occurred both in the advanced economies where labourers functioned as a distinct category of powerless, easily controlled labor in the tertiary sector, and in the secondary sector of the developing countries with their growing demand for both external and internal migrant labor (Sassen, 1988; Sharapov, 2017).

This first phase of postwar global capitalist consolidation ended around the mid-1980s, at which time barriers to immigration emerged in the advanced economies. However, by then the process had greatly disrupted traditional patterns of employment in the less developed world, which, along with rapidly growing populations partly due to the globalization of modern medical and public health practices, and the sudden entry of three of the world's largest population blocs into the capitalist system, led to a great surge in the global supply of labor. Between 1980 and 2005, there had been a quadrupling of the global labor force (IMF, 2007). Indeed, between 1990 and 1995 there was a remarkable "great doubling" of the global labor market, from 1.46 to 2.93 billion, with the entry of China, India, and the former Soviet bloc countries in the capitalist system (Freeman, 2008). Beginning about this time, supply would appear to generate demand, especially in the service, including sex work, sector (Anderson and Davidson, 2003). Simultaneously, there was a steep decline in labor income shares across the world, a deeper disruption of traditional means of employment and sources of security, a rapid rise in global value share participation, and an even greater increase in the movement of workers both internally and internationally (IMF, 2017). All this happened just as the advanced economies were placing severe limits on labor immigration. It is striking, and perhaps not coincidental, that at precisely this time there was a sudden escalation in reports on, and activism around, the issue of labor and sexual trafficking, smuggling, and abusive migration (see Limoncelli, 2017: figure 1).

One way of demonstrating the link between globalization and the growth of forced labor, including slavery, is to track the value chain between industries in the advanced world and exploited labor in poor and developing countries following this massive expansion of the global labor force. For example, the auto and other industries of the advanced world depend heavily on imported steel, which requires the transformation of iron into steel, which, in turn, requires the production of vast quantities of charcoal, usually using exploited labor verging on or passing into outright modern-day slavery, as in the case of Brazil (Hale, 2012). Kara (2014) documents in some detail bond labor supply chains between South Asia and the Western economies in the frozen shrimp and carpet weaving industries. Similarly, as indicated earlier, the large growth of demand in the advanced world both for chocolate and for cheap fish for pet food has been directly linked to child and sea slavery, respectively. Globalization also led to much greater and cheaper means of transportation and communication, facilitating the work of human smugglers and traffickers, and especially of international criminal organizations, what Doomernik (2006) calls the "globalization, migration and trafficking nexus."

Globalization, market privatization, and economic growth also greatly increased inequality both within and between nations (IMF, 2017). At the same time, the massive increase in channels of communication made people aware of their relative impoverishment and of opportunities elsewhere, spurring their desire to migrate, sometimes under circumstances that made them vulnerable to exploitation (Liang and Ye, 2001).

The commercial sex industry was transformed by the internet in both positive and negative ways (*The Economist*, 2014; Pettinger, 2014). It made it easier for sex workers to get in touch with their clients, thereby reducing the dangers of relying on street prostitution and on pimps; at the same time, pimps and traffickers have used it to facilitate both the domestic and international buying and selling of sex and the exploitation of women.

Closely linked to these broader macro-economic changes have been several sociological developments that facilitated the growth of migration, smuggling, and trafficking. In many areas, the condition of women has been relatively worsened initially by modernization. While development in the long run, and often in the medium run, does lead to improvement in women's lives, the initial effects are often negative or mixed in many parts of the world. Not only have their roles in traditional economic systems been disrupted, leading to the disproportionate rise of female unemployment in rural areas, but often the worst jobs in the service sector and new labor-intensive industries fall into their hands (Farr, 2005; Mammen and Paxson, 2000; Oishi, 2005; Shah, 2017). Women move within their countries to engage in exploitative work in domestic service and sweatshop operations, and they make up the majority of the millions of international migrants across the globe, a significant number of whom end up in forced labor situations. One striking gendered aspect of migration in the vast Asian region, documented by Oishi (2005) is that women migrate from the more developed of the sending countries (the Philippines, Sri Lanka, Indonesia), whereas men migrate from the least developed economies

(Bangladesh, Pakistan). One reason for this was a major new feature of the sociology of globalization earlier identified by Rhacel Parreñas (2015) in her seminal study of Filipina domestic-labor migrants: the international division of reproductive labor, in which women of the advanced economies come to rely on educated women from the less developed world to perform their childcaring services.

Traditional racial or ethnic discrimination also greatly contributes to trafficking and modern servitude. Indeed, contrary to what some have claimed, modern trafficking and servitude are as racial and ethnic in their causes and impact as ancient and traditional slavery (Bedoya et al., 2009; Dank et al., 2014; Kara, 2014).

Several major political and regional changes during the last third of the twentieth century also facilitated the growth of forced labor. The most dramatic of these has been the collapse of the Soviet Union and the emergence of the post-Soviet successor states (Wylie and McRedmond, 2010), which ushered in a new era of economic and social insecurity. It is no accident that a substantial proportion of trafficked prostitutes in Turkey and Western Europe come from these states (Farr, 2005; Kligman and Limoncelli, 2005). The other major political development that enabled trafficking and smuggling was the emergence of the EU, which removed border controls within the Schengen Area and thereby made it much easier for persons to be moved within the Union and from Eastern Europe and the less-developed world (UNODC, 2016).

In addition to changes in Eastern Europe, we have also seen the proliferation of civil wars across the world. These wars, especially in Africa, Asia, and the Middle East, have reached extraordinary levels of savagery and violence, forcing the movement of vast numbers of people as refugees. Women and children have been especially vulnerable to statelessness and warfare (UN Security Council, 2016; Bunting, 2017).

Personal factors account for the seeming ease with which women have been deceived into accompanying their traffickers across borders. One is simply the desire for a better life. A second factor is the desire to escape abuse, especially from traditional households where they are oppressed by patriarchal older men or sexually abused. A third personal factor is that many trafficked women have been betrayed by relatives and friends who are paid by traffickers. In America a large number of teenagers and young women are forced into homelessness and sex work in order to escape dysfunctional families, or are lured into prostitution, sometimes resulting in modern-day slavery, by relatives and friends, as is the case with some men who become pimps.

Conclusion

As noted earlier, trafficking and servitude in the modern world have generated considerable interest and a vigorous antitrafficking and antislavery movement encompassing some 2,569 organizations that operate both within countries and internationally (Polaris, 2023). Most countries of the world have now signed on to the Palermo Protocol and other decrees calling for measures to reduce and ultimately eliminate modern trafficking and servitude (see Gallagher, 2017; ILO et al., 2017b). Among the advanced nations, the United States has taken the lead, with its State Department's annual TIP Report and its Labor Department's Worst Cases of Child Labor Report, in promoting awareness of the problem and encouraging countries to take action against it. The EU and the major global institutions, most notably the UN, have been active in documenting and promoting similar programs against the problem (e.g. UNODC, 2013, 2022). Indeed, the eradication of trafficking and forced labor has been formally adopted by the UN as one of the major goals of its 2030 agenda for sustainable development.

Encouraging as these movements have been, the fact is that they have so far had relatively little impact on the growth and persistence of modern trafficking and servitude. For example, although there are estimated millions of victims across the world, only a few thousand traffickers have been indicted, and even fewer have been successfully prosecuted. Across the world, the UNODC (2016: 50) found that in 2016 the criminal justice system "appears to be stagnating at a low level." The Covid-19 pandemic made matters worse. The 2022 UNODC report found that the global slowdown in convictions had accelerated; that trafficking for sexual exploitation was detected less; that there was "increased impunity in home countries resulting in more victims trafficked to more destinations"; that climate change was multiplying trafficking risks; that women and children were suffering greater violence at the hands of traffickers; and that "more highly organized traffickers exploit more victims, more violently and for longer periods of time." The report pondered whether "women were more likely than men to be traffickers or more likely than men to be convicted."

Prosecutions for violations of laws against forced labor are also rare, even in blatantly visible cases such as bonded labor in South Asia. The main reasons for this failure have been, on the one hand, the lack of commitment of states and their prosecutors to pursue trafficking and labor violation cases and, on the other, the enormous profits to be made from modern trafficking and forms of forced labor. According to the 2014 ILO report on the economics of forced labor, "modern-day slavery" is a US$150 billion-a-year industry, with the sex servitude sector being the most profitable, generating average profit of US$21,800 per year per victim (see also Kara, 2017). The UK-based Hope for Justice group (2023) has updated these figures, estimating that, as of 2021, total illicit profits amounted to US$245.81 billion, of which US$169.9 billion was from sexual exploitation and US$75.9 billion from the private sector forced labor, including domestic servitude. This estimate was quite close to the updated estimate of the ILO issued in March 2024, which found that total annual illegal profits from forced labor amounted to US$236 billion, a 37 percent increase in the ten years between 2014 and 2024. Per victim annual illegal profits had also increased to US$10,000 (ILO, 2024).

In many countries, corruption and conflicts of interest prevent effective action. Even in the United States, where the government has expressed genuine commitment to fighting trafficking and forced labor, the number of convictions of traffickers each year has been strikingly small. Between 2000, when the first major antitrafficking law was passed (TVPA 2000–23, or the Trafficking Victims Protection Act of 2000, reauthorized repeatedly, most recently in January 2023; see also FOSTA, or Allow States and Victims to Fight Online Sex Trafficking Act of 2018) and 2015, by which time all fifty states, as well as the federal government, had antitrafficking laws, only 1,876 suspects had been prosecuted at the federal level for antitrafficking crimes, and only 450 had been prosecuted at the state level (see also Peters, 2018). The failure to convict anyone on criminal charges for the clear enslavement of four hundred Thai farm workers in Hawaii between 2004 and 2005, which the FBI called the largest human trafficking case in US history, is a telling example of the ineffectiveness of the antitrafficking laws (a civil action by the Equal Employment Opportunity Commission eventually succeeded after eight years) (Heller, 2014). If America, for all its commitment to the antitrafficking and modern antiservitude cause, can perform so poorly in bringing violators to justice, in spite of the thousands of reported victims, it is hardly surprising that other countries have been so ineffective. The EU, we should note, has a somewhat better, though hardly impressive, record.

Nonetheless, social scientists, and especially sociologists, should be careful not to become too skeptical about the entire movement and the serious problems it addresses. It has now been reasonably

HUMAN TRAFFICKING, MODERN-DAY SLAVERY, AND SERVITUDE

estimated that nearly 50 million persons are presently in servitude around the world, many in genuine modern-day slavery and hundreds of thousands still in traditional, descent-based enslavement. Indeed, if we are to take marital and child servitude seriously, as we should, this is likely a conservative estimate. Public state-based slavery, on a par with ancient imperial Rome, thrives in at least three states: North Korea, Eritrea, and Myanmar.

Out of the conceptual muddles have emerged valuable models of forced labor and other forms of servitude that we have drawn on and sought to clarify in this chapter. From the admittedly hegemonic scrutiny of the US State and Labor Departments and their European counterparts, as well as from transnational and domestic advocacy networks, have emerged clearly defined and legally binding international and domestic norms prompting forceful local activism that have placed the plight of the forgotten dispossessed on the agenda of national and global consciousness, even if real changes are yet to materialize. To measure the effectiveness of the antitrafficking and antiservitude movement purely in terms of number of convictions per country is to embrace the very "criminal justice paradigm" for which J. A. Chuang (2014) has rightly criticized American state authorities as well as some fellow scholars. If exaggerated outrage over sexual trafficking has spilled over to long-overdue awareness and indignation about the oppression of laborers and women in forced marriage throughout the world, that is all for the good. A recent global study of NGOs that work in the trenches of antitrafficking advocacy found them "surprisingly sanguine about American State Department efforts," viewing the US government support as "powerful allies in [their] own anti-trafficking work" (Heiss and Kelley, 2017).

Understudied types of forced labor and their mechanisms call for further research. One area that urgently needs further study, noted recently by Rhacel Parreñas, is domestic servitude, especially among female migrant workers. In view of ageing populations in the advanced world, not only its children but also its elderly will be turning to the women of the less developed world for care. The "international division of reproductive labor" (Parreñas, 2015) is likely to become the international division of dependent care, and this increases the possibility of growing abuse as more restrictions are placed on these migrants in the interest of controlling them. The number of children in sexual servitude in the advanced world, especially America, child labor in agriculture, and the use of children in the military are all in need of more scholarly research. More work is also needed on bonded labor, the most widespread form of forced labor in the world. Kara's

275

(2014) study provides a valuable point of departure; what is badly needed now is an approach that does not prejudge the issue of slavery but attempts to estimate the differences between voluntarily initiated, though exploitative, relationships, on the one hand, and the cross-over to genuine modern-day slavery, on the other.

For sociologists particularly, antitrafficking activism presents the exciting case of a global social movement potentially on a par with its nineteenth-century abolitionist counterpart. For example, a study of the first international movement to combat the sexual exploitation of women showed the relation between the early antitrafficking movement and the development of the nation-state, imperialism, and the politics of women's sexuality (Limoncelli, 2010). Like that and all subsequent social movements, antitrafficking activism has deployed the strategies of awakening, exposing and shaming, metaphoric extension, numeric exaggeration, heartrending narratives, and cognitive reframing (see DeStefano, 2007; Limoncelli, 2016; Doorninck, 2017) in order to fracture and reshape our views of taken-for-granted evils around the world. It has already served the three purposes that Stephen Risse and Kathryn Sikkink (1999: 5) consider "necessary conditions for sustainable domestic change in the human rights area": it has exposed norm-violating states to the full glare of the international community, empowered and legitimated domestic activists and provided them some measure of protection from repression, and created "a transnational structure pressuring such regimes simultaneously 'from above' and 'from below.'" To cite a dramatic recent example, gender-equality and anti-forced marriage advocates can take much credit for the landmark ruling of the Indian Supreme Court that sex with a wife under eighteen years of age constitutes rape, a decision handed down, significantly, on October 11, 2017, the International Day of the Girl Child (Meixler, 2017).

The movement is crying out for more studies that go beyond critical evaluations of its discursive strategies and moral crusading. Limoncelli's (2017) study is an admirable move in this direction, demonstrating its substantive importance as a major case of a transnational social movement, and its theoretical significance in the way its non-Western origins and partly bottom-up development challenge some of the predictions of both world polity- and state-centered or coercion studies concerning the Western sources of issue-based advocacy and the institutionalization of global norms. Sadly, the persistent parochialism and presentism of American sociology remains an obstacle to badly needed sociological work on this inherently transnational problem.

The late sociologist, Helen Fein, one of the most distinguished scholars of genocide, wrote in her last work that:

> The victims of twentieth-century slavery come from the most varied points of origin. They might be outside (aliens) or inside the nation (citizens/residents); snatched, sentenced, enlisted, or born into servitude, conquered in war, serving in peace, or volunteering for a job abroad. They might be housed in camps, brothels, factory hostels, or private homes. They might be racially distinct or similar to their enslavers . . . Mostly they are invisible, strangers below the social radar screen, only detected by international, state, and local human rights nongovernmental organizations. (2007: 212)

Both the messengers and their message, then – global servitude, the subterranean suffering of those whom Fanon called the wretched of the earth – should animate the sociological imagination and rouse it from its sometimes too-myopic focus on the visible, present problems of the advanced world.

CREDITS

Chapter 1, "On the Institution of Slavery and Its Consequences," is a revised and substantially expanded version of my paper "Slavery as Social Institution," published in *International Encyclopedia of the Social and Behavioral Sciences*, vol. 21 (2001), pp. 14146–14152.

Chapter 2, "Revisiting Slavery and Property as a 'Bundle of Rights,'" is a revised and greatly expanded part of my chapter "Revisiting Slavery, Property, and Social Death," in J. Bodel and W. Scheidel, eds., *On Human Bondage: After Slavery and Social Death*. Wiley-Blackwell (2017), pp. 266–281.

Chapter 3, "Beyond 'Slave Society': The Structural Articulations of Slavery in Pre-Capitalist and Capitalist Social Formations," draws in part from two previously published papers: "Slavery: Comparative Aspects," *International Encyclopedia of the Social and Behavioral Sciences*, vol. 21 (2001), pp. 49–53; "Slavery in Human History," *New Left Review*, vol. 1, no. 117 (1979).

Chapter 4, "The Denial of Slavery in American Sociology," was previously published in *Theory and Society*, vol. 48 (2019): pp. 903–914.

Chapter 5, "The Origins of Slavery and Slave Society: A Critique of the Nieboer-Domar Hypothesis and Case Study of Ancient Athens," is a completely rewritten and greatly expanded version, using updated methodology, of a paper originally published as "The Structural Origins of Slavery: A Critique of the Nieboer-Domar Hypothesis from a Comparative Perspective," in V. Rubin and A. Tuden, eds.,

CREDITS

Comparative Perspectives on Slavery in New World Plantation Societies, New York Academy of Sciences (1977), pp. 12–34.

Chapter 6, "The Social and Symbolic Uses of Slavery in Ancient Rome and Early Christianity," is adapted and expanded from a section of my chapter, "Revisiting Slavery, Property, and Social Death," in J. Bodel and W. Scheidel, eds., *On Human Bondage: After Slavery and Social Death*, Wiley-Blackwell (2017), pp. 266–281.

Chapter 7, "Slavery and Slave Revolts: The Maroon Slave Wars of Jamaica, 1655–1739," is reproduced with the permission of the Sir Arthur Lewis Institute of Social and Economic Studies, The University of the West Indies, Mona, Jamaica, publisher of the *Social and Economic Studies* journal in which the article was originally published: "Slavery and Slave Revolts: A Socio-historical Analysis of the First Maroon War Jamaica, 1655–1740," *Social and Economic Studies*, vol. 19, no. 3 (September 1970), pp. 289–325.

Chapter 8, "Slavery and Genocide: The US South, Jamaica, and the Historical Sociology of Evil." Parts of the second section were previously published in the Introduction to the 2022 edition of my book, *The Sociology of Slavery: Black Slave Society in Jamaica, 1655–1832*, Polity, pp. xlviii–lxii.

Chapter 9, "Human Trafficking, Modern-Day Slavery, and Other Forms of Servitude," is a revised and updated version of the paper, "Modern Trafficking, Slavery, and Other Forms of Servitude," with Xiaolin Zhuo, published in *The Annual Review of Sociology*, vol. 44 (2018), pp. 407–439.

REFERENCES

"A Planter," 1733. "Paragraph in a Letter from Jamaica," CO 137/21, f. 11.

Abdelkader, G. K., ed., 2004. *Slavery in Niger: Historical, Legal and Contemporary Perspectives*. Anti–Slavery International.

Acemoglu, D., C. Garcia-Jimeno, and J. A. Robinson, 2012. "Finding Eldorado: Slavery and Long–run Development in Colombia," *Journal of Comparative Economics*, vol. 40: 534–564.

Acemoglu, D., S. Johnson, and J. A. Robinson, 2001. "The Colonial Origins of Comparative Development: An Empirical Investigation," *American Economic Review*, vol. 91, no. 5: 1369–1401.

Acemoglu, D., S. Johnson, and J. A. Robinson, 2005. "The Rise of Europe: Atlantic Trade, Institutional Change and Economic Growth," *American Economic Review*, vol. 95, no. 3: 546–579.

Acharya, A., M. Blackwell, and M. Sen, 2018. *Deep Roots: How Slavery Still Shapes Southern Politics*. Princeton University Press.

Agoston, G., 2017. "Janissaries," in K. Fleet et al., eds., *Encyclopedia of Islam*. Brill.

Agustin, L. 2007. *Sex at the Margins: Migration, Labour Markets and the Rescue Industry*. Zed Books.

Ahmet, I., and S. Toktas, 2002. *How Do Smuggling and Trafficking Operate via Irregular Border Crossings in the Middle East? Evidence from Fieldwork in Turkey. International Migration*, vol. 40, no. 6: 25–54.

Alesina, A., P. Giuliano, and N. Nunn, 2011. "On the Origins of Gender Roles: Women and the Plough." NBER Working Paper 17098.

Alexander, M., 2010. *The New Jim Crow: Mass Incarceration in the Age of Colorblindness*. The New Press.

Allain, J., ed., 2012. *The Legal Understanding of Slavery: From the Historical to the Contemporary*. Oxford University Press.

Allain, J., 2017. "Genealogies of Human Trafficking and Slavery," in R. Piotrowicz, C. Rijken, and B. Uhl, eds., *Routledge Handbook of Human Trafficking*. Routledge, pp. 3–12.

Anderson, A., S. Chilczuk, K. Nelson, R. Ruther, and C. Wall-Scheffler, 2023. "The Myth of Man the Hunter: Women's Contribution to the Hunt across Ethnographic Contexts," *PLoS ONE*, June 28. https://doi.org/10.1371/journal.pone.0287101.

REFERENCES

Anderson, B., 2000. *Doing Dirty Work? The Global Politics of Domestic Labor.* Zed Books.

Anderson, B., and J. Davidson, 2003. *Is Trafficking in Human Beings Demand Driven? A Multi-Country Pilot Study.* International Organization for Migration.

Anderson, K., 2007. "Marx's Late Writings on Russia Re–examined," *News and Letters.* https://www.kevin-anderson.com/wp-content/uploads/docs/anderson-article-marx-late-writings-russia-re-examined.pdf.

Anderson, P., 1974. *Passages from Antiquity to Feudalism.* New Left Books.

Andrews, A., 1967. *The Greeks.* Hutchinson.

Andrews, G., 1980. *The Afro-Argentines of Buenos Aires, 1800–1900.* University of Wisconsin Press.

Andrews, G., 2004. *Afro-Latin America, 1800–2000.* Oxford University Press.

Andrijasevic, R., 2010. *Migration, Agency and Citizenship in Sex Trafficking.* Palgrave Macmillan.

Anon., n.d. "Account of the Maroons and the Late War." C.E. Long Papers, 12431, BM, Sl.

Anon., 1693. *The Truest and Largest Account of the Late Earthquake in Jamaica, June the 7th, 1692.* T. Parkhurst.

Aptheker, H., 1939. "Maroons within the Present Limits of the United States." *Journal of Negro History,* vol. 24: 167–184.

Aptheker. H., 1969. *American Negro Slave Revolts.* International Publishers.

Aronowitz, A. A., 2009. *Human Trafficking, Human Misery: The Global Trade in Human Beings.* Praeger.

Ayalon, D., 1951. *L'Esclavage du Mamelouk.* Israel Oriental Society.

Aykan, Y., 2017. "On Freedom, Kinship and the Market Rethinking Property and Law in the Ottoman Slave System," *Quaderni storici,* vol. 52: 13–39.

Bahrami-Rad, D., A. Becker, and J. Henrich, 2021. "Tabulated Nonsense? Testing the Validity of the Ethnographic Atlas," *Economics Letters,* vol. 204: 1–5.

Bailey, C., and P. O'Neill, 2023. "The Evolution of Anti-Blackness in the American South: How Slavery and Segregation Perpetuates the Victimization of Black People," *Journal of Research in Crime and Delinquency,* vol. 60, no. 1.

Baker, B., and N. Rytina, 2012. *Estimates of the Unauthorized Immigrant Population Residing in the United States: January 2012.* US Office of Immigration Statistics.

Baker, H., 2017. "Slavery and Personhood in the Neo-Assyrian Empire," in J. Bodel and W. Scheidel, eds., *On Human Bondage: After Slavery and Social Death,* Wiley-Blackwell, pp. 15–30.

Baker, R., 2022. "The Historical Racial Regime and Racial Inequality in Poverty in the American South," *American Journal of Sociology,* vol. 127: 1721–1781.

Bales, K., 2007. *Ending Slavery: How We Free Today's Slaves.* University of California Press.

Bales, K., 2012. *Disposable People: New Slavery in the Global Economy.* University of California Press.

Bales, K., and R. Soodalter, 2009. *The Slave Next Door: Human Trafficking and Slavery in America Today.* University of California Press.

Bales, K., O. Hesketh, and B. Silverman, 2015. "Modern Slavery in the UK: How Many Victims?" *Significance,* vol. 12, no. 3: 16–21.

281

REFERENCES

Baptist, E., 2014. *The Half Has Never Been Told*. Basic Books.

Barbieri-Low, A., 2017. "Becoming Almost Somebody: Manumission and its Complications in the Early Han Empire," in J. Bodel and W. Scheidel, eds., *On Human Bondage: After Slavery and Social Death*. Wiley-Blackwell, pp. 122–135.

Barham, H., 1722. "The Most Correct and Particular Account of the Island of Jamaica." BM, Sl., Ms. 3918.

Baron, J., 2014. "Rescuing the Bundle-of-Rights Metaphor in Property Law," *University of Cincinnati Law Review*, vol. 82, no. 1.

Barrick, K., 2016. "Human Trafficking, Labor Exploitation and Exposure to Environmental Hazards," in J. F. Donnermeyer, ed., *Routledge International Handbook of Rural Criminology*. Routledge, pp. 147–156.

Barrick, K., P. Lattimore, W. Pitts, and S. Zhang, S., 2014. "Labor Trafficking Victimization among Farmworkers in North Carolina: Role of Demographic Characteristics and Acculturation," *International Journal of Rural Criminology*, vol. 2, no. 1: 225–243.

Barrick, K., W. J. Pitts, J. P. McMichael, W. D. Wheaton, and B. M. Evans, 2015. "Developing a Sampling Frame of Potential Trafficking Victims Using Geo-Mapping Techniques," *Forum Crime Society*, vol. 8: 95–108.

Barrientos, S. 2011. "Labour Chains: Analysing the Role of Labour Contractors in Global Production Networks." Working Paper 153, Brookings World Poverty Institute., University of Manchester. http://www.capturingthegains.org/pdf/bwpi–wp–15311.pdf.

Barry, K., 1996. *The Prostitution of Sexuality*. New York University Press.

Barsalou, L. W., 1985. "Ideals, Central Tendency, and Frequency of Instantiation as Determinants of Graded Structure in Categories," *Journal of Experimental Psychology: Learning, Memory and Cognition*, vol. 11, no. 4: 629–654.

Bassiouni, M. C., 1999. *Crimes Against Humanity in International Criminal Law*. Martinus Nijhoff Publishers.

Bauman, Z., 1989. *Modernity and the Holocaust*. Cornell University Press.

Becker, C., 1959. "What are Historical Facts?" in H. Meyerhoff, ed., *The Philosophy of History in Our Time*. Doubleday.

Beckert, S., 2014. *Empire of Cotton: A Global History*. Knopf.

Beckert, S., and S. Rockman, eds., 2016. *Slavery's Capitalism: A New History of American Economic Development*. University of Pennsylvania Press.

Beckford to Lords, CSP, 1702, nos. 912, 928.

Beckles, H., 1997. "Capitalism, Slavery and Caribbean Modernity," *Callaloo*, vol. 20, no. 4: 777–789.

Bedoya, E., A. Bedoya, and P. Belser, 2009. "Debt Bondage and Ethnic Discrimination in Latin America," in B. Andrees and P. Belser, eds., *Forced Labor: Coercion and Exploitation in the Private Economy*. International Labour Office, pp. 35–50.

Belanger, D., 2014. "Labor Migration and Trafficking among Vietnamese Migrants in Asia," *Annals of the American Academy of Political and Social Sciernce*, vol. 653, no. 1: 87–106.

Bell, D., 1976. *The Coming of Post-Industrial Society*. Basic Books.

Beneria, L., and Sen, G., 1981. "Accumulation, Reproduction, and Women's Role in Economic Development," *Journal of Women in Culture and Society*, vol. 7, no. 2: 279–298.

282

REFERENCES

Benveniste, E., 1973. *Indo-European Language and Society*. University of Miami Press.

Bérard, J., 1960. *L'Expansion et la colonisation grecques jusqu'aux guerres médiques*. Aubier.

Bergad, L., 2017."Slavery in Cuba and Puerto Rico, 1804 to Abolition," in D. Eltis, S. Engerman, and S. Drescher, eds.,*The Cambridge World History of Slavery*. Cambridge University Press, vol. 4, Ch. 5.

Berlin, I., 1998. *Many Thousands Gone: The First Two Centuries of Slavery in North America*. Harvard University Press.

Bernstein, E., 2007. "The Sexual Politics of the 'New Abolitionism'," *Differences*, vol. 18, no. 3: 128–151.

Bertocchi, G., 2016. "The Legacies of Slavery in and out of Africa," *IZA Journal of Migration*, vol. 5, no. 1: 1–19.

Bertocchi, G., and A. Dimico, 2012. "The Racial Gap in Education and the Legacy of Slavery," *Journal of Comparative Economics*, vol. 40: 581–595.

Bertocchi, G., and A. Dimico, 2014. "Slavery, Education, and Inequality," *European Economic Review*, vol. 70: 197–209.

Bertrand, W., E. de Buhr, and S. Dudis, S., 2015. *Survey Research on Child Labor in West African Cocoa-Growing Areas*. Tulane University School of Public Health and Tropical Medicine.

Best, L., 1968. "Outline of a Model of Pure Plantation Economy," *Social and Economic Studies*, vol. 17: 283–324.

Beyond Borders et al. 2014. "The Plight of Restavèk (Child Domestic Servants)." Republic of Haiti. http://www.ijdh.org/wp-content/uploads/ 2014/09/HRC_ Restavek-Sept-12.pdf.

Biermann, F., and M. Jankowiac, eds., 2021. *The Archeology of Slavery in Early Medieval Northern Europe: The Invisible Community*. Springer.

Bilger, V., M. Hoffman, and M. Jandl, 2006. "Human Smuggling as a Transnational Service Industry: Evidence from Austria," *International Migration*, vol. 44, no. 4: 59–93.s

Black, C., 1966. *Tales of Old Jamaica*. Collins.

Blackburn, R., 2010 [1997]. *The Making of New World Slavery: From the Baroque to the Modern, 1492–1800*, 2nd ed. Verso.

Blackett, R. J. M., 2018. *The Captive's Quest for Freedom: Fugitive Slaves, the 1850 Fugitive Slave Law, and the Politics of Slavery*. Cambridge University Press.

Blackhawk, N., 2023a. "The Centrality of Dispossession: Native American Genocide and Settler Colonialism," in N. Blackhawk, B. Kiernan, B. Madley, and R. Taylor, eds., *The Cambridge World History of Genocide*, vol. 2. Cambridge University Press, pp. 23–45.

Blackhawk, N., 2023b. "The Destruction of Wendake (Huronia), 1647–1652," in N. Blackhawk, B. Kiernan, B. Madley, and R. Taylor, eds., *The Cambridge World History of Genocide*, vol. 2. Cambridge University Press, pp. 243–266.

Blackmon, D. A., 2008. *Slavery By Another Name: The Re-Enslavement of Black Americans from the Civil War to World War II*. Doubleday.

Blackstone, W., 1979 [1766]. *Commentaries on the Laws of England*. Vol. 2: Of the Rights of Things. University of Chicago Press.

Blagbrough, J., 2017. "Child Domestic Labour: Work Like Any Other, Work Like No Other," in A. Bunting and J. Quirk, eds., *Contemporary Slavery:*

283

REFERENCES

Popular Rhetoric and Political Practice. University of British Columbia Press, pp. 301–328.

Blanton, J., 2016. "This Species of Property: Slavery and the Properties of Subjecthood in Anglo-American Law and Politics, 1619–1783," PhD thesis, Department of History, City University of New York Graduate Center.

Blassingame, J. W., 1972. *The Slave Community: Plantation Life in the Antebellum South*. Oxford University Press.

Bloch, M., 1966. "The Rise of Dependent Cultivation and Seignorial Institutions," in M. Postan, ed., *Cambridge Economic History of Europe*. Cambridge University Press, Ch. VI.

Bloome, D., 2014. "Racial Inequality Trends and the Intergenerational Persistence of Income and Family Structure," *American Sociological Review*, vol. 79: 1196–1225.

Bloome, D., and C. Muller, 2015. "Tenancy and African American Marriage in the Postbellum South," *Demography*, vol. 52: 1409–1430.

Bloome, D., and G. Pace, 2024. "Family Tree Branches and Southern Roots: Contemporary Racial Differences in Marriage in Intergenerational and Contextual Perspective," *American Journal of Sociology*, vol. 129, no. 4: 1084–1135.

Bloxham, D., and A. D. Moses, eds., 2010. *The Oxford Handbook of Genocide Studies*. Oxford University Press.

Bodel, J., 2017. "Death and Social Death in Ancient Rome," in J. Bodel and W. Scheidel, eds., *On Human Bondage: After Slavery and Social Death*. Wiley-Blackwell, pp. 81–108.

Bok-rae, K., 2003. "Nobi: A Korean System of Slavery," *Slavery and Abolition*, vol. 24, no. 2: 144–168.

Bok-rae, K., 2018. "A Microhistorical Analysis of Korean Nobis through the Prism of the Lawsuit of Damulsari," in N. Lenski and C. Cameron, eds., *What Is a Slave Society?* Cambridge University Press, pp. 383–409.

Bonassie, P., 1985. *Survie et extinction du régime esclavagiste dans l'Occident du haut moyen âge*. Cahiers de Civilisation Médiévale, vol. 28, no. 112: 307–343.

Boserup, E., 2007 [1970]. *Woman's Role in Economic Development*. Cromwell Press.

Boserup, E., 2017 [2005]. *The Conditions of Agricultural Growth: The Economics of Agrarian Change Under Population Pressure*. Routledge.

Bradley, K. R., 1987. *Slaves and Masters in the Roman Empire*. Oxford University Press.

Brennan, D., 2004. "Selling Sex for Visas: Sex Tourism as a Stepping-Stone to International Migration," in B. Ehrenreich and A. Hochschild, eds., *Global Woman: Nannies, Maids and Sex Workers in the New Economy*. Henry Holt, pp. 154–168.

Bresson, A., 2015. *The Making of the Ancient Greek Economy: Institutions, Markets, and Growth in the City-States*. Princeton University Press.

Briggs, S., 1989. "Can an Enslaved God Liberate? Hermeneutical Reflections on Phil 2:6–11," *Semeia*, vol. 47: 137–153.

Brodkin, K., 1998. *How Jews Became White Folks and What that Says About Race in America*. Rutgers University Press.

Brown, V., 2009. "Social Death and Political Life in the Study of Slavery," *American Historical Review*, vol. 114, no. 5: 1231–1249.

REFERENCES

Brunovskis, A., and G. Tyldum, 2004. *Crossing Borders: An Empirical Study of Transnational Prostitution and Trafficking in Human Beings*. Fafo Research Foundation.

Bunting, A., 2017. "Narrating Wartime Enslavement, Forced Marriage and Modern Slavery," in A. Bunting and J. Quirk, eds., *Contemporary Slavery: Popular Rhetoric and Political Practice*. University of British Columbia Press, pp. 129–157.

Bunting, A., and J. Quirk, 2017. "Contemporary Slavery as More than Rhetorical Strategy? The Politics and Ideology of a New Political Cause," in A. Bunting and J. Quirk, eds., *Contemporary Slavery: Popular Rhetoric and Political Practice*. University of British Columbia Press, pp. 5–35.

Burford, A., 1972. *Craftsmen in Greek and Roman Society*. Cornell University Press.

Burford, A., 1993. *Land and Labor in the Greek World*. Johns Hopkins University Press.

Burn, A. R., 1966 [1936]. *The World of Hesiod*. Ayer Co.

Burnard, T., 2001. "'Prodigious Riches': The Wealth of Jamaica Before the American Revolution," *Economic History Review*, vol. 54, no. 3: 506–524.

Burnard, T., 2004. *Mastery, Tyranny, and Desire: Thomas Thistlewood and His Slaves in the Anglo-Jamaican World*. University of North Carolina Press.

Burnard, T., and G. Riello, 2020. "Slavery and the New History of Capitalism," *Journal of Global History*, vol. 15, no. 2: 1–20.

Burnard, T., and J. Garrigus, 2016. *The Plantation Machine: Atlantic Capitalism in French Saint-Domingue and British Jamaica*. University of Pennsylvania Press.

Busch-Armendariz, N., N. Nale, M. Kammer-Kerwick, B. Kellison, M. Torres et al., 2016. *Human Trafficking by the Numbers: The Initial Benchmark of Prevalence and Economic Impact for Texas*. Institute of Domestic Violence and Sexual Assault, University of Texas, Austin.

Bush, M. L., 2000. *Servitude in Modern Times*. Polity.

Cameron, C., 2016. *Captives: How Stolen People Changed the World*. University of Nebraska Press.

Cameron, C., 2017. "Slavery and Freedom in Small-Scale Societies," in J. Bodel and W. Scheidel, eds., *On Human Bondage: After Slavery and Social Death*. Wiley-Blackwell, pp. 210–225.

Cameron, C., 2018. "The Nature of Slavery in Small-Scale Societies," in N. Lenski and C. Cameron, *What Is a Slave Society?* Cambridge University Press, pp. 151–168.

Cameron, S., and Newman, E., eds. 2008. *Trafficking in Humans: Social, Cultural and Political Dimensions*. UN University Press.

Camus, A., 1954. *The Rebel: An Essay on Man in Revolt*. Alfred A. Knopf.

Card, C., 2003. "Genocide and Social Death," *Hypatia*, vol. 18, no.1: 63–79.

Carolino, B., 2020. "Nevsun Settles with Eritrean Plaintiffs in Relation to Landmark Supreme Court of Canada Case," *Canadian Lawyer*, vol. 11, no. 5.

Cartledge, P. A., 1985. "Rebels and 'Sambos' in Classical Greece: A Comparative View," *History of Political Thought*, vol. 6, nos. 1/2: 16–46.

Cartledge, P., 2023. "Urbicide in the Ancient Greek World, 480–330 BCE," in B. Kiernan, T. M. Lemos, and T. S. Taylor, eds., *The Cambridge World History of Genocide*, vol. 1. Cambridge University Press, pp. 235–256.

Cash, W. J., 1960. *The Mind of the South*. Vintage.

REFERENCES

Cassidy, F. G., 1961. *Jamaica Talk: Three Hundred Years of the English Language In Jamaica*. Macmillan.

Chantavanich, C., S. Laodumrongchai, and C. Stringer, 2016. "Under the Shadow: Forced Labour among Sea Fishers in Thailand," *Marine Policy*, vol. 68: 1–7.

Cheng, C. M. C., 2014. "Migrant Workers or Trafficked Victims? Structural Vulnerabilities of Women Migrant Workers in Contemporary China," in K. K. Hoang and R. S. Parreñas, eds., *Human Trafficking Reconsidered: Rethinking the Problem, Envisioning New Solutions*. International Debate Education Association, pp. 50–57.

Chevaleyre, C., 2023. "Slavery in Late Ming China," in D. A. Pargas and J. Schiel, eds., *The Palgrave Handbook of Global Slavery throughout History*. Palgrave Macmillan.

Child Soldiers International, 2017–18. Annual Report. https://reliefweb.int/report/world/child-soldiers-international-annual-report-2017-18.

Chin, K., and J. Finckenauer, 2012. *Selling Sex Overseas: Chinese Women and the Realities of Prostitution and Global Sex Trafficking*. New York University Press.

Chuang, J. A., 2010. "Rescuing Trafficking from Ideological Capture: Prostitution Reform and Anti-trafficking Law and Policy," *University of Pennsylvania Law Review*, vol. 158, no. 6: 1655–1728.

Chuang, J. A., 2014. "Exploitation Creep and the Unmaking of Human Trafficking," *American Journal of International Law*, vol. 108, no. 4: 609–649.

Chuang, J., 2014. "Chains of Debt: Labor Trafficking as a Career in China's Construction Industry," in K. K. Hoang and R. S. Parreñas, eds., 2014. *Human Trafficking Reconsidered: Rethinking the Problem, Envisioning New Solutions*. International Debate Education Association, pp. 58–68.

Cicero, 1913. *de Officiis*, trans. W. Miller. Harvard University Press.

Claeys, E., 2011. "Bundle-of-Sticks Notions in Legal and Economic Scholarship," *Economic Journal Watch*, vol. 8, no. 3: 205–214.

Claridge, W., 1964. *A History of the Gold Coast and Ashanti*. F. Cass.

Clark, K. B., 1965. *Dark Ghetto: Dilemmas of Social Power*. Harper Torchbooks.

Cofino, M., 1963. *Domaines et seigneurs en Russie vers la fin du XVIIIe siècle. Étude de structures agraires et de mentalités économiques*. Collection historique de l'Institut d'études slaves, vol. XVIII. Repr. in *Revue d'histoire moderne et contemporaine*, vol. 11, no. 4, 1964: 309–313.

Conrad, A., and J. Meyer, 1958. "The Economics of Slavery in the Ante Bellum South," *Journal of Political Economy*, vol. LXVI: 95–130.

Cooper, A., 2012. "From Slavery to Genocide: The Fallacy of Debt in Reparations Discourse," *Journal of Black Studies*, vol. 43, no. 2: 107–126.

Craig, G., 2010. "Introduction: Child Slavery Worldwide," in G. Craig, ed., *Child Slavery Now: A Contemporary Reader*. Policy Press, pp. 1–20.

Crone, P., 1980. *Slaves on Horses: The Evolution of the Islamic Polity*. Cambridge University Press.

CTDC. 2022. "Age of Victims: Children and Adults." Counter Trafficking Data Collaborative. https://www.ctdatacollaborative.org/story/age-victims-children-and-adults.

"Cudjoe's Fidelity," 1739. C. E. Long Papers, 12431, BM, Sl.

Cundall, F., ed., 1939. *The Journal of Lady Nugent*. Institute of Jamaica.

REFERENCES

Curtin, P., 1969. *The Atlantic Slave Trade: A Census*. University of Wisconsin Press.

Curtis, R., K. Terry, M. Dank, K. Dombrowski, and B. Khan, 2008. *Commercial Sexual Exploitation of Children in New York City*, vol. 1: *The CSEC Population in New York City: Size, Characteristics, and Needs*. John Jay College of Criminal Justice.

Dallas, R., 1803. *The History of the Maroons*. T. N. Longman.

Dalzel, A.,1793. *The History of Dahomy: An Inland Kingdom of Africa*. T. Spilsbury and Sons.

Daniel P. 1972. *The Shadow of Slavery: Peonage in the South 1901–1969*. University of Illinois Press.

Danieli, Y., 1998. *The International Handbook of Multigenerational Legacies of Trauma*. Plenum Press.

Dank, M., B. Khan, P. M. Downey, C. Kotonias, D. Mayer et al., 2014. *Estimating the Size and Structure of the Underground Commercial Sex Economy in Eight Major US Cities*. Urban Institute, Washington, DC.

Datta, M. N., and K. Bales, 2013. "Slavery in Europe: Part 1, Estimating the Dark Figure," *Human Rights Quarterly*, vol. 35, no. 4: 817–829.

David, P., and P. Temin, 1974. "Slavery: The Progressive Institution?" *Journal of Economic History*, vol. 34, no. 3: 739–783.

Davidson, B., 1966. *A History of West Africa*. Anchor Books.

Davidson, J., and B. Anderson, 2006. "The Trouble with 'Trafficking,'" in C. van den Anker and J. Doomernik, eds., *Trafficking and Women's Rights*. Palgrave Macmillan, pp. 11–26.

Davis, D. B., 1966. *The Problem of Slavery in Western Culture*. Cornell University Press.

Davis, D. B., 1975. *The Problem of Slavery in the Age of Revolution, 1770–1823*. Cornell University Press.

Davis, D. B., 1986. *Slavery and Human Progress*. Oxford University Press.

de la Fuente, A., 2004. "Sugar and Slavery in Early Colonial Cuba," in S. B. Schwartz, ed., *Tropical Babylons: Sugar and the Making of the Atlantic World, 1450–1680*. University of North Carolina Press.

de Lisser, H. G., 1929. *The White Witch of Rosehall*. E. Benn,

de Ste Croix, G. E. M., 1981. *The Class Struggles in the Ancient Greek World*. Cornell University Press.

Delvaux, M., 2019. "Transregional Slave Networks of the Northern Arc, 700–900 C.E.," PhD thesis, Department of History, Boston University.

Desborough, V. R. d'A., 1972. *The Greek Dark Ages*. St. Martin's Press.

DeStefano, A., 2007. *The War on Human Trafficking: U.S. Policy Assessed*. Rutgers University Press.

Dewey, S., 2014. "Understanding Force and Coercion: Perspectives from Law Enforcement, Social Service Providers, and Sex Workers," in K. K. Hoang and R. S. Parreñas, eds., *Human Trafficking Reconsidered: Rethinking the Problem, Envisioning New Solutions*. International Debate Education Association, pp. 102–115.

Dickenson, D., 2006. "Philosophical Assumptions and Presumptions about Trafficking for Prostitution," in C. van den Anker and J. Doomernik, eds., *Trafficking and Women's Rights*. Palgrave Macmillan, pp. 43–53.

Dikötter, F., 2023. "China under Mao, 1949–1976," in B. Kiernan, W. Lower, N. Naimark, and S. Straus, eds., *The Cambridge World History of Genocide*, vol. 3. Cambridge University Press, pp. 429–449.

REFERENCES

Dinan, K. A., 2002. "Migrant Thai Women Subjected to Slavery-like Abuses in Japan," *Violence Against Women*, vol. 8, no. 9: 1113–1139.

Divale, W., 2004. "Codebook of Variables for the Standard Cross-Cultural Sample (Variables v1 to v2000 as of May, 2004)," *World Cultures: The Journal of Cross Cultural and Comparative Research*, vol. 14, no. 2.

Dockes, P., 1982. *Medieval Slavery and Liberation*. University of Chicago Press.

Dodds, E., 1973. *The Ancient Concept of Progress*. Oxford University Press.

Domar, E. D., 1970. "The Causes of Slavery or Serfdom: A Hypothesis," *Journal of Economic History*, vol. XXX, no. 1: 18–32.

Doomernik, J., 2006. "The Globalisation, Migration and Trafficking Nexus: European Outcomes," in C. van den Anker and J. Doomernik, eds., *Trafficking and Women's Rights*. Palgrave Macmillan, pp. 200–18.

Doorninck, M., 2017. "Changing the System from Within: The Role of NGOs in the Flawed Anti-trafficking Framework," in R. Piotrowicz, C. Rijken, and B. Uhl, eds., *Routledge Handbook of Human Trafficking*. Routledge, pp. 419–430.

Dore, E., 2006. *Myths of Modernity: Peonage and Patriarchy in Nicaragua*. Duke University Press.

Douglass, F., 1855. *My Bondage and My Freedom*. Miller, Orton, and Mulligan.

Dovring, F., 1965. "Bondage, Tenure and Progress: Reflections on the Economics of Forced Labor," *Comparative Studies in Society and History*, vol. 7, no. 3: 309–323.

Drescher, S., 1996. "The Atlantic Slave Trade and the Holocaust: A Comparative Analysis," in A. Rosenbaum, ed., *Is the Holocaust Unique? Perspectives on Comparative Genocide*. Westview Press, pp. 65–85.

DuBois, W. E. B., 1935. *Black Reconstruction in America, 1860–1880*. Atheneum

Dunn, R., 2014. *A Tale of Two Plantations: Slave Life and Labor in Jamaica and Virginia*. Harvard University Press.

Dwork, D., 2023. "Jewish Life and Death Under Nazi Rule Across Europe and Around the Globe," in B. Kiernan, W. Lower, N. Naimark, and S. Straus, eds., *The Cambridge World History of Genocide*, vol. 3. Cambridge University Press, pp. 258–280

Edwards, B., 1807 [1796]. "Observations on the Disposition, Character, Manners, and Habits of Life, of the Maroon Negroes of the Island of Jamaica," in B. Edwards, *The History, Civil and Commercial, of the British Colonies in the West Indies*, vol. I. London, pp. 522–576.

EJF, 2015. *Thailand's Seafood Slaves: Human Trafficking, Slavery and Murder in Kantang's Fishing Industry*. Environmental Justice Foundation, London.

Elkins, S., 1959. *Slavery: A Problem in American Institutional and Intellectual Life*. University of Chicago Press.

Elkins, S., 1975. "The Slavery Debate," *Commentary*, vol. 60, no. 6: 40–54.

Eltis, D., F. D. Lewis, and K. L. Sokoloff, eds., 2004. *Slavery in the Development of the Americas*. Cambridge University Press.

Engels, F., 1962. *Anti-Dühring*. Foreign Languages Publishing House.

Engerman, S., 1973. "Some Considerations Relating to Property Rights in Man," *Journal of Economic History*, vol. 33, no. 1: 43–65.

Engerman, S., 1976. "Some Economic and Demographic Comparisons of Slavery in the United States and the British West Indies," *Economic History Review*, vol. 29, no. 2: 258–275.

REFERENCES

Engerman, S., S. Drescher, and R. Paquette, eds., 2001. *Slavery*. Oxford University Press.

Engerman, S., K. Sokoloff, M. Urquiola, and D. Acemoglu, 2002. "Factor Endowments, Inequality, and Paths of Development among New World Economies (with Comments)," *Economia*, vol. 3, no. 1: 41–109.

Epstein, S. A., 2001. *Speaking of Slavery: Color, Ethnicity and Human Bondage in Italy*. Cornell University Press.

Ermakoff, I., 2019. "Causality and History: Modes of Causal Investigation in Historical Social Sciences," *Annual Review of Sociology*, vol. 45: 581–606.

Eurostat, 2015. *Trafficking in Human Beings*. Publications Office of the European Union.

Extract, 1734. "Extract of a Letter from Jamaica," CO 137/21, f. 57.

Fanon, F., 1963. *The Wretched of the Earth*. Grove Press.

Fanon, F., 2008 [1952]. *Black Skin, White Masks*. Grove Press. [*Peau Noire, Masques Blancs*, Éditions du Seuil.]

Farias, P., 1985. "Models of the World and Categorical Models: The 'Enslavable Barbarian' as a Mobile Classificatory Label," in J. R. Willis, ed., *Slaves and Slavery in Muslim Africa*. Vol.1: *Islam and the Ideology of Enslavement*. Frank Cass and Co., pp. 27–46.

Farley, M., 2004. "Bad for the Body, Bad for the Heart: Prostitution Harms Women even if Legalized or Decriminalized," *Violence Against Women*, vol. 10, no. 10: 1087–1125.

Farley, M., A. Cotton, J. Lynne, A. Zumbeck, F. Spiwak et al., 2004. "Prostitution and Trafficking in Nine Countries: An Update on Violence and Posttraumatic Stress Disorder," *Journal of Trauma Practice*, vol. 2, nos. 3–4: 33–74.

Farr, K., 2005. *Sex Trafficking: The Global Market in Women and Children*. Worth.

Farrag, H., R. Flory, and B. Loskota, 2014. "Evangelicals and Human Trafficking: Rescuing, Rehabilitating, and Releasing One Individual at a Time," in K. K. Hoang and R. S. Parreñas, eds., *Human Trafficking Reconsidered: Rethinking the Problem, Envisioning New Solutions*. International Debate Education Association, pp. 116–122.

Fede, A. T., 2017. *Homicide Justified: The Legality of Killing Slaves in the United States and the Atlantic World*. Georgia University Press.

Fein, H., 2007. *Human Rights and Wrongs: Slavery, Terror, Genocide*. Paradigm Publishers.

Fernando, B.. 2013. *In Contempt of Fate: The Tale of a Sri Lankan Sold into Servitude, Who Survived to Tell It*. BeaRo Publishing.

Feurtado, W. A., 1896. *Official and Other Personages of Jamaica from 1655 to 1790*. Feurtado's Sons.

Finley, M. I., 1956. *The World of Odysseus*. Chatto and Windus.

Finley, M. I., ed., 1960. "Was Greek Civilization Based on Slave Labour?," in Finley, ed., *Slavery in Classical Antiquity: Views and Controversies*. William Heffer and Sons.

Finley, M. I., 1962. "The Black Sea and Danubian Regions and the Slave Trade in Antiquity," *Klio*, vol. 40: 51–59.

Finley, M. I., 1964. "Between Slavery and Freedom," *Comparative Studies in Society and History*, vol. 6, no. 3: 233–249.

Finley, M. I., 1968. "Slavery," in David Sills, ed., *International Encyclopedia of the Social Sciences*. Macmillan, pp. 307–313.

REFERENCES

Finley, M., 1973. *The Ancient Economy*. Chatto and Windus.

Finley, M., 1980. *Ancient Slavery and Modern Ideology*. Viking Press.

Finley, M., 1981. *Economy and Society in Ancient Greece*, ed. B. D. Shaw and R. P. Saller. Chatto & Windus.

Firth, R., 1959. *Primitive Economics of the New Zealand Maori*. New Zealand Government, Wellington.

Fiske, S. T., 2010. *Social Beings: Core Motives in Social Psychology*. Wiley.

Fitzhugh, G., 1857. *Cannibals All! Or, Slaves Without Masters*. A. Morris.

Fogel, R., and S. Engerman, 1974. *Time on the Cross: Economics of American Negro Slavery*, vol. 1. Little, Brown.

Fogel, R., and S. Engerman, 1979. "Recent Findings in the Study of Slave Demography and Family Structure," *Sociology and Social Research*, vol. 63: 567–568.

Foner, E., 1995. *Free Soil, Free Labor, Free Men: The Ideology of the Republican Party before the Civil War*. Oxford University Press.

Foote, P., and D. Wilson, 1970. *The Viking Achievement*. Hurst and Co.

Forand, P. G., 1962. "Military Slavery in Ninth Century Bagdad," PhD thesis, Princeton University.

Forced Marriage Unit, 2017. *Forced Marriage Unit Statistics 2016*. Forced Marriage Unit, London.

Forde, D., 1941. *Marriage and the Family Among the Yako in South-Eastern Nigeria*. Routledge.

Fraginals, M., 1976. *The Sugar Mill: The Socio-Economic Complex of Sugar in Cuba*. Monthly Review Press.

Frazier, E. F., 1951 [1939]. *The Negro Family in the United States*. Dryden Press.

Frederick, J., 1998. "Deconstructing Gita." *Himal South Asian Magazine*, September 30.

Freeman, K., 2014 [1926]. *The Works and Life of Solon. With a Translation of His Poems*. University of Wales Press Board. Repr. in the Legal Classics Library.

Freeman, R. B., 2008. "The New Global Labor Market," *Focus*, vol. 26, no. 1: 1–6

Fried, B., 1998. *The Progressive Assault on Laissez Faire: Robert Hale and the First Law and Economics Movement*. Harvard University Press.

Funakoshi, M., 2013. "China's 'Re-education Through Labor' System: The View from Within," *The Atlantic*, February 6.

Furstenberg, F. Jr., T. Hershberg, and J. Modell, 1975. "The Origins of the Female-headed Black Family: The Impact of the Urban Experience," *Journal of Interdisciplinary History*, vol. 6, no. 2: 211–233.

Furtado, J., 2017. "Honor and Dishonor in the Slavery of Colonial Brazil," in J. Bodel and W. Scheidel, eds., *On Human Bondage: After Slavery and Social Death*. Wiley-Blackwell, pp. 167–192.

Gallagher, A., 2014. "The Global Slavery Index is Based on Flawed Data: Why Does No One Say So?" *Guardian*, November 28.

Gallagher, A., 2017. "Trafficking in Transnational Criminal Law," in R. Piotrowicz, C. Rijken, and B. Uhl, eds., 2017. *Routledge Handbook of Human Trafficking*. Routledge, pp. 21–40.

Gallagher, A., and F. David, 2014. *The International Law of Migrant Smuggling*. Cambridge University Press.

REFERENCES

Galvan, J., 2002. "Urban Slavery in Argentina after Independence, 1810–1860," *Proceedings of the Pacific Coast Council on Latin American Studies*, vol. 20.

Gardner, W. J., 1873. *The History of Jamaica*. T. Fisher Unwin.

Garlan, Y., 1982. *Les Esclaves en grèce ancienne*. Éditions la Découverte.

Gayi, S. K., and K. Tsowou, 2016. *Cocoa Industry: Integrating Small Farmers into the Global Value Chain*. UN Conference on Trade and Development.

Genovese, E., 1961. "The Slave South: An Interpretation," *Science and Society*, vol. 25: 320–337.

Genovese, E., 1965. *The Political Economy of Slavery: Studies in the Economy and Society of the Slave South*. Oxford University Press.

Genovese, E., 1967. "Rebelliousness and Docility in the Negro Slave: A Critique of the Elkins Thesis," *Civil War History*, vol. 13: 293–314.

Genovese, E., 1969. *The World the Slaveholders Made*. Pantheon.

Genovese, E., 1976. *Roll, Jordan Roll: The World the Slaves Made*. Vintage.

Genovese, E., 1980. *From Rebellion to Revolution: Afro-American Slave Revolts in the Making of the Modern World*. Louisiana State University Press.

Gershman, B., 2020. "Witchcraft Beliefs as a Cultural Legacy of the Atlantic Slave Trade: Evidence from Two Continents," *European Economic Review*, vol. 122.

Ghosh, R., 2005. *CODE: Collaborative Ownership and the Digital Economy*. MIT Press.

Gillingham, J., 2012."Women, Children and the Profits of War," in J. L. Nelson, S. Reynolds, and S. Johns, *Gender and Historiography: Studies in the Earlier Middle Ages in Honour of Pauline Stafford*. University of London Press, pp. 61–74.

Giobbe, E., 1993. "An Analysis of Individual, Institutional, and Cultural Pimping," *Michigan Journal of Gender and Law*, vol. 1: 33–57.

Giri, B. R., 2010. "Haliya and Kamaiya Bonded Child Labourers in Nepal," In G. Craig, ed., *Child Slavery Now: A Contemporary Reader*. Policy Press, pp. 227–242.

Glancy, J. A., 2006. *Slavery in Early Christianity*. Fortress Press.

Global Slavery Index, 2017. *Mauritania Country Study*. Walk Free, Nedlands, WA.

Gluckman, M., 2012 [1965]. *Politics, Law and Ritual in Tribal Society*. Transaction Books.

Goad, K., 2017. *Columbia University and Incarcerated Worker Labor Unions under the National Labor Relations Act*. Cornell Law Library Prize for Exemplary Student Research Papers, 14. http://scholarship.law.cornell.edu/cllsrp/14.

Goldhagen, D., 1997. *Hitler's Willing Executioners*. Knopf.

Goni, U., 2021. "The Hidden History of Black Argentina," *New York Review of Books*, February 8.

Goody, J., 1973. "Bridewealth and Dowry in Africa and Eurasia," in J. Goody and S. J. Tambiah, eds., *Bridewealth and Dowry*. Cambridge University Press.

Goody, J., 1980. "Slavery in Time and Place," in J. L. Watson, ed., *Asian and African Systems of Slavery*. Oxford University Press.

Gordon, M., 1990. *Slavery in the Arab World*. New Amsterdam Books.

Gottlieb, A., and K. Flynn, 2021. "The Legacy of Slavery and Mass Incarceration: Evidence from Felony Case Outcomes," *Social Service Review*, vol. 95, no. 1.

REFERENCES

Gouda, M., and A. Rigterink, 2017. "The Long-Term Effect of Slavery on Violent Crime: Evidence from US Counties." https://papers.ssrn.com/sol3/papers.cfm?abstract_id=2358389.

Gourevitch, A., 2013. "Wage-Slavery and Republican Liberty." https://jacobin.com/2013/02/wage–slavery–and–republican–liberty/.

Goździak, E., 2016. *Trafficked Children and Youth in the United States: Reimagining Survivors*. Rutgers University Press.

Goździak, E., and M. Bump, 2008. "Data and Research on Human Trafficking: Bibliography of Research Based Literature." Institute for the Study of International Migration, Georgetown University. https://www.ncjrs.gov/pdffiles1/nij/grants/224392.pdf.

Graff, G., 2014. "The Intergenerational Trauma of Slavery and Its Aftermath," *The Journal of Psychohistory*, vol. 41, no. 3: 181–197.

Green, E. 2012. "Slavery, Land and Capital in 18th-Century Cape Colony: Revising the Nieboer-Domar hypothesis." https://portal.research.lu.se/en/publications/slavery-land-and-capital-in-18th-century-cape-colony-revising-the.

Greenberg, K., 1997. *Honor and Slavery*. Princeton University Press.

Greene, S., 2017. "Child Slavery in Africa as Social Death? Responses Past and Present," in J. Bodel and W. Scheidel, eds., *On Human Bondage: After Slavery and Social Death*. Wiley-Blackwell, pp. 193–209.

Greenhalgh, P., 1973. *Early Greek Warfare: Horsemen and Chariots in the Homeric and Archaic Ages*. Cambridge University Press.

Greenland, F., 2019. "Long-Range Continuities in Comparative and Historical Sociology: The Case of Parasitism and Women's Enslavement," *Theory and Society*, vol. 48, no. 6: 883–902.

Grey, T., 1980. "The Disintegration of Property," in J. R. Pennock and J. W. Chapman, eds., *Property*. New York University Press.

Guilmoto, C. Z., 2007. "Sex Ratio Imbalance in Asia: Trends, Consequences, and Policy Responses." Paper presented at Fourth Asia Pacific Conference on Reproductive Sexual Health and Rights, Hyderabad, India, October 29–31.

Gulati, G., 2012. "Representing Trafficking: Media in the United States, Great Britain, and Canada," in A. Brysk, ed., *From Human Trafficking to Human Rights: Reframing Contemporary Slavery*. University of Pensylvania Press, pp. 44–72.

Gunadi, C., 2019. "The Legacy of Slavery on Hate Crime in the United States," *Research in Economics*, vol. 73: 339–344.

Guth, A., R. Anderson, K. Kinnard, and H. Tran, 2014. "Proper Methodology and Methods of Collecting and Analyzing Slavery Data: An Examination of the Global Slavery Index," *Social Inclusion*, vol. 2, no. 4: 14–22.

Gutman, H., 1976. *The Black Family in Slavery and Freedom, 1750–1925*. Pantheon.

Haas, S. S., 1977. "The Contribution of Slaves to and their Influence upon Early Islam," PhD thesis, Princeton University.

Hale, E., 2012. "Ford, GM and BMW Linked to Illegal Logging and Slave Labour in Brazil," *Guardian*, May 17.

Hall, C., N. Draper, K. McClelland et al., 2014. *Legacies of British Slave-ownership: Colonial Slavery and the Formation of Victorian Britain*. Cambridge University Press.

Hall, D., 1962. "Slaves and Slavery in the British West Indies," *Social and Economic Studies*, vol. 11, no. 4: 305–318.

REFERENCES

Hall, D., 1989. *In Miserable Slavery: Thomas Thistlewood in Jamaica, 1750–86.* University of the West Indies Press.

Hallgrimsdottir, H., and C. Benoit, 2007. "From Wage Slaves to Wage Workers: Cultural Opportunity Structures and the Evolution of the Wage Demands of the Knights of Labor and the American Federation of Labor, 1880–1900," *Social Forces*, vol. 85, no. 3.

Hammer, C., 2002. *A Large-Scale Slave Society of the Early Middle Ages: Slaves and their Families in Early Medieval Bavaria.* Ashgate.

Hammond, N. G. L., 1973. *Studies in Greek History.* Oxford University Press.

Handler, J., and F. Lange, 1978. *Plantation Slavery in Barbados: An Archeological and Historical Investigation.* Harvard University Press.

Hannah-Jones, N., ed., 2019. *The 1619 Project: A New Origin Story.* One World.

Harper, K., 2011. *Slavery in the Late Roman World,* AD *275–425.* Cambridge University Press.

Harper, K., and W. Scheidel, 2018. "Roman Slavery and the Idea of 'Slave Society'," in N. Lenski and C. Cameron, eds., *What is a Slave Society?* Cambridge University Press, pp. 86–105.

Harrill, A., 1995. *The Manumission of Slaves in Early Christianity.* J. C. B. Mohr.

Harris, E., 2012. "Homer, Hesiod, and the 'Origins' of Greek Slavery," *REA*, vol. 114, no. 2: 345–366.

Harris, E., 2020. "Slavery in Homer and Hesiod," in C. O. Pache, ed., *The Cambridge Guide to Homer.* Cambridge University Press.

Harris, G., 1972. "Taita Bridewealth and Affinal Relationships," in M. Fortes, ed., *Marriage in Tribal Societies.* Cambridge University Press, pp. 55–87.

Harroff-Tavel, H., and A. Nasri, 2013. *Tricked and Trapped: Human Trafficking in the Middle East.* International Labour Organization.

Harsh, P. W., 1955. "The Intriguing Slave in Greek Comedy," *Transactions and Proceedings of the American Philological Association*, vol. 86: 135–142.

Hart, R., 1950. "Cudjoe and the First Maroon War in Jamaica," *Caribbean Historical Review*, vol. 1: 46–79.

Hartman, S., 2007. *Lose Your Mother: A Journey Along the Atlantic Slave Route.* Farrar, Straus and Giroux.

Haskell, T., 1975. "The True and Tragical History of 'Time on the Cross,'" *New York Review of Books*, October 2.

Haynes, D. F., 2009. "Exploitation Nation: The Thin and Gray Legal Lines between Trafficked Persons and Abused Migrant Laborers," *Notre Dame Journal of Law, Ethics, and Public Policy*, vol. 23, no. 1: 1–71.

Haynes, D. F., 2014. "The Celebritization of Human Trafficking," *Annals of the American Academy of Political and Social Science*, vol. 653, no. 1: 25–45.

Heckathorn, D., 1997. "Respondent–driven Sampling: A New Approach to the Study of Hidden Populations," *Social Problems*, vol. 44, no. 2: 174–199.

Hegel, G., 2016 [1807]. *Phenomenology of Mind*, trans J. B. Baillie. Swan Sonnenschein and Co.

Heichelheim, F., 1958. *An Ancient Economic History*, 3 vols. A. W. Sijthoff.

Heiss, A., and J. Kelley, 2017. "From the Trenches: A Global Survey of Anti-TIP NGOs and their Views of US Efforts," *Journal of Human Trafficking*, vol. 3, no. 3: 1500–1528.

REFERENCES

Heller, M., 2014. "Thai Workers Claim Vindication in Long Battle with Farm Labor Contractor," *MPN News*, March 31.

Henderson, G., 1968. *Korea: The Politics of the Vortex*. Harvard University Press.

Herf, J., 2007. "Comparative Perspectives on Anti-Semitism, Radical Anti-Semitism in the Holocaust and American White Racism," *Journal of Genocide Research*, vol. 9, no. 4: 575–600.

Herzig-Yoshinaga, A., 2009. "Words Can Lie or Clarify: Terminology of the World War II Incarceration of Japanese Americans," Manzanar Committee Blog, March 4.

Higman, B. W., 1984. *Slave Populations of the British Caribbean, 1807–1834*. University Press of the West Indies.

Higman, B. W., 2017. "Demographic Trends," in D. Eltis, S. Engerman, S. Drescher, and D. Richardson, eds., *The Cambridge World History of Slavery*, vol. 4. Cambridge University Press, pp. 20–48.

Hinton, A., 2022. *It Can Happen Here*. New York University Press.

Hoang, K. K., 2015. *Dealing in Desire: Asian Ascendancy, Western Decline, and the Hidden Currencies of Global Sex Work*. University of California Press.

Hoang, K. K., and R. S. Parreñas, eds., 2014. *Human Trafficking Reconsidered: Rethinking the Problem, Envisioning New Solutions*. International Debate Education Association.

Hoffman, J., 2017. "Hunting a Killer: Sex, Drugs and the Return of Syphilis," *New York Times*, August 24.

Hohfeld, W., 1913, "Some Fundamental Legal Conceptions as Applied in Judicial Reasoning," *Yale Law Journal*, vol. 23, no. 1: 16–59.

Holness, A., 2021. "Emancipation Day 2021. Message by Prime Minister, the Most Honorable Andrew Holness, August 1, 2021." Jamaica Information Service. https://jis.gov.jm/speeches/emancipation–day–2021–message–by–pri me–minister–the–most–hon–andrew–holness–on–pc–mp/.

Hondagneu-Sotelo, P., 2007. *Domestica: Immigrant Workers: Cleaning and Caring in the Shadows of Affluence*. University California Press.

Hong, S., 1979. *The Legal Status of the Private Slaves in the Koryo Dynasty*. (Privately translated for the author from the Korean.)

Honore, A. M., 1961. "Ownership," in A. G. Guest, ed., *Oxford Essays in Jurisprudence*. Oxford University Press.

Hope For Justice, 2023. "Updated Estimate of the Illicit Monetary Profits of Modern Slavery and Human Trafficking." https://hopeforjustice.org/wp-con tent/uploads/2023/08/Hope-for-Justice-estimated-global-profits-from-modern -slavery-July-2023-update.pdf.

Hopkins, K., 1993. "Novel Evidence for Roman Slavery," *Past and Present*, vol. 138: 3–27.

Hopkins, K., 2010 [1978]. *Conquerors and Slaves*. Cambridge University Press

Hopper, M., 2018. "Was Nineteenth-Century Eastern Arabia a 'Slave Society'?" in N. Lenski and C. Cameron, eds., *What is a Slave Society?* Cambridge University Press, pp. 313–336.

Horsley, R., 1998. "Paul and Slavery: A Critical Alternative to Recent Readings," *Semeia*, vol. 83/84: 153–200.

Horsley, R., 2004. *Paul and the Roman Imperial Order*. T. and T. Clark.

REFERENCES

Hossain, M., C. Zimmerman, M. Abas, M. Light, and C. Watts, 2010. "The Relationship of Trauma to Mental Disorders among Trafficked and Sexually Exploited Girls and Women," *American Journal of Public Health*, vol. 100, no. 12: 2442–2449.

Howard-Hassmann, R. E., 2017. "State Enslavement in North Korea," in A. Bunting and J. Quirk, eds., *Contemporary Slavery: Popular Rhetoric and Political Practice*. University of British Columbia Press, pp. 255–278.

Hudson, P. J., 2018. "The Racist Dawn of Capitalism: Unearthing the Economy of Bondage," *Boston Review*, March.

Hudson, Z., 2010. "With Friends Like These: Ongoing Legal Challenges to the Anti-prostitution Loyalty Oath Requirement in PEPFAR under the Obama Administration," in *Human Trafficking, HIV/AIDS and the Sex Sector: Human Rights for All*. CHANGE and Center for Human Rights and Humanitarian Law, American University, Washington College of Law.

Huijsmans, R., and S. Baker, 2012. "Child Trafficking: 'Worst Form' of Child Labour, or Worst Approach to Young Migrants?" *Development and Change*, vol. 43, no. 4: 919–946.

Human Rights Watch, 2013. *Uzbekistan: Forced Labor Widespread in Cotton Harvest*. News Release, January 25. https://www.hrw.org/news/2013/01/25/uzbekistan-forced-labor-widespread-cotton-harvest.

Human Rights Watch, 2014. *Sudan: Stop Deporting Eritreans. 30 Forced Back to Eritrea, Including 6 Registered Refugees*. News Release, May 8. https://www.hrw.org/news/2014/05/08/sudan-stop-deporting-eritreans.

Human Rights Watch, 2017. *Human Rights Watch Submission on the Democratic People's Republic of Korea to the Committee on the Rights of the Child*. News Release, February 13. https://www.hrw.org/news/2017/02/13/human-rights-watch-submission-democratic-peoples-republic-korea-committee-rights.

Human Rights Watch, 2019. *"They Are Making Us Into Slaves, Not Educating Us": How Indefinite Conscription Restricts Young People's Rights, Access to Education in Eritrea*, August 8. https://www.hrw.org/report/2019/08/09/they-are-making-us-slaves-not-educating-us/how-indefinite-conscription-restricts.

Hunt, P., 2017. "Slaves or Serfs? Patterson on the Thetes and Helots of Ancient Greece," in J. Bodel and W. Scheidel, eds., *On Human Bondage: After Slavery and Social Death*. Wiley-Blackwell, pp. 55–80.

Hunter, R., 1730–4. "Various statements to the Jamaica House of Assembly." *JHA*, vol. 3.

Hvistendahl, M., 2012. *Unnatural Selection: Choosing Boys Over Girls, and the Consequences of a World Full of Men*. Public Affairs.

Ibanez, M., and D. D. Suthers, 2014. "Detection of Domestic Human Trafficking Indicators and Movement Trends Using Content Available on Open Internet Sources," *2014 47th Hawaii International Conference on System Sciences (HICSS)*, Waikoloa, HI, pp. 1556–1565.

Ignatiev, N., 1995. *How the Irish Became White*. Routledge.

ILO, 2001. *Stopping Forced Labour: Global Report Under the Follow-Up to the ILO Declaration on Fundamental Principles and Rights at Work*. International Labour Office. https://www.ilo.org/global/publications/ilo-bookstore/order-online/books/WCMS_PUBL_9221119483_EN/lang--en/index.htm.

ILO, 2005. *A Global Alliance Against Forced Labour*. International Labour Conference, 93rd Session. https://www.ilo.org/public/english/standards/relm/ilc/ilc93/pdf/rep-i-b.pdf.

REFERENCES

ILO, 2011. *Children in Hazardous Work: What We Know, What We Need to Do*. International Labour Office. http://www.ilo.org/wcmsp5/groups/public/@dgreports/@dcomm/@publ/documents/publication/wcms_155428.pdf.

ILO, 2012. *Global Estimate of Forced Labour: Results and Methodology*. International Labour Office. https://www.ilo.org/global/topics/forced-labour/publications/WCMS_182004/lang--en/index.htm.

ILO, 2014. *Profits and Poverty: The Economics of Forced Labour*. International Labour Office. https://www.ilo.org/wcmsp5/groups/public/---ed_norm/---declaration/documents/publication/wcms_243391.pdf.

ILO, 2015. *Global Estimates on International Migrant Workers*. International Labour Office. https://www.ilo.org/publications/ilo-global-estimates-migrant-workers.

ILO, 2017a. *Global Estimates of Child Labor: Results and Trends, 2012–2016*. International Labour Office. https://www.ilo.org/global/publications/books/WCMS_575499/lang--en/index.htm.

ILO, 2017b. *Global Estimates of Modern Slavery: Forced Labor and Forced Marriage*. International Labour Office. https://www.ilo.org/global/publications/books/WCMS_575479/lang--en/index.htm.

ILO, 2023. *Myanmar Commission of Inquiry Finds Far-reaching Violations of Freedom of Association and Forced Labour Conventions*. International Labour Office. https://www.ilo.org/global/about-the-ilo/newsroom/news/WCMS_896572/lang--en/index.htm.

ILO, 2024. *Profits and Poverty: The Economics of Forced Labor*. International Labour Office. https://www.ilo.org/publications/profits-and-poverty-economics-forced-labour-1.

ILO, Walk Free, and IOM, 2022. *Global Estimates of Modern Slavery: Forced Labour and Forced Marriage*. ILO Publications. https://www.ilo.org/global/topics/forced-labour/publications/WCMS_854733/lang--en/index.htm.

IMF, 2007. *World Economic Outlook, October 2007: Globalization and Inequality*. International Monetary Fund. https://www.imf.org/en/Publications/WEO/Issues/2016/12/31/World-Economic-Outlook-October-2007-Globalization-and-Inequality-20354.

IMF, 2017. *World Economic Outlook, April 2017: Gaining Momentum?* International Monetary Fund. https://www.imf.org/en/Publications/WEO/Issues/2017/04/04/world-economic-outlook-april-2017.

Inikori, J. I., and S. Engerman, eds., 1992. *The Atlantic Slave Trade: Effects on Economies, Societies and Peoples in Africa, the Americas and Europe*. Duke University Press.

IOM, 2010. *World Migration Report 2010: The Future of Migration*. International Organization for Migration. https://publications.iom.int/system/files/pdf/wmr_2010_english.pdf.

IOM, 2012. *Gender and Migration*. International Organization for Migration. https://www.iom.int/gender-and-migration.

IOM, 2016. *Mediterranean Human Trafficking and Exploitation Prevalence Survey*. News Release, August 12. International Organization for Migration. https://www.iom.int/news/mediterranean-human-trafficking-and-exploitation-prevalence-survey-iom.

IOM, 2017. *Global Trafficking Trends in Focus, 2006–2016*. International Organization for Migration. https://www.iom.int/sites/g/files/tmzbdl486/files/our_work/DMM/MAD/A4-Trafficking-External-Brief.pdf.

REFERENCES

Irish, M., 2023. "Genocidal Massacres of Jews in Medieval Western Europe, 1096–1392," in B., Kiernan, T. M. Lemos, and T. S. Taylor, eds., *The Cambridge World History of Genocide*, vol. 1. Cambridge University Press, pp. 425–447.

Ismard, P., 2017. *Democracy's Slaves: A Political History of Ancient Greece*. Harvard University Press.

Jackson, M., and I. Smith, 2013. "Ownership or Tenure? A Case Study of Tribal Land Use from the Cusp of Prehistory," in M. Relaki and D. Catapoti, eds., *An Archeology of Land Ownership*. Routledge.

Jacobs, H., 1861. *Incidents in the Life of a Slave Girl. Written by Herself*. Thayer & Eldridge.

Jacobs, J. S., 2024 [1855]. *The United States Governed by Six Hundred Thousand Despots*, ed. J. Schroeder. University of Chicago Press.

Jacoby, H. G., 1995. "The Economics of Polygyny in Sub-Saharan Africa: Female Productivity and the Demand for Wives in the Cote d'Ivoire," *Journal of Political Economy*, vol. 103, no. 5: 938–971.

James, C. L. R., 1963 [1938]. *The Black Jacobins: Toussaint L'Ouverture and the San Domingo Revolution*. Vintage Books.

Jameson, M., 1977–8. "Agriculture and Slavery in Classical Athens," *The Classical Journal*, vol. 73, no. 2: 122–145.

Jelly, T., 1826. *Remarks on the Condition of the Whites and Free Coloured Inhabitants of Jamaica: With observations on the causes which either facilitate, or retard the progress of civilization amongst the slaves of the West-Indies*. Office of the Montego Bay Gazette.

Johnson, D., 2007. "Reflections on the Bundle of Rights," *Vermont Law Review*, vol. 32: 247–272.

Johnson, W., 2013. *River of Dark Dreams: Slavery and Empire in the Cotton Kingdom*. Harvard University Press.

Jok, J. M., 2001. *War and Slavery in Sudan*. University of Pennsylvania Press.

Jones, A., 2000. "Gendercide and Genocide," *Journal of Genocide Research*, vol. 2, no. 2: 185–211.

Jordan, W., 1968. *White Over Black: American Attitudes toward the Negro, 1550–1812*. University of North Carolina Press.

Jung, Y., 2019. "How the Legacy of Slavery Survives: Labour Market Institutions and Human Capital Investment." https://www.semanticscholar.org/paper/How-the-Legacy-of-Slavery-Survives%3A-Labor-Market-Jung/1dd1bbe00a61 71845b3a734c8a1a35f2f211b515.

Jusseret, S., J. Driessen, and Q. Letesson, 2013. "Minoan Lands? Some Remarks on Land Ownership on Bronze Age Crete," in M. Relaki and D. Catapoti, eds., *Archeology of Land Ownership*. Routledge.

Kaplan, D., 2000. "The Darker Side of the Original Affluent Society," *Journal of Anthropological Research*, vol. 56, no. 3: 301–324.

Kaplan, M., 1998. *Between Dignity and Despair: Jewish Life in Nazi Germany*. Oxford University Press.

Kara, S., 2014. *Bonded Labor: Tackling the System of Slavery in South Asia*. Columbia University Press.

Kara, S., 2017. *Sex Trafficking: Inside the Business of Modern Slavery*. Columbia University Press.

Kardiner, A., and L. Ovesey, 1951. *The Mark of Oppression: Explorations in the Personality of the American Negro*. Norton.

REFERENCES

Karras, R. M., 1988. *Slavery and Society in Medieval Scandinavia.* Yale University Press.

Karras, R. M., 1990. "Concubinage and Slavery in the Viking Age," *Scandinavian Studies,* vol. 62, no. 2: 141–162.

Karras, R. M., 1994. "Desire, Descendants and Dominance: Slavery, the Exchange of Women, and Masculine Power," in A. J. Frantzen and D. Moffat, eds., *The Work of Work: Servitude, Slavery and Labour in Medieval England.* Cruithne Press, pp. 16–29.

Karras, R. M., 2023. "Injection: A Gender Perspective on Domestic Slavery," in D. A. Pargas and J. Schiel, eds., *The Palgrave Handbook of Global Slavery throughout History.* Palgrave Macmillan, pp. 215–224.

Keeley, L., 1997. *War Before Civilization: The Myth of the Peaceful Savage.* Oxford University Press.

Kempadoo, K., J. Sanghera, and B. Pattanaik, eds., 2012. *Trafficking and Prostitution Reconsidered: New Perspectives on Migration, Sex Work and Human Rights.* Routledge.

Kennedy, M. A., C. Klein, J. T. K. Bristowe, B. S. Cooper, and J. C. Yuille, 2007. "Routes of Recruitment: Pimps' Techniques and Other Circumstances that Lead to Street Prostitution," *Journal of Aggression, Maltreatment and Trauma,* vol. 15, no. 2: 1–19.

Kesler, K., 2002. "Is a Feminist Stance in Support of Prostitution Possible? An Exploration of Current Trends," *Sexualities,* vol. 5, no. 2: 219–235.

Kiernan, B., 2023. "Genocide: Its Causes, Components, Connections and Continuing Challenges," in B. Kiernan, T. Lemos, and T. Taylor, eds., *The Cambridge World History of Genocide,* vol. 1. Cambridge University Press, pp. 1–30.

Kiernan, B., W. Lower, N. Naimark, and S. Straus, eds., 2023. *The Cambridge World History of Genocide.* Vol. 3: *Genocide in the Contemporary Era, 1914–2020.* Cambridge University Press.

Kim, S., 2023. "Slavery in Chosŏn Korea," in D. A. Pargas and J. Schiel, eds., *The Palgrave Handbook of Global Slavery throughout History.* Palgrave Macmillan

Kiple, K., 1985. *The Jamaican Slave: A Biological History.* Cambridge University Press.

Klein, A., 1981. "The Two Asantes," in P. Lovejoy, ed., *The Ideology of Slavery in Africa.* Sage.

Klein, D., and J. Robinson, eds., 2011. "Property: A Bundle of Rights? Prologue to the Property Symposium," *Economic Journal Watch,* vol. 8, no. 3: 193–204.

Klein, H., 1986. *African Slavery in Latin America and the Caribbean.* Oxford University Press.

Kligman, G., and S. Limoncelli, 2005. "Trafficking Women after Socialism: From, To, and Through Eastern Europe," *Social Politics,* vol. 12, no. 1: 118–140.

Knight, F., 1970. *Slave Society in Cuba during the Nineteenth Century.* University of Wisconsin Press.

Kochan, D., 2013. "The Property Platform in Anglo-American Law and the Primacy of the Property Concept," *Georgia State University Law Review,* vol. 29, no. 2: 475–482.

Koettl, J., 2009. *Human Trafficking, Modern Day Slavery and Economic Exploitation.* Discussion Paper 0911, World Bank, Washington, DC. https://documents1.worldbank.org/curated/en/208471468174880847/pdf/498020N WP0SP0d10Box341969B01PUBLIC1.pdf.

REFERENCES

Kolchin, P., 1983. "Reevaluating the Antebellum Slave Community: A Comparative Perspective," *The Journal of American History*, vol. 70, no. 3: 579–601.

Kolchin, P., 1993. *American Slavery, 1619–1877*. Hill and Wang.

Korotayev, A., 2003. "Form of Marriage, Sexual Division of Labor, and Postmarital Residence in Cross-Cultural Perspective: A Reconsideration," *Journal of Anthropological Research*, vol. 59, no. 1: 69–89.

Kramer, M., N. Black, S. Matthews, and S. James, 2017. "The Legacy of Slavery and Contemporary Declines in Heart Disease Mortality in the US South," *SSM – Population Health*: 609–617.

Kristof, N. D., and S. WuDunn, 2010. *Half the Sky: Turning Oppression into Opportunity for Women Worldwide*. Vintage.

Kropiwnicki, Z., 2011. "Female Adolescent Prostitutes' Strategies of Resistance in Cape Town, South Africa," in S. Dewey and P. Kelly, eds., *Policing Pleasure: Sex Work, Policy, and the State in Global Perspective*. New York University Press, pp. 100–114.

Krugman, P., 2003. "Serfs Up!" Entry of 5/8/2003 on the *Unofficial Paul Krugman Blog*, cited in J.-J. Rosa, "Freedom and Serfdom," https://papers. ssrn.com/sol3/papers.cfm?abstract_id=1428729.

Kuper, L., 1981. *Genocide: Its Political Use in the Twentieth Century*. Yale University Press.

Kurasawa, F., 2017. "Show and Tell: Contemporary Anti–slavery Advocacy as Symbolic Work," in A. Bunting and J. Quirk, eds., *Contemporary Slavery: Popular Rhetoric and Political Practice*. University of British Columbia Press, pp. 158–179.

Kye, S., 2021. "Slavery in Medieval Korea," in C. Perry, D. Eltis, S. Engerman, and D. Richardson, eds., *The Cambridge World History of Slavery*, vol. 2. Cambridge University Press, pp. 295–312.

Kyle, D., and R. Koslowski, eds., 2001. *Global Human Smuggling: Comparative Perspectives*. Johns Hopkins University Press.

La Rue, G., 2007. "African Slave Women in Egypt, *ca.* 1820 to the Plague of 1834–1835," in G. Campbell, S. Miers, and J. C. Miller, eds., *Women and Slavery: Africa, the Indian Ocean World, and the Medieval North Atlantic*. Ohio University Press.

Laing, R. D., 1965. *The Divided Self: An Existential Study in Sanity and Madness*. Penguin.

Lakoff, G., and M. Johnson, 1980. *Metaphors We Live By*. University of Chicago Press.

Lakoff, G., and M. Johnson, 1999. *Philosophy in the Flesh: The Embodied Mind and its Challenge to Western Thought*. Basic Books.

Lane, A., ed., 1971. *The Debate over Slavery: Stanley Elkins and His Critics*. University of Illinois Press.

Lane, P., and K. MacDonald, eds., 2011. *Slavery in Africa: Archeology and Memory*, Oxford University Press.

Lauffer, S., 1979. *Die Bergwerkssklaven von Laureion (Forschungen zur antiken Sklaverei)*, Franz Steiner Verlag GMBH.

Lawrence, B., 2017. "Asylum Courts and the 'Forced Marriage Paradox': Gender-based Harm and Contemporary Slavery in Forced Conjugal Associations," in A. Bunting and J. Quirk, eds., *Contemporary Slavery: Popular Rhetoric and Political Practice*. University of British Columbia Press, pp. 97–128.

REFERENCES

Le Page, R. B., and D. De Camp, 1960. *Jamaican Creole: An Historical Introduction to Jamaican Creole*. Macmillan and Co.

Lemkin, R., 2008 [1944]. *Axis Rule in Occupied Europe: Laws of Occupation, Analysis of Government, Proposals for Redress*. Lawbook Exchange.

Lemonius, M., 2017. "'Deviously Ingenious': British Colonialism in Jamaica," *Peace Research*, vol. 49, no. 2: 79–103.

Lencman, J., M. Bräuer-Pospelova, H. Bräuer, and J. Vogt, 1967. *Die Sklaverei im mykenischen und homerischen Griechenland*. Franz Steiner.

Lenski, N., and C. Cameron, eds., 2018. *What is a Slave Society?* Cambridge University Press.

Lepore, J., 2018. *These Truths: A History of the United States*. Norton.

Levison, D., and A. Langer, 2010. "Counting Child Domestic Servants in Latin America," *Population and Development Review*, vol. 36, no. 1: 125–149.

Levitt, S. D., and S. A. Venkatesh, 2007. "An Empirical Analysis of Street-level Prostitution." Paper presented at the Annual Meeting of the American Economic Association, New Orleans. https://www.semanticscholar.org/paper/An-Empirical-Analysis-of-Street-Level-Prostitution-Levitt-Venkatesh/13c53cf55f0151d663045a09ed11ee49bf9c9894?p2df.

Lewis, D., 2017. "Orlando Patterson, Property, and Ancient Slavery: The Definitional Problem Revisited," in J. Bodel and W. Scheidel, eds., *On Human Bondage: After Slavery and Social Death*. Wiley-Blackwell, pp. 31–54.

Liang, Z., and W. Ye, 2001. "From Fujian to New York: Understanding the New Chinese Immigration," in D. Kyle and R. Koslowski, eds., *Global Human Smuggling: Comparative Perspectives*. Johns Hopkins University Press, pp. 204–232.

Limoncelli, S., 2010. *The Politics of Trafficking: The First International Movement to Combat the Sexual Exploitation of Women*. Stanford University Press.

Limoncelli, S., 2016. "What in the World are Anti-Trafficking NGOs Doing? Findings from a Global Study," *Journal of Human Trafficking*, vol. 2, no. 4: 316–328.

Limoncelli, S., 2017. "The Global Development of Contemporary Anti-human Trafficking Advocacy," *International Sociology*, vol. 32, no. 6: 814–834.

Linder, D. O., 1995. "Celia, A Slave, Trial (1855): An Account." https://famous-trials.com/celia/180-home.

Long, E., 1774. *The History of Jamaica or, General Survey of the Antient and Modern State of That Island*. T. Lowndes.

Loria, A., 1893. *Les Bases économiques de la constitution sociale*. F. Alcan.

Lorimer, H., 1947. "The Hoplite Phalanx," *The Annual of the British School at Athens*, vol. 42, pp. 76–138.

Lott, E., 2013. *Love and Theft: Blackface Minstrelsy and the American Working Class*. Oxford University Press.

Lovejoy, P. E., 2000. *Transformations in Slavery: A History of Slavery in Africa*, Cambridge University Press.

Lovejoy, P., 2018. "Slavery in Societies on the Frontiers of Centralized States in West Africa," in N. Lenski and C. Cameron, eds., *What is a Slave Society?* Cambridge University Press, pp. 220–247.

Machel, G., 2001. *The Impact of War on Children*. Palgrave.

MacKinnon, C. A., 1993. "Prostitution and Civil Rights," *Michigan Journal of Gender and Law*, vol. 1: 13–31.

REFERENCES

MacKinnon, C. A., 2011. "Trafficking, Prostitution and Inequality," *Harvard Civil Rights–Civil Liberties Law Review*, vol. 46: 271–309.

Madison, J., 1962 [1792]. "Property," in William T. Hutchinson et al., eds., *The Papers of James Madison*, vol. 14. University of Chicago Press, pp. 266–268.

Madley, B., 2023a. "'Too Furious': The Genocide of Connecticut's Pequot Indians, 1636–1640," in N. Blackhawk, B. Kiernan, B. Madley, and R. Taylor, eds., *The Cambridge World History of Genocide*, vol. 2. Cambridge University Press, pp. 215–242.

Madley, B., 2023b. "'A War of Extermination': The California Indian Genocide, 1846–1873," in N. Blackhawk, B. Kiernan, B. Madley, and R. Taylor, eds., *The Cambridge World History of Genocide*, vol. 2. Cambridge University Press, pp. 412–443.

Magness, P. W., 2019. "The New History of Capitalism Has a 'Whiteness' Problem," *American Institute for Economic Research*, December 10.

Magubane, Z., 2016. "American Sociology's Racial Ontology: Remembering Slavery, Deconstructing Modernity, and Charting the Future of Global Historical Sociology," *Cultural Sociology*, vol. 10, no. 3. https://doi.org/10.1177/1749975516641301.

Magubane, Z., 2017. "Following 'the Deeds of Men': Race, 'the Global', and International Relations," in J. Go and G. Lawson, eds., *Global Historical Sociology*. Cambridge University Press.

Mahon, B., 1839. *Jamaica Plantership*. E. Wilson.

Malik, N., 2017. *Trafficking Terror: How Modern Slavery and Sexual Violence Fund Terrorism*. Henry Jackson Soc.

Malowist, I. B., 1968. "Les recherches sur l'esclavage ancien et le mouvement abolitioniste européen," in J. Burian and L. Vidman, eds., *Antiquitas Graeco-Romana ac Tempora Nostra*. Academia, pp. 161–167.

Mammen, K., and C. Paxson, 2000. "Women's Work and Economic Development," *Journal of Economic Perspectives*, vol. 14, no. 4: 141–164.

Mandic, D., 2017. "Trafficking and Syrian Refugee Smuggling: Evidence from the Balkan Route," *Social Inclusion*, vol. 5, no. 2: 28–38.

Mann, M., 2005. *The Dark Side of Democracy: Explaining Ethnic Cleansing*. Cambridge University Press

Manning, P., 1990. *Slavery and African Life: Occidental, Oriental and African Slave Trades*. Cambridge University Press.

Manning, P., 1992. "The Slave Trade: The Formal Demography of a Global System," in J. E. Inikori and S. Engerman, eds., *The Atlantic Slave Trade: Effects on Economies, Societies and Peoples in Africa, the Americas and Europe*. Duke University Press, pp. 117–141.

Marcel, G., 1963. *The Existential Background of Human Dignity*. Harvard University Press.

Marmon, S. E., ed., 1999. *Slavery in the Islamic Middle East*. Wiener Publishers.

Marschke, M., and P. Vandergeest, 2016. "Slavery Scandals: Unpacking Labour Challenges and Policy Responses within the Off-shore Fisheries Sector," *Marine Policy*, vol. 68: 39–46.

Martin, D., 1990. *Slavery as Salvation: The Metaphor of Slavery in Pauline Christianity*. Yale University Press.

Martin, J., 2004. *Divided Mastery: Slave Hiring in the American South*. Harvard University Press.

Marx, K., 1934. "A Letter on Russia," *New International*, vol. 1, no. 4: 110–111.

301

REFERENCES

Marx, R., 1967. *Pirate Port: The Story of the Sunken City of Port Royal.* World Publishing Co.

Maxwell, C. V. H., 2000. "'The Horrid Villainy': Sarah Bassett and the Poisoning Conspiracies in Bermuda, 1727–30," *Slavery & Abolition*, vol. 21, no. 3: 48–74.

McAuliffe, M. L., and F. Laczko, eds., 2016. *Migrant Smuggling Data and Research: A Global Review of the Emerging Evidence Base.* International Organization for Migration.

McBride, P., 2023. "Lessons from Canada. The Question of Genocide in US Boarding Schools for Native Americans," *Cambridge World History of Genocide*, vol. 2. Cambridge University Press, pp. 434–460.

McCain Institute, 2021. *A Six-Year Analysis of Sex Traffickers of Children.* ASU School of Social Work, University of Arizona.

McCarthy, K., 2004. "The Joker in the Pack: Slaves in Terence," *Ramus*, vol. 33: 100–119.

McClendon, D., and A. Sandstrom, 2016. "Child Marriage Is Rare in the U.S., Though This Varies by State." Pew Research Center, November 1. https://www.pewresearch.org/short-reads/2016/11/01/child-marriage-is-rare-in-the-u-s-though-this-varies-by-state/.

McCormick, M., 2001. *Origins of the European Economy: Communications and Commerce AD 300–900.* Cambridge University Press.

McCormick, M., 2002. "New Light on the 'Dark Ages': How the Slave Trade Fuelled the Carolingian Economy," *Past and Present*, vol. 177: 17–54.

McKee, S., 2004. "Inherited Status and Slavery in Late Medieval Italy and Venetian Crete," *Past and Present*, vol. 182: 31–53.

McKee, S., 2016. "Slavery," in R. M. Karras and J. Bennett, eds., *Oxford Handbook of Women and Gender in Medieval Europe.* Oxford University Press.

Meier, C., 2011. *A Culture of Freedom: Ancient Greece and the Origins of Europe.* Oxford University Press.

Meillassoux, C., 1975. *L'Esclavage en Afrique précoloniale.* François Maspero.

Meillassoux, C., 1991. *The Anthropology of Slavery: The Womb of Iron and Gold*, trans. A. Dasnois. Athlone.

Meixler, E., 2017. "India's Supreme Court Rules Sex with Child Brides Is Rape," *Time*, October 12.

Mellafe, R., 1975. *Negro Slavery in Latin America.* University of California Press.

Mendelsohn, I., 1949. *Slavery in the Ancient Near East.* Oxford University Press.

Menell, P., 2011. "Governance of Intellectual Resources and Disintegration of Intellectual Property in the Digital Age," UC Berkeley Public Law Research Paper No. 1615193. https://papers.ssrn.com/sol3/papers.cfm?abstract_id=1615193.

Merrill, T. W., 2011. "The Property Prism," *Economic Journal Watch*, vol. 8: 247–254.

Merrill, T. W., and H. E., Smith. 2007. *Property: Principles and Policies.* Foundation Press.

Métraux, A., 1948. "The Tupinamba," in J. H. Seward, ed., *Handbook of South American Indians*, vol. 3. US Government Printing Office, pp. 95–133.

Migrant-Rights.Org., 2018. *Reform the Kafala System.* https://www.migrant-rights.org/campaign/end-the-kafala-system/.

REFERENCES

Miller, J. C., 1977. "Imbangala Lineage Slavery," in S. Miers and I. Kopytoff, eds., *Slavery in Africa*. University of Wisconsin Press.

Miller, J., 2002. "Violence and Coercion in Sri Lanka's Commercial Sex Industry: Intersections of Gender, Sexuality, Culture and the Law," *Violence Against Women*, vol. 8, no. 9: 1044–1073.

Miller, J., 2008. *Getting Played: African American Girls, Urban Inequality, and Gendered Violence*. New York University Press.

Miller, K. L., 2014. "The Semantic Field of Slavery in Old English: Wealh, Esne, Præl," PhD thesis, School of English, University of Leeds.

Molesworth, H., 1685–8. Molesworth to Whitehall, CO 138/5, ff. 87.

Mommsen, T., 1878–1905. *The History of Rome*. Scribner.

Mondolfo, R., and D. S. Duncan, 1954. "The Greek Attitude to Manual Labor," *Past & Present*, vol. 6: 1–5.

Monk, E., 2021. "The Unceasing Significance of Colorism: Skin Tone Stratification in the United States," *Daedalus*, vol. 150, no. 2: 76–90.

Moore, B., 1993 [1966]. *The Social Origins of Dictatorship and Democracy*. Beacon Press.

Morgan, E., 2003 [1975]. *American Slavery, American Freedom*. Norton.

Morgan, K., 2000. *Slavery, Atlantic Trade and the British Economy, 1660–1800*. Cambridge University Press.

Morris, A., 2015. *The Scholar Denied: W. E. B. DuBois and the Birth of Modern Sociology*. University of California Press.

Morris, I., 2011. "Archaeology and Greek Slavery," in K. Bradley and C. Cartledge, eds., *The Cambridge World History of Slavery*, vol. 1. Cambridge University Press, pp. 176–193.

Morris, M., 2016. *Pushout: The Criminalization of Black Girls in School*. The New Press.

Moses, A., 2010. "Raphael Lemkin, Culture, and the Concept of Genocide," in D. Bloxham and A. Moses, eds., *The Oxford Handbook of Genocide Studies*. Oxford University Press, pp. 19–41.

Mossé, C., 1970. *La Colonisation dans l'antiquité*. Fernand Nathan.

Mouritsen, H., 2011. *The Freedman in the Roman World*. Cambridge University Press

Muller, C., 2018. "Freedom and Convict Leasing in the Postbellum South," *American Journal of Sociology*, vol. 124: 367–405.

Muller, C., 2021. "Exclusion and Exploitation: The Incarceration of Black Americans from Slavery to the Present," *Science*, vol. 374: 282–286.

Muller, C., and D. Schrage, 2021. "The Political Economy of Incarceration in the Cotton South, 1910–1925," *American Journal of Sociology*, vol. 127: 828–866.

Murdock, G., and D. White, 1969. "The Standard Cross-Cultural Sample," *Ethnology*, vol. 8: 329–369.

Mustakeem, S., 2016. *Slavery at Sea: Terror, Sex, and Sickness in the Middle Passage*. University of Illinois Press.

Myrdal, G., 1944. *An American Dilemma: The Negro Problem and Modern Democracy*. Harper and Brothers.

Naimark, N., 2023. "Geocide in Stalinist Russia and Ukraine, 1930–1938," in B. Kiernan, W. Lower, N. Naimark, and S. Straus, eds., *The Cambridge World History of Genocide*, vol. 3. Cambridge University Press, pp. 162–185.

REFERENCES

Naroll, R., 1970. "What Have We Learned from Cross-Cultural Surveys?" *American Anthropologist*, vol. 72: 1227–1288.

Neubauer, F., and N. C. Kim, 2022. "Tupinamba Practices of Violence, Warfare, and Cannibalism in Sixteenth-Century Brazil through Ethnohistory and Archeology," *Revista Habitus – Revista do Instituto Goiano de Pré-História e Antropologia*, vol. 19, no. 2: 189–213.

Nieboer, H. J., 1900. *Slavery as an Industrial System*. Cambridge University Press.

Novic, E., 2016. *The Concept of Cultural Genocide: An International Law Perspective*. Oxford University Press.

Nunn, N., 2008. "Slavery, Inequality, and Economic Development in the Americas," in E. Helpman, ed., *Institutions and Economic Performance*. Harvard University Press.

Nunn, N., 2011. "The Slave Trade and the Origins of Mistrust in Africa," *American Economic Review*, vol. 101: 3221–3252.

Nurse, K., and M. Crichlow, 2011. Review of, "Essays on the Theory of Plantation Economy," *Social and Economic Studies*, vol. 60, nos. 3 & 4: 203–214.

Nussbaum, G., 1960. "Labour and Status in the Works and Days," *The Classical Quarterly*, vol. 10, no. 2: 213–220.

O'Connell, H. A., 2012. "The Impact of Slavery on Racial Inequality in Poverty in the Contemporary U.S. South," *Social Forces*, vol. 90, no. 3: 713–734.

O'Sullivan, M., 2018. "The Intelligent Woman's Guide to Capitalism," *Enterprise and Society*, vol. 19, no. 4: 751–802.

Ober, J., 2015. *The Rise and Fall of Classical Greece*. Princeton University Press

OHCHR, 2022. "Assessment of Human Rights Concerns in the Xinjiang Uyghur Autonomous Region, People's Republic of China." https://www.ohchr.org/en/documents/country-reports/ohchr-assessment-human-rights-concerns-xinjiang-uyghur-autonomous-region.

Oishi, N., 2005. *Women in Motion: Globalization, State Policies, and Labor Migration in Asia*. Stanford University Press

Oliver, L., 2002. *The Beginnings of English Law*. University of Toronto Press.

Olmstead, A. L., and P. W. Rhode, 2018. "Cotton, Slavery, and the New History of Capitalism," *Explorations in Economic History*, vol. 67, no. 1: 1–17.

O'Malley, M., 2012. *Face Value: The Entwined Histories of Money and Race in America*. University of Chicago Press.

Osborne, R., 2010. *Athens and Athenian Democracy*. Cambridge University Press.

Owens, C., M. Dank, A. Farrell, J. Breaux, I. Banuelos et al., 2014. *Understanding the Organization, Operation, and Victimization Process of Labor Trafficking in the United States*. Urban Institute.

Palais, J., 1984. "Slavery and Slave Society in the Koryŏ Period," Review article on *Koryŏ Kwijok sahoe wa nobi (The Aristocratic Society of Koryŏ and Slavery)* by Hong Sŭnggi, *The Journal of Korean Studies*, vol. 5: 173–190.

Palmer, C., 1976. *Slaves of the White God: Blacks in Mexico, 1570–1650*. Harvard University Press.

Panikkar, K. M., 1963. *The Serpent and the Crescent: A History of the Negro Empires of West Africa*. Asia Publishing House.

Papanikos, G., 2022. "Hesiod's Place in the Economics Literature," *Athens Journal of Business and Economics*, vol. 8: 1–31.

REFERENCES

Park, M., 2023 [1807]. *Travels in the Interior Districts of Africa in the Years 1795, 1796, and 1797*. Legare Street Press.

Parreñas, R. S., 2011. *Illicit Flirtations: Labor, Migration, and Sex Trafficking in Tokyo*. Stanford University Press.

Parreñas, R. S., 2015. *Servants of Globalization: Migration and Domestic Work*. Stanford University Press.

Pateman, C., 2002. "Self-Ownership and Property in the Person," *Journal of Political Philosophy*, vol. 10, no. 2: 20–53.

Paton, D., 2012. "Witchcraft, Poison, Law, and Atlantic Slavery," *William and Mary Quarterly*, vol. 69, no. 2: 235–264.

Patterson, O., 1966a. "Frantz Fanon," *New World Quarterly*, vol. 2, no. 3: 93–95.

Patterson, O., 1966b. "Slavery, Acculturation and Social Change," *The British Journal of Sociology*, vol. 17, no. 2: 151–164.

Patterson, O., 1967. *The Sociology of Slavery*. Associated University Press.

Patterson, O., 1972. *Die the Long Day*. William Morrow.

Patterson, O., 1977. "Slavery," *Annual Review of Sociology*, vol. 3: 407–449.

Patterson, O., 1987. "The Unholy Trinity: Freedom, Slavery and the American Constitution," *Social Research: An International Quarterly*, vol. 54, no. 3: 543–577.

Patterson, O., 1991. *Freedom in the Making of Western Culture*. Basic Books

Patterson, O., 1998a. "Feast of Blood: Race Religion and Human Sacrifice in the Postbellum South," in O. Patterson, *Rituals of Blood: Consequences of Slavery in Two American Centuries*. Civitas, pp. 171–232.

Patterson, O., 1998b. "Paul, Slavery and Freedom: Personal and Socio-Historical Reflections," *Semeia*, vol. 83/84: 263–280.

Patterson, O., 1998c. *Rituals of Blood: Consequences of Slavery in Two American Centuries*. Civitas.

Patterson, O., 1999. *Chronology of World Slavery*. ABC-CLIO Press.

Patterson, O., 2003. "Reflections on Helotic Slavery and Freedom," in N. Luraghi and S. E. Alcock, eds., *Helots and Their Masters in Laconia and Messenia: Histories, Ideologies, Structures*. Cambridge Center for Hellenic Studies, pp. 289–309.

Patterson, O., 2004. "Culture and Continuity: Causal Structures in Sociocultural Persistence," in J. Mohr and R. Friedland, eds., *Matters of Culture: Cultural Sociology in Practice*. Cambridge University Press, p. 71–109.

Patterson, O., 2012. "Trafficking Gender and Slavery: Past and Present," in J. Allain, ed., *The Legal Understanding of Slavery: From the Historical to the Contemporary*. Oxford University Press, pp. 322–359.

Patterson, O., 2014. "Making Sense of Culture,' *Annual Review of Sociology*, vol. 40: 1–30.

Patterson, O., 2016. "Sklaverei in globalhistorischer Perspektive. Von der Antike bis in die Gegenwart," in W. Schmitz, ed., *Die Sklaverei setzen wir mit dem Tod Gleich: Slaven in globalhistorischer Perspektive*. Franz Steiner Verlag.

Patterson, O., 2018. "Freedom, Slavery, and Identity in Renaissance Florence: The Faces of Leon Battista Alberti," in D. Schmidtz and C. Pavel, eds., *The Oxford Handbook of Freedom*. Oxford University Press.

Patterson, O., 2018 [1982]. *Slavery and Social Death: A Comparative Study*, 2nd ed. Harvard University Press.

REFERENCES

Patterson, O., 2019. *The Confounding Island: Jamaica and the Postcolonial Predicament*. Harvard University Press.

Patterson, O., 2022 [1967]. *The Sociology of Slavery: Black Society in Jamaica, 1655–1838*. Polity.

Patterson, O., and X. Zhuo, 2018. "Modern Trafficking, Slavery, and Other Forms of Servitude," *Annual Review of Sociology*, vol. 44: 407–439.

Patterson, W., ed., 1970. *We Charge Genocide: The Crime of Government against the Negro People*. International Publishers.

Pečirka, J., 1973. "Homestead Farms in Classical and Hellenistic Hellas," in M. I. Finley, ed., *Problèmes de la terre en Grèce ancienne*. Mouton, pp. 113–147.

Peirce, C., 1931–58. *Collected Writings*, 8 vols., ed. C. Hartshorne, P. Weiss, and A. Burks. Harvard University Press.

Pelteret, D., 1995. *Slavery in Early Medieval England: From the Reign of Alfred until the Twelfth Century*. Boydell Press.

Peng, I., 2017. *Transnational Migration of Domestic and Care Workers in Asia Pacific*. International Labour Organization. https://www.ilo.org/global/topics /labour-migration/publications/WCMS_547228/lang--en/index.htm.

Penner, J. E., 2011. "Potentiality, Actuality, and 'Stick' Theory," *Economic Journal Watch*, vol. 8, no. 3: 274–278.

Peters, A., 2014. "Challenging the Sex/Labor Trafficking Dichotomy with Victim Experience," in K. K. Hoang and R. S. Parreñas, eds., *Human Trafficking Reconsidered: Rethinking the Problem, Envisioning New Solutions*. International Debate Education Association, pp. 30–40.

Peters, A., 2018. *Responding to Human Trafficking: Sex, Gender, and Culture in the Law*. University of Pennsylvania Press.

Pettinger, L., 2014. "The Judgement Machine: Markets, Internet Technologies and Policies in Commercial Sex," *Social Policy and Society*, vol. 14, no. 1: 1–9.

Phillips, U. B., 1918. *American Negro Slavery: A Survey of the Supply, Employment and Control of Negro Labor as Determined by the Plantation Regime*. Appleton.

Pierson, W. D., 1976. "Puttin' down Ole Massa: African Satire in the New World," *Research in African Literatures*, vol. 7, no. 2: 166–180.

Piketty, T., 2014. *Capital in the Twenty-First Century*. Harvard University Press.

Pinker, S., 2011. *The Better Angels of Our Nature: Why Violence Has Declined*. Viking.

Pipes, D., 1981. *Slave Soldiers and Islam*. Yale University Press.

Pitman, F. W., 1917. *The Development of the British West Indies*. Yale University Press.

Pohl, D., 1923. "The Nazi Camps and Killing Centers," in B. Kiernan, W. Lower, N. Naimark, and S. Straus, eds., *The Cambridge World History of Genocide*, vol. 3. Cambridge University Press, pp. 281–307.

Pohlenz, M., 1966. *Freedom in Greek Life and Thought: The History of an Ideal*. D. Reidel Publishing Company.

Polanyi, K., 1944. "The Self-Regulating Market and the Fictitious Commodities: Labor, Land, and Money," in *The Great Transformation*, Rinehart & Co., pp. 68–76.

Polaris, 2023. *Global Modern Slavery Directory*. Polaris, Washington, DC.

Pope Francis, 2022. "Pope Francis: It Was a Genocide against Indigenous Peoples," *Vatican News*, July 30.

REFERENCES

Price, R., 1996. *Maroon Societies: Rebel Slave Communities in the Americas.* Johns Hopkins University Press.

Pulleyblank, E. G., 1958. "The Origins and Nature of Chattel Slavery in China," *Journal of the Economic and Social History of the Orient*: 285–220.

Quarrell, W., 1730. "The Deposition of W. Quarrell." CO 137/18, f. 100.

Raaflaub, K., 2004. *The Discovery of Freedom in Ancient Greece.* University of Chicago Press.

Raffield, B., 2018. "Raiding, Slaving, and the Economies of Unfreedom in the Viking Diaspora," *SAA Archaeological Record*, vol. 18, no.3: 32–35.

Ragatz, L., 1928. *The Fall of the Planter Class in the British Caribbean.* Century.

Ragatz, L., 1931. "Absentee Landlordism in the British Caribbean," *Agricultural History*, vol. 5, no. 1: 7–24.

Rainwater, L., and W. Yancey, 1967. *The Moynihan Report and the Politics of Controversy.* MIT Press.

Raza, D., 2014. "The Marriage Bazaar: How Female Foeticide Has Made Bride Trade a Roaring Business," *Hindustan Times*, December 28.

Reece, R., 2017. "Legacies of Slavery: An Analysis of the Dimensions of Slavery's Post-Emancipation Effects," PhD thesis, Department of Sociology, Duke University. https://dukespace.lib.duke.edu/dspace/bitstream/handle/10161/14399/Reece_duke_0066D_13847.pdf?sequence=1andisAllowed=y.

Reece, R. L., 2018. "Genesis of U.S. Colorism and Skin Tone Stratification: Slavery, Freedom, and Mulatto-Black Occupational Inequality in the Late 19th Century," *The Review of Black Political Economy*, vol. 45, no. 1: 3–21.

Reece, R. L., and H. A. O'Connell, 2016. "How the Legacy of Slavery and Racial Composition Shape Public School Enrollment in the American South," *Sociology of Race and Ethnicity*, vol. 2, no. 1: 42–57.

Reis, J., and F. dos Santos, 2010. "Quilombo: Brazilian Maroons During Slavery." https://www.culturalsurvival.org/publications/cultural-survival-quarterly/quilombo-brazilian-maroons-during-slavery.

Richardson, D., 2001. "Shipboard Revolts, African Authority, and the Atlantic Slave Trade," *William and Mary Quarterly*, vol. 58, no. 1: 69–92.

Rio, A., 2012. "Self-sale and Voluntary Entry into Unfreedom, 300–1100," *Journal of Social History*, vol. 45, no. 3: 661–685.

Rio, A., 2017. *Slavery After Rome, 500–1100.* Oxford University Press.

Risse, T., and K. Sikkink, 1999. "The Socialization of International Human Rights Norms into Domestic Practices: Introduction," in T. Risse, S. C. Ropp, and K. Sikkink, eds., *The Power of Human Rights: International Norms and Domestic Change.* Cambridge University Press, pp. 1–38.

Roberts, G., 1957. *The Population of Jamaica.* Cambridge University Press.

Robinson, C., 1969. *The Fighting Maroons of Jamaica.* Collins and Sangster (Jamaica).

Robinson, C., 1983. *Black Marxism: The Making of the Black Radical Tradition.* University of North Carolina Press.

Rockman, S., 2009. *Scraping By: Wage Labor, Slavery and Survival in Early Baltimore.* Johns Hopkins University Press.

Rockman, S., 2012. "Slavery and Capitalism," *Journal of the Civil War Era*, vol. 2, no. 1: 5.

Rockman, S., 2014. 'What Makes the History of Capitalism Newsworthy?', *Journal of the Early Republic*, vol. 34, no. 3: 439–468.

REFERENCES

Rodriguez, J. P., ed., 1997. *The Historical Encyclopedia of World Slavery.* ABC–CLIO.

Roediger, D., 1991. *The Wages of Whiteness: Race and the Making of the American Working Class.* Verso.

Roediger, D., 2018. *Working Toward Whiteness: How America's Immigrants Became White: The Strange Journey from Ellis Island to the Suburbs.* Basic Books.

Roediger, D., and E. D. Esch, 2012. *The Production of Difference: Race and the Management of Labor in U.S. History.* Oxford University Press.

Rome Statute, 1998. *Rome Statute of the International Criminal Court, In force 2002.* UN Treaty Series, vol. 2187, no. 38544.

Rosa, J.-J., 2011. "The Causes of Serfdom: Domar's Puzzle Revisited." https://papers.ssrn.com/sol3/papers.cfm?abstract_id=1428729.

Rosen, D., 2005. *Armies of the Young: Child Soldiers in War and Terrorism.* Rutgers University Press.

Rosen, D., 2012. *Child Soldiers: A Reference Handbook.* ABC–CLIO.

Rosenbaum, A., ed., 1996. *Is the Holocaust Unique? Perspectives on Comparative Genocide.* Westview Press.

Rothman, J. D., 2012. *Flush Times and Fever Dreams: A Story of Capitalism and Slavery in the Age of Jackson.* University of Georgia Press.

Ruef, M., 2014. *Between Slavery and Capitalism: The Legacy of Emancipation in the American South.* Princeton University Press.

Ruef, M., and B. Fletcher, 2003. "Legacies of American Slavery: Status Attainment among Southern Blacks after Emancipation," *Social Forces*, vol. 82, no. 2: 445–480.

Ruggles, S., 1994. "The Origins of the African-American Family Structure," *American Sociological Review*, vol. 59, no.1: 136–151.

Ruwanpura, K. N., and P. Rai, 2004. "Forced Labour: Definitions, Indicators and Measurement." Working Paper, International Labour Organization. https://www.ilo.org/wcmsp5/groups/public/---ed_norm/---declaration/documents/publication/wcms_081991.pdf.

Sacerdote, B., 2005. "Slavery and the Intergenerational Transmission of Human Capital," *Review of Economics and Statistics*, vol. 87, no. 2: 217–234.

Sahlins, M., 1968. "Notes on the Original Affluent Society," in R. B. Lee and I. DeVore, eds., *Man the Hunter.* Aldine Publishing Company, pp. 85–89.

Sahlins, M., 1974. *Stone Age Economics.* Tavistock Publishing.

Salem, E., 1978. "Slavery in Medieval Korea." Ph.D. dissertation, Columbia University.

Sana, alias Ned, 1733. "The Further Examination of Sana, alias Ned," CO 137/21, f. 42.

Sanghera, J., 2016. "Unpacking the Trafficking Discourse," in K. Kempadoo, J. Sanghera, and B. Pattanaik, eds., *Trafficking and Prostitution Reconsidered: New Perspectives on Migration, Sex Work and Human Rights.* Routledge, pp. 3–24.

Santos-Granero, F., 2017. "Rituals of Enslavement and Markers of Servitude: Orlando Patterson in the American Tropics," in J. Bodel and W. Scheidel, eds., *On Human Bondage: After Slavery and Social Death.* Wiley-Blackwell, pp. 226–248.

Sargent, R. L., 1927. "The Use of Slaves by the Athenians in Warfare," *Classical Philology*, vol. 22, no. 3: 264–279.

REFERENCES

Sartre, J.-P., 1968. "Genocide," *New Left Review*, vol. 1, no. 48.

Sassen, S., 1988. *The Mobility of Labor and Capital*. Cambridge University Press.

Savage, J., 2007. "'Black Magic' and White Terror: Slave Poisoning and Colonial Society in Early 19th-Century Martinique," *Journal of Social History*, vol. 40, no. 3: 635–662.

Saxton, A., 1990. *The Rise and Fall of the White Republic: Class, Politics and Mass Culture in 19th-Century America*. Verso.

Schaps, D., 2004. *The Invention of Coinage and the Monetization of Ancient Greece*. University of Michigan Press.

Scheidel, W., 2001. "Progress and Problems in Roman Demography," in W. Scheidel, ed., *Debating Roman Demography*. K. Brill, pp. 1–81.

Scheidel, W., ed., 2012. *The Cambridge Companion to the Roman Economy*. Cambridge University Press.

Scheidel, W., ed., 2015. *State Power in Ancient China and Rome*. Oxford University Press.

Schermerhorn, C., 2015. *The Business of Slavery and the Rise of American Capitalism, 1815–1860*. Yale University Press.

Schutz, A., and T. Luckmann, 1980. *The Structures of the Life World: Studies in Phenomenology and Existential Philosophy*, trans. Richard M. Zaner and J. Tristam. Northwestern University Press.

Scott, D., and O. Patterson, 2023. *The Paradox of Freedom: A Biographical Dialogue*. Polity.

Scott, J. C., 1985. *Weapons of the Weak: Everyday Forms of Peasant Resistance*. Yale University Press.

Scullion, L., H. Lewis, P. Dwyer, and L. Waite, 2014. "Explaining the Link between Forced Labor and Immigration Status in the United Kingdom," in K. K. Hoang and R. S. Parreñas, eds., *Human Trafficking Reconsidered: Rethinking the Problem, Envisioning New Solutions*. International Debate Education Association, pp. 149–157.

Seeberg, M., and E. Goździak, 2016. "Contested Childhoods: Growing Up in Migrancy," in M. Seeberg and E. Goździak, eds., *Contested Childhoods: Growing up in Migrancy: Migration, Governance, Identities*. Springer, pp. 1–19.

Sersen, W., 1985. "Stereotypes and Attitudes Towards Slaves in Arabic Proverbs: A Preliminary View," in J. R. Willis, ed., *Slaves and Slavery in Muslim Africa*. Vol. 1: *Islam and the Ideology of Enslavement*. Frank Cass and Co.

Shah, S., 2017. "Sex and Work: Understanding Sexual Commerce in an Era of 'Globalisation'," in R. Piotrowicz, C. Rijken, and B. Uhl, eds., *Routledge Handbook of Human Trafficking*. Routledge, pp. 319–327.

Sharapov, K., 2017. "Trafficking in Human Beings and the Informal Economy," in R. Piotrowicz, C. Rijken, and B. Uhl, eds., *Routledge Handbook of Human Trafficking*. Routledge, pp. 526–534.

Shaw, M., 2015. *What Is Genocide?* Polity.

Shelley, L., 2010. *Human Trafficking: A Global Perspective*. Cambridge University Press.

Sheridan, R. B., 1965. "The Wealth of Jamaica in the Eighteenth Century," *Economic History Review*, vol. 18, no. 2: 292–311.

Siegel, B. J., 1945 "Some Methodological Considerations for a Comparative Study of Slavery," *American Anthropologist*, vol. 47, no. 3: 357–392.

REFERENCES

Singer, A., and D. S. Massey, 1998. "The Social Process of Undocumented Border Crossing among Mexican Migrants," *International Migration Review*, vol. 32, no. 3: 561–592.

Singer, P. W., 2006. *Children at War*. University of California Press.

Skocpol, T., ed., 1984. *Vision and Method in Historical Sociology*. Cambridge University Press.

Skrivankova, K. 2017. "Defining Exploitation in the Context of Trafficking: What Is a Crime and What Is Not," in R. Piotrowicz, C. Rijken, and B. Uhl, eds., 2017. *Routledge Handbook of Human Trafficking*. Routledge, pp. 109–119.

Sloan, B. 2010. "The Prison Industries Enhancement Certification Program: Why Everyone Should Be Concerned," *Prison Legal News*, vol. 21, no. 3: 1–9.

Smedley, A., and B. Smedley, 2011. *Race in North America: Origin and Evolution of a Worldview*. Routledge.

Smith, H., 2011. "Property Is Not Just a Bundle of Rights," *Economic Journal Watch*, vol. 8, no. 3: 279–291.

Smith, J. D., 1980. "A Different View of Slavery: Black Historians Attack the Proslavery Argument, 1890–1920," *Journal of Negro History*, vol. 65, no. 4.

Smith, M. G., 1954. "Slavery and Emancipation in Two Societies," *Social and Economic Studies*, vol. 3, no. 3: 239–290.

Smith, R. W., 1945. "The Legal Status of the Jamaican Slaves Before the Anti-Slavery Movement," *Journal of Negro History*, vol. 30, no. 3: 293–303.

Smith, S., 2010. "Race and Trust," *Annual Review of Sociology*, vol. 36: 453–475.

Smucker, G. R., Y.-F. Pierre, and J.-F. Tardieu, 2009. *Lost Childhoods in Haiti: Quantifying Child Trafficking, Restaveks and Victims of Violence*. Pan American Development Foundation.

Snodgrass, A., 1971. *The Dark Age of Greece*. University of Edinburgh Press.

Snow, J., 2016. "Claudia Card's Concept of Social Death: A New Way of Looking at Genocide," *Metaphilosophy*, vol. 47, nos. 4–5: 607–626.

Snyder, C., 2018. "Native American Slavery in Global Context," in N. Lenski and C. Cameron, eds., *What Is a Slave Society?* Cambridge University Press, pp. 169–190.

Snyder, T., 2015. *The Power to Die: Slavery and Suicide in British North America*. University of Chicago Press.

Soares, R., J. Assuncao, and T. F. Goulart, 2010. "A Note on Slavery and the Roots of Inequality," *Journal of Comparative Economics*, vol. 40: 565–580.

Solow, B., ed., 1991. *Slavery and the Rise of the Atlantic System*. Harvard University Press.

Sommar, M., 2020. *The Slaves of the Churches: A History*. Oxford University Press.

Sommerfelt, T., ed., 2015. *Child Fosterage and Child Domestic Work in Haiti in 2014: Analytical Report*. Fafo.

Son, L., L. Cai, and Q. Ninh, 2011. *Human Trafficking Sentinel Surveillance: Vietnam–China Border 2010*. UN Inter-Agency Project on Human Trafficking.

Spurdle, F., 1962. *Early West Indian Government: Showing the Progress of Government in Barbados, Jamaica, and the Leeward Islands, 1600–1783*. Whitcombe and Tombs.

Srivastava, R., 2005. *Bonded Labor in India: Its Incidence and Pattern*. International Labour Organization.

Stampp, K., 1989 [1956].*The Peculiar Institution*. Vintage.

REFERENCES

Standard Cross-Cultural Sample, 2004. *Codebook: Variables 1–2000*. https://www.academia.edu/590083/Standard_Cross_Cultural_Sample_Codebook_variables_1_to_2000.

Stannard, D., 1993. *American Holocaust: The Conquest of the New World*. Oxford University Press.

Starr, C., 1961. *The Origins of Greek Civilization*. Knopf.

Stein, S., 1986. *Vassouras: A Brazilian Coffee County, 1850–1900: The Roles of Planter and Slave in a Plantation Society*. Princeton University Press.

Steinfatt, T., 2011. "Sex Trafficking in Cambodia: Fabricated Numbers versus Empirical Evidence," *Crime Law and Social Change*, vol. 56: 443–462.

Steinfatt, T., 2015. "Calculations versus Counting of Human Trafficking Numbers," *Forum on Crime and Society*, vol. 8: 63–84.

Steinfeld, R., 1991. *The Invention of Free Labor: The Employment Relation in English and American Law and Culture, 1350–1870*. University of North Carolina Press.

Steinmetz, G., ed., 2013. *Sociology and Empire. The Imperial Entanglements of a Discipline*. Duke University Press.

Steinmetz, G., 2018. "Arguments for a Comparative and Historical Sociology Section of the ASA," *Trajectories: Newsletter of the ASA Comparative and Historical Sociology Section*, vol. 29, no. 3.

Steinmetz, G., 2019. "Sociology and Sisyphus: Postcolonialism, Anti-positivism, and Modernist Narrative in Patterson's Oeuvre," *Theory and Society*, vol. 48, no. 6: 799–822.

Stone, D., 2010. "Genocide and Memory," in D. Bloxham and A. D. Moses, eds., *The Oxford Handbook of Genocide Studies*. Oxford University Press, pp. 102–119.

Strathern, M., 2005. *Kinship, Law and the Unexpected: Relatives Are Always a Surprise*. Cambridge University Press.

Stuard, S. M., 1995. "Ancillary Evidence for the Decline of Medieval Slavery," *Past & Present*, vol. 149: 3–28.

Sunderland, J., 2006. *Swept Under the Rug: Abuses Against Domestic Workers Around the World*. Human Rights Watch.

Surtees, R., 2012. *Trafficked at Sea: The Exploitation of Ukrainian Seafarers and Fishers*. Nexus Institute and International Organization for Migration. https://publications.iom.int/books/trafficked-sea-exploitation-ukrainian-sea farers-and-fishers-2012.

Sutherland, S., 2017. "Mancipia Dei: Slavery, Servitude, and the Church in Bavaria, 975–1225," PhD thesis, Ohio State University.

Swanton, Lieutenant, *c.* 1733. "Extract out of Lieut. Swanton's Journal." CO 137/20, ff. 192–193.

Tadman, M., 2000. "The Demographic Cost of Sugar: Debates on Slave Societies and Natural Increase in the Americas," *The American Historical Review*, vol. 105, no. 5: 1534–1575.

Tahirih Justice Center, 2011. *Forced Marriage in Immigrant Communities in the United States: 2011 National Survey Results*. https://preventforcedmarriage .org/wp-content/uploads/2014/07/REPORT-Tahirih-Survey-on-Forced-Marriage-in-Immigrant-Communities-in-the-United-States-September-201151.pdf.

Tannenbaum, F., 1946. *Slave and Citizen*. Alfred A. Knopf.

REFERENCES

Taylor, A., 2014. *The Internal Enemy: Slavery and War in Virginia 1772–1832.* Norton.

Taylor, S., 1965. *The Western Design: An Account of Cromwell's Expedition to the Caribbean.* Institute of Jamaica.

Taylor, T., 2023a. "A Tale of Three Cities: The Roman Destruction of Carthage, Corinth and Numantia," in B. Kiernan, T. Lemos, and T. Taylor, eds., *The Cambridge World History of Genocide*, vol. 1. Cambridge University Press, pp. 278–308

Taylor, T., 2023b. "Caesar's Gallic Genocide: A Case Study in Ancient Mass Violence," in B. Kiernan, T. Lemos, and T. Taylor, eds., *The Cambridge World History of Genocide*, vol. 1. Cambridge University Press, pp. 309–329.

Tello, J., 1730. "The Deposition of John Tello," CO 137/18, f. 98.

Teulon, A. E., n.d. *Report on Expedition to Nanny Town.* Mimeo, pamphlet. Institute of Jamaica.

The Economist, 2010. "Gendercide: The War on Baby Girls," March 5.

The Economist, 2014. "Prostitution and the internet: more bang for your buck," August 17.

Thomas, L., 1993. *Vessels of Evil: American Slavery and the Holocaust.* Temple University Press.

Thomas, M., and Smith, H., 2007. *Property: Principles and Policies.* Foundation Press.

Thompson, F. H., 2003. *The Archeology of Greek and Roman Slavery.* Duckworth.

Thomson, I., 2011. *The Dead Yard: A Story of Modern Jamaica.* Nation Books.

Thornton, R., 1990. *American Indian Holocaust and Survival: A Population History since 1492.* University of Oklahoma Press.

Thorpe, A., N. Pouw, A. Baio et al., 2014. "'Fishing Na Everybody Business': Women's Work and Gender Relations in Sierra Leone's Fisheries," *Feminist Economics*, vol. 20, no. 3: 53–77.

Tiefenbrun, S., and C. J. Edwards, 2008. "Gendercide and the Cultural Context of Sex Trafficking in China," *Fordham International Law Journal*, vol. 32, no. 3: 731–780.

Tippett, E., 2021. "Enslaved Agents: Business Transactions Negotiated by Slaves in the Antebellum South," *Arizona Law Review*, vol. 63, no. 4.

Tizon, A., 2017. "My Family's Slave," *The Atlantic*, June. https://www.the atlantic.com/magazine/archive/2017/06/lolas-story/524490/.

Toledano, E., 2017. "Ottoman Elite Enslavement and 'Social Death'," in J. Bodel and W. Scheidel, eds., *On Human Bondage: After Slavery and Social Death*, Wiley-Blackwell, pp. 136–150.

Tostado, I., 2023. "The Spanish Destruction of the Canary Islands: A Template for the Caribbean Genocide," in B. Kiernan, T. Lemos, and T. Taylor, eds., *The Cambridge World History of Genocide*, vol. 1. Cambridge University Press, pp. 594–621.

Toutain, J., 1968. *The Economic Life of the Ancient World.* Routledge & Kegan Paul.

Tran, M., 2012. "Mali Conflict Puts Freedom of 'Slave Descendants' in Peril," *Guardian*, October 23.

Tregear, E., 1904. *The Maori Race.* A. D. Willis.

Turley, D., 2000. *Slavery.* Blackwell.

REFERENCES

Turner, B., 2017. "The Anthropology of Property," in M. Graziadei and L. Smith, eds., *Comparative Property Law. Global Perspective.* Edward Elgar.

Turner, C., 2013. *Out of the Shadows: Child Marriage and Slavery.* Anti-Slavery International.

UN, 1951. Convention on the Prevention and Punishment of the Crime of Genocide. https://www.un.org/en/genocideprevention/documents/atrocity-crimes/Doc.1_Convention%20on%20the%20Prevention%20and%20Punishment%20of%20the%20Crime%20of%20Genocide.pdf.

UN, 1966. The General Assembly resolution 2200A, International Covenant on Civil and Political Rights. https://www.ohchr.org/en/instruments–mechanisms/instruments/international–covenant–civil–and–political–rights.

UN, 2007. United Nations Declaration on the Rights of Indigenous Peoples. https://www.un.org/development/desa/indigenouspeoples/wp-content/uploads/sites/19/2018/11/UNDRIP_E_web.pdf.

UN, 2019. *Global Study of Homicide, 2019.* UN Office on Drugs and Crime.

UN, 2020. *United Nations Population Fund, State of the World Population, 2020. Against My Will: Defying the Practices that Harm Women and Girls and Undermine Equality.* https://www.unfpa.org/sites/default/files/pub-pdf/UNFPA_PUB_2020_EN_State_of_World_Population.pdf.

UN General Assembly Resolution 44/25, 1989. *Convention on the Rights of the Child.* http://www.ohchr.org/en/professionalinterest/pages/crc.aspx.

UN Human Rights, 2023. "Mali, Slavery by Descent Must Be Criminalized, UN Experts Say." Press Release, May 8. https://www.ohchr.org/en/press-releases/2023/05/mali-slavery-descent-must-be-criminalised-un-experts-say.

UN OHCHR, 1926. *Slavery Convention.* http://www.ohchr.org/EN/Professional Interest/Pages/SlaveryConvention.aspx.

UN OHCHR, 2000. *Protocol to Prevent, Suppress and Punish Trafficking in Persons Especially Women and Children.* https://www.ohchr.org/en/instruments-mechanisms/instruments/protocol-prevent-suppress-and-punish-trafficking-persons.

UN Security Council, 2016. *Children and Armed Conflict: Report of the Secretary General.* April 20. https://www.refworld.org/reference/themreport/unsecgen/2016/en/110458.

Unchained at Last, 2023. *Forced/Arranged/Child Marriage.* https://www.unchainedatlast.org/about-arranged-forced-marriage/.

UNESCO, 1981. *UNESCO and the Struggle Against Ethnocide: 1981 Declaration of San José.* https://unesdoc.unesco.org/ark:/48223/pf0000049951.

UNICEF, 2014. *Ending Child Marriage: Progress and Prospects.* https://data.unicef.org/wp–content/uploads/2015/12/Child–Marriage–Brochure–HR_164.pdf.

UNICEF, 2023. *Child Marriage.* Global Databases. https://data.unicef.org/topic/child-protection/child-marriage/.

United Nations Population Division, 2017. "Migration and Population Change: Drivers and Impacts." https://www.un.org/en/development/desa/population/migration/publications/populationfacts/docs/MigrationPopFacts20178.pdf.

UNODC, 2004. *United Nations Convention Against Transnational Organized Crime and the Protocols Thereto.* UN Press. https://www.unodc.org/documents/treaties/UNTOC/Publications/TOC%20Convention/TOCebook–e.pdf.

313

REFERENCES

UNODC, 2013. *India: Country Assessment Report. Current Status of Victim Service Providers and Criminal Justice Actors in India on Anti-Human Trafficking.* https://www.unodc.org/southasia/frontpage/2013/July/india_-country-assessment-highlights-status-of-victim-assistance-and-criminal-justice-initiatives-on-anti-human-trafficking.html.

UNODC, 2016. *Global Report on Trafficking in Persons.* http://www.unodc.org/unodc/data–and–analysis/glotip.html.

UNODC, 2018. *Trafficking in Persons in the Context of Armed Conflict.* https://www.unodc.org/documents/data-and-analysis/glotip/2018/GloTIP2018_BOOKLET_2_Conflict.pdf.

UNODC, 2022. *Global Report on Trafficking in Persons 2022.* https://www.unodc.org/documents/data-and-analysis/glotip/2022/GLOTiP_2022_web.pdf.

UNODC, 2023. *Working Group on the Smuggling of Migrants,* 5 and 6 October. https://www.unodc.org/unodc/en/treaties/CTOC/working-group-on-the-smuggling-of-migrants-2023.html.

Urbainczyk, T., 2008. *Slave Revolts in Antiquity,* University of California Press.

Urbina, I., 2015, "The Outlaw Ocean, Parts 1–6," *New York Times,* July 25.

US Department of Labor, 2015. *Findings on the Worst Forms of Child Labor.* https://www.dol.gov/agencies/ilab/resources/reports/child-labor/findings.

US State Department, 2017. *Trafficking in Persons Report, 2017.* https://www.state.gov/reports/2017-trafficking-in-persons-report/.

US State Department, 2021. *Trafficking in Persons Report, 2021.* https://www.state.gov/reports/2021-trafficking-in-persons-report/.

US State Department, 2023. *Trafficking in Persons Report, 2023.* https://www.state.gov/reports/2023-trafficking-in-persons-report/.

van Cleve, G. W., 2010. *A Slaveholders' Union: Slavery, Politics, and the Constitution in the Early American Republic.* University of Chicago Press.

van den Anker, C., ed., 2004. *Political Economy of the New Slavery.* Palgrave Macmillan.

van der Heijden, P. G. M., I. de Vries, D. Bohning, and M. Cruyff, 2015. "Estimating the Size of Hard-to-Reach Populations Using Capture–Recapture Methodology, with a Discussion of the International Labour Organization's Global Estimate of Forced Labor," *Forum on Crime and Society,* vol. 8: 109–136.

van Dijk, J., and C. Campistol, 2017. "Work in Progress: International Statistics on Human Trafficking," in R. Piotrowicz, C. Rijken, and B. Uhl, eds., 2017. *Routledge Handbook of Human Trafficking.* Routledge, pp. 381–394.

van Dijk, J., and P.G. M. van der Heijden, 2016. *Multiple Systems Estimation for Estimating the Number of Victims of Human Trafficking across the World.* United Nations Office on Drugs and Crime.

van Liempt, I., 2006. "Trafficking in Human Beings: Conceptual Dilemmas," in C. van den Anker and Doomernik, J., eds., *Trafficking and Women's Rights.* Palgrave Macmillan, pp. 27–42.

van Lunteren, F., 2019. "Historical Explanation and Causality," *Isis,* vol. 110, no. 2: 321–324.

Vandiver, M., D. Giacopassi, and W. Lofquist, 2007. "Slavery's Enduring Legacy: Executions in Modern America," *Journal of Ethnicity in Criminal Justice,* vol. 4, no. 4: 19–36.

Vargas-Silva, C., ed., 2012. *Handbook of Research Methods in Migration.* Edward Elgar.

REFERENCES

Vaughn, J., 1977. "Mafakur: A Limbic Institution of the Margi," in S. Miers and I. Kopytoff, eds., *Slavery in Africa*. University of Wisconsin Press.

Verlinden, C., 1970. *The Beginnings of Modern Colonization*, NCROL.

Verlinden, C., 1995. *L'Esclavage dans l'Europe médiévale*, vols. 1 and 2. Bruges.

Vésteinsson, O., and H. Gestsdóttir, 2014. "The Colonization of Iceland in Light of Isotope Analyses," *Journal of the North Atlantic*, vol. 7: 137–145.

Vogt, J., 1957. *Struktur Der Antiken Sklavenkriege*. Akademie der Wissenschaften und der Literatur.

Vogt, J., 1965. *Sklaverei und Humanität*, Weisbaden: Steiner.

Vogt, J., 1973. *Bibliographie zur Antiken Sklaverei*. Brockmeyer.

Vujcic, N., 2021. "A Numbers Game: The Size of the Slave Population in Classical Athens," *Journal of Classical Studies*, vol. 23: 87–112.

Wacquant. L., 2002. "From Slavery to Mass Incarceration," *New Left Review*, vol. 13: 41–60.

Wagner, E., 1974. "Social Stratification in 17th-Century Korea." Occasional Papers on Korea 1.

Wakefield, E. G., 1849. *A View of the Art of Colonization*. J. W. Parker.

Walk Free, 2016. *Global Slavery Index 2016*. Walk Free Foundation.

Walk Free, 2023a. *Global Slavery Index 2023*. Walk Free Foundation.

Walk Free, 2023b. *Methodology Behind the Global Slavery Index*. https://www.walkfree.org/global-slavery-index/methodology/methodology-content/.

Walker, A., 1978. *Marx: His Theory and its Context*. London.

Wallerstein, I., 1974. *The Modern World System*, vol. 1. Academic Press.

Walton, G. M., ed., 1975. "A Symposium on 'Time on the Cross'," *Explorations in Economic History*, January.

Ward, M., 2022. "The Legacy of Slavery and Contemporary Racial Disparities in Arrest Rates," *Sociology of Race and Ethnicity*, vol. 8, no. 4: 534–552.

Ward, R., and E. Kingdon, eds., 1995. *Land, Custom and Practice in the South Pacific*. Cambridge University Press.

Warren, M., 1985. *Gendercide: The Implications of Sex Selection*. Roman and Allanheld.

Waschefort, G., 2017. "Child Soldiering in Relation to Human Trafficking," in R. Piotrowicz, C. Rijken, and B. Uhl, eds., *Routledge Handbook of Human Trafficking*. Routledge, pp. 135–156.

Weaver, K. K., 2006. *Medical Revolutionaries: The Enslaved Healers of Eighteenth-Century Saint Domingue*. University of Illinois Press.

Watson, A., 1989. *Slave Law in the Americas*. University of Georgia Press.

Weber, M., 1964. *The Theory of Social and Economic Organization*. Free Press.

Weitzer, R., 2007. "The Social Construction of Sex Trafficking: Ideology and Institutionalization of a Moral Crusade," *Politics and Society*, vol. 35: 447–475.

Weitzer, R., 2011. "Sex Trafficking and the Sex Industry: The Need for Evidence-based Theory and Legislation," *Journal of Criminal Law and Criminology*, vol. 101, no. 4: 1337–1369.

Weitzer, R., 2014. "New Directions in Research on Human Trafficking," *Annals of the American Academy of Political and Social Science*, vol. 653, no. 1: 6–24.

Weitzer, R., 2015. "Human Trafficking and Contemporary Slavery," *Annual Review of Sociology*, vol. 41: 223–242.

REFERENCES

Westermann, W. L., 1955a. "Slave Maintenance and Slave Revolts," *Classical Philology*, vol. 40, no. 1: 1–10.

Westermann, W. L., 1955b. *The Slave Systems of Greek and Roman Antiquity*. American Philosophical Society.

Whelan, F., 1980. "Property as Artifice: Hume and Blackstone," in J. Pennock and J. Chapman, eds., *Property*. New York University Press.

White, H. R., 2005. "Between the Devil and the Inquisition: African Slaves and the Witchcraft Trials in Cartagena de Indies," *The North Star: Journal of African American Religious History*, vol. 8, no. 2: 1–15.

Whitman, J. Q., 2018. *Hitler's American Model: The United States and the Making of Nazi Race Law*. Princeton University Press

Whitsun, A. M., 1929. *The Constitutional Development of Jamaica, 1660–1729.* Manchester.

WHO, 2005. *Violence Against Women and HIV/AIDS: Critical Intersections.* World Health Organization.

Wijers, M., 2017. "Fifteen Years Lifting of the Ban on Brothels: The Struggle of Policy Makers between Sex Workers as Agents or Victims," in R. Piotrowicz, C. Rijken, and B. Uhl, eds., *Routledge Handbook of Human Trafficking*. Routledge, pp. 487–498.

Wilderson, F. B., 2021. *Afropessimism*. Liveright Publishing.

Wilks, I., 1975. *Asante in the Nineteenth Century*. Cambridge University Press.

Williams, C., 1733. "The Substance of Capt. Williams' Examination," CO 137/20, f. 154.

Williams, C. O., 1937. *Thraldom in Ancient Iceland*. University of Chicago Press.

Williams, E., 2021 [1944]. *Capitalism and Slavery*, 3rd ed. University of North Carolina Press.

Williams, J. B., 1995. *From the Commercial Revolution to the Slave Revolution: The Development of Slavery in Medieval Genoa*. University of Chicago Press.

Williams, J., 1938 "The Maroons of Jamaica." *Anthropological Series of the Boston College Graduate School*, vol. 3, no. 4: 379–480.

Williamson, C., and T. Cluse-Tolar, 2002. "Pimp-Controlled Prostitution: Still an Integral Part of Street Life," *Violence Against Women*, vol. 8, no. 9: 1074–1092.

Williamson, K., ed., 2006 [1828]. *Marly: Or, A Planter's Life in Jamaica*. Macmillan.

Willis, J., 1985. "Introduction: The Ideology of Enslavement in Islam," in J. R. Willis, ed., *Slaves and Slavery in Muslim Africa*. Vol. 1: *Islam and the Ideology of Enslavement*. Frank Cass and Co., pp. 1–15.

Willis, P., 1981. *Learning to Labor: How Working Class Kids Get Working Class Jobs*. Columbia University Press.

Winter, M., 1984. "Slavery and the Pastoral Twareg of Mali," *The Cambridge Journal of Anthropology*, vol. 9, no. 2: 4–30.

Wolfe, P. 2006. "Settler Colonialism and the Elimination of the Native," *Journal of Genocide Research*, vol. 8, no. 4: 387–409.

Woodhouse, W. J., 1938. *Solon the Liberator*. Oxford University Press.

Wright, G., 2016. Review of S. Beckert and S. Rockman, eds., *Slavery's Capitalism*. https://eh.net/book_reviews/slaverys–capitalism–a–new–history–of–american–economic–development/.

Wright, G., 2022. "Slavery and the Rise of the Nineteenth-Century American Economy," *Journal of Economic Perspectives*, vol. 36, no. 2: 123–148.

REFERENCES

Wyatt, D., 2002. "Slavery, Patriarchy and Power in Medieval Britain and Ireland." PhD thesis, Cardiff University.

Wyatt, D., 2009. *Slaves and Warriors in Medieval Britain and Ireland, 800–1200.* Brill.

Wyatt-Brown, B., 1988. "The Mask of Obedience: Male Slave Psychology in the Old South," *The American Historical Review*, vol. 93, no. 5: 1228–1252.

Wylie, G., and P. McRedmond, eds., 2010. *Human Trafficking in Europe: Character, Causes and Consequences.* Palgrave Macmillan.

Zanker, P., 1990. *The Power of Images in the Age of Augustus.* University of Michigan.

Zhang, S. X., 2009. "Beyond the 'Natasha' Story: A Review and Critique of Current Research on Sex Trafficking," *Global Crime*, vol. 10: 178–195.

Zhang, S. X., 2012. *Looking for a Hidden Population: Trafficking of Migrant Laborers in San Diego County.* US Department of Justice.

Zhang, S. X., M. W. Spiller, B. K. Finch, and Y. Qin, 2014. "Estimating Labor Trafficking among Unauthorized Migrant Workers in San Diego," *Annals of the American Academy of Political and Social Science*, vol. 653, no. 1: 65–86.

Zheng, T., 2014. "Migrant Sex Workers and Trafficking in China," in K. K. Hoang and R. S. Parreñas, eds., *Human Trafficking Reconsidered: Rethinking the Problem, Envisioning New Solutions.* International Debate Education Association, pp. 139–148.

INDEX

Abbasid caliphate, 80
absolute property, 59–60, 62
abusive migration, 233, 241–2
Accompong (rebel leader), 171,
    171n7, 196, 198
Accompong, Jamaica
    photograph, *181*
Acemoglu, Daron, 40, 87
Aegina (ancient town), 214
Afghanistan
    child soldiers in, 253
Africa
    child labor in, 254
    child soldiers in, 253
    forced marriages in, 256
    slavery in, 39, 73
"Afropessimism," 37, 40
agency of slaves, 16, 31–2
agriculture
    slavery and, 104, 113–14, 143
Alexander, Michelle, 38
Algeria
    forced labor in, 258
Allow States and Victims to Fight
    Online Sex Trafficking Act
    (FOSTA, 2018), 274
American Civil War, 231, 254
American Community Survey, 264

American sociology
    denial of slavery in, 83–5, 87–92
    pervasive presentism of, 88
ancient slave latifundia, 76
Anderson, Perry, 65, 79, 88
Andrews, Antony, 129
anti-Semitism, 203
Aptheker, Herbert, 185n10
Arab states
    demand for slave women, 121
    forced marriages in, 255
Arendt, Hannah, 227n11
Arisba (ancient town), 214
Armenian genocide, 202
articulation of slavery in society
    capitalist plantation mode of,
        76–7
    embedded demesne mode of,
        73–4
    passive and active, 74, 75,
        78–81
    predatory circulation mode of,
        73
    urban-industrial mode of, 74–5
    urban-latifundic mode of, 75–6
Asante state, 72
Ashworth (White commander), 173,
    176

INDEX

Asiatic mode of production, 79
Athens
  arable farming, 128, 129, 134
  aristocracy, 130–1
  citizens, 100
  commercial class, 133
  economy, 127, 128–9, 130
  "imperial colonization," 130
  indebted bondsmen, 54, 55, 56
  kinship system, 127
  land hunger, 129, 131
  landless laborers, 54, 55, 131–2,
    134
  peasants, 131–2
  population, 127, *128,* 132
  poverty, 127
  public slaves, 138–9
  scholarship on, 126–7
  serfs, 132, 134
  slavery, 65–6, 75, 78, 126–40
  social classes, 54, 127, 130, 131
  Solonic reforms, 78, 133, 136
  standard of living, 133
  state structure, 130
  unskilled and skilled laborers,
    133
  upward mobility, 131
Atlantic slave trade, 1, 2, 30, 125,
    129
Attica, 136
Ayscough, John, 178
Azerbaijan
  forced labor in, 258

Backpage Hawaii, 267
Baker, Heather, 53, 54
Ball, John, 153
Bangladesh
  bonded labor in, 244
Barbados slave society, 217, 218
Barbieri-Low, Anthony, 150
Bassett, Sarah, 35
Bauman, Zygmunt, 203

Bavaria
  slavery in, 71, 74
Beckert, Sven, 5, 76
Bellagio-Harvard Guidelines on the
    Legal Parameters of Slavery,
    236, 238
belonging, 19–20
Benin
  forced labor in, 258
Bennett, Robert, 198–200
Best, Lloyd, 77
bi-partite estate, 74
Black Americans
  ethnocide of, 215, 215n5
  legacy of slavery, 38
  mass incarceration of, 38
  pattern of early marriage, 39
Black Death, 100, 207
Blackburn, Robin, 88
Blackhawk, Ned, 205, 210
Blackstone, W., 46, 47
  *Commentaries on the Laws of
    England,* 46
Blassingame, John, 4
  The Slave Community, 90
Bloc, Fred, 91
Bloome, Dierdre, 37, 38, 40, 84
Bodel, John, 9, 145, 146, 148
Boeotia, 129
Boko Haram, 249
bonded labor
  causes of, 245
  definition of, 242, 243–4
  statistics of, 244
  study of, 275
  use of the term, *232*
Boserup, Ester, 97, 98–9, 115, 117,
    122
  *The Conditions of Agricultural
    Growth,* 98
Brazil
  debt bondage in, 245
  slavery in, 25, 26, 34, 36, 77, 110

319

INDEX

Bresson, A., 138
bride-buying, 257
bridewealth payments, 117–18
British law, 43
Brunovskis, A., 267
brydhlop ("bride-running"), 123
Buenos Aires
  as slave-trading port, 75
Bulley (rebel leader), 170
Burford, Alison, 135
Burlamaqui, Jean-Jacques, 43
Burn, A. W., 131
Burnard, Trevor, 6, 215, 218, 219, 224
Burundi
  forced labor in, 258
Byzantium Empire
  slavery in, 86

California
  underage prostitution in, 248
Calinago Caribs war, 112
Cambodia
  genocide, 207
  sex workers, 264
Cambridge World History of Genocide, The (Kiernan), 206, 210
Cameron, Catherine, 53, 70, 72, 109, 111, 114, 122–3
Cameron, David, 2
Cameroon
  child labor in, 254
Campistol, C., 261
Canada
  human rights violations, 259
Canary Islands
  protracted genocide in, 216
  Spanish conquest of, 214, 216n7
Canon law, 43
Card, Claudia, 208, 209
Caribbean islands

manumission, 30
proportion of slaveholders, 30
slavery in, 25, 26, 36, 72
Carthage (ancient town), 214
Catholic Church
  treatment of Indigenous people, 207, 210
Charlemagne's empire, 56
Chevaleyre, Claude, 22
child labor
  in chocolate industry, 254
  in cotton harvesting, 259
  in domestic sphere, 254–5
  drivers of, 252–3
  statistics of, 252, 262, 268
child servitude
  vs. child labor, 251–2
  definition of, 242, 251
child soldiers, 253–4, 275
child trafficking, 232, 238, 263
children
  forced marriages of, 252, 255–6, 257
  sexual exploitation of, 248, 252, 253, 267
China
  cultural revolution, 205
  economic system, 270
  ethnic minorities, 259, 260
  forced labor, 259, 260–1
  gendercide, 256
  human smuggling, 256–7
  human trafficking, 239
  manumission, 150
  nubi revolts in, 22
  punishment for crimes in, 109
  slave population, 22
Chosŏn period, 78
Christianity
  early congregations, 9
  metaphor of redemption in, 10
  notion of true freedom, 151–2
  slavery and, 27–8, 86, 152

320

INDEX

Chuang, J. A., 233, 239, 275
Cicero, 62
civil wars, 272
Claeys, Eric, 49
Clark, Kenneth, 4, 89, 90
Clegg, John, 84
Codler, Captain, 170
Colombia
  sex trafficking, 248
  slavery, 40
commendation ("voluntary"
  enslavement), 22
commercially sexually exploited
  children (CSEC), 267
common law, 46, 47
concubinage, 28–9, 124
Confino, Michael, 97
Congo, Democratic Republic of
  child soldiers, 253
  sex trafficking, 248
Congo Free State, 202
consensual exploitation, 236–7
Corinth (ancient town), 214
Coromantee slaves
  origin of the term, 166n3
  population of, 192
  revolt of, 166–7, 170, 171, 173,
    177
  stereotype of, 192, 192n15,
    192n16
Corpus Juris Civilis, 59
Côte d'Ivoire
  child labor, 254
COVID-19 pandemic, 235, 248,
  263, 269
crimes against humanity, 202
Cromwell, Oliver, 159
Cropping Index, 103, 141
Crusades
  as case of genocide, 207
Cuban slavery, 215
Cudjoe (rebel leader)
  attitude toward Whites, 187

peace negotiations with British,
  159, 171, 179–80, *180,*
  182–5, 186–7, 196–8
personality, 171, 172, 186
settlement in St. James, 179
Windward refugees and, 178–9,
  180–1
Cuffee (rebel leader), 168,
  171–2n7, 196
cultural genocide, *see*
  ethnocide
Cunningham, Henry, 178
Curacao colony, 30

Dark Age pastoral heroes, 113
Davis, Ossie, 213
death, *see* social death
debt bondage, 21, *232,* 244–5
Declaration of San Jose, 209
degree of dependence on slavery,
  70–1
Desborough, Vincent, 127
Desmond, Matt, 5
deterior condicio principle, 23
Die the Long Day (Patterson),
  216, 227
direction of dependence on
  slavery, 71–2
Diriomenos, 244
dis-enslavement, 150
Dogrib Indians, 106
Domar, Evsey D., 9, 95, 96, 98,
  100, 101
domestic (household) servitude,
  242, 247
Dominican Republic
  slave revolts, 36
Doomernik, J., 271
Douglas, Massey, 240
Douglass, Frederick, 19, 33, 37
Dovring, Folke, 97, 98
Drescher, Seymour, 212
Du Casse, Jean-Baptiste, 160

321

INDEX

DuBois, W. E. B., 4, 18, 19, 89
Black Reconstruction in America, 1860–1880, 85
Duncan, D. S., 134
Dunn, Richard, 217
Dutch slave laws, 59–60

Edward VI, King of England, 110
Edwards, Bryan, 191n14
Egypt
 child soldiers in, 253
elite slaves, 58
Elkins, Stanley, 4, 33, 186, 187, 212
Emancipation Act, 162
Emergency Conference Committee, 213
Engels, Friedrich, 3, 65
Engerman, Stanley, 4, 31, 69, 73, 90, 97, 99–100
England, medieval
 food insecurity, 109
 punishment for crimes, 109–10
 "resource polygyny," 123
 serfdom, 100–1
 slavery, 74, 100–1
 warfare, 106–7
enslaved, *see* slaves
enslaved women, 224, 225–6
enslavement
 by birth, 22–3
 food insecurity and, 108–9
 modes of, 20–4
 punishment for crimes and, 109–10
 through capture in warfare, 20
Equal Employment Opportunity Commission, 274
Eritrea
 human rights in, 259
 modern-day slavery, 258
 state-imposed forced labor, 258–9
ethnic cleansing, 202, 203
ethnicity, 207

ethnocide
 of Black Americans, 215, 215n5
 concept of, 201, 207, 208
 vs. genocide, 10, 209–10
 legal norms on, 209
Ethnographic Atlas database, 102–3
eunuchs, 58
Europe
 antitrafficking and antislavery laws, 274
 forced marriages, 255
 human trafficking, 263
 modern-day slavery, 264
 refugee crisis, 240
 sex trafficking, 272
Eurostat Report on Trafficking in Human Beings, 262, 264
Evans, Peter B., 91
exploitation creep, 233
ex-slaves
 social status of, 63
"extrusive" slavery, 22

Fanon, F., 277
farming systems, 118, 119
Fein, Helen, 202–3, 206, 213, 224, 225, 226, 277
"fiction of separability," 51
Fiji
 forced labor in, 258
Finley, Moses, 8, 16, 35, 51, 54, 65, 66, 67, 68, 85, 126, 186, 194
First Maroon War
 Black revolts, 177–8
 history, 36, 159, 171
 major figures, 171, 186
 peace negotiations, 159, 179–80, *180,* 181, 182–5
 White parties actions in, 176–7
fishing communities
 slavery in, 112–13, 116, 143
Fitzhugh, George, 62

INDEX

Fletcher, Ben, 38
Floyd, George, 205
Fogel, Robert, 4, 31, 90
Forand, Paul, 69
forced labor
    in agriculture and rural areas,
        244–5
    definition of, 233, 234–5
    economics of, 274
    globalization and, 269–71
    laws against, 273–4
    migrants and, 265
    in prisons, 259
    statistics of, 235, 262, 264,
        265–6, 269, 272
    study of, 275–6
    use of the term, 231, *232*
    see also state-imposed forced
    labor
Forced Labor Convention (1957),
    258
forced marriages
    in Asia, 255
    of children, 252
    estimates of, 248
    as form of servitude, 233–4, 237,
        255
    movement against, 276
    paradox of, 257
    as violation of human rights,
        256
FOSTA, *see* Allow States and
    Victims to Fight Online Sex
    Trafficking Act
Francis, Pope, 210
Frazier, E. Franklin, 89
free persons
    vs. enslaved, 52–3, 147
freedom
    idea of, 52, 53, 151–2, 203
Freeman, Kathleen, 133
French slave law, 59
Furtado, Junia, 147

Gaul
    Roman conquest of, 214
gendercide, 210–12, 222, 256
genocide
    as collateral damage, 207
    vs. crimes against humanity, 202
    definitions of, 202–4, 206
    ideological motives of, 207
    intent to exterminate and, 222
    motivation for, 207
    as organized violence, 205–7
    vs. other forms of mass killings,
        208–9
    as physical killing, 204–5
    prevention of births as, 204,
        205–6, 222
    slavery and, 201, 202, 212–14,
        221–2
    social death and, 208
    sociological conception of, 206
genocide by attrition, 226
Genovese, Eugene, 185n10, 186,
    187
genuine slave societies, 8, 67, 126
Ghosh, Rishab, 50
Gillingham, John, 107
Global Slavery Index, 243, 260,
    268
globalization, 269–72
Gluckman, Max, 50
Gold Coast (Ghana) slave trade, 25
Goldhagen, Daniel
    Hitler's Willing Executioners, 213
Goldthorpe, John, 91
Goody, J., 117, 119
Google Books Ngram Viewer, 231
"Graeculus" stereotype, 34
grand historical sociology, 91
Great Britain
    occupation of Jamaica, 226
    Royal decree of 1789, 59
Greco-Roman world, *see* Greece
    (ancient)

323

INDEX

Greece (ancient)
  agriculture, 134, 135, 137
  artists and craftsmen, 135
  Dark Age era, 126, 127
  demand for wood, 136
  division of labor, 138
  fruit farms, 137
  genocidal episodes, 214
  manual labor, 134–5
  manumission rates, 30
  murder of enslavers, 35
  pastoral heroes, 113
  population growth, 139
  productivity, 138
  public servants, 31
  slavery, 3, 18, 26, 34, 75, 85–6,
    130, 137–8, 214
  socioeconomic order, 137, 138
Green, Erik, 101
Greene, Sandra, 147
Greenland, Fiona, 84
Gregory, John, 180, 181
Grey, T., 49, 50
Grotius, Hugo, 43
Guanaboa Vale, Jamaica
  maroon settlements, *158,* 164,
    165
Guthrie, John, 182, 196–8
Gutman, Herbert, 4
Guy's Town group, 172, 176

Haas, Samuel, 69–70
Haida peoples, 26
Haiti
  child labor, 254–5
  slavery, 36, 88, 215, 215n4
Hall, Catherine, 77
Hammer, Carl, 71
Hammond, N. G. L., 131
Handler, Jerome, 150
Harper, Kyle, 68, 75
Harris, Edward, 133
Harroff-Tavel, Hélène, 242

Hartman, Saidiya, 37
Hegel, Georg Wilhelm Friedrich, 45,
  185
Heichelheim, Fritz, 133
Helots revolt, 190
Henderson, G., 79
Herf, Jeffrey, 212
Herodotus, 214
herrenvolk democracy, 61, 62–3
Herring, Julines, 169, 169n6
Hesiod, 54, 55, 129, 131
Higman, BarryW., 77, 217n8
Hinton, Alex, 204, 213
Hobby's plantation, 177
Hobsbawm, Eric, 88
Holness, Andrew, 226
Holocaust, 203, 211, 213, 221–2
Holodomor, 205
Homeric poems, 113, 126–7
Honore, A. M., 48, 49, 50
Honore, Tony, 42
"honorific trap," 120
Hopkins, Keith, 66, 67, 75, 88
Human Rights Watch, 259
human smuggling
  definition of, 233, 240
  experiences of, 240–1
  statistics of, 240, 242
  as transnational service industry,
    241
  use of the term, 232
human soul, 153
human trafficking
  Covid-19 pandemic and, 239
  data collection on, 261
  definition of, 233, 238, 242
  estimated statistics of, 264
  gender and, 273
  local-level analysis of, 264
  migration and, 271–2
  movement against, 231, 273, 276
  patterns of, 264
  personal factors of, 272

324

prevention of, 239–40
statistics of, 235, 239, 242, 262–3
targeted ethnic groups, 235
use of the term, 231, *232*
Hume, David, 47
Hunt, Peter, 54
Hunter, Robert, 173–4, 177, 178
hunter-gathering societies
slavery in, 111–12, 116
Husserl, Edmund, 148

Iceland
colonization of, 108
ideology of slavery, 147
illegal adoptions, 242
India
bonded labor in, 244, 245
bride-buying in, 257
economic system, 270
forced marriages, 276
gendercide, 256
Jamadar labor contracting system, 245
marginalized groups, 244
seasonal labor migration, 244
Supreme Court, 276
women's workshare in, 116
Indian Ocean slave trade, 24
Indigenous peoples
destruction of culture of, 209
mass killings of, 205, 207, 210, 214
pre-Columbian population of, 210n3
removal of children, 209
wars between, 106
institutional reproduction of inequality, 38
intensive farming, 122
intent to destroy, 222–3
International Association of Genocide Scholars, 202

International Court of Justice (ICJ), 204
International Criminal Tribunal for the former Yugoslavia (ICTY), 202
International Day of the Girl Child, 276
International Labour Office (ILO)
report on child labor and migrant workers, 251, 252–3, 260, 268
report on debt bondage, 244
report on forced labor, 244, 245, 257–8, 260, 265, 269, 274
report on forced marriage, 255
report on human trafficking and smuggling, 242
report on modern servitude, 233, 234, 235, 235n3, 242, 249, 252, 263, 264
report on sexual exploitation, 248
international migrant forced laborers (IMFL), 242, 245–6, 265, 268
International Organization for Migration (IOM), 235, 235n3, 240, 247, 249, 268
internecine warfare, 106
Irish, Maya, 203
ISIS, 249, 253
Islamic *Ghilman*, 58
Islamic societies
character of, 69–70
conception of property, 57
concubinage in, 73
polygamy, 120
slave revolts, 35–6
slavery, 26, 27, 56–8, 73, 121
slavery/property relations, 41
Ismard, Paulin, 31, 75, 135, 138

Jacobs, Harriet, 19
Jacobs, John, 16, 17, 20, 153

INDEX

Jamaica
    abuse of women and children,
        91–2
    British control of, 157, 159–62,
        164
    civil government, 160
    climate, 160, 192
    earthquake of 1692, 160
    economic system, 33, 218
    history of, 226–7
    Indigenous population, 207
    internal autonomy, 161
    legal system, 161–2
    Maroon settlements, *158*
    norms and values, 162
    plantation system, 10, 160, 161,
        185, 193
    post-genocidal memories, 226–7
    poverty, 92
    practice of herbalism, 35
    provision ground system, 32
    size of, 218
    Spanish rule, 157, 159–60, 164,
        165
    violence, 227
Jamaican slave revolts
    on Captain Ducke's plantation,
        167
    causes of, 153, 157, 187–8,
        190–3, 195
    on Downs's plantation, 170
    execution of rebels, 167, 183–4
    guerrilla warfare, 176
    on Herring estate, 169
    history of, 157, 159, 163–9
    on Hobby's plantation, 177
    intelligence system, 172–3
    leading figures, 164, 168, 171–2,
        171n7
    vs. marronage, 187–90
    rebel towns, 179
    social-psychological explanation
        of, 185–6

solidarity between rebels and
    slaves, 169–73
Spaniards and, 157, 164–5, 174
on Sutton's plantation, 168
tribal composition during, 171,
    173
violence, 167
White parties actions against,
    167–8, 169–70, 173–6, 177,
    178
Jamaican slavery
    abolition of, 226–7
    as case of genocide, 201, 215–16,
        220–1, 223–4, 226
    vs. Nazi holocaust, 221–2
    vs. US slave system, 215–18,
        219–20, *220*
Jamaican slaves
    of African origin, 191
    death toll, 10, 217
    denial of reproduction of, 223–4
    mass rape of, 224–5
    population, 159, 160–1, 162–3,
        166, 190, 219–21, 223
    psychological trauma of, 147,
        186–7, 218–19
    ratio of local to foreign-born,
        190–1
    resistance of, 34
    sorcerers among, 110
    tribal and cultural diversity, 163,
        192
Jamaican White settlers
    absenteeism among slaveholders,
        193, 195
    cultural disintegration, 193,
        194–5
    emergency meeting of the
        legislature, 174–5
    insecurity, 160
    population statistics, 159–61,
        162, 174
    sex ratio, 194, 194n18

326

INDEX

slave revolts and, 166, 174
social relationships, 162, 193–4
violence against, 170–1, 194
wealth, 161
James, C. L. R., 5, 87
The Black Jacobins, 88
Jameson, M., 136, 137
Jamestown, Jamaica, 61
Janissaries, 58
Japanese Americans, 239
Jennings, Paul, 45
Jim Crow system, 4, 38, 68, 83, 84, 87, 204, 214
Johnny (rebel leader), 171, 171n7, 196, 198
Johnson, Mark, 148
Jones, A., 211
Journal of United Labor, 62

kafala (sponsorship system), 242
Kampuchean genocide, 226
Kaplan, David, 112
Kaplan, Marion, 212
Kara, Siddharth, 245, 270, 275
Karras, Ruth, 120, 124, 224
Kazakhstan
forced labor in, 258
Keeley, Lawrence, 106
kidnapping, 20–1
Kiernan, Ken, 227
Kikotan massacre, 210
Kim Jun, 80
Kim Yun-seong, 80
kinless persons, 17
Kiple, Kenneth, 219
Kishee (rebel leader), 172, 172n7
Kissey (rebel leader), 176, 184
Kochan, Donald, 44
Kolchin, Peter, 4
Korea
coup d'état against Ch'pe Ui, 80
economy, 78, 79–80
food insecurity, 109

Mongol domination, 80
punishment for crimes in, 109
religion, 79
slavery in, 56–7, 67, 74, 78–81
Korotayev, Andrey, 118
Koryŏ period, 78
Krugman, Paul, 100

Labor Convention (1930), 232
labor trafficking, 245
Laing, R. D., 187n12
Lakoff, George, 148
Lange, Frederick, 150
Langer, A., 265
Lares Augusti cult, 152
large-scale slave societies, 71, 126, 140
Las Siete Partidas, 59
Latin America
child domestic servants, 265
forced marriage, 256
manumission, 29
resistance of slaves, 34
slave inheritance laws, 24
law of slavery, 59–60
Lawrence, Benjamin, 257
League of Nations Slavery Convention (1926), 235, 236
Lei, Ya-Wen, ix
Leeward band
efforts to defeat, 175
formation of, 167
growing number of, 178–9
internecine disputes, 170
leading figures, 171, 171n7
settlements, 176
strength of, 168, 173
treaty with British, 182–3, 184
tribal composition, 171
Lemkin, Raphael, 202, 203, 207, 213–14, 221
Lenski, Noel, 68
Leopold II, King of Belgium, 202

INDEX

Levison, D., 265
Lewis, David, 41–2
Lewis, Oscar, 89
life-integrity rights, 202–3
Limoncelli, Stephanie, 231, 270, 272, 276
Lluidas Vale, Jamaica, 165
Locke, John, 44, 47
Loria, Achille, 95
Los Vermejales, Jamaica, 164
Louisiana
  slave population, 217
Lubola, Juan (a.k.a. Juan de Bolas), 164, 165
Lunteren, Frans van, 38

Madagascar slaves, 163, 168, 170
Madison, James, 44–5
Madley, B., 210
Magubane, Zine, 85
Mali
  slavery in, 73, 243
Mamluk Sultanate, 81
Mandic, Danilo, 241
Mann, Michael, 203
Manning, P., 121
manumission
  for acts of heroism, 29
  by adoption, 29
  forms of, 28
  personal characteristics of enslaved and, 29–30
  postmortem, 28
  rates of, 30, 73
  studies of, 150–1
  supply of slaves and, 30
Mao Zedong, 205
Maori, 51, 70, 112, 120
Marghi people, 120
marital servitude, 6, 242, 255–7
maroons
  artists' impressions of, 192n17
  identity, 188

origin of the term, 166n2
population, 188, 189
settlements, *158*, 164, 169, 179
vs. slaves, 188, 189
solidarity between rebels and, 169
tribal composition of, 189
marriage instigated by rape, 123
marronage, 157, 159, 163–9, 187–90
Marx, Karl, 3, 52, 56, 81–2
mass killing
  vs. genocide, 204–5, 208–9
Masters and Servants Act, 61
Mauritania
  slavery in, 243
McCormick, M., 56
melior condicio, see slave inheritance
Mendelsohn, Isaac, 190
Menell, Peter, 50
Merrill, Thomas, 49
Middle East
  forced marriages in, 256
military slavery, 69
Miller, Katherine, 153
Ming dynasty, 22
modern slavery
  criminal justice system and, 273–4
  definition of, 233–4, 236–7, 242
  estimates of, 242, 248
  globalization and, 269–71
  rise of, 269–71
  terminology, 231–2
  vs. traditional slavery, 231, 243.
  see also servitude
Mondolfo, Rodolfo, 134
Moore, Barrington
  The Social Origins of Dictatorship and Democracy, 91
Morgan, Edmund, 61, 62
Morris, Ian, 128

328

INDEX

Morrison (White commander), 176
Mossé, Claude, 130
Mouritsen, Henrik, 146
Moynihan, Daniel Patrick, 89
Moynihan, Patrick, 4
Moynihan report, 89, 90
mulatto people, 225
Muller, Christopher, viii, 38, 64, 84
Muntzer, Thomas, 153
Murdock, George, 9, 102, 110, 115, 122
Myanmar
  child soldiers, 253
  forced labor, 258
  sex trafficking, 248
Mycenaean civilization, 126
Myrdal, Gunnar
  An American Dilemma, 89

Nanny (Jamaican rebel leader), 172, 172n8
Nanny Town, Jamaica, *158,* 172, 176–7, 180
Nasri, Alix, 242
nature of dependence on slavery, 69
Nazis
  concentration camps, 212, 259
  influence of American race practices, 216n5
  treatment of Jews, 212–13
Nepal
  bonded labor in, 244
  kamaliri system, 255
Nevsun Resources, 259
New Grenada, Colombia
  slavery in, 110
New History of Capitalism (NHC) school, 5–6
New World slave systems
  genocidal aspect of, 222–3
  history of, 214–17
  variations among, 215–16, 217n8
New York Times, 1

New Zealand
  slavery-property relations, 41
Newcastle, Thomas Pelham-Holles, Duke of, 194
Nieboer, H. J., 9, 95, 96
Nieboer-Domar hypothesis, 96–7, 99–100, 104, 125–6, 134, 139
Niger
  slavery in, 73
Nigeria
  child labor in, 254
The 1619 Project, 1, 5
non-slave labor, 60–1
North America
  forced marriages, 255
  manumission, 29
  slavery, 72
North Korea
  forced labor in, 258, 260–1
Novic, Elisa, 209
Numantia (ancient town), 214
Nuremberg Tribunal, 202

Ober, Josiah, 127, 128–9, 133
O'Connell, Heather, 84
Oishi, N., 271
Optional Protocol to the Convention of the Rights of the Child, 253
organ trafficking, 242
Osborne, Robin, 137
Ottoman empire, 58

Pace, G., 37
Pakistan
  bonded labor in, 244
Palermo Protocol, 238, 273
Papanikos, Gregory, 130
Papaw slaves, 173, 192, 192n15
Paraguay
  debt bondage in, 245
Park, Mungo, 191n14
Parreñas, Rhacel, 272, 275

INDEX

pastoralist societies
  division of labor in, 116–17
  slavery in, 113, 116–17, 143
Pateman, Carol, 51
Patterson, Orlando
  Die the Long Day, 216, 227
  *Freedom in the Making of
    Western Culture,* 52
  Slavery and Social Death, 8, 41,
    51, 55, 70, 91, 145, 146, 147,
    150, 212, 235
  The Sociology of Slavery, 89, 91,
    216, 227
Patterson, William, 213
  We Charge Genocide, 213, 214
Paul, Saint
  Christology of, 10, 151–2
  on death, 151
  on God of liberty, 153
Peirce, Charles, 10, 149
Penner, J. E., 44
peonage, 244
People's Army of Vietnam (PAVN),
  205
Pequot massacre, 210
Peru
  debt bondage in, 245
Peters, Thomas, 174, 176
Philippines
  domestic-labor migrants, 272
Phillips, Ulrich, 3
plantation slavery, 10, 76, 77–8,
  212
polycoity, 124
polygyny
  agriculture type and, 144
  bridewealth and, 144
  female workload and, 144
  slavery and, 119–20, 144
  in small-scale societies, 123
  warfare and, 118–19, 144
  women's role in subsistence and,
    117–18

population density
  slavery and, 103, 104, *105,* 139,
    140
population growth
  theory of, 98–9
Poseidonios, 190
premodern societies
  punishment for crimes, 110
  slavery in, 106, 124–5
prevention of births, 204, 222,
  225
property
  absolutist conceptions of, 41,
    42–3, 51
  Anglo-American legal thought on,
    44–8
  bundle-of-rights theory of,
    42–51
  vs. contract, 46
  digital technology revolution and,
    50
  essentialists' view of, 48
  Locke on, 44, 47
  Madison on, 44–5
  mixed notions of, 53–8
  nominalists' view of, 48
  personalistic notions of, 53–8
  in premodern societies, 43
  relational approach to, 42
  residuary character of, 48
  slavery and, 8, 41, 43
  traditional common law view of,
    46–7
prostitution
  legal aspects, 249–50
  socioeconomic aspects, 250, 251
  underage, 248
protracted genocide, 11, 201, 215,
  216
public slavery, 135–6
Pufendorf, Samuel von, 43
punishment for crimes
  enslavement through, 20, 21

330

INDEX

Qing dynasty, 22
Quaco (rebel leader), 171n7, 196, 198
Quao (rebel leader), 171, 172n7, 184, 189, 198–200
Quashee stereotype, 34, 186

racial capitalism, 76, 101
racial education gap, 39
racism, 63, 207
Raffield, Ben, 108
rape of enslaved women, 123, 223–5
Reece, Robert, 84
resistance of slaves
  covert and overt, 33
  cultural forms of, 33–4
  running away as form of, 34
  satire and trickery as, 33–4
  suicide as form of, 34
  violent, 34–6
resource polygyny, 123
respondent-driven sampling (RDS), 266–7
rights
  taxonomy of, 48–9
Rio, Alice, 22, 74
Risse, Stephen, 276
Robeson, Paul, 213
Robinson, C., 76, 192n17
Rockman, Seth, 6
Rohingya minority, 258
Roman law, 43
Rome
  familia Caesaris, 58
  freedmen in, 149–50
  genocidal episodes, 214
  law on slavery, 59, 60
  manumission, 29, 30–1, 75, 146–7
  notion of absolute property, 59
  slave revolts, 35
  slavery in, 17, 18–19, 65–9, 76, 147–8, 222–3

sociological sequence of statuses in, 148–9
  treatment of slaves, 26, 35, 145–7
  working class, 76
Rome Statute of the International Criminal Court, 202
Rosa, Jean-Jacques, 100, 101
Rosen, D., 253
Ruef, Martin, 38, 84
Rueschemeyer, Dietrich, 91
Ruggles, Steve, 90
Russia
  child soldiers, 253
  forced labor, 258
  servile system, 96, 97
Russo-Ukrainian War, 248

Sadler, Francis, 182, 196–8
Sahel
  slavery in, 73, 113, 117, 121
Sahlins, Marshall, 52, 111
Saint-Domingue
  slavery in, 110, 159, 215
Sambo (Black freedman), 173, 176
Sambo stereotype, 33, 34, 186, 187
Santos-Granero, Fernando, 53
Sartre, Jean-Paul, 204
Scandinavia
  polygyny in, 124
  slaveholding system in, 123–4
Scheidel, Walter, viii, 49, 54, 75, 86, 146
Scipio (rebel), 172
Scott, James, 33
Sebly, Major, 166
Second Maroon War, 189
self-enslavement, 21–2
Seneca, 36
serfdom, 98, 100–1
Serras, Juan de, 164, 164n1, 165–6
Sersen, William, 58
"servile concubinage," 124

331

INDEX

servitude
  data collection on, 262–3, 263–4,
    267–9
  definition of, 233, 234, 234n2
  estimates of, 232, 234–5, 261,
    261–2, 265, 266, 268, 275
  forms of, 11, 234, 242–61, 277
  interdisciplinary literature on,
    232–3
  local-level analysis of, 264
  longevity of, 235
  macro-level analysis of, 261
  multiplier method analysis of,
    264
  racial and ethnic discrimination
    and, 272
  respondent-driven sampling,
    266–7
sex industry, 271
sex ratio of population, 211–12
sexual slavery
  average duration of, 249
  definition of, 242
  estimates of, 248, 249
  minors and, 248, 250–1
  scholarship on, 249–50
  social death and, 237
  use of the term, 232
sexual trafficking
  conflict zones and, 248
  COVID-19 pandemic and, 248
  criminalization of, 250
  definition of, 247–8
  estimates of, 262
  as family survival strategy, 239
  of minors, 249
  use of the term, 232
  victimization rate, 264
Shari'a, 57
Sharp, Daddy, 28
Sharpe, Samuel, 153, 226–7
Shaw, B. D., 205, 206n1, 211
Shaw, Martin, 202

Sicilian slave revolts, 191
Siegel, Bernard, 96
Sikkink, Kathryn, 276
Singer, Audrey, 240
Skocpol, Theda, 91
slave inheritance *(melior condicio)*,
    23–4
slave labor, 65, 231, 232
slave revolts, 10, 28, 34, 35, 36,
    190–3
slave societies
  approaches to study of, 65–78,
    81
  examples of, 70
  "genuine," 65, 67, 126
  "large-scale," 71, 126, 140
  law of agency in, 16
  problem of, 8
  proportion of the enslaved in,
    70–1
  theories of, 66–8
slave trade
  historical significance of, 86–7
  routes of, 24–5
  Trans-Atlantic, 25, 217, 219–20,
    220
slaveholders
  glorification of, 18
  total power of, 16, 17
slavery
  in agricultural societies, 104,
    113–14, 118
  in cannibal societies, 17
  consequences of, 36–40
  critics of, 2, 3
  cropping index and, 141
  definition of, 15, 235–6
  distinctive features of, 15–20
  economic factors of, 96, 98
  as extreme form of degradation,
    18
  feminists' view of, 6, 208
  vs. forced labor, 231

332

INDEX

as form of domination, 8, 15, 16
"free labor" and, 62–3
gender and, 114–16, 119, 121, 125
vs. genocide, 201, 202, 212–14
hereditary, 22–3, 113, 237, 243
historical significance of, 1, 3, 4, 65, 83, 85–7, 214–15
illegal status of, 6
industrial capitalism and, 60–4
inequality and, 8–9
as institution, 95–140
labor supply and, 96, 97
laws against, 11
legacy of, 38, 39
legal theory of, 8
logistic models of, 140–5
in medieval societies, 86
modes of articulation of, 72
moral problem of, 2, 3
notions of property and, 8, 41, 53–8, 59–60
population density and, 103, 104, *105*, 125, 139, 140
in premodern world, 9, 106
probability by Cropping Index, 103, *105*, 105–6
racism and, 89, 90–1
in renaissance states, 86
scholarship on, 1–6, 7–8, 87, 90, 95, 102–3, 149
vs. serfdom, 86, 98, 100–1
sexual division of labor and, 114–16
as social death, 9, 19, 32, 145, 148–50
starvation and, 108–9, 142
statistics of, 11, 243
structural and cultural passivity of, 71
theories of origins of, 9, 37–8, 66, 95–6, 101, 114
by warfare, 106–8, *108*, 141

Western conception of, 41
witchcraft and, 110–11, 143
Slavery and Social Death (Patterson), 8, 41, 51, 55, 70, 91, 145, 146, 147, 150, 212, 235
slaves
acquisition of, 24–5
categories of, 15–16
dehumanization of, 18, 185–6
demand for, 66
female *vs.* male, 120, 121, 225
vs. free persons, 52–3, 147
honorlessness of, 18
vs. impoverished non-slaves, 56
lack of agency, 31–2
lack of power, 16
mental suffering of, 17–18, 186–7
as outsiders, 17
personal characteristics of, 26–7, 53
possession of the body of, 17
resiliency of, 32
slaveholders and, 53–4, 186, 187n12, 191
treatment of, 25–8
Slavic slaves, 25
small-scale societies
comparative study of, 111
life expectancies, 112
male power in, 123
violence in, 123
women in, 122
Smith, Adam, 31
Wealth of Nations, 97
Snodgrass, Anthony, 126, 127, 129
Snow, James, 208
Snyder, Christina, 53
Snyder, Terry, 34
social death, 9, 19, 145, 146, 148, 149, 151, 208, 236
sociology, *see* American sociology

333

INDEX

Sociology of Slavery, The
    (Patterson), 88, 91, 216, 227
soft trafficking, 239
Solon, *55, 56*, 133
Somalia
    sex trafficking in, 248
Somers, Margaret, 91
South America
    debt bondage, 244, 245
    forced marriages, 255
    slavery, 71–2, 77–8
South Asia
    bonded labor, 244
    forced marriages, 255, 256
South Korea
    gendercide, 256
Soviet Gulags, 259
Soviet Union
    collapse of, 270, 272
Spain
    New World possessions, 159
    slave laws, 59
Spartacus, 192n15, 194
Spartan public slaves, 100
Srivastava, R., 244
St. George's parish, 179, 184
Stalin, Joseph, 205
Stampp, Kenneth, 4
Stannard, David, 210, 210n3
Starr, Chester, 132
state servitude, 242
state-imposed forced labor
    causes of, 258, 259–60
    ethnic groups and, 258, 260
    in prisons, 259
    statistics of, 257–8, 260–1
Steinfatt, T., 264
Steinmetz, George, 85, 88, 91
Stone, Dan, 226
"Stop Gendercide Act," 212
Strathern, Dame Marilyn, 46
Straus, Scott, ix, 207
structural genocide, 213

Stuard, Susan, 122
subsistence mode of premodern
    societies
    type of slavery and, 111, *112*
    women's workshare and, 114,
    115
Sudan
    genocide by attrition, 226
    sex trafficking, 248
    slavery, 243
Sutherland, 71, 124
Sweden
    slave inheritance laws, 24
Syria
    child soldiers, 253
    sex trafficking, 248
    slavery, 192n16

Tadman, Michael, 217, 218
Tainos people, 207
Taliban, 253
Tanzania
    forced labor in, 258
Taylor, Tristan, 222
Thai fishing industry, 246
Thetes (landless laborers), 54, 55,
    56
Third Servile War, 194
Thirteenth Amendment, 63
Thomas, Laurence, 213
Time on the Cross (Fogel and
    Engerman), 90
Tlingit tribe, 26, 109
Toledano, E., 57
Toutain, Jules, 136
Trafficking in Persons Report (TIP
    Report), 242, 253, 260, 263,
    273
Trafficking Victims Protection Act
    (TVPA, 2000), 212, 274
Treaty of 1739
    articles of, 182–3, 196–8
    impact on slavery, 183–4

INDEX

negotiations of, 179–80, 181, 182
plot against, 183
signing of, 159
Treaty of 1740, 198–200
Trelawny, Edward, 182
Trent, Battle of, 107
tribal societies, 106
Trinidad slave society, 218
Truth and Reconciliation Commission of Canada (TRC), 209
Tupinamba people, 18, 112
Turkey
child soldiers, 253
sex trafficking, 272
Turner, Bertram, 43
Turner, Nat, 28, 153
Tyldum, G., 267

Ukraine
sexual trafficking, 248
Umayyad caliphate, 70
UN Convention on the Elimination of All Forms of Discrimination against Women, 255
UN Convention on the Prevention and Punishment of the Crime of Genocide, 203–4, 205, 206–7, 209, 222
UN Declaration of Human Rights, 205, 256
UN Declaration on the Rights of Indigenous Peoples, 207–8
UN Office on Drugs and Crime (UNODC), 239, 240, 248, 260, 264, 273
UN Protocol on Smuggling, 240, 241
underground commercial sex economy, 267–8
United Arab Emirates
forced labor, 258

United Kingdom
Forced Marriage Unit, 257
migrant labor, 246
United States
antitrafficking and antislavery laws, 273, 274, 275
arrest rates, 39
child marriages, 257
child sex exploitation, 248, 267
dedication to human liberty, 61
Department of Homeland Security, 264
Department of Labor, 252
disease environment, 218
economy, 67
forced labor, 274
free labor, 61–2, 67
gang-raping, 92
human trafficking, 264
migrant labor, 245–6
mortality rates, 217, 218
peonage, 244
prison system, 259
prostitution, 248, 250
racial inequality, 83
school segregation, 89
sex trafficking and sexual servitude, 250–1
United States slavery
as case of genocide, 11, 201, 214, 215–16
establishment of, 87
impact on society, 63–4, 83
vs. Jamaican slave system, 10, 215–18, 219–20, 220
legacy of, 39–40
revolts against, 35, 36
statistics of, 25, 77, 216, 217
study of, 3–4
treatment of slaves, 26
universities
role of slavery in development of, 1, 2

335

INDEX

"unjust servitude," 22
UN's Committee of Experts on the Application of Conventions and Recommendations (CEAR), 258
Urbainczyk, Theresa, 35
urban slavery, 66
US Trafficking in Persons Report (TIP Report), 239
Uzbekistan
forced labor, 259–60

van der Heijden, P. G. M., 266
van Dijk, J., 261, 266
Vassouras, Brazil, 215
Venezuela
child soldiers, 253
sex trafficking, 248
Vermahalis band, 164
Vietnam
human trafficking, 256–7
mass killings during war in, 204–5
Viking age slavery, 107, 108, 121, 124
Virginia
slave population, 217
violent conflict in, 61
Vision and Method in Historical Sociology, 91
Vogt, Joseph, 190

Wacquant, Loïc, viii, 85
Wakefield, E. G., 95
Walk Free Foundation, 233, 268
Walker, Angus, 81, 82
Wallerstein, Immanuel
The Modern World System, 91
war crimes, 202
War of the Spanish Succession, 168
warfare
female participation and, 119

pastoral systems and, 119
polygyny and, 118–19
slavery and, 119, 141
Warren, Mary, 211, 222
Warsaw Ghetto, 226
Watson, Alan, 59, 60
We Charge Genocide (W. Patterson), 213, 214
Weaver, Karol, 35
Weber, Max, 66
West Indian slave systems, 29, 77
West-Central Africa slave trade, 25
Whelan, Frederick, 47
Whiles Town, 176
Whitman, James, 216n5
Wilderson, Frank, 37
Williams, Eric, 5, 6
Willis, John, 58
Willis, Paul, 91
Windward band
claim to land, 181
leading figures of, 171–2n7, 184
meeting with Cudjoe, 178–9
raids of, 181
refugees, 178–9
strength of, 173
struggle with the Whites, 170, 175, 176, 177–80, 186
Treaty of 1739 and, 184–5
witchcraft
slavery and, 110–11, 143
Wittgenstein, Ludwig, 237, 238
Wolfe, Patrick, 213
women
contribution to subsistence, 114–16, 117, 118
as primary producers, 121
sexual exploitation of, 248, 249–50
slave ownership of, 120
in small-scale societies, 122
targeted killings of, 211–12
Woodhouse, W. J., 131, 132

336

INDEX

World Bank, 236
Wright, Gavin, 5
Wyatt, David, 123
Wyatt-Brown, Bertram, 33

Yemen
  child soldiers, 253
  human smuggling, 241

Yi Sung-gye, 78
Ysassi (Spanish guerrilla leader), 165

Zhang, S. X., 266, 267
Zheng, T., 246
Zimbabwe
  forced labor, 258